Machine Learning in the AWS Cloud

Machine Learning in the AWS Cloud

Add Intelligence to Applications with Amazon SageMaker and Amazon Rekognition

Abhishek Mishra

ISBN: 978-1-119-55671-8
ISBN: 978-1-119-55673-2 (ebk.)
ISBN: 978-1-119-55672-5 (ebk.)

Manufactured in the United States of America

For general information on our other products and services or to obtain technical support, please contact our Customer Care Department within the U.S. at (877) 762-2974, outside the U.S. at (317) 572-3993 or fax (317) 572-4002.

Wiley publishes in a variety of print and electronic formats and by print-on-demand. Some material included with standard print versions of this book may not be included in e-books or in print-on-demand. If this book refers to media such as a CD or DVD that is not included in the version you purchased, you may download this material at http://booksupport.wiley.com. For more information about Wiley products, visit www.wiley.com.

Library of Congress Control Number: 2019940774

C10012744_080519

Acknowledgments

This book would not have been possible without the support of the team at Wiley, including Jim Minatel, Kenyon Brown, David Clark, Kim Cofer, and Pete Gaughan. I would also like to thank Chaim Krause for his keen eye for detail. It has been my privilege to work with all of you. Thank you.

About the Author

Abhishek Mishra has been active in the IT industry for over 19 years and has extensive experience with a wide range of programming languages, enterprise systems, service architectures, and platforms.

He holds a master's degree in computer science from the University of London and currently provides consultancy services to Lloyds Banking Group in London as a security and fraud solution architect. He is the author of several books, including *Amazon Web Services for Mobile Developers*.

About the Technical Editor

Chaim Krause is a lover of computers, electronics, animals, and electronic music. He's tickled pink when he can combine two or more in some project. He has come by the vast majority of his knowledge through independent learning. He jokes with everyone that the only difference between what he does at home and what he does at work is the logon he uses. As a lifelong learner he is often frustrated with technical errors in documentation that waste valuable time and cause unnecessary frustration. One of the reasons he works as the technical editor on books is to help others avoid those same pitfalls.

Contents at a Glance

Contents

Introduction

Amazon Web Services (AWS) is one of the leading cloud-computing platforms in the industry today. At the time this book was written, AWS offered more than 100 services, each of which resided in one of 18 different service categories. For someone who is new to cloud computing or to the AWS ecosystem, the sheer number of services on offer can be daunting. It can be difficult to know where to begin and what services to focus on.

Developers who are new to machine learning as well as experienced data scientists are often not aware of the power of the public cloud and AWS's offerings in the machine learning space in particular. In the past, cloud-based machine learning offerings have been limited in the types of algorithms they could support and the level of customization that was possible. All of this changed when Amazon announced SageMaker—a service that provided the ability to build machine learning models based on Amazon's implementation of cutting-edge algorithms, as well as the option to build custom models with frameworks such as Scikit-learn and Google TensorFlow.

Real-world use cases of cloud-based machine learning models are not based on using the model in isolation, but instead rely on a number of supporting systems such as databases, load balancers, API gateways, and identity providers, all of which are provided by AWS. This book is written to provide both seasoned machine learning experts and enthusiasts alike an introduction to a selection of AWS machine learning services that are based on pre-trained models, as well as step-by-step examples of how to train and deploy your own custom models on Amazon SageMaker. For enthusiasts who are new to machine learning, this book also provides a selection of chapters that cover the fundamentals of machine learning such as data preprocessing, visualization, feature engineering, and the use of common Python libraries such as NumPy, Pandas, and Scikit-learn.

This book at all times attempts to balance between theory and practice, giving you enough visibility into the underlying concepts and providing you with the best practices and practical advice that you can apply at your workplace right away. I have also made every attempt to keep the content up-to-date and relevant. Even though this makes the book susceptible to being outdated in a few rare instances, I am confident the content will remain useful and relevant through the next versions of the AWS services.

Who This Book Is For

This book is best suited for software developers who wish to learn about machine learning in general and how to leverage machine learning–specific offerings from AWS. The book is also useful to data scientists, system architects, and application architects, who want to get an introduction to some of the commonly used AWS services in the machine learning space.

If you are new to both machine learning and AWS, I advise that you read all chapters from start to finish. If you are an experienced data scientist, you may want to skip ahead to Part 2 to learn about machine learning–specific AWS services.

What This Book Covers

This book covers building and training machine learning models with Python on the AWS cloud, as well as a number of ready-to-use machine learning services such as Amazon Rekognition, Amazon Comprehend, and Amazon Lex.

The book also covers general high-level concepts of machine learning, including feature engineering, data visualization, as well as supporting AWS services that are used to build machine learning systems such as Amazon IAM, Amazon Cognito, Amazon S3, Amazon DynamoDB, and AWS Lambda.

The model-building and evaluation code in this book is written in Python 3. Services provided by Amazon, Apple, and Google are updated frequently and therefore sometimes you may encounter a newer version of a screen when you follow the instructions in a chapter.

How This Book Is Structured

This book consists of 18 chapters that are grouped into two parts, and four appendices. The first part consists of five chapters and covers the fundamentals of machine learning using Python. This part covers techniques for feature engineering, data visualization, model building, and model evaluation using Pandas, NumPy, Matplotlib, and Scikit-learn. The examples developed in this part make use of Jupyter Notebook and are aimed at readers who are new to machine learning.

Part 2 covers building machine learning applications using AWS services. This part starts with introducing the basics of commonly used AWS services such as Amazon S3, Amazon DynamoDB, and AWS Lambda. It then proceeds to AWS services that deal specifically with machine learning such as Amazon Comprehend, Amazon Lex, Amazon Machine Learning, and Amazon SageMaker. Two chapters are dedicated to Amazon SageMaker; the first one covers building and deploying models using built-in algorithms and Scikit-learn, and the second one covers building and deploying a model with Google TensorFlow. Not all chapters in this part include source code, but where applicable, you can download the source code that accompanies each chapter using a GitHub link. Some of the chapters in this part require you to upload files to Amazon S3; you will need to substitute the names of buckets in the examples with those from your own account.

The chapters in Part 1 include:

Introduction to Machine Learning (Chapter 1) This is an introduction to the types of machine learning systems, their applications, and tools used to build machine learning systems.

Data Collection and Preprocessing (Chapter 2) This chapter covers sources that can be used to obtain training data, techniques to explore datasets, and basic feature engineering.

Data Visualization with Python (Chapter 3) This chapter covers techniques to visualize datasets using Matplotlib.

Creating Machine Learning Models with Scikit-learn (Chapter 4) This chapter covers techniques to build and train classification and regression models using Scikit-learn.

Evaluating Machine Learning Models (Chapter 5) This chapter covers techniques to evaluate the quality of a machine learning model.

The chapters in Part 2 include:

Introduction to Amazon Web Services (Chapter 6) This chapter is a brief primer on cloud computing and Amazon Web Services. It also covers commonly encountered service and deployment models.

AWS Global Infrastructure (Chapter 7) This chapter introduces AWS regions, availability zones, and edge locations.

Identity and Access Management (Chapter 8) This chapter introduces one of the key services provided by AWS to secure your resources in the Amazon cloud. It also provides instructions to sign up for an account under the AWS free tier.

Amazon S3 (Chapter 9) This chapter introduces one the most commonly used storage services provided by AWS, Amazon Simple Storage Service (S3).

Amazon Cognito (Chapter 10) This chapter introduces Amazon's cloud-based OAuth2.0-compliant identity management solution, Amazon Cognito.

Amazon DynamoDB (Chapter 11) This chapter introduces Amazon's managed NoSQL database service, Amazon DynamoDB.

AWS Lambda (Chapter 12) This chapter introduces AWS Lambda, a service designed to allow you to run code in the Amazon cloud without having to provision or manage any infrastructure.

Amazon Comprehend (Chapter 13) This chapter introduces Amazon Comprehend, a cloud-based natural language processing service that you can integrate into your applications to analyze the contents of text documents.

Amazon Lex (Chapter 14) This chapter introduces Amazon Lex, a cloud-based service that you can use to create chatbots and integrate them into your applications.

Amazon Machine Learning (Chapter 15) This chapter introduces Amazon Machine Learning, a fully managed cloud-based service that you can use to build and deploy simple machine learning models without any programming.

Amazon SageMaker (Chapter 16) This chapter introduces Amazon SageMaker, a cloud-based machine learning service that can be used to train and deploy both built-in and custom machine learning models.

Using Google Tensorflow with Amazon SageMaker (Chapter 17) This chapter introduces Google's Tensorflow framework and covers the use of Amazon SageMaker to build and deploy Tensorflow models.

Amazon Rekognition (Chapter 18) This chapter introduces Amazon Rekognition, a fully managed cloud-based service that can be used to add computer vision capabilities to your applications.

The appendices cover the following topics:

Anaconda and Jupyter Notebook Setup (Appendix A)   This appendix provides instructions to install the Anaconda distribution and set up a Jupyter Notebook server on your local computer.

AWS Resources Needed to Use This Book (Appendix B)   This appendix provides information on the AWS resources that you need to set up in your account in order to follow along with the examples in the book.

Installing and Configuring the AWS CLI (Appendix C)   This appendix provides instructions to download and install the AWS CLI tool.

Introduction to NumPy and Pandas (Appendix D)   This appendix provides an introduction to two Python libraries commonly used by data scientists: NumPy and Pandas.

What You Need to Use This Book

- A suitable Mac or Windows computer for development
- Basic knowledge of Python programming
- An AWS account that you can administer

Conventions

To help you get the most from the text and keep track of what's happening, we've used a number of conventions throughout the book.

NOTE   Notes, tips, hints, tricks, and asides to the current discussion are offset like this.

As for styles in the text:

- We *italicize* new terms and important words when we introduce them.
- We show keyboard strokes like this: Ctrl+A.
- We show filenames, URLs, and code within the text like so: `persistence.properties`.
- We present code in two different ways:

```
We use a monofont type with no highlighting for most code examples.
```

We use bold type to emphasize code that is of particular importance in the present context.

Source Code

As you work through the examples in this book, you may choose either to type in all the code manually or to use the source code files that accompany the book. All of the source code used in this book is available for download at www.wiley.com/go/machinelearningawscloud. Also, you can download the code files at GitHub.

Errata

We make every effort to ensure that there are no errors in the text or in the code. However, no one is perfect, and mistakes do occur. If you find an error in one of our books, like a spelling mistake or faulty piece of code, we would be very grateful for your feedback. By sending in errata you may save another reader hours of frustration and at the same time you will be helping us provide even higher quality information.

To report errata, email to errata@wiley.com and include

- The book's title and ISBN (*Machine Learning in the AWS Cloud*, 9781119556718)

- The page number of the relevant content

- A description of just what's wrong

Part 1

Fundamentals of Machine Learning

Chapter 1

Introduction to Machine Learning

WHAT'S IN THIS CHAPTER

- ◆ Introduction to the basics of machine learning
- ◆ Tools commonly used by data scientists
- ◆ Applications of machine learning
- ◆ Types of machine learning systems
- ◆ Comparison between a traditional and a machine learning system

Hello and welcome to the exciting world of machine learning with Amazon Web Services (AWS). If you have never heard of machine learning until now, you may be tempted to think that it is a recent innovation in computer science that will result in sentient computer programs, significantly more intelligent than humans, that will one day make humans obsolete. There is very little truth in that idea of machine learning. For starters, it is not a recent development. For decades computer scientists have been researching ways to make computers more intelligent, attempting to find ways to teach computers to reason and to make decisions, generalizations, and predictions much like humans do.

Machine learning specifically deals with the problem of creating computer programs that can generalize and predict information reliably, quickly, and with accuracy resembling what a human would do with similar information. Building machine learning models can require a lot of processing power and storage space, and until recently was only possible to implement in very large companies or in academic institutions. Recent advances in storage, processor speeds, GPU technology, and the ability to rapidly create new virtual computing resources in the cloud have finally provided the processing power require to build and deploy machine learning systems at scale, and get results in real time.

Another factor that has contributed to the recent increase in machine learning applications is the availability of excellent tools such as Pandas, Matplotlib, TensorFlow, Scikit-learn, PyTorch, and Jupyter Notebook, which have made it possible for newcomers to start building real-world machine learning applications without having to delve into the complex underlying mathematical concepts.

Cloud computing as we know it today was born in 2006 when Amazon launched its Elastic Compute Cloud (EC2) service. Soon after in 2008, Microsoft launched its Azure service. This was followed by competing offers from other players, including Rackspace, Google, Oracle, and Apple. Building and deploying machine learning applications in the cloud is extremely popular. Most major cloud providers offer services to build and deploy some kind of machine learning applications.

You can find more information on the basics of cloud computing and Amazon Web Services in Chapters 6 and 7. In this chapter you will learn about what machine learning is, how machine learning systems are classified, and examples of real-world applications of machine learning.

What Is Machine Learning?

Machine learning is a discipline within Artificial Intelligence (AI) that deals with creating algorithms that learn from data. Machine learning traces its roots to a computer program created in 1959 by the computer scientist Arthur Samuel while he was working for IBM. Samuel's program could play a game of checkers and was based on assigning each position on the board a score that indicated the likelihood of leading toward winning the game. The positional scores were refined by having the program play against itself, and with each iteration the performance of the program improved. The program was, in effect, learning from experience, and the field of machine learning was born.

A machine learning system can be described as a set of algorithms based on mathematical principles that can mine data to find patterns in the data and then make predictions on new data as it is encountered. Rule-based systems can also make predictions on new data; however, rule-based systems and machine learning systems are not the same. A rule-based system requires a human to find patterns in the data and define a set of rules that can be applied by the algorithm. The rules are typically a series of if-then-else statements that are executed in a specific sequence. A machine learning system, on the other hand, discovers its own patterns and can continue to learn with each new prediction on unseen data.

Tools Commonly Used by Data Scientists

In this section you will learn about some of the tools commonly used by data scientists to build machine learning solutions. Most machine learning scientists use one of two programming languages: Python or R. R is a language commonly used by statisticians. While R has historically been the more popular choice, availability of machine learning–specific libraries in Python have made Python the more popular choice today. This book uses Python 3.6.5 and the rest of this section will focus on the most popular machine learning tools for Python:

◆ *Jupyter Notebook:* This is a very popular web-based interactive development environment for data science projects. A notebook combines code, execution results, and visualization results all in a single document. Jupyter Notebook is a successor to an older project called IPython Notebook. You can find out more about Jupyter Notebook at http://jupyter .org. Appendix A contains instructions on installing Anaconda Navigator and setting up Jupyter Notebook on your own computer.

◆ *Anaconda Navigator:* This is a commonly used package manager for data scientists. It allows users to conveniently install and manage Python and R libraries and quickly switch between different sets of libraries and language combinations. It also includes popular tools such as Jupyter Notebook, Spyder Python IDE, and R Studio. You can find more information on Anaconda at https://www.anaconda.com.

◆ *Scikit-learn:* This is a Python library that provides implementations of several machine learning algorithms for classification, regression, and clustering applications. It also provides powerful data preprocessing and dimensionality reduction capabilities. You can find more information on Scikit-learn at https://www.scikit-learn.org.

◆ *NumPy:* This is a Python library that is commonly used for scientific computing applications. It contains several useful operations such as random number generation and Fourier transforms. The most popular NumPy features for data scientists are N-dimensional data arrays (known as ndarrays) and functions that manipulate these arrays. NumPy ndarrays allow you to perform vector and matrix operations on arrays, which is significantly faster than using loops to perform element-wise mathematical operations. You can find more information on NumPy at `https://www.numpy.org`.

◆ *Pandas:* This is a Python library that provides a number of tools for data analysis. Pandas builds upon the NumPy ndarray and provides two objects that are frequently used by data scientists: the Series and the DataFrame. You can find more information on Pandas at `https://pandas.pydata.org`.

◆ *Matplotlib:* This is a popular 2D plotting library. It is used by data scientists for data visualization tasks. You can find more information on Matplotlib at `https://matplotlib.org`.

◆ *Pillow:* This is a library that provides a variety of functions to load, save, and manipulate digital images. It is used when the machine learning system needs to work with images. You can find more information on Pillow at `https://python-pillow.org`.

◆ *TensorFlow:* This is Python library for numerical computation. It was developed by Google and eventually released as an open source project in 2015. TensorFlow is commonly used to build deep-learning systems. It uses a unique computation-graph–based approach and requires users to build a computation graph where each node in the graph represents a mathematical operation and the connections between the nodes represent data (tensors). You can find more information on TensorFlow at `https://www.tensorflow.org`.

◆ *PyTorch:* This is another popular Python library for training and using deep-learning networks. It was built by Facebook, and many newcomers find it easier to work with than TensorFlow. You can find more information on PyTorch at `https://pytorch.org`.

Common Terminology

In this section we will examine some of the common machine learning–specific terminology that you are likely to encounter. While this list is not exhaustive, it should be useful to someone looking to get started:

◆ *Machine learning model:* This is the algorithm that is used to make predictions on data. It can also be thought of as a function that can be applied to the input data to arrive at the output predictions. The machine learning algorithm often has a set of parameters associated with it that influence its behavior, and these parameters are determined by a process known as *training*.

◆ *Data acquisition:* The process of gathering the data needed to train a machine learning model. This could include activities ranging from downloading ready-to-use CSV files to scraping the web for data.

◆ *Input variables:* These are the inputs that your machine learning model uses to generate its prediction. A collection of N input variables are generally denoted by lowercase x_i with i = 1, 2, 3, ...N. Input variables are also known as *features*.

- *Feature engineering:* This is the process of selecting the best set of input variables and often involves modifying the original input variables in creative ways to come up with new variables that are more meaningful in the context of the problem domain. Feature engineering is predominantly a manual task.

- *Target variable:* This is the value you are trying to predict and is generally denoted by a lowercase y. When you are training your model, you have a number of training samples for which you know the expected value of the target variable. The individual values of the target variable for N samples are often referred to as y_i with i = 1, 2, ...N.

- *Training data:* A set of data that contains all the input features as well as any engineered features and is used to train the model. For each item in the set, the value of the target variable is known.

- *Test data:* A set of data that contains all the input features (including engineered features), as well as the values of the target variable. This set is not used while training the model, but instead is used to measure the accuracy of the model's predictions.

- *Regression:* A statistical technique that attempts to find a mathematical relationship between a dependent variable and a set of independent variables. The dependent variable is usually called the target, and the independent variables are called the features.

- *Classification:* The task of using an algorithm to assign observations a label from a fixed set of predefined labels.

- *Linear regression:* A statistical technique that attempts to fit a straight line, plane, or hyperplane to a set of data points. Linear regression is commonly used to create machine learning models that can be used to predict continuous numeric values (such as height, width, age, etc.)

- *Logistic regression:* A statistical technique that uses the output of linear regression and converts it to a probability between 0 and 1 using a sigmoid function. Logistic regression is commonly used to create machine learning models that can predict class-wise probabilities. For example, the probability that a person will develop an illness later in life, or the probability that an applicant will default on a loan payment.

- *Decision tree:* A tree-like data structure that can be used for classification and prediction problems. Each node in the tree represents a condition, and each leaf represents a decision. Building a decision tree model involves examining the training data and determining the node structure that achieves the most accurate results.

- *Error function:* A mathematical function that takes as input the predicted and actual values and returns a numerical measure that captures the prediction error. The goal of the training function is to minimize the error function.

- *Neural networks:* A machine learning model that mimics the structure of the human brain. A neural network consists of multiple interconnected nodes, organized into distinct layers—the input layer, the in-between layers (also known as the hidden layers), and the output layer. Nodes are commonly known as neurons. The number of neurons in the input layer correspond to the number of input features, and the number of neurons in the output layer correspond to the number of classes that are being predicted/classified.

◆ *Deep learning:* A branch of machine learning that utilizes multi-layer neural networks with a large number of nodes in each layer. It is also quite common for deep-learning models to use multiple deep neural networks in parallel.

Real-World Applications of Machine Learning

Machine learning is transforming business across several industries at an unprecedented rate. In this section you will learn about some of the applications of machine learning–based solutions:

◆ *Fraud detection:* Machine learning is commonly used in banks and financial institutions to make a decision on the overall risk associated with a payment instruction. Payments in this context include money transfers and purchases (payments to providers) using cards. The risk decision is based on several factors, including the transactional history. If the risk is low, the transaction is allowed to proceed. If the risk is too high, the transaction is declined. If the risk is deemed to lie in an acceptable threshold, the customer may be asked to perform some form of step-up authentication to allow the transaction to proceed.

◆ *Credit scoring:* Whenever a customer applies for a credit product such as a loan or credit card, a machine learning system computes a score to indicate the overall risk of the customer not being able to repay the loan.

◆ *Insurance premium calculation:* Machine learning systems are commonly used to compute the insurance premium that is quoted to customers when they apply to purchase an insurance product.

◆ *Behavioral biometrics:* Machine learning systems can be trained to build a profile of users based on the manner in which they use a website or a mobile application. Specifically, such systems create a profile of the user based on analyzing information on the location of the user at the time when the system was accessed, the time of the day, the precise click locations on a page, the length of time spent on a page, the speed at which the mouse is moved across the page, etc. Once the system has been trained, it can be used to provide real-time information on the likelihood that someone is impersonating a customer.

◆ *Product recommendations:* Machine learning systems are commonly used by online retailers (such as Amazon) to provide a list of recommendations to customers based on their purchase history. These systems can even predict when a customer is likely to run out of groceries or consumables and send reminders to order the item.

◆ *Churn prediction:* Machine learning systems are commonly used to predict which customers are likely to cancel their subscription to a product or service in the next few days. This information gives businesses an opportunity to try to retain the customer by offering a promotion.

◆ *Music and video recommendations:* Online content providers such as Netflix and Spotify use machine learning systems to build complex recommendation engines that analyze the movies and songs you listen to and provide recommendations on other content that you may like.

Types of Machine Learning Systems

There are several different types of machine learning systems today. The classification of a machine learning system is usually based on the manner in which the system is trained and the manner in which the system can make predictions. Machine learning systems are classified as follows:

◆ Supervised Learning

◆ Unsupervised Learning

◆ Semi-supervised Learning

◆ Reinforcement Learning

◆ Batch Learning

◆ Incremental Learning

◆ Instance-based Learning

◆ Model-based Learning

These labels are not mutually exclusive; it is quite common to come across a machine learning system that falls into multiple categories. For example, a system that uses behavioral usage data to detect potential fraudsters on a banking website could be classified as a supervised model–based machine learning system. Let's examine these classification labels in more detail.

Supervised Learning

Supervised learning refers to the training phase of the machine learning system. During the supervised training phase, the machine learning algorithm is presented with sets of training data. Each set consists of inputs that the algorithm should use to make predictions as well as the desired (correct) result (Figure 1.1).

FIGURE 1.1
Supervised learning

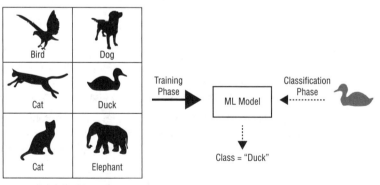

Labeled training set

Training consists of iterating over each set, presenting the inputs to the algorithm, and comparing the output of the algorithm with the desired result. The difference between the actual output and the desired output is used to adjust parameters of the algorithm so as make the output of the algorithm closer to (or equal to) the desired output.

Human supervision is typically needed to define the desired output for each input in the training set. Once the algorithm has learned to make predictions on the training set, it can be used to make predictions on data it has not previously encountered.

Most real-world machine learning applications are trained using supervised learning techniques. Some applications of supervised learning are:

◆ Finding objects in digital images

◆ Spam filtering

◆ Predicting the possibility of developing a medical condition based on lifestyle factors

◆ Predicting the likelihood of a financial transaction being fraudulent

◆ Predicting the price of property

◆ Recommending a product to a customer based on historical purchasing data

◆ A music streaming servicing suggesting a song to a customer based on what the customer has been listening to

Unsupervised Learning

Unsupervised learning also refers to the training phase of a machine learning system. However, unlike supervised learning, the algorithm is not given any information on the class/category associated with each item in the training set. Unsupervised learning algorithms are used when you want to discover new patterns in existing data. Unsupervised learning algorithms fall into two main categories:

Clustering These algorithms group the input data into a number of clusters based on patterns in the data. Visualizing these clusters can give you helpful insight into your data. Figure 1.2 shows the results of a clustering algorithm applied to the data on the heights and ages of children under 6 years of age. Some of the most popular clustering algorithms are k-means clustering, and Hierarchical Cluster Analysis (HCA).

FIGURE 1.2
Clustering technique
used to find patterns
in the data

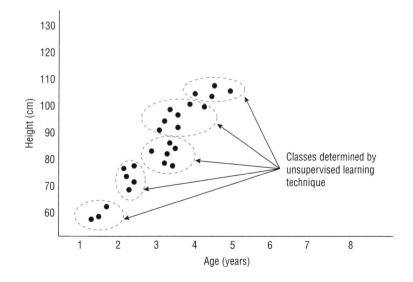

Dimensionality reduction   These algorithms are used to combine a large number of input features into a smaller number of features without losing too much information. Typically, the features that are combined have a high degree of correlation with each other. Dimensionality reduction reduces the number of input features and therefore the risk of overfitting; it also reduces the computational complexity of a machine learning model. Some examples of algorithms in this category are Principal Component Analysis (PCA), Linear Discriminant Analysis (LDA), and Autoencoding. Dimensionality reduction is often used when the number of features in a dataset is too large for a data scientist to meaningfully analyze.

Semi-Supervised Learning

Semi-supervised learning is a mix of both supervised and unsupervised learning. In many situations it is practically impossible for a data scientist to label millions of samples for a super-vised learning approach; however, the data scientist is already aware that there are known classifications in the data. In such a case, the data scientist labels a small portion of the data to indicate what the known classifications are, and the algorithm then processes the unlabeled data to better define the boundaries between these classes as well as potentially discover new classes altogether. Figure 1.3 depicts the results of applying semi-supervised learning to the same data on the heights and ages of children under 6 years of age, with some of the samples labeled to indicate the level of education.

FIGURE 1.3
Semi-supervised learning

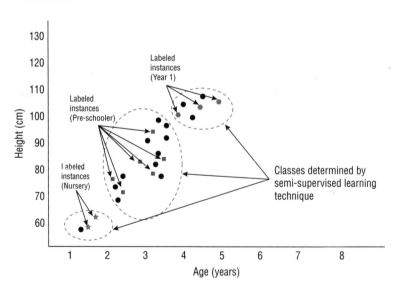

Real-world problems that involve extremely large datasets use this approach. Applications include speech recognition, natural language parsing, and gene sequencing.

A distinct advantage of semi-supervised learning is that it is less prone to labeling bias than supervised learning. This is because a data scientist is only labeling a small portion of the data, and the effects of any personal labeling bias introduced by the scientist can be corrected by the unsupervised learning part of the algorithm based on the sheer number of unlabeled samples it will process.

Semi-supervised learning algorithms make an assumption that the decision boundaries are geometrically simple; in other words, points that are close to each other are actually related in some way.

Reinforcement Learning

Reinforcement learning is a computational approach that attempts to learn using techniques similar to how humans learn: by interacting with their environment and associating positive and negative rewards with different actions. For instance, human beings have learned over time that touching a fire is a bad thing; however, using the same fire for cooking or providing warmth is a good thing. Therefore when we come across a fire we use it in positive ways.

A reinforcement learning–based system is typically called an *agent* and has a number of fixed actions that it can take at any given point in time, and with each action is an associated reward or penalty. The goal of the system is to maximize the cumulative reward over a series of actions. The knowledge gained by the agent is represented as a set of policies that dictate the actions that must be taken when the agent encounters a given situation. Reinforcement learning–based systems are used with two types of tasks:

- **Episodic tasks:** This is when the problem has a finite end point, such as winning a game.

- **Continuous tasks:** This is when the problem has no end point, such as maximizing the value of a stock portfolio.

Reinforcement learning algorithms often work in an environment where the results of choices are often delayed. Consider, for instance, an automated stock trading bot. It has several real-time inputs, manages several stocks, and can take one of three given actions at any point in time: buy a stock, sell a stock, or hold on to the stock. The result of several buy and sell decisions could be an eventual increase in the value of the portfolio (reward), or decrease in the value of the portfolio (penalty).

The bot does not know beforehand if taking a given action will result in reward or penalty. The bot must also incorporate a delay mechanism and not attempt to gauge reward/penalty immediately after making a transaction. The goal of the bot is to maximize the number of rewards.

In time the bot would have learned of trading strategies (policies) that it can apply in different situations. Reinforcement learning coupled with deep learning neural networks is a hotly researched topic among machine learning scientists.

Batch Learning

Batch learning refers to the practice of training a machine learning model on the entire dataset before using the model to make predictions. A batch learning system is unable to learn incrementally from new data it encounters in the future. If you have some new additional data that you want to use to train a batch learning system, you need to create a new model on all the data you have used previously plus the new additional data, and replace the older version of the model with this newly trained one.

Batch learning systems work in two distinct modes: learning and prediction. In learning mode the system is in training and cannot be used to make predictions. In prediction mode the system does not learn from observations.

The training process can be quite lengthy, and require several weeks and several computing resources. You also need to retain all training data in the event that you need to train a new version of the model. This can be problematic if the training data is large and requires several gigabytes of storage.

Incremental Learning

Incremental learning, also known as online learning, refers to the practice of training a machine learning model continuously using small batches of data and incrementally improving the performance of the model. The size of a mini batch can range from a single item to several hundred items. Incremental learning is useful in scenarios where the training data is available in small chunks over a period of time, or the training data is too large to fit in memory at once. The aim of incremental learning is to not have to retrain the model with all the previous training data; instead, the model's parameters (knowledge) are updated by a small increment with each new mini batch that it encounters. Incremental learning is often applied to real-time streaming data or very large datasets.

Instance-based Learning

Instance-based learning systems make a prediction on new unseen data by picking the closest instance from instances in the training dataset. In effect the machine learning system memorizes the training dataset and prediction is simply a matter of finding the closest matching item. The training phase of instance-based learning systems involves organizing all the training data in an appropriate data structure so that finding the closest item during the prediction phase will be quicker. There is little (if any) model tuning involved, although some level of preprocessing may have been performed on the training data before presenting it to the machine learning system.

The advantage of an instance-based learning system is that both training and prediction are relatively quick, and adding more items to the training set will generally improve the accuracy of the system. It is important to note that the prediction from an instance-based system will be an instance that exists in the training set. For example, consider an instance-based machine learning system that predicts the shoe size of an individual given a height and weight value as input. Let's assume this system is trained using a training set of 100 items, where each item consists of a height, weight, and shoe size value.

If this instance-based machine learning system were to be used to predict the shoe size for a new individual given a height and weight of the new individual as input values, the predicted shoe size would be the value of the closest matching item in the training set. To put it another way, the machine learning system would never output a shoe size that was not in the training set to start with.

Model-based Learning

Model-based learning systems attempt to build a mathematical, hierarchical, or graph-based model that models the relationships between the inputs and the output. Prediction involves solving the model to arrive at the result. Most machine learning algorithms fall in this category.

While model-based systems require more time to build, the size of the model itself is a fraction of the size of the training data, and the training data need not be retained (or presented to the model) in order to get a prediction. For example, a model built from a training dataset of over a million items could be stored in a small five-element vector.

The Traditional Versus the Machine Learning Approach

As humans, all of us are familiar with the concept of learning. Learning takes two major forms: memorization and understanding. There is a clear difference between memorizing your password and learning to drive a car. The latter involves understanding how the vehicle works, and how to react in different situations on the road. You do not memorize the exact sequence of activities you need to perform to drive between your home and your place of work; instead, you apply the understanding you have gained while assessing the situation on the road.

The capabilities of machine learning algorithms are not as sophisticated as human learning. Machines do not have the capability to understand and reason; however, they can predict and generalize, and they are capable of processing data much faster than humans. In this section you will examine a hypothetical situation and understand how a machine learning system can be applied to solve the problem at hand.

Imagine you have been hired by the credit cards team at a bank and tasked with creating a solution to offer a new credit card product to customers. Eligible customers can, under this new product, get cards with credit limits up to $25,000 at low interest rates. The bank would like to keep its losses to a minimum and requires that the credit card only be offered to customers who are likely to pay the money back to the bank.

To start with, you decide to create a new application form that customers will need to fill out to apply for this credit card. On the application form, you ask for the following information:

◆ Name

◆ Age

◆ Sex

◆ Number of years lived at current address

◆ Number of addresses in the last 5 years

◆ Number of credit cards held with other banks

◆ Total amount of loan (excluding mortgage)

◆ Total income after tax

◆ Estimated regular monthly outgoings

◆ Total monthly repayments

◆ Homeowner status

◆ Marital status

◆ Number of dependents in the household

In a real-world scenario you would ask for a lot more information and would also use a credit scoring company to provide the applicant's credit rating, but for the purposes of this example this list will do. Let's also assume that the mechanism to allow customers to apply for the credit card is available on the bank's website, and data from all application forms is available in a table in a SQL database within the bank.

When the product is launched, your bank expects it to be popular with customers and you need to have a plan in place to process a large number of applications each week. It is also crucial for your bank to remain competitive in the credit card space, and therefore you cannot keep applicants waiting for weeks to find out the outcome of a credit card application. You need to ensure that the bank's standard terms of service apply to your new product and therefore at least 51% of all credit applications need to be decided within a few minutes of the application being received by the bank.

Clearly, it is not cost effective to a hire few hundred analysts to scrutinize each loan application and make the necessary checks to arrive at a decision. You have two choices before you:

◆ You can build a rule-based decisioning system

◆ You can build a machine learning system

Let's first examine how a rule-based system could be used to help with this problem.

A Rule-based Decision System

Faced with the prospect of choosing between an easy-to-understand rule-based approach, and a somewhat unknown, black-box machine learning system, you decide to go with a rule-based decision system.

The business rules themselves are to be stored in a database, and the business logic to apply the rules to a loan application will be encapsulated into a server-side application. You plan to have a cluster of these servers that can be scaled up as necessary to deal with increased volumes. Figure 1.4 depicts the architecture of the proposed system.

FIGURE 1.4
Architecture of a rule-based decision system

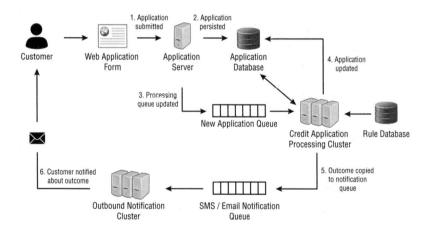

When an applicant submits a credit card application on the bank's website, a unique card application identifier is generated, and a row is added to a database by the web application. The web application also publishes a message onto a message queue; the content of the message contains the unique application identifier. A cluster of loan processing servers subscribe to the message queue and the first available servers will pick up the message and begin processing the credit card application. When the server reaches a decision, it will update the loan application in the database and publish a message on another message queue. The contents of this new message will contain all the information needed to send an SMS or email notification to the customer, informing the customer of the outcome.

How do you define the rules that will be used to make the decision? To start with you will need to create the rules based on your experience of the problem domain and qualities of the loan application form that you feel are favorable. If your business has another rule-based system that your solution is trying to replace, you may also be able to port some of the rules from the existing system.

Let's assume you do not have access to an existing system and need to define the business rules yourself. Looking at the fields in your loan application form, you decide that the following fields can be discarded from the decision-making process as you feel they are not likely to have any impact on the ability of individuals to keep up their monthly repayments:

◆ Name

◆ Sex

◆ Marital status

◆ Number of dependents in the household

◆ Homeowner status

You are now left with the following information that you can use to build your rules:

◆ Number of years lived at current address

◆ Number of addresses in the last 5 years

◆ Number of credit cards held with other banks

◆ Total amount of loan (excluding mortgage)

◆ Total income after tax

◆ Estimated regular monthly outgoings

◆ Total monthly repayments

You decide to create rules that will reject applications that meet any of the following criteria:

1. Applicants that have lived less than 1 year at their current address.

2. Applicants that have had more than three addresses in the last 5 years.

3. Applicants that have two or more credit cards with other banks.

4. Applicants whose disposable monthly income is less than 15% of their total income after tax.

These rules can be coded in any programming language using `if-then-else` statements. Figure 1.5 contains a flowchart that depicts the decision-making process using the rules you have defined.

FIGURE 1.5
A flowchart depicting
the decision-making
process for a rule-
based system

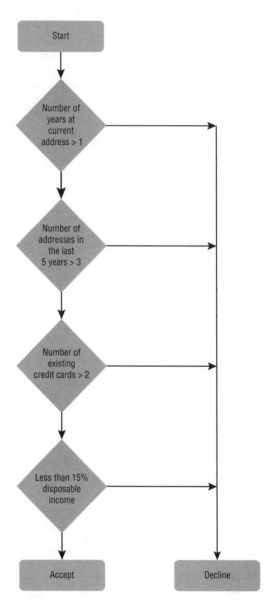

There is a possibility that the rules you have created and the initial assumptions you have made were not optimal, but you can always tailor the rules if you observe the losses due to missed payments exceed the bank's risk threshold. In time, as the volume of credit applications increases you will need to tailor your business rules to deal with the increased volume, and you are likely to encounter a few problems:

◆ Your rules become very complicated and interdependent; it becomes increasingly complex to replace old rules with new ones.

◆ Your rules have not been based on any numerical analysis; they have been created ad hoc to address increasing demand.

◆ Your rules do not account for changing patterns in the economy; for example, in the midst of a recession a larger number of people may end up missing their payments even though your rules predict that they should not. You will need to constantly keep updating your rules and that can be a costly and time-consuming process.

Let's now see how a machine learning–based system could be used to address these problems.

A Machine Learning–based System

Unlike a rule-based solution, you cannot create a machine learning solution without historical data from previous applicants. It is important to have data that is accurate and relevant to the problem you are trying to solve. You may be tempted to build your machine learning model using data from a different loan product, such as a personal loan. This is not recommended, as there could be trends in that data that are applicable only for personal loan applications.

You may be wondering why there was no need for historical data while building the rule-based system, and why defining the rules based on an intuitive understanding of the questions alone was sufficient. The reason is that in the rule-based approach, you were defining the rules based on your personal knowledge and experience of the problem domain. A machine-learning system, on the other hand, does not start with any prior knowledge of the problem domain. It does not have the intuitive capability of a human being. Instead, a machine learning system attempts to make its own inferences purely from the data it encounters. Not only do you need data, but also relevant data. If the data that is used to train the machine learning system is significantly different from what the system will encounter when asked to make predictions, the predictions are likely to be incorrect.

Just how much data will you need? There is no simple answer to that question. In general, machine learning algorithms require a lot of data to be trained effectively, but it is not just the quantity that matters; it is also the quality of the data. If your data has too many samples that follow a particular trend, then your machine learning system will be biased toward that trend.

For the purpose of this example, let's assume you have decided to pick the data for 5000 applicants randomly from your database, and exported these rows to a CSV file. These are all applicants that have applied for your credit card product and have either kept up with their regular payments or missed at most one payment. The input variables in this case would be answers to the questions asked on the form; the target variable will be a Boolean that indicates whether the applicant missed at most one payment.

Such type of data, where you already know the value of the target variable, is known as *labeled data* and is commonly used for training machine learning models. Not all data is labeled; in fact, the vast majority of data in the world is unlabeled. Using unlabeled (or partially labeled) data to train machine learning algorithms is an active area of research.

What if you want to build a machine learning solution, but have absolutely no data of your own, and can't wait months (or years) to collect high-quality labeled data? Your best option in this case would be to try to find existing datasets from free or paid sources on the Internet that are as close as possible to the problem domain you are working in. Chapter 2 provides links to several public machine learning datasets.

PICKING INPUT FEATURES

Once you have collected the labeled input data, you will need to perform basic statistical analysis on the data to pick input variables that are most likely to be relevant and prepare the input data for the machine learning model. Having the data in a CSV file makes it easy to load into data analysis tools. Most cloud-based data analysis tools allow you to upload CSV files, and some also support importing data from cloud-based relational databases.

Data visualization techniques are commonly used to get an indication of the spread and correlation of individual features. You will most likely build and train a model using an initial set of features and calculate the value of a performance metric while making predictions with the model. You will then retrain the model with additional input features and repeat as necessary as long as you observe a significant improvement in the value of the performance metric.

The number of features you choose will also impact the size of the training dataset you are likely to need. A model with 3 features could be built using a dataset of 500 items, whereas a model with 10 features will likely need a training dataset that consists of several thousands of items.

It may surprise you to learn that the bulk of a data scientist's job is looking at data and working out ways to use it. This work is often referred to as *data munging*, and involves several steps, including but not limited to:

◆ Finding out if there are any missing values in the data

◆ Working out the best way to handle missing values

◆ Examining the statistical distribution of the data

◆ Examining the correlation between input variables

◆ Creating new input variables by splitting or combining existing input variables

NOTE *Munge* is a technical term coined by MIT students and means to transform data using a series of reversible steps to arrive at a different representation. Data munging is also known as data wrangling and feature engineering.

R, Python, Jupyter Notebook, NumPy, Pandas, and Matplotlib are commonly used for statistical analysis and feature engineering. Chapters 2 and 3 cover a number of techniques that can be used for feature engineering and data visualization to arrive at the final list of input features.

Let's now examine the questions on the application form and perform some simple feature engineering, based on your experience with the rule-based approach, to arrive at the inputs to our first machine learning model. Table 1.1 lists all the questions on the loan application form with their data types, range of expected values, and range of actual values as observed in 5000 samples.

It is quite clear that some of the answers are categorical while others are numeric. The numeric features themselves are either discrete or continuous and have different ranges of values.

TABLE 1.1:   Type and Range of Data across 100 Sample Applications

QUESTION	TYPE OF DATA	ACTUAL RANGE	MAXIMUM RANGE
Name	Free Text	Characters A–Z, some special characters	Characters A–Z, some special characters
Age	Continuous Numeric	22–45	18–150
Sex	Categorical	Male, Female, Undisclosed	Male, Female, Undisclosed
Number of years lived at current address	Continuous Numeric	0–7	0–150
Number of addresses in the last 5 years	Continuous Numeric	1–6	1–10
Number of credit cards held with other banks	Discrete Numeric	1, 2, 3	1, 2, 3, 4, 5, 6, 7, 8, 9, 10
Total amount of loan (excluding mortgage)	Continuous Numeric	0–17500	0–10 million
Total income after tax	Continuous Numeric	50000–200000	0–10 million
Estimated regular monthly outgoings	Continuous Numeric	3000–15000	0–10 million
Total monthly repayments	Continuous Numeric	0–1500	0–10 million
Homeowner status	Categorical	Yes or No	Yes or No
Marital status	Categorical	Single, Married, Undisclosed	Single, Married, Undisclosed
Number of dependents in the household	Discrete Numeric	1, 2, 3	1, 2, 3, 4, 5, 6, 7, 8, 9, 10

Most machine learning models are designed to perform better on one type of feature over the other. Some statistical-based learning models are also sensitive to large numeric values. After examining the type of questions on the application form, the range of input values, and sample data for 5000 applicants, you decide that you want to use all of the answers on the application form as input features, except for the following:

◆ Name of the applicant

◆ Number of dependents

◆ Number of credit cards held with other banks

You also decide to engineer a new feature called Total Disposable Income, and split three categorical features into discrete numeric features as listed in Table 1.2.

TABLE 1.2:   Transforming Categorical Features into Numeric Features

ORIGINAL CATEGORICAL FEATURE	NEW NUMERIC FEATURE	ALLOWED VALUES/RANGE
Sex	SexIsMale	0 or 1
	SexIsFemale	0 or 1
	SexIsUndisclosed	0 or 1
Homeowner status	IsHomeOwner	0 or 1
	IsNotHomeOwner	0 or 1
Marital status	MaritalStatusIsSingle	0 or 1
	MaritalStatusIsMarried	0 or 1
	MaritalStatusIsUndisclosed	0 or 1

The new engineered feature Total Disposable Income is defined as:

Total Disposable Income = Total Income After Tax – Regular Monthly outgoings – Monthly Loan Repayments

Feature engineering techniques are covered in Chapter 2, but it is worth noting that some of the questions that have been answered as *undisclosed* are being treated as first-class values, as opposed to treating the question as missing an answer.

Table 1.3 lists the new set of input and engineered features, the expected range of values for each feature, and the actual range of values as observed in 5000 sample application forms.

TABLE 1.3:   Modified Input Features

FEATURE NAME	FEATURE DESCRIPTION	TYPE OF DATA	OBSERVED RANGE	MAXIMUM RANGE
F1	Age	Continuous Numeric	22–45	18–150
F2	SexIsMale	Discrete Numeric	0, 1	0 or 1
F3	SexIsFemale	Discrete Numeric	0, 1	0 or 1
F4	SexIsUndisclosed	Discrete Numeric	0, 1	0 or 1
F5	Number of years lived at current address	Continuous Numeric	0–7	0–150

TABLE 1.3:   Modified Input Features *(CONTINUED)*

FEATURE NAME	FEATURE DESCRIPTION	TYPE OF DATA	OBSERVED RANGE	MAXIMUM RANGE
F6	Number of addresses in the last 5 years	Continuous Numeric	1–6	0–150
F7	Total Disposable Income	Continuous Numeric	0–5000	0–10 million
F8	Total amount of loan (excluding mortgage)	Continuous Numeric	0–17500	0–10 million
F9	Total income after tax	Continuous Numeric	50000–200000	0–10 million
F10	Estimated regular monthly outgoings	Continuous Numeric	3000–15000	0–10 million
F11	Total monthly repayments	Continuous Numeric	0–1500	0–10 million
F12	IsHomeOwner	Discrete Numeric	0, 1	0 or 1
F13	IsNotHomeOwner	Discrete Numeric	0, 1	0 or 1
F14	MaritalStatusIsSingle	Discrete Numeric	0, 1	0 or 1
F15	MaritalStatusIsMarried	Discrete Numeric	0, 1	0 or 1
F16	MaritalStatusIsUndisclosed	Discrete Numeric	0, 1	0 or 1

It is quite clear that the range of allowed values for the features are not all the same. For example, F1 (Age) values lie in the range [18,100], whereas other feature values lie in the ranges [0,1], [0, 150], [1,10] and [0, 10000000]. Before you can use this data you will need to normalize the values of all the features to lie in the same range [0, 1]. Normalization is covered in Chapter 2, and involves transforming the value of each feature so that it lies in the interval [0, 1]. You will need to normalize both the training data as well as data on which your solution will make predictions.

You could also have chosen to transform the numeric features into categorical features by defining ranges of allowed values. For example, a given response to the *total income after tax* question, which is a continuous value between 0 and 10 million, could be converted into the following categorical value:

◆   Between0and100000

◆   Between100001and500000

◆   Above500001

There is no right or wrong way to engineer features. Sometimes the choice of machine learning algorithm dictates the type of features (numerical or categorical). Some algorithms, such as linear regression, work with numeric features; others that are based on decision trees work better with categorical features. Sometimes you start with a set of features only to realize that the predictive accuracy of the model trained on those features is not good enough and you need to start from scratch with new features, or perhaps a different algorithm or training technique.

PREPARING THE TRAINING AND TEST SET

Before you can build a machine learning model, you need to create separate training and testing datasets. The training set is used to build the model, whereas the test set is used to evaluate the performance of the model. The reason to have a separate training and test set is that a well-trained model will always perform well on the training set, as it has learned all the items in the training set. To truly measure the performance of the model, you need to present it data that it has not encountered during training.

Typically you will use 70% of the data for training and hold out 30% of the data for testing; however, other splits, such as 60:40, are also commonly used. When preparing the training and test set it is important to ensure that the members of the test set are well distributed, and do not exhibit bias toward any particular trend. For instance, if the training set consisted of a large proportion of applicants that were female and had annual incomes exceeding $100,000, the model is likely to incorporate this trend as part of its learning and perform poorly on other types of applicants. When a model performs well on the training set and poorly on the test set, the model is said to overfit the training data.

Cross-validation can help minimize the possibility of the model picking up on unexpected bias in the training set. The idea behind cross-validation is to shuffle the entire dataset randomly and divide it into a number of smaller sets (known as folds). If, for instance, the data were divided into 10 equal folds, the model would be trained and evaluated 10 times. During each training and evaluation cycle, one of the folds will be held out as the test set and the remaining nine will make the training set. This is illustrated in Figure 1.6.

FIGURE 1.6
Cross-validation using multiple folds

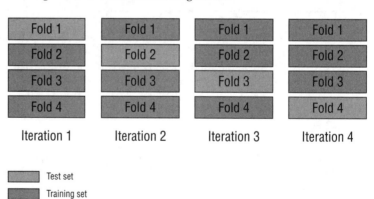

Sometimes the bias is introduced during the data collection phase (also known as sampling bias), and no amount of cross-validation can help remove it. For instance, you may be building a model based on a dataset that contains information on consumer shopping trends collected during the Christmas holiday season. This data will be biased toward trends that are specific to holiday shopping, and a model built using this data will perform poorly if used to predict what consumers may buy over the course of the entire year. In such cases the best option is to collect more data to remove the sampling bias.

PICKING A MACHINE LEARNING ALGORITHM

There are a number of machine learning algorithms that can be used for classification tasks. In the current example, the objective is to decide, at the point of application, whether an applicant should be issued a credit card. The machine learning system that makes this decision is to be trained on data that is labeled to indicate if the customer has historically missed any payments (negative outcome), or if the customer did not miss a single payment (positive outcome).

The decision to issue the credit card is directly related to whether the machine learning system indicates the customer will default or not. This is a typical classification problem and a number of algorithms could be used:

♦ Logistic regression

♦ Decision trees

♦ Random forests

♦ XGBoost

♦ Neural networks

♦ Clustering-based techniques

The choice of algorithm is often influenced by factors such as desired accuracy, number of classes desired (binary vs. multi-class classification), availability of sufficient training data, time taken to train the model, memory footprint of the trained model, and resources required to deploy the model into production.

In this example we will make use of an algorithm called *logistic regression*, which is an algorithm that performs well for binary classification problems—problems that involve classifying something into one of two classes. Logistic regression builds upon the output of an algorithm called *linear regression*. Linear regression is a simple and effective algorithm for predicting continuous numeric values and assumes that the output variable can be expressed as a linear combination of the input features.

In effect, linear regression attempts to find the best line (or hyperplane in higher dimensions) that fits all the data points. The output of linear regression is a continuous, unbounded value. It can be a positive number or a negative number. It can have any value, depending on the inputs with which the model was trained.

In order to use a continuous value for binary classification, logistic regression converts it into a probability value between 0.0 and 1.0 by feeding the output of linear regression into a sigmoid function. The graph of the sigmoid function is presented in Figure 1.7. The output of the sigmoid function will never go below 0.0 or above 1.0, regardless of the value of the input.

The output of the sigmoid function can be used for binary classification by setting a threshold value and treating all values below that as class A and everything above the threshold as class B (Figure 1.8).

While logistic regression is simple to understand, it may fail to provide good results if the relationship between the target variable and the input features is complex. In such a case you can consider using a tree-based model such as decision trees or an instance learning–based clustering model. You will learn more about model building in Chapter 4.

FIGURE 1.7
The sigmoid function

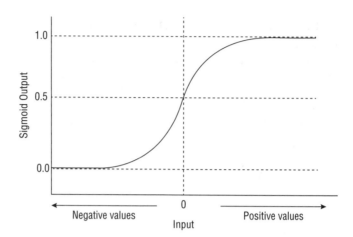

FIGURE 1.8
Using the sigmoid
function for binary
classification

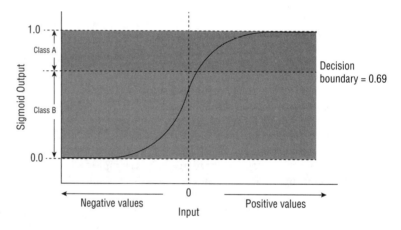

EVALUATING MODEL PERFORMANCE

Once you have built a model that can be used to determine if an applicant should be issued a credit card, you need to be able to quantitatively measure its performance. The purpose of evaluating a model is to determine how well it works on new data—models are evaluated using the labeled test set that was set aside during the training phase.

Since the model in this example attempts to solve a classification problem, you could simply count the number of times the model predicted the correct outcome and use this as an evaluation metric.

If issuing a credit card to an applicant is considered as the positive outcome, you can create a few additional metrics that go beyond simple counting:

◆ **True positive count:** The number of times the model predicted that a credit card should be issued to an applicant, and this decision matched the outcome in labeled test dataset.

◆ **False positive count:** The number of times the model predicted that a credit card should be issued to an applicant where the labeled test data indicated that applicant should not have been successful.

◆ **True negative count:** The number of times the model predicted that a credit card should not be issued to an applicant, and this decision matched the outcome in test dataset.

◆ **False negative count:** The number of times the model predicted that a credit card should not be issued to an applicant, and this decision was not correct according to the labeled test data.

You will learn to use these metrics and other performance evaluation and model tuning techniques in Chapter 5.

Summary

◆ Machine learning is a discipline within artificial intelligence that deals with creating algorithms that learn from data.

◆ Machine learning deals with the problem of creating computer programs that can generalize and predict information reliably and quickly.

◆ Machine learning is commonly used to implement fraud-detection systems, credit-scoring systems, authentication-decision engines, behavioral biometric systems, churn prediction, and product-recommendation engines.

◆ The type of training data that is required to train a machine learning system can be used to classify the machine learning system into supervised, unsupervised, or semi-supervised learning.

◆ Batch learning refers to the practice of training a machine learning model on the entire dataset before using the model to make predictions.

◆ Incremental learning, also known as online learning, refers to the practice of training a machine learning model continuously using small batches of data and incrementally improving the performance of the model.

◆ Instance-based learning systems make a prediction on new unseen data by picking the closest instance from instances in the training dataset.

◆ Model-based learning systems attempt to build a mathematical, hierarchical, or graph-based model that models the relationships between the inputs and the output.

Chapter 2

Data Collection and Preprocessing

WHAT'S IN THIS CHAPTER

◆ Sources to obtain training data

◆ Techniques to explore data

◆ Techniques to impute missing values

◆ Feature engineering techniques

In the previous chapter, you were given a general overview of machine learning, and learned about the different types of machine learning systems. In this chapter you will learn to use NumPy, Pandas, and Scikit-learn to perform common feature engineering tasks.

NOTE To follow along with this chapter ensure you have installed Anaconda Navigator and Jupyter Notebook as described in Appendix A.

You can download the code files for this chapter from www.wiley.com/go/ machinelearningawscloud or from GitHub using the following URL:

https://github.com/asmtechnology/awsmlbook-chapter2.git

Machine Learning Datasets

Training a machine learning model requires high-quality data. In fact, lack of quality training data can result in the poor performance of models built using the best-known machine learning algorithms. Quality in this case refers to the ability of the training data to accurately capture the nuances of the underlying problem domain, and to be reasonably free of errors and omissions.

Some of the common sources for publicly available machine learning data are explored next.

Scikit-learn Datasets

The datasets package within Scikit-learn includes down-sampled versions of popular machine learning datasets such as the Iris, Boston, and Digits datasets. These datasets are often referred to as *toy datasets*. Scikit-learn provides functions to load the toy dataset into a dictionary-like object with the following attributes:

◆ *DESCR*: Returns a human-readable description of the dataset.

◆ *data*: Returns a NumPy array that contains the data for all the features.

◆ *feature_names*: Returns a NumPy array that contains the names of the features. Not all toy datasets support this attribute.

◆ *target*: Returns a NumPy array that contains the data for the target variable.

◆ *target_names*: Returns a NumPy array that contains the values of categorical target variables. The digits, Boston house prices, and diabetes datasets do not support this attribute.

The following snippet loads the toy version of the popular Iris dataset and explores the attributes of the dataset:

```
#load Scikit-learn's downsampled iris dataset
from sklearn import datasets
iris_dataset = datasets.load_iris()

# explore the dataset
print (iris_dataset.DESCR)
Iris Plants Database
====================


Notes
-----

Data Set Characteristics:
    :Number of Instances: 150 (50 in each of three classes)
    :Number of Attributes: 4 numeric, predictive attributes and the class
    :Attribute Information:
        - sepal length in cm
        - sepal width in cm
        - petal length in cm
        - petal width in cm
        - class:
                - Iris-Setosa
                - Iris-Versicolour
                - Iris-Virginica
    :Summary Statistics:

    ============== ==== ==== ======= ===== ====================
                    Min  Max  Mean    SD    Class Correlation
    ============== ==== ==== ======= ===== ====================
    sepal length:   4.3  7.9  5.84   0.83    0.7826
    sepal width:    2.0  4.4  3.05   0.43   -0.4194
    petal length:   1.0  6.9  3.76   1.76    0.9490  (high!)
    petal width:    0.1  2.5  1.20   0.76    0.9565  (high!)
    ============== ==== ==== ======= ===== ====================

    :Missing Attribute Values: None
    :Class Distribution: 33.3% for each of 3 classes.
    :Creator: R.A. Fisher
```

```
    :Donor: Michael Marshall (MARSHALL%PLU@io.arc.nasa.gov)
    :Date: July, 1988

This is a copy of UCI ML iris datasets.
http://archive.ics.uci.edu/ml/datasets/Iris

.....

print (iris_dataset.data.shape)
(150, 4)

print (iris_dataset.feature_names)
['sepal length (cm)', 'sepal width (cm)', 'petal length (cm)', 'petal
width (cm)']

print (iris_dataset.target.shape)
['sepal length (cm)', 'sepal width (cm)', 'petal length (cm)', 'petal
width (cm)']

print (iris_dataset.target_names)
['setosa' 'versicolor' 'virginica']
```

The list of toy datasets included with Scikit-learn are:

◆ *Boston house prices dataset*: This is a popular dataset used for building regression models. The toy version of this dataset can be loaded using the `load_boston()` function. You can find the full version of this dataset at `https://archive.ics.uci.edu/ml/machine-learning-databases/housing/`.

◆ *Iris plants dataset*: This is a popular dataset used for building classification models. The toy version of this dataset can be loaded using the `load_iris()` function. You can find the full version of this dataset at `https://archive.ics.uci.edu/ml/datasets/iris`.

◆ *Onset of diabetes dataset*: This is a popular dataset used for building regression models. The toy version of this dataset can be loaded using the `load_diabetes()` function. You can find the full version of this dataset at `http://www4.stat.ncsu.edu/~boos/var.select/diabetes.html`.

◆ *Handwritten digits dataset*: This is a dataset of images of handwritten digits 0 to 9 and is used in classification tasks. The toy version of this dataset can be loaded using the `load_digits()` function. You can find the full version of this dataset at `http://archive.ics.uci.edu/ml/datasets/Optical+Recognition+of+Handwritten+Digits`.

◆ *Linnerud dataset*: This is a dataset of exercise variables measured in middle-aged men and is used for multivariate regression. The toy version of this dataset can be loaded using the `load_linnerud()` function. You can find the full version of this dataset at `https://rdrr.io/cran/mixOmics/man/linnerud.html`.

◆ *Wine recognition dataset*: This dataset is a result of chemical analysis performed on wines grown in Italy. It is used for classification tasks. The toy version of this dataset can be loaded using the `load_wine()` function. You can find the full version of this dataset at `https://archive.ics.uci.edu/ml/machine-learning-databases/wine/`.

◆ *Breast cancer dataset*: This dataset describes the characteristics of cell nuclei of breast cancer tumors. It is used for classification tasks. The toy version of this dataset can be loaded using the `load_breast_cancer()` function. You can find the full version of this dataset at `https://archive.ics.uci.edu/ml/datasets/Breast+Cancer+Wisconsin+ (Diagnostic)`.

AWS Public Datasets

Amazon hosts a repository of public machine learning datasets that can be easily integrated into applications that are deployed onto AWS. The datasets are available as S3 buckets or EBS volumes. Datasets that are available in S3 buckets can be accessed using the AWS CLI, AWS SDKs, or the S3 HTTP query API. Datasets that are available in EBS volumes will need to be attached to an EC2 instance. Public datasets are available in the following categories:

◆ *Biology*: Includes popular datasets such as the Human Genome Project.

◆ *Chemistry*: Includes multiple versions of PubChem and other content. PubChem is a database of chemical molecules that can be accessed at `https://pubchem.ncbi .nlm.nih.gov`.

◆ *Economics*: Includes census data and other content.

◆ *Encyclopedic*: Includes Wikipedia content and other content.

You can browse the list of AWS public datasets at `https://registry.opendata.aws`.

Kaggle.com Datasets

`Kaggle.com` is a popular website that hosts machine learning competitions. `Kaggle.com` also contains a large number of datasets for general use that can be accessed at `https://www .kaggle.com/datasets`. In addition to the general-use datasets listed on the page, competitions on `Kaggle.com` also have their own datasets that can be accessed by taking part in the competition. The dataset files can be downloaded onto your local computer and can then be loaded into Pandas dataframes. You can get a list of current and past competitions at `https://www.kaggle .com/competitions`.

UCI Machine Learning Repository

The UCI machine learning repository is a public collection of over 450 datasets that is maintained by the Center for Machine Learning and Intelligent Systems at UC Irvine. It is one of the oldest sources of machine learning datasets and is often the go-to destination for beginners and experienced professionals alike. The datasets are contributed by the general public and vary in the level of preprocessing you will need to perform in order to use them for model building. The datasets can be downloaded onto your local computer and then processed using tools like Pandas and Scikit-learn. You can browse the complete list of datasets at `https://archive.ics .uci.edu/ml/datasets.php`.

A small selection of the most popular UCI machine learning repository datasets is also hosted at `Kaggle.com` and can be accessed at `https://www.kaggle.com/uciml`.

Data Preprocessing Techniques

In Chapter 1, you learned about the different types of machine learning systems and the general process in building a machine learning–based solution. It should come as no surprise that the performance of a machine learning system is heavily dependent on the quality of training data. In this section, you will learn some of the common ways in which data is prepared for machine learning models. The examples in this section will use datasets commonly found on the Internet and included with the downloads that accompany this lesson.

Obtaining an Overview of the Data

When building a machine learning model, one of the first things you will want to do is explore the data to get an overview of the variables and the target. This section uses the Titanic dataset in a Jupyter notebook with NumPy and Pandas. The dataset and the notebook files are included with the lesson's code resources.

The Titanic dataset is a very popular dataset that contains information on the demographic and ticket information of 1309 passengers on board the Titanic, with the goal being to predict which of the passengers were more likely to survive. The full dataset is available from the Department of BioStatistics at Vanderbilt University (`https://biostat.mc.vanderbilt.edu/wiki/Main/DataSets`). Versions of the titanic3 dataset are also available from several other sources, including a popular `Kaggle.com` competition titled Titanic: Machine Learning From Disaster (`https://www.kaggle.com/c/titanic`). The Kaggle version is included with the resources that accompany this chapter and has the benefit of being shuffled and pre-split into a training and validation set. The training set is contained in a file named `train.csv` and the validation set is `test.csv`.

The description of the attributes of the Kaggle version of the Titanic dataset are as follows:

- *PassengerId*: A text variable that acts as a row identifier.

- *Survived*: A Boolean variable that indicates if the person survived the disaster. 0 = No, 1 = Yes.

- *Pclass*: A categorical variable that indicates the ticket class. 1 = 1st class, 2 = 2nd class, 3 = 3rd class.

- *Name*: The name of the passenger.

- *Sex*: A categorical variable that indicates the sex of the passenger.

- *Age*: A numeric variable that indicates the age of the passenger.

- *SibSp*: A numeric variable that indicates the number of siblings/spouses traveling together.

- *Parch*: A numeric variable that indicates the number of parents and children traveling together.

- ◆ *Ticket*: A text variable containing the ticket number.

- ◆ *Fare*: A numeric variable that indicates the fare paid in Pre-1970 British pounds.

- ◆ *Cabin*: A textual variable that indicates the cabin number.

- ◆ *Embarked*: A categorical variable that indicates the port of embarkation. C = Cherbourg, Q = Queenstown, S = Southampton.

To load the Titanic training set from a CSV file located on your computer into a Pandas dataframe, use the following snippet:

```
import numpy as np
import pandas as pd


# load the contents of a file into a pandas Dataframe
input_file = './datasets/titanic_dataset/original/train.csv'
df_titanic = pd.read_csv(input_file)
```

The first thing to do is to get information on the number of rows and columns of the dataset. The shape attribute of the dataframe can be used to provide this information:

```
df_titanic.shape

(891, 12)
```

You can see that the dataframe has 891 rows and 12 columns (or attributes). The following snippet can be used to get the names of the columns:

```
# titles of the 12 columns
print (df_titanic.columns.values)

['PassengerId' 'Survived' 'Pclass' 'Name' 'Sex' 'Age' 'SibSp' 'Parch'
 'Ticket' 'Fare' 'Cabin' 'Embarked']
```

One of the most common problems that data scientists have to deal with is that of missing values. Raw datasets often have missing values in one or more columns. There can be a number of reasons why the values are missing, ranging from human error to data simply being unavailable for that observation. When you load a CSV file into a Pandas dataframe, Pandas uses NaN as a marker to signify missing values. There are various ways to find out if a column in a dataframe contains missing values. One way is to use the info() function as illustrated in the following snippet:

```
# how many missing values?
df_titanic.info()

<class 'pandas.core.frame.DataFrame'>
Int64Index: 891 entries, 1 to 891
Data columns (total 11 columns):
Survived    891 non-null int64
Pclass      891 non-null int64
```

```
Name         891 non-null object
Sex          891 non-null object
Age          714 non-null float64
SibSp        891 non-null int64
Parch        891 non-null int64
Ticket       891 non-null object
Fare         891 non-null float64
Cabin        204 non-null object
Embarked     889 non-null object
dtypes: float64(2), int64(4), object(5)
memory usage: 83.5+ KB
```

Looking at the results of the info() function, it is clear that most columns have 891 values, whereas three columns—Age, Cabin, and Embarked—have less than 891 values. The use of the info() function to detect missing values only works if the value is truly missing in the CSV file, which means Pandas has been able to detect the missing value and substitute it with a NaN marker in the dataframe. If, however, the process by which the data was generated used a blank space, or a special character such as ! to represent a missing value, then Pandas will not automatically interpret these characters to represent missing data.

Another way to get information on missing values is to chain the output of the Pandas isnull() function with the sum() function. The isnull() function, when applied on a dataframe, returns a dataframe of boolean values that has the same dimensions as the original dataframe. Each position in the new dataframe has a value of True if the corresponding position in the original dataframe has a value of None or NaN. The sum() function, when applied to the new dataframe of boolean values, will returns a list with the number of values in each column that are True. The following snippet shows the result of chaining the isnull() and sum() functions to obtain the number of missing values in each column of the dataframe:

```
# another way to determine the number of missing
# values in a dataframe.
df_titanic.isnull().sum()

PassengerId     0
Survived        0
Pclass          0
Name            0
Sex             0
Age           177
SibSp           0
Parch           0
Ticket          0
Fare            0
Cabin         687
Embarked        2
dtype: int64
```

It is quite clear from the results that a significant number of Age and Cabin values are missing. We will look at ways to deal with missing values later in this chapter.

Sometimes the best way to get a feel for the data is to visually inspect the contents of the dataframe. You can use the head() function of the dataframe object to view the contents of the first few rows of the dataframe (Figure 2.1).

FIGURE 2.1
The head() function displays rows from the beginning of a Pandas dataframe.

```
In [12]:  # view the first 5 rows of the dataframe
          df_titanic.head()
```

```
Out[12]:
```

	PassengerId	Survived	Pclass	Name	Sex	Age	SibSp	Parch	Ticket	Fare	Cabin	Embarked
0	1	0	3	Braund, Mr. Owen Harris	male	22.0	1	0	A/5 21171	7.2500	NaN	S
1	2	1	1	Cumings, Mrs. John Bradley (Florence Briggs Th...	female	38.0	1	0	PC 17599	71.2833	C85	C
2	3	1	3	Heikkinen, Miss. Laina	female	26.0	0	0	STON/O2. 3101282	7.9250	NaN	S
3	4	1	1	Futrelle, Mrs. Jacques Heath (Lily May Peel)	female	35.0	1	0	113803	53.1000	C123	S
4	5	0	3	Allen, Mr. William Henry	male	35.0	0	0	373450	8.0500	NaN	S

If the number of columns is too many for Pandas to fit horizontally into a single line, then Pandas, by default, displays a subset of the columns of the dataframe. The subset consists of a few columns from the left of the dataframe, and a few from the right. Figure 2.2 illustrates the effect of using the head() function on a dataframe with 30 columns.

FIGURE 2.2
The head() function displays truncated data for large dataframes.

```
In [13]:  # load a 30 column dataset, to examine the behaviour of the head() function
          input_file = './datasets/random_30column.csv'
          df_random30 = pd.read_csv(input_file)
          df_random30.head()
```

```
Out[13]:
```

	attribute_1	attribute_2	attribute_3	attribute_4	attribute_5	attribute_6	attribute_7	attribute_8	attribute_9	attribute_10	...	attribute_21	attribute_22	attribute
0	457	430	295	778	420	420	560	821	362	116	...	360	652	
1	679	597	940	859	590	304	22	444	514	32	...	827	687	
2	278	326	998	885	974	387	238	288	22	251	...	846	964	
3	909	604	10	876	845	100	119	72	718	955	...	743	599	
4	622	26	272	67	520	837	804	236	679	689	...	948	881	

5 rows × 30 columns

You can change the maximum number of columns that will be displayed by Pandas by setting the display.max_columns Pandas property. For example, the following snippet will ensure Pandas displays no more than four columns:

```
pd.set_option('display.max_columns', 4)
df_random30.head()

      attribute_1.   attribute_2    ...   attribute_29.   target
0.    457.           430.           ...   8               1
1.    679.           597.           ...   253.            1
2.    278.           326.           ...   706.            0
3.    909.           604.           ...   263.            1
4     622.           26.            ...   675.            1

5 rows × 30 columns
```

If you would like all columns to be displayed, set the value of display.max_columns to None:

```
pd.set_option('display.max_columns', None)
```

Astute readers may have noticed that the `PasengerId` attribute of the Titanic dataset is a numeric row identifier and does not provide any useful input as far as model building is concerned. Every Pandas dataframe can have an index that contains a unique value for each row of the dataframe. By default, Pandas does not create an index for a dataframe; you can find out if a dataframe has an index by using the following snippet:

```
# Does this dataframe have a named index? If so, what is it?
print (df_titanic.index.name)

None
```

To make the `PassengerId` attribute the index of the `df_titanic` dataframe, use the following snippet:

```
df_titanic.set_index("PassengerId", inplace=True)
```

If you were to examine the index of the dataframe after executing the `set_index()` function, you would see that the `PassengerId` attribute is now the index:

```
# Does this dataframe have a named index? If so, what is it?
print (df_titanic.index.name)

PasengerId
```

Figure 2.3 shows the results of applying the `head()` function to the `df_titanic` dataframe before and after the index has been set up.

FIGURE 2.3

Impact of the `set_index` function on a dataframe

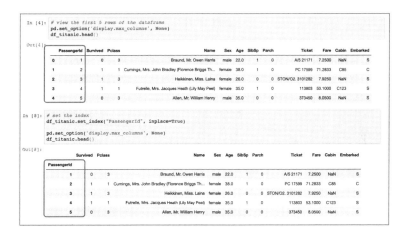

If you now use the shape attribute of the dataframe to get the number of rows and columns, you will notice that the number of columns is now reported as 11 instead of 12. This is illustrated in the following snippet:

```
# how many rows and columns in the dataframe
# after the index has been set?
df_titanic.shape

(891, 11)
```

You may have noticed that the `Survived` attribute is one of the 11 remaining attributes in the `df_titanic` dataframe after `PassengerId` has been used as the index. During the training process, you need to ensure you do not include the target attribute as one of the input features. There are various means by which you could ensure this, but perhaps the simplest option is to separate the feature variables and the target variables into separate dataframes. The following snippet will extract the `Survived` attribute from the `df_titanic` dataframe into a separate dataframe called `df_titanic_target`, and the 10 feature variables from the `df_titanic` dataframe into a separate dataframe called `df_titanic_features`:

```
# extract the target attribute into its own dataframe
df_titanic_target = df_titanic.loc[:,['Survived']]

# create a dataframe that contains the 10 feature variables
df_titanic_features = df_titanic.drop(['Survived'], axis=1)
```

The `Survived` attribute is a binary attribute in which a value of 1 implies that the individual survived. When the target that your machine learning model is trying to predict is categorical (binary or multi-class), it is useful to know the distribution of values in the training dataset per category. You can get the distribution of target values in this example by using the following snippet:

```
# what is the split between the two classes of the target variable?
df_titanic_target['Survived'].value_counts()

0    549
1    342
Name: Survived, dtype: int64
```

The `value_counts()` function can be used on numeric columns in addition to categorical columns. However, by default, the `value_counts()` function will not pick out NaN values. To have the `value_counts()` function include counts of NaN markers, include the `dropna=false` parameter as demonstrated in the following snippet:

```
# unique values and counts of categorical attribute 'Embarked'
# includes NaN markers
df_titanic_features['Embarked'].value_counts(dropna=False)

S      644
C      168
Q       77
NaN      2
Name: Embarked, dtype: int64
```

If you prefer a visual representation of the distribution of target values, you can use the following snippet to create a histogram. The histogram is depicted in Figure 2.4.

```
# histogram of target variable
%matplotlib inline
import matplotlib.pyplot as plt
df_titanic_target.hist(figsize=(5,5))
```

FIGURE 2.4
Distribution of values
for the
Survived attribute

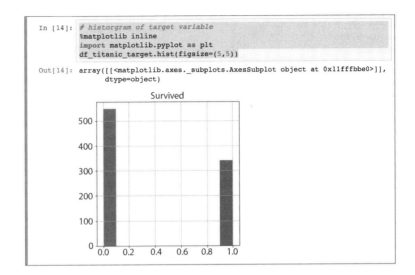

```
In [14]: # historgram of target variable
         %matplotlib inline
         import matplotlib.pyplot as plt
         df_titanic_target.hist(figsize=(5,5))

Out[14]: array([[<matplotlib.axes._subplots.AxesSubplot object at 0x11fffbbe0>]],
               dtype=object)
```

In addition to a histogram of the target variables, it is also useful to use histograms to get an overview of the distribution of feature values. The `hist()` function provided by the Pandas dataframe object will only generate histograms for numeric values. The only numerical features in the Titanic dataset are `Age`, `Fare`, `Pclass`, `Parch`, and `SibSp`. The following snippet can be used to generate histograms of numeric features. The resulting feature histograms are depicted in Figure 2.5.

```
#histogram of features
df_titanic_features.hist(figsize=(10,10))
```

If you have a background in statistics, then you will be aware that the appearance of a histogram is influenced by the width of the bins. Data scientists often generate multiple histograms of the same variable with different bin widths to get a better understanding of the distribution of the data. The following snippet can be used to create a histogram of a single numeric attribute and specify the number of equal-width bins along the x-axis. Figure 2.6 depicts the histograms obtained by choosing a number of different bin widths for the same numerical feature.

```
#histogram of single feature - Age
# it is a good idea to try different bin widths to get a better idea of
# the distribution of values.
df_titanic_features.hist(column='Age', figsize=(5,5), bins=2)
```

Since the `value_counts()` function works on both numeric and categorical features, you could generate a histogram of a categorical feature by using the output of the `value_counts()` function. The following snippet demonstrates this approach on the Embarked categorical feature. The resulting histogram is depicted in Figure 2.7.

```
# histogram of categorical attribute 'Embarked'
# computed from the output of the value_counts() function
vc = df_titanic_features['Embarked'].value_counts(dropna=False)
vc.plot(kind='bar')
```

FIGURE 2.5
Histogram of
numeric features

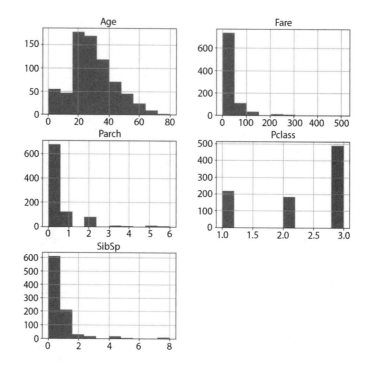

FIGURE 2.6
Histogram of numeric
feature "Age" using
different bin widths
(2, 3, 5, 80)

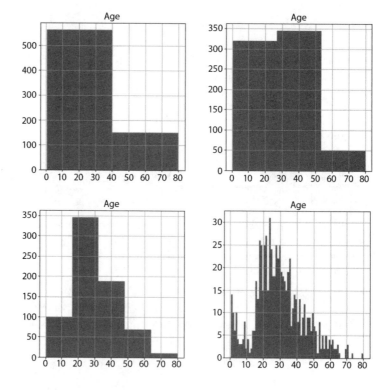

FIGURE 2.7

Histogram of categorical
feature "Embarked"

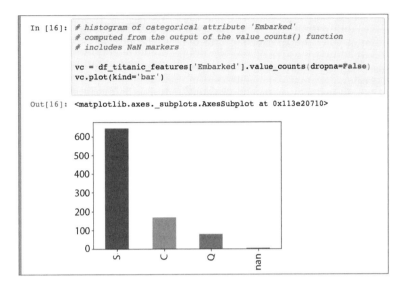

```
In [16]:  # histogram of categorical attribute 'Embarked'
          # computed from the output of the value_counts() function
          # includes NaN markers

          vc = df_titanic_features['Embarked'].value_counts(dropna=False)
          vc.plot(kind='bar')
```

Out[16]: <matplotlib.axes._subplots.AxesSubplot at 0x113e20710>

In addition to information on the distribution of features and target variables, the statistical characteristics of these variables and the correlation between them can provide useful insights into the training data. Pandas provides a `describe()` function that can be used on dataframes to obtain statistical information on the numerical attributes within the dataframe. The following snippet shows the results of the `describe()` function on the `df_titanic_features` dataset:

```
# get statistical characteristics of the data
df_titanic_features.describe()
```

	Pclass	Age.	SibSp.	Parch	Fare
Count.	891.000000	714.000000.	891.000000.	891.000000.	891.000000
Mean.	2.308642.	29.699118.	0.523008.	0.381594.	32.204208
Std.	0.836071.	14.526497.	1.102743.	0.806057.	49.693429
Min.	1.000000.	0.420000.	0.000000.	0.000000.	0.000000
25%.	2.000000	20.125000.	0.000000.	0.000000.	7.910400
50%.	3.000000.	28.000000.	0.000000.	0.000000.	14.454200
75%.	3.000000.	38.000000	1.000000.	0.000000.	31.000000
Max.	3.000000.	80.000000.	8.000000.	6.000000.	512.329200

Information provided by the `describe()` function includes the minimum value, maximum value, mean value, standard deviation, and the quartiles of each numerical feature. A quartile is a value below which a certain percent of observations can be found. For example, the first quartile is the value below which 25% of the observations can be found. The first quartile of the Age feature is 20.12, which means that 25% of the people captured by the dataset have ages less than 20 years. Information on quartiles and statistical characteristics of a feature is often represented using a box plot. Box plots are covered in Chapter 4; however, you can use the `boxplot()` function of the dataframe to create a box plot of all numeric features. The following snippet demonstrates the use of the `boxplot()` function. The resulting box plot is depicted in Figure 2.8.

```
# create a box plot of numeric features.
df_titanic_features.boxplot(figsize=(10,6))
```

FIGURE 2.8

Box plot of
numeric features

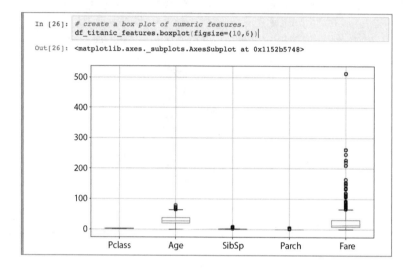

Information on the correlation between input features and the target can be helpful in picking out the best features from the data to use for model building and predictions. Information on the correlation between the features themselves can be helpful in reducing the number of features and the general risk of overfitting. Pandas provides a `corr()` function that can be used to compute Pearson's correlation coefficient between the columns of a dataframe. The results of applying the `corr()` function on the `df_titanic` dataframe is depicted in Figure 2.9.

FIGURE 2.9

Linear correlation
between
numeric columns

```
In [39]:  # correlation between the target variable and the features
          df_titanic.corr()
Out[39]:
```

	Survived	Pclass	Age	SibSp	Parch	Fare
Survived	1.000000	-0.338481	-0.077221	-0.035322	0.081629	0.257307
Pclass	-0.338481	1.000000	-0.369226	0.083081	0.018443	-0.549500
Age	-0.077221	-0.369226	1.000000	-0.308247	-0.189119	0.096067
SibSp	-0.035322	0.083081	-0.308247	1.000000	0.414838	0.159651
Parch	0.081629	0.018443	-0.189119	0.414838	1.000000	0.216225
Fare	0.257307	-0.549500	0.096067	0.159651	0.216225	1.000000

It is important to note that Pearson's correlation coefficient will only detect linear correlation between variables. The `corr()` function allows you to choose from standard correlation coefficients such as Pearson, Kendall, and Spearman. You can find more information at `https://pandas.pydata.org/pandas-docs/stable/reference/api/pandas.DataFrame.corr.html`.

The following snippet lists the correlation between the numeric features and the target variable, sorted by descending value:

```
# what features show the strongest correlation with the target variable?
corr_matrix = df_titanic.corr()
corr_matrix['Survived'].sort_values(ascending=False)


Survived    1.000000
Fare        0.257307
Parch       0.081629
SibSp      -0.035322
Age        -0.077221
Pclass     -0.338481
Name: Survived, dtype: float64
```

Computing correlation coefficients between pairs of attributes is not the only way to get information on the correlation between features. You can also create scatter plots between pairs of features to visualize their relationship. The following snippet uses the Pandas `scatter_matrix()` function to create scatter plots of all numeric features with each other. The resulting scatter plot is depicted in Figure 2.10.

```
# visualize relationship between features using a
# matrix of scatter plots.
from pandas.plotting import scatter_matrix
scatter_matrix(df_titanic, figsize=(12,12))
```

FIGURE 2.10

Matrix of scatter plots between pairs of numeric attributes

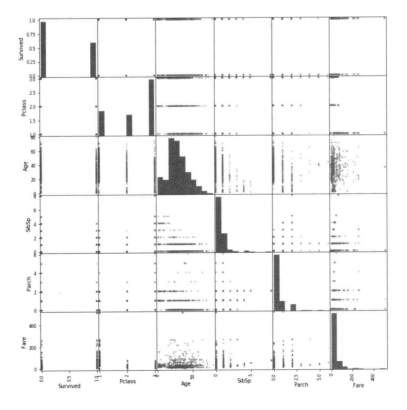

Handling Missing Values

In the previous section, you learned of techniques that can be used to explore the data. While exploring the Titanic dataset, you learned that the Age, Cabin, and Embarked classes have missing values. Age is a numeric feature, and we can use a box plot to get a quick overview of the statistical characteristics of the values that make up this feature using the following snippet. Figure 2.11 depicts a box plot of the Age feature variable.

```
# boxplot of 'Age'
%matplotlib inline
import matplotlib.pyplot as plt
df_titanic_features.boxplot(column='Age', figsize=(7,7))
```

FIGURE 2.11

Box plot of the Age feature variable

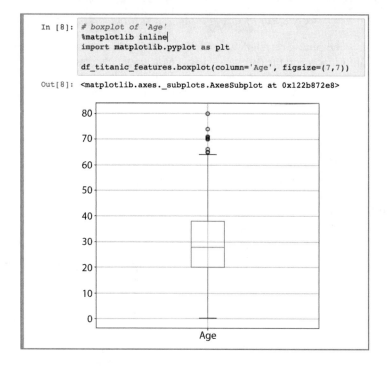

The median value of the age, according to the box plot, is just under 30. Pandas provides the `fillna()` function that can be used to replace missing values with a new value. The following snippet uses the `fillna()` function to replace the missing values of the Age attribute with the median value:

```
# fill missing values with the median
median_age = df_titanic_features['Age'].median()
print (median_age)
28.0

df_titanic_features["Age"].fillna(median_age, inplace=True)
```

NOTE Although it is not demonstrated in this section, you must ensure that any feature engineering or imputation that is carried out on the training data is also carried out on the test data.

The Embarked attribute is categorical, and since the number of missing values is small (just 2), a reasonable approach is to substitute the missing values with the most frequently occurring value in the Embarked column. The following snippet uses the fillna() function to achieve this:

```
# fill missing values of the Embarked attribute
# with the most common value in the column
embarked_value_counts = df_titanic_features['Embarked'].value_counts(dropna=True)
most_common_value = embarked_value_counts.index[0]

print (most_common_value)
S

df_titanic_features["Embarked"].fillna(most_common_value, inplace=True)
```

The Cabin attribute is also categorical but has a very large number of missing values (687). Using the same strategy that was used to impute missing values for the Embarked attribute will not work in this case as you will create a significant bias in the data. The best approach in this situation is to create a new boolean feature CabinIsKnown, which will have a value of True if the Cabin attribute is known, and False otherwise. You may be tempted to use the integer 1 to signify known cabin values and 0 to signify missing cabin values, but if you were to do this you would create an unintentional order in the data (1 being greater than 0), and this could influence the output of some models. The following snippet creates a new column called CabinIsKnown and drops the original Cabin column from the dataframe:

```
# create a boolean feature 'CabinIsKnown'
# which will have True if the Cabin column
# does not have missing data
df_titanic_features['CabinIsKnown'] = ~df_titanic_features.Cabin.isnull()

# drop the Cabin column from the dataframe
df_titanic_features.drop(['Cabin'], axis=1, inplace=True)
```

With the changes described in this section, you have imputed missing values where possible and created a new column in the dataframe. There should be no missing values in the dataframe, a new column called CabinIsKnown should be visible in the dataframe, and the Cabin column should have been deleted from the dataframe. All of this can be validated by executing the following snippet:

```
# display the columns of the dataframe.
print (df_titanic_features.columns.values)

# display number of missing values in the columns
df_titanic_features.isnull().sum()

['Pclass' 'Name' 'Sex' 'Age' 'SibSp' 'Parch' 'Ticket' 'Fare' 'Embarked'
 'CabinIsKnown']
Out[10]:
```

```
          Pclass         0
          Name           0
          Sex            0
          Age            0
          SibSp          0
          Parch          0
          Ticket         0
          Fare           0
          Embarked       0
          CabinIsKnown   0
          dtype: int64
```

Creating New Features

If you observe the descriptions of the columns of the Titanic dataset, you will come across the SibSp and Parch columns. From the description of the dataset:

◆ *SibSp*: A numeric variable that indicates the number of siblings/spouses traveling together.

◆ *Parch*: A numeric variable that indicates the number of parents and children traveling together.

It may make sense to combine these values into a single numeric value that represents the size of the family traveling together. It is not possible to tell at this stage if the model will perform better with this additional synthesized feature, but having this new feature in the data will give you more options when it comes to building and evaluating models. The following snippet creates a new attribute in the dataframe called FamilySize, which is computed as the arithmetic sum of the SibSp and Parch attributes:

```
# create a numeric feature called FamilySize that is
# the sum of the SibSp and Parch features.
df_titanic_features['FamilySize'] = df_titanic_features.SibSp + df_titanic_features.Parch
```

NOTE Although it is not demonstrated in this section, you must ensure that any feature engineering that is carried out on the training data is also carried out on the test data.

The Age and Fare features are numeric and take on a range of values; it may be useful to bin the value of these features and create categorical features. During model building you may discover that the categorical (binned) values of Age and Fare provide better results. To create a new categorical feature called AgeCategory, you can use the Pandas cut() function as demonstrated in the following snippet:

```
# generate new categorical feature AgeCategory
bins_age = [0,20,30,40,50,150]
labels_age = ['<20','20-30','30-40','40-50','>50']
```

```
df_titanic_features['AgeCategory'] = pd.cut(df_titanic_features.Age,
                                            bins=bins_age,
                                            labels=labels_age,
                                            include_lowest=True)
```

Figure 2.12 depicts the output of the head() function on the df_titanic_features dataframe after the AgeCategory feature has been created.

FIGURE 2.12
Dataframe with engineered feature AgeCategory

The cut() function has several parameters. In this example, the bins parameter contains a sequence of numbers that define the edges of the bins; the lowest and highest values are deliberately chosen to be outside the range of values observed in the Age feature. The labels parameter contains a list of strings that serve as the labels of the bins (and the values of the categorical feature that will be generated as a result of executing the cut() function). The include_lowest parameter is set to True to indicate that the first interval is left-inclusive. You can find information on the full list of parameters for the cut() function at https://pandas.pydata.org/pandas-docs/version/0.23.4/generated/pandas.cut.html.

There is no set formula to determine the correct number of bins and the widths of the bins. During the model-building process, you may find yourself experimenting with different binning strategies and pick the strategy that results in the best-performing model. If you want to split a continuous numeric variable into a categorical variable by using the quantiles as bin boundaries, you can use the Pandas qcut() function. The following snippet uses the qcut() function to create a new categorical feature called FareCategory using the quartiles as bin boundaries:

```
# generate new categorical feature FareCategory
df_titanic_features['FareCategory'] = pd.qcut(df_titanic_features.Fare,
                                              q=4,
                                              labels=['Q1', 'Q2', 'Q3', 'Q4'])
```

The second parameter, q=4, indicates that you want to use the quartiles as bin boundaries. Information on the qcut() function is available at https://pandas.pydata.org/pandas-docs/stable/reference/api/pandas.qcut.html.

Figure 2.13 depicts the output of the head() function on the df_titanic_features dataframe after the FareCategory feature has been created.

FIGURE 2.13
Dataframe with
engineered feature
FareCategory

```
In [27]:  # examine the first 10 rows of the dataset
          df_titanic_features.head(10)
```

Out[27]:

PassengerId	Pclass	Name	Sex	Age	SibSp	Parch	Ticket	Fare	Embarked	CabinIsKnown	FamilySize	AgeCategory	FareCategory
1	3	Braund, Mr. Owen Harris	male	22.0	1	0	A/5 21171	7.2500	S	False	1	20-30	Q1
2	1	Cumings, Mrs. John Bradley (Florence Briggs Th...	female	38.0	1	0	PC 17599	71.2833	C	True	1	30-40	Q4
3	3	Heikkinen, Miss. Laina	female	26.0	0	0	STON/O2. 3101282	7.9250	S	False	0	20-30	Q2
4	1	Futrelle, Mrs. Jacques Heath (Lily May Peel)	female	35.0	1	0	113803	53.1000	S	True	1	30-40	Q4
5	3	Allen, Mr. William Henry	male	35.0	0	0	373450	8.0500	S	False	0	30-40	Q2
6	3	Moran, Mr. James	male	28.0	0	0	330877	8.4583	Q	False	0	20-30	Q2
7	1	McCarthy, Mr. Timothy J	male	54.0	0	0	17463	51.8625	S	True	0	>50	Q4
8	3	Palsson, Master. Gosta Leonard	male	2.0	3	1	349909	21.0750	S	False	4	<20	Q3
9	3	Johnson, Mrs. Oscar W (Elisabeth Vilhelmina Berg)	female	27.0	0	2	347742	11.1333	S	False	2	20-30	Q2
10	2	Nasser, Mrs. Nicholas (Adele Achem)	female	14.0	1	0	237736	30.0708	C	False	1	<20	Q3

Transforming Numeric Features

After having created the categorical features AgeCategory and FareCategory in the previous section, you may wish to drop the original Age and Fare attributes from the dataset. The decision to drop the original numerical values will largely depend on the type of model you are going to build.

When building a model with continuous numeric variables, you may need to transform numeric attributes. Several machine learning models converge faster and work better when the values of numeric attributes are small and have a distribution that is close to a standard normal distribution with mean 0 and variance 1.

Normalization and standardization are the two most common types of transformations performed on numerical attributes. The result of normalizing a feature is that the values of the feature will be scaled to fall within 0 and 1. The result of standardizing a feature is that the distribution of the new values will have a mean of 0 and a standard deviation of 1, but the range of the standardized values is not guaranteed to be between 0 and 1. Standardization is used when the model you want to build assumes the feature variables have a Gaussian distribution. Normalization is often used with neural network models, which require inputs to lie within the range [0, 1].

Scikit-learn provides a number of classes to assist in scaling numeric attributes. The MinMaxScaler class is commonly used for normalizing features, and the StandardScaler class is commonly used for standardization. The following snippet creates two new columns, NormalizedAge and StandardizedAge, in the df_titanic_features dataframe. Figure 2.14 compares the histogram of the Age, NormalizedAge, and StandardizedAge features:

```
# generate new feature NormalizedAge using MinMaxScaler
from sklearn import preprocessing

minmax_scaler = preprocessing.MinMaxScaler()
ndNormalizedAge = minmax_scaler.fit_transform(df_titanic_
features[['Age']].values)
df_titanic_features['NormalizedAge']  = pd.DataFrame(ndNormalizedAge)

# generate new feature StandardizedAge using StandardScaler
standard_scaler = preprocessing.StandardScaler()
```

```
ndStandardizedAge = standard_scaler.fit_transform(df_titanic_
features[['Age']].values)
df_titanic_features['StandardizedAge']  = pd.DataFrame(ndStandardizedAge)

# histogram of Age, NormalizedAge, StandardizedAge
df_titanic_features[['Age', 'NormalizedAge', 'StandardizedAge']].
hist(figsize=(10,10), bins=5)
```

FIGURE 2.14

Histogram of Age, NormalizedAge, and StandardizedAge

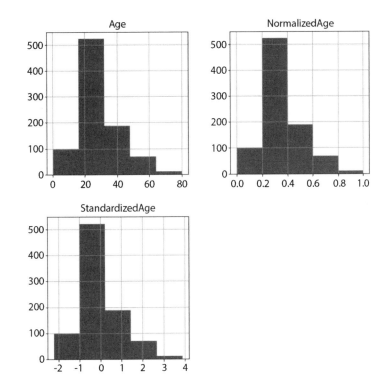

One-Hot Encoding Categorical Features

The final topic that we will look at in this chapter will be converting categorical features into numeric features using *one-hot encoding*. You may be wondering why you would want to convert categorical features to numeric, especially since a previous section in this chapter has discussed techniques to do the opposite—converting numeric features into categorical.

Not all machine learning algorithms can deal with categorical data. One-hot encoding is a technique that converts a categorical feature into a number of binary numeric features, one per category. For example, linear regression and logistic regression are only capable of using numeric features. Algorithms like XGBoost and random forests are capable of using categorical features without any problems.

Pandas provides the `get_dummies()` function to help with one-hot encoding. The following snippet will convert the categorical features Sex, Embarked, CabinIsKnown, AgeCategory, and FareCategory into binary numeric features and list the columns of the dataframe:

```
# use one-hot encoding to convert categorical attributes
# into binary numeric attributes
df_titanic_features = pd.get_dummies(df_titanic_features,
columns=['Sex','Embarked','CabinIsKnown','AgeCategory','FareCategory'])

# display the columns of the dataframe.
print (df_titanic_features.columns.values)

['Pclass' 'Name' 'Age' 'SibSp' 'Parch' 'Ticket' 'Fare' 'FamilySize'
 'NormalizedAge' 'StandardizedAge' 'Sex_female' 'Sex_male' 'Embarked_C'
 'Embarked_Q' 'Embarked_S' 'CabinIsKnown_False' 'CabinIsKnown_True'
 'AgeCategory_<20' 'AgeCategory_20-30' 'AgeCategory_30-40'
 'AgeCategory_40-50' 'AgeCategory_>50' 'FareCategory_Q1' 'FareCategory_Q2'
 'FareCategory_Q3' 'FareCategory_Q4']
```

As can be seen from the preceding snippet, the original categorical attributes are no longer present in the `df_titanic_features` dataframe; however, a number of new columns have been added. To understand how Pandas has created the additional columns, consider the Sex categorical attribute. This attribute has two values: male, and female. To convert this categorical attribute into a binary numeric attribute, Pandas has created two new columns in the dataframe called Sex_male and Sex_female. Other categorical attributes such as Embarked, CabinIsKnown, etc. have been processed using a similar approach. The following snippet lists the values of the Sex_male and Sex_female columns for the first five rows of the dataframe:

```
df_titanic_features[['Sex_male', 'Sex_female']].head()

               Sex_male        Sex_female
PassengerId
1                 1               0
2                 0               1
3                 0               1
4                 0               1
5                 1               0
```

Astute readers may notice that since the values taken by the Sex attribute in the original `df_titanic_features` dataset is either male or female, you don't need both Sex_male and Sex_female attributes because you can infer one from the other. These two attributes have a very strong negative correlation of −1.0 and you should not use both of them as inputs to a machine learning model. The following snippet demonstrates the strong negative correlation between the two attributes:

```
# strong negative correlation between Sex_male and Sex_female.
# one of these can be dropped.
corr_matrix = df_titanic_features[['Sex_male', 'Sex_female']].corr()
print(corr_matrix)
```

```
           Sex_male  Sex_female
Sex_male        1.0        -1.0
Sex_female     -1.0         1.0
```

The situation is similar with the CabinIsKnown_False and CabinIsKnown_True features. The following snippet drops the Sex_female and CabinIsKnown_False attributes along with non-numeric attributes Name and Ticket to arrive at a dataframe that contains only numeric attributes:

```
# drop the Name, Ticket, Sex_female, CabinIsKnown_False features
# to get a dataframe that can be used for linear or logistic regression
df_titanic_features_numeric = df_titanic_features.drop(['Name', 'Ticket',
'Sex_female', 'CabinIsKnown_False'], axis=1)
```

If you compute the correlation between the target attribute Survived and these numeric features, you will see a significantly better correlation than achieved earlier in this chapter prior to feature engineering. The following snippet demonstrates this:

```
# what features show the strongest correlation with the target variable?
corr_matrix = df_temporary.corr()
corr_matrix['Survived'].sort_values(ascending=False)

Survived              1.000000
CabinIsKnown_True     0.316912
Fare                  0.257307
FareCategory_Q4       0.233638
Embarked_C            0.168240
FareCategory_Q3       0.084239
Parch                 0.081629
AgeCategory_<20       0.076565
AgeCategory_30-40     0.057867
FamilySize            0.016639
Embarked_Q            0.003650
AgeCategory_40-50    -0.000079
NormalizedAge        -0.001654
StandardizedAge      -0.001654
AgeCategory_>50      -0.022932
SibSp                -0.035322
Age                  -0.064910
AgeCategory_20-30    -0.093689
FareCategory_Q2      -0.095648
Embarked_S           -0.149683
FareCategory_Q1      -0.221610
Pclass               -0.338481
Sex_male             -0.543351
Name: Survived, dtype: float64
```

Note the particularly strong negative correlation between the chances of survival and `Sex_male`, and the strong positive and negative correlation with `FareCategory_Q4` and `FareCategory_Q1`, respectively.

Feature engineering is the most laborious and time-consuming aspect of data science, and there is no set formula that can be applied to a given situation. In this chapter you have learned some of the techniques that can be used to explore data, impute missing values, and engineer features.

NOTE To follow along with this chapter ensure you have installed Anaconda Navigator and Jupyter Notebook as described in Appendix A.

You can download the code files for this chapter from `www.wiley.com/go/machinelearningawscloud` or from GitHub using the following URL:

`https://github.com/asmtechnology/awsmlbook-chapter2.git`

Summary

- A number of sources of datasets can be used to create machine learning models. Some of the popular sources are the UCI machine learning repository, `Kaggle.com`, and AWS public datasets.

- Scikit-learn includes subsampled versions of popular datasets that are often used by beginners.

- Pandas provides the `read_csv()` function that allows you to load a CSV file into a dataframe.

- You can use the Pandas `isnull()` and `sum()` functions together to obtain the number of missing values in each column of a dataframe.

- The `hist()` function exposed by the Pandas dataframe object will only generate histograms for numeric values.

- Pandas provides a `describe()` function that can be used on dataframes to obtain statistical information on the numerical attributes within the dataframe.

- Pandas provides a `corr()` function that can be used to compute Pearson's correlation coefficient between the columns of a dataframe.

- You can also create scatter plots between pairs of features to visualize their relationship.

- Pandas provides the `fillna()` function that can be used to replace missing values with a new value.

Chapter 3

Data Visualization with Python

WHAT'S IN THIS CHAPTER

◆ Introduction to Matplotlib

◆ Learn to create histograms, bar charts, and pie charts

◆ Learn to create box plots and scatter plots

◆ Learn to use Pandas plotting functions

In the previous chapter, you learned about techniques to explore data and perform feature engineering with NumPy, Pandas, and Scikit-learn. In this chapter you will learn to use Matplotlib to visualize data. Data visualization helps to understand the characteristics and relationships between the features during the data exploration phase but becomes particularly important when you are dealing with very large datasets that have several hundreds of features.

NOTE To follow along with this chapter ensure you have installed Anaconda Navigator and Jupyter Notebook as described in Appendix A.

You can download the code files for this chapter from `www.wiley.com/go/machinelearningaws-cloud` or from GitHub using the following URL:

`https://github.com/asmtechnology/awsmlbook-chapter3.git`

Introducing Matplotlib

Matplotlib is a plotting library for Python that offers functionality to generate numerous types of plots and the ability to customize these plots. It was created by John Hunter to provide Python users with a plotting library with capabilities similar to MATLAB. MATLAB is the standard for data visualization in the scientific community. The Matplotlib package has an extensive codebase and was designed to address the needs of a variety of users and provide capabilities at different levels of abstraction. Some users may want to simply present Matplotlib with some data in an array and ask for a specific type of plot (such as a scatter plot) to be created using as few commands as possible; these users may not want to control detailed attributes of the plot (such as positioning, scaling, line style, color). On the other hand, some users may want the ability to control every single attribute of a plot, down to the level of individual pixels.

For most common plotting tasks, you will use the `pyplot` module within Matplotlib, which provides the highest level of abstraction. The `pyplot` module implements a functional interface, powered by a state-machine design—you use functions to set up attributes of the plotting engine such as colors and fonts, and these apply to all subsequent plots until you issue commands to change them. Beneath the `pyplot` level of abstraction is the object-oriented interface, which offers more flexibility.

A NOTE ABOUT SEABORN

Seaborn is another Python plotting package that builds on top of Matplotlib. Seaborn provides additional plot types and some individuals may find the figures it generates to be more visually appealing. Matplotlib and Seaborn are complementary packages; the one you end up using in a given situation can come down to various factors including aesthetics, personal preferences, or the ease of making a specific type of plot with one package over the other. Seaborn is not covered in this chapter. If you are interested in learning about Seaborn, visit `https://seaborn.pydata.org`.

The conventional alias for the `pyplot` module is `plt`, the alias for the Matplotlib package is `mpl`, and the alias for the Seaborn package is `sns`. The following statements demonstrate how to import Matplotlib and Seaborn in a Python project:

```
import matplotlib.pyplot as plt
import matplotlib as mpl
import seaborn as sns
```

The reason to import both the `pyplot` submodule and the `matplotlib` package is to allow you to use functions from both the higher level of abstraction provided by `pyplot` and the lower-level object-oriented API exposed by Matplotlib. If you are using Matplotlib in a Jupyter Notebook, you must also add the `%matplotlib inline` statement before drawing any figures to ensure that plots render within the cells of the notebook.

Before looking at the components of a Matplotlib figure, let's examine the code to plot a simple curve using the `pyplot` module. The following snippet plots the function $y_1 = 4x^2 + 2x + 2$ and the function $y_2 = 3x + 4$ for values of x between 1 and 7. Figure 3.1 depicts the figure generated by these statements.

```
%matplotlib inline
import matplotlib.pyplot as plt
import matplotlib as mpl

import numpy as np
import pandas as pd

# prepare x values
x = np.linspace(1, 7, 10)

# prepare y1 and y2
y1 = 4*x*x + 2*x + 2
y2 = 3*x + 4

# create a new figure
plt.figure(figsize=(7,7))
```

```
# plot y1 = 4*x*x + 2*x + 2
plt.plot(x, y1)

#y2 = 3*x + 4
plt.plot(x, y2)

# set up axis labels
plt.xlabel('X values')
plt.ylabel('Y values')

# show the plot.
plt.show()
```

FIGURE 3.1
Plotting two curves
using Matplotlib

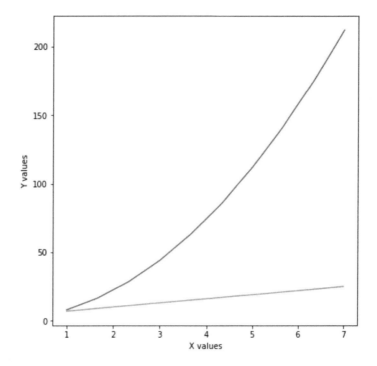

The code snippet uses NumPy functions to generate ndarrays x, y1, and y2. A Matplotlib figure object with dimensions 7 × 7 inches is then created using the statement plt .figure(figsize=(7,7)). The first curve $y_1=4x^2 + 2x + 2$ is plotted using the plt.plot(x, y1) statement; the inputs to the plot function are 2D coordinates of the points that need to be plotted. The plt.xlabel('X values') and plt.ylabel('Y values') statements are for aesthetic purposes and add labels along the x- and y-axes of the plot, respectively. Finally, the plt.show() statement is used to render the figure.

Components of a Plot

Regardless of the type of plot you make with Matplotlib or whether you use the high-level pyplot interface or the lower-level object-oriented interface, there are common components and terminology associated with plots. This section presents an overview of these concepts. Figure 3.2 depicts the parts of a plot.

FIGURE 3.2

Components of a Matplotlib plot

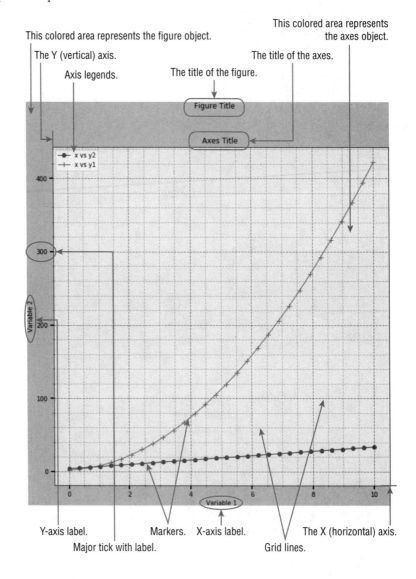

Figure

A figure object can be thought of as the entire diagram, with all the lines and text. You can think of it as the container; everything you plot using Matplotlib must belong to a figure. Figures are generally created using a `pyplot` function, even if you then want to manipulate the figure with the lower-level object-oriented API. Use the following `pyplot` command to create an empty figure:

```
plt.figure()
```

If you want the figure to have specific dimensions, you can provide a tuple with the x-axis and y-axis dimensions in inches:

```
plt.figure(figsize=(10,5))
```

Besides the `figsize` attribute, the `pyplot` figure function can accept various other attributes that you can use to customize aspects of the figure at the point of creation. You can find out more about these attributes at https://matplotlib.org/api/_as_gen/matplotlib.pyplot.figure.html.

The `pyplot` figure function creates a figure and makes it the active figure on which subsequent drawing operations will have effect. The figure is not displayed until there is something drawn to it. If you want to use the object-oriented API to control aspects of the figure after it has been created, you need to store a reference to the figure object in your code and then use the object-oriented API with this reference. The following code snippet creates a figure using the `pyplot` `figure()` function and then uses the object-oriented API to change the background color of the figure:

```
figure1 = plt.figure(figsize=(5,3))
figure1.suptitle('Figure Title')
figure1.set_facecolor('#c3badc')
```

Axes

An axes object is what you would normally consider as a plot. It is the actual graph with various characteristics commonly associated with plots, such as data points, markers, colors, scales, etc. A figure object can contain multiple axes, which in effect are multiple subplots within a larger diagram. The following snippet uses `pyplot` to create a figure with a 2 × 2 grid of axes (subplots), and stores references to both the figure and the axes objects. Each axes object has its own title, which is different from the figure title. The object-oriented API is used to set the title for the figure and the four subplots within the figure. Figure 3.3 depicts the figure generated by executing the code snippet.

```
# create a figure with a 2 x 2 grid of axes objects
figure, axes_list  = plt.subplots(2,2, figsize=(9,9))

# title for the figure object
figure.suptitle('This is the title of the figure')

# title for each axis
axes_list[0,0].set_title('Subplot 0')
axes_list[0,1].set_title('Subplot 1')
axes_list[1,0].set_title('Subplot 2')
axes_list[1,1].set_title('Subplot 3')
```

FIGURE 3.3
A figure object with four
axes objects

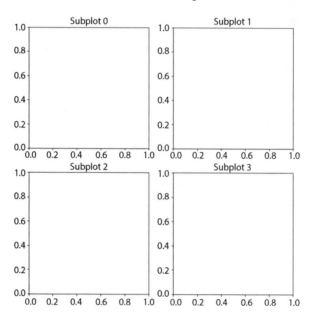

The Matplotlib `figure` and `axes` classes are the primary entry points for working with the lower-level object-oriented API.

Axis

The axis object represents a dimension within a subplot. Two-dimensional plots have two axis objects: one for the horizontal direction and the other for the vertical direction. The `axes` class, which is part of the object-oriented interface, provides several methods to modify attributes of the underlying x- and y-axis.

Axis Labels

The axis label is displayed beneath (or beside) each axis of the plot. Axis labels can be configured by calling the `set_xlabel()` and `set_ylabel()` methods on an axes object. The following snippet demonstrates the use of these methods:

```
figure, axes  = plt.subplots(figsize=(10,10))
axes.set_xlabel('Variable 1')
axes.set_ylabel('Variable 2')
```

If you do not want to use the object-oriented API exposed by the axes object, you can use the `xlabel()` and `ylabel()` functions from the `pyplot` high-level interface that set the axis labels for the active plot. The use of these functions is demonstrated in the following snippet:

```
plt.figure(figsize=(7,7))
plt.xlabel('X values')
plt.ylabel('Y values')
```

Grids

A grid is a set of horizontal and vertical lines inside the plot area that helps in reading values. The axes object provides a method called `grid()` that can be used to customize the appearance of the grid. You can find out more about the `grid()` method of the `axes` class at `https://matplot-lib.org/api/_as_gen/matplotlib.axes.Axes.grid.html`. The `pyplot` module also provides a `grid()` function that is identical to the similarly named method of the `axes` class.

The following snippet demonstrates the use of the `grid()` method of the `axes` class:

```
figure, axes  = plt.subplots(figsize=(10,10))
axes.grid(b=True, which='both', linestyle='--', linewidth=1)
```

Figure 3.4 depicts two plots side by side, one with a grid and one without.

FIGURE 3.4

Comparison of plots with and without grids

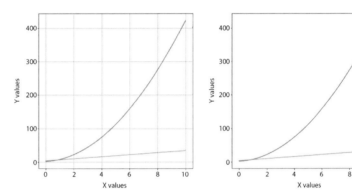

Title

The title is a string that is displayed on top of a plot. Both the figure object and the axes objects within the figure can have titles. Titles are displayed, by default, at the top of the figure or axes object, center aligned. The figure title can be changed use the `suptitle()` method of the `figure` class, or the `suptitle()` function of the `pyplot` module. These functions are identical to each other in syntax and function. You can find more information on the `pyplot suptitle()` function at `https://matplotlib.org/api/_as_gen/matplotlib.pyplot.suptitle.html#matplotlib .pyplot.suptitle`.

The following snippet demonstrates the use of the `suptitle()` method of the `figure` class, and the `suptitle()` function of the `pyplot` module:

```
# create a figure with one axes object.
# Call the suptitle() method on the figure instance.
figure, axes  = plt.subplots(figsize=(10,10))
figure.suptitle('Figure Title')

# create a new figure with one axes object
# use the pyplot suptitle() function
plt.figure(figsize=(7,7))
plt.suptitle('Figure Title')
```

The title of the axes object can be changed by calling the `set_title()` method on the axes object. You can find more information on using the `set_title()` method at `https://matplotlib .org/api/_as_gen/matplotlib.axes.Axes.set_title.html#matplotlib.axes .Axes.set_title`.

The `pyplot` module provides a convenience function called `title()`, which operates on the active axes object and has the same signature as the `set_title()` method of the axes class. The following snippet demonstrates the use of the `set_title()` method of the axes class and the `title()` function of the pyplot module:

```
# create a figure with one axes object.
# Call the set_title() method on the axes instance.
figure, axes  = plt.subplots(figsize=(10,10))
axes.suptitle(Axes Title')

# create a new figure with one axes object
# use the pyplot suptitle() function
plt.figure(figsize=(7,7))
plt.title(Axes Title')
```

Common Plots

In the previous section you learned the aspects of a typical Matplotlib plot, and that there are often different ways to configure a plot. The high-level `pyplot` API provides a functional interface and the lower-level Matplotlib API operates using an object-oriented interface. In this section, you will learn to create common types of plots using Matplotlib.

Histograms

A histogram is commonly used to visualize the distribution of a numeric variable. Histograms are not applicable when dealing with a categorical variable. The following snippet uses functions from the pyplot module to generate a histogram of the Age attribute of the popular Titanic dataset. The resulting figure is depicted in Figure 3.5.

```
import numpy as np
import pandas as pd

# load the contents of a file into a pandas Dataframe
input_file = './datasets/titanic_dataset/original/train.csv'
df_titanic = pd.read_csv(input_file)

# set the index
df_titanic.set_index("PassengerId", inplace=True)

# use pyplot functions to plot a histogram of the 'Age' attribute
fig = plt.figure(figsize=(7,7))
plt.xlabel('Passenger Age')
plt.ylabel('Count')
plt.grid()
```

```
n, bins, patches = plt.hist(df_titanic['Age'], histtype='bar',
                            color='#0dc28d', align='mid',
                            rwidth=0.90, bins=7)
```

FIGURE 3.5

Histogram of Passenger
Age values

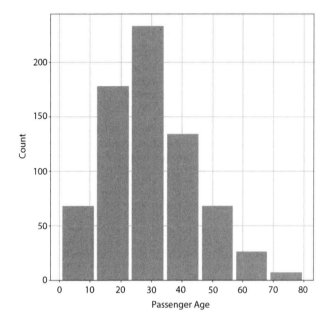

The pyplot hist() function is used to create a histogram. The function takes several arguments. Some of the arguments that have been used in the preceding snippet are histtype='bar', which signifies that you want a standard histogram; rwidth=0.9, which leaves space between the bars; and bins=7, which is the number of bars. You can find a full list of parameters supported by the hist() function at https://matplotlib.org/api/_as_gen/matplotlib.pyplot.hist.html#matplotlib.pyplot.hist.

The appearance of the histogram is influenced by the binning strategy, which in turn is controlled by the value you pass into the bins parameter. If you pass an integer (as in the preceding snippet), Matplotlib will create the specified number of equal-width bins and use the boundaries (edges) of the bins to determine the number of values in each bin. You can optionally specify the bin edges instead of the number of bins. In most cases you simply specify the number of bins.

The pyplot hist() function returns a tuple, (n, bins, patches). The first element of the tuple, n, is an array with the counts for each bin. The second element, bins, is an array of floating-point values that contains the bin edges, and the third element, patches, is an array of rectangle objects that represent the low-level drawing primitives used by Matplotlib to make the bars. You can use the print() statement to inspect the contents of the tuple:

```
print (n)
[ 68. 178. 233. 134.  68.  26.   7.]

print (bins)
[0.42
```

```
     11.78857143
     23.15714286
     34.52571429
     45.89428571
     57.26285714
     68.63142857
     80.0]

print (patches[0])
Rectangle(xy=(0.988429, 0), width=10.2317, height=68, angle=0)
```

The following snippet uses pyplot functions to create a figure with four subplots (axes objects) and uses the object-oriented API to create histograms of the same data in each of the subplots, but with different numbers of bins. The result of this snippet is depicted in Figure 3.6.

```
# use pyplot functions and matplotlib object-oriented API
# to plot multiple histograms of the same data, with different
# binning strategies.

fig, axes_list = plt.subplots(2,2, figsize=(11,11))

# plot a histogram with 3 bins
axes_list[0,0].set_xlabel('Passenger Age')
axes_list[0,0].set_ylabel('Count')
axes_list[0,0].grid()

n1, bins1, patches1 = axes_list[0,0].hist(df_titanic['Age'], histtype='bar',
                         color='#0dc28d', align='mid',
                         rwidth=0.90, bins=3)


# plot a histogram with 10 bins
axes_list[0,1].set_xlabel('Passenger Age')
axes_list[0,1].set_ylabel('Count')
axes_list[0,1].grid()
n2, bins2, patches2 = axes_list[0,1].hist(df_titanic['Age'], histtype='bar',
                         color='#0dc28d', align='mid',
                         rwidth=0.90, bins=10)

# plot a histogram with 30 bins
axes_list[1,0].set_xlabel('Passenger Age')
axes_list[1,0].set_ylabel('Count')
axes_list[1,0].grid()
n3, bins3, patches3 = axes_list[1,0].hist(df_titanic['Age'], histtype='bar',
                         color='#0dc28d', align='mid',
                         rwidth=0.90, bins=30)
```

```
# plot a histogram with 100 bins
axes_list[1,1].set_xlabel('Passenger Age')
axes_list[1,1].set_ylabel('Count')
axes_list[1,1].grid()
n4, bins4, patches4 = axes_list[1,1].hist(df_titanic['Age'], histtype='bar',
                            color='#0dc28d', align='mid',
                            rwidth=0.90, bins=100)
```

FIGURE 3.6

Histograms of Passenger Age values created using different binning strategies

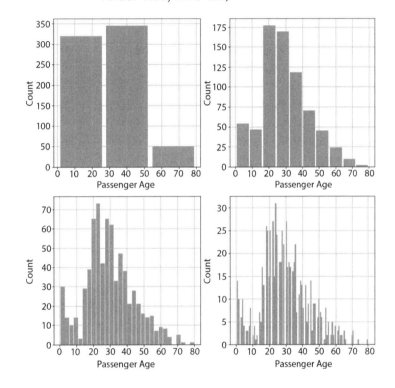

As you can infer, the binning strategy significantly affects the appearance of the histogram and the inferences that you can make from the histogram. There is no set rule to the number of bins that must be used; often data scientists use a number of different binning strategies to reveal characteristics of the data that were not previously visible. A common rule of thumb is to set the number of bins to be the square root of the number of values as a starting point, and then update as necessary. A commonly used approach in statistics to select the bin width for histograms was proposed in 1981 by David Freedman and Persi Diaconis and is known as the Freedman-Diaconis rule. The general idea is to set the bin width to be $2 \times IQR /$ (number of observations) $^{1/3}$. Using this equation to compute the bin width, you can divide the range of values by the bin width to work out the number of bins. You can get more information on this rule from the original paper published in 1981 titled "On the histogram as a density estimator." You can access a copy of the paper at `https://statistics.stanford.edu/sites/g/files/sbiybj6031/f/EFS%20NSF%20159.pdf`.

The Pandas dataframe object also provides limited plotting capabilities. These capabilities are built on top on Matplotlib, but in some situations, you may find the Pandas plotting functions simpler to use. The following snippet shows how you could create a simple histogram using the Pandas dataframe plot function:

```
%matplotlib inline
import matplotlib.pyplot as plt
import matplotlib as mpl
import numpy as np
import pandas as pd

# load the contents of a file into a pandas Dataframe
input_file = './datasets/titanic_dataset/original/train.csv'
df_titanic = pd.read_csv(input_file)

# set the index
df_titanic.set_index("PassengerId", inplace=True)

fig = plt.figure(figsize=(7,7))
plt.xlabel('Passenger Age')
plt.ylabel('Count')

df_titanic['Age'].plot.hist(color='#0dc28d', align='mid',
                            rwidth=0.90, bins=7, grid=True)
```

Bar Chart

Bar charts are commonly used when you are dealing with a categorical variable. Each bar in a bar chart represents some information about a categorical attribute, such as a count, mean, or other measure. Bar charts can be used with both nominal and ordinal categorical data. When plotting a bar chart for nominal categorical data it is common practice to order the bars so that the height (or length) of the bars increases in an orderly fashion.

This is possible because a category that contains nominal data does not have any inherent order between the values, and hence you can freely order the placement of the bars to create a visually pleasing figure. Continuing with the use of the Titanic dataset from the previous section, the following snippet creates a bar plot of the Embarked attribute. The resulting bar chart is depicted in Figure 3.7.

```
# use pyplot functions to plot a bar chart of the 'Embarked' attribute
fig = plt.figure(figsize=(9,9))
plt.xlabel('Embarkation Point')
plt.ylabel('Count')
plt.grid()

values = df_titanic['Embarked'].unique()
counts = df_titanic['Embarked'].value_counts(dropna=False)
x_positions = np.arange(len(values))

plt.bar(x_positions, counts, align='center')
plt.xticks(x_positions, values)
```

FIGURE 3.7
Bar chart of the
Embarked attribute

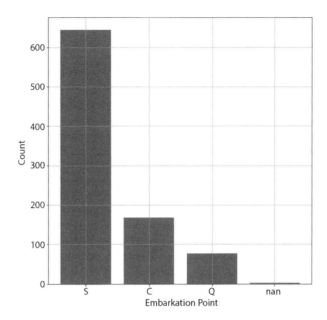

Plotting bar charts is significantly simpler with the Pandas dataframe plot function. The following snippet demonstrates how you can create the same bar chart using Pandas functions:

```
# use Pandas dataframe functions to plot a bar chart of the 'Embarked' attribute
fig = plt.figure(figsize=(7,7))
plt.xlabel('Embarkation Point')
plt.ylabel('Count')
plt.grid()

df_titanic['Embarked'].value_counts(dropna=False).plot.bar(grid=True)
```

Grouped Bar Chart

If you want to show information about different subgroups within each category, a grouped bar chart can be used. A grouped bar chart, as its name suggests, is a chart with groups of bars clustered together. Each bar group provides information on one category, and the length of bars within the group provides information on the individual subgroups within the category.

For example, a grouped bar chart could be used to visualize the distribution of the number of individuals who survived and the number who did not, for each embarkation point. The following snippet creates a grouped bar chart for the Embarked attribute with two bars in each group. The resulting bar chart is depicted in Figure 3.8.

```
# a grouped bar chart for the Embarked attribute with
# two bars per group.
survived_df = df_titanic[df_titanic['Survived']==1]
not_survived_df = df_titanic[df_titanic['Survived']==0]
```

```
values = df_titanic['Embarked'].dropna().unique()
embarked_counts_survived = survived_df['Embarked'].value_counts(dropna=True)
embarked_counts_not_survived =
not_survived_df['Embarked'].value_counts(dropna=True)

x_positions = np.arange(len(values))

fig = plt.figure(figsize=(9,9))
plt.xlabel('Embarkation Point')
plt.ylabel('Count')
plt.grid()

bar_width = 0.35

plt.bar(x_positions, embarked_counts_survived, bar_width, color='#009bdb',
label='Survived')
plt.bar(x_positions + bar_width, embarked_counts_not_survived, bar_width,
color='#00974d', label='Not Survived')

plt.xticks(x_positions + bar_width, values)
plt.legend()

plt.show()
```

FIGURE 3.8
Grouped bar chart of the
Embarked attribute

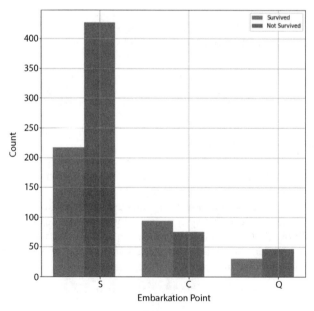

The following snippet shows how to use the Pandas plotting functions to draw the same grouped bar chart:

```
# a grouped bar chart for the Embarked attribute with
# two bars per group.
survived_df = df_titanic[df_titanic['Survived']==1]
not_survived_df = df_titanic[df_titanic['Survived']==0]

values = df_titanic['Embarked'].dropna().unique()
embarked_counts_survived = survived_df['Embarked'].value_counts(dropna=True)
embarked_counts_not_survived =
not_survived_df['Embarked'].value_counts(dropna=True)

embarked_counts_survived.name = 'Survived'
embarked_counts_not_survived.name = 'Not Survived'
df = pd.concat([embarked_counts_survived, embarked_counts_not_survived],
axis=1)

fig, axes = plt.subplots(figsize=(9,9))
plt.xlabel('Embarkation Point')
plt.ylabel('Count')

df.plot.bar(grid=True, ax=axes, color=['#009bdb', '#00974d'])
```

Stacked Bar Chart

A stacked bar chart provides another way to visualize the same information. Instead of having multiple bars in clustered groups, a stacked bar chart uses one bar per categorical value and splits the bar to depict the distribution of subgroups within the category.

The following snippet creates a stacked bar chart for the Embarked attribute showing the distribution of survivors from each embarkation point. The resulting bar chart is depicted in Figure 3.9.

```
# a stacked bar chart for the Embarked attribute
# showing the number of survivors in each category
survived_df = df_titanic[df_titanic['Survived']==1]
not_survived_df = df_titanic[df_titanic['Survived']==0]

values = df_titanic['Embarked'].dropna().unique()
embarked_counts_survived = survived_df['Embarked'].value_counts(dropna=True)
embarked_counts_not_survived =
not_survived_df['Embarked'].value_counts(dropna=True)

x_positions = np.arange(len(values))

fig = plt.figure(figsize=(9,9))
plt.xlabel('Embarkation Point')
plt.ylabel('Count')
plt.grid()

plt.bar(x_positions, embarked_counts_survived, color='#009bdb',
label='Survived')
plt.bar(x_positions, embarked_counts_not_survived, color='#00974d', label='Not
Survived', bottom=embarked_counts_survived)
```

```
plt.xticks(x_positions, values)
plt.legend()

plt.show()
```

FIGURE 3.9
Stacked bar chart of the
Embarked attribute

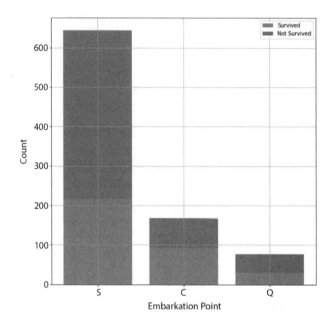

Creating a stacked bar chart with Pandas plotting functions is simply a matter of adding the `stacked=True` attribute to the argument list of the `dataframe.plot.bar()` function. The following snippet using Pandas plotting functions to draw the same stacked bar chart:

```
# a stacked percentage bar chart for the Embarked attribute
# showing the number of survivors in each category
survived_df = df_titanic[df_titanic['Survived']==1]
not_survived_df = df_titanic[df_titanic['Survived']==0]

values = df_titanic['Embarked'].dropna().unique()
embarked_counts_survived = survived_df['Embarked'].value_counts(dropna=True)
embarked_counts_not_survived =
not_survived_df['Embarked'].value_counts(dropna=True)

embarked_counts_survived.name = 'Survived'
embarked_counts_not_survived.name = 'Not Survived'
df = pd.concat([embarked_counts_survived, embarked_counts_not_survived],
axis=1)

fig, axes = plt.subplots(figsize=(9,9))
plt.xlabel('Embarkation Point')
plt.ylabel('Count')

df.plot.bar(stacked=True, grid=True, ax=axes, color=['#009bdb', '#00974d'])
```

The power of Pandas plotting functions over pyplot and Matplotlib is evident with stacked bar charts, especially if you have more than two groups per bar. With Matplotlib and pyplot functions, you will have to plot each group on top of the other using multiple plt.bar() statements. With Pandas, all you need to do is get your data in a dataframe and make a single call to dataframe.plot.bar().

Stacked Percentage Bar Chart

If you want to show the percentage contribution of each subgroup within the categories, you can use a stacked percentage bar chart. The bars in a stacked percentage bar chart are all the same height. The following snippet creates a stacked percentage bar chart for the Embarked attribute showing the percentage of survivors from each embarkation point. The resulting bar chart is depicted in Figure 3.10.

```
# a stacked percentage bar chart for the Embarked attribute
# showing the number of survivors in each category
survived_df = df_titanic[df_titanic['Survived']==1]
not_survived_df = df_titanic[df_titanic['Survived']==0]

values = df_titanic['Embarked'].dropna().unique()
counts = df_titanic['Embarked'].value_counts(dropna=True)

embarked_counts_survived = survived_df['Embarked'].value_counts(dropna=True)
embarked_counts_not_survived =
not_survived_df['Embarked'].value_counts(dropna=True)

embarked_counts_survived_percent = embarked_counts_survived / counts * 100
embarked_counts_not_survived_percent = embarked_counts_not_survived / counts *
100

x_positions = np.arange(len(values))

fig = plt.figure(figsize=(9,9))
plt.xlabel('Embarkation Point')
plt.ylabel('Percentage')
plt.grid()

plt.bar(x_positions, embarked_counts_survived_percent, color='#009bdb',
label='Survived')
plt.bar(x_positions, embarked_counts_not_survived_percent, color='#00974d',
label='Not Survived', bottom=embarked_counts_survived_percent)

plt.xticks(x_positions, values)
plt.legend()

plt.show()
```

FIGURE 3.10
Stacked percentage bar
chart of the
Embarked attribute

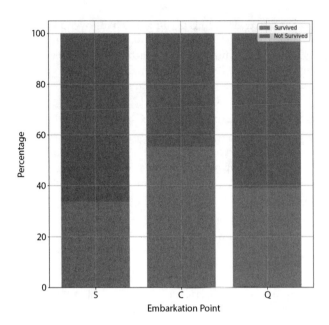

FIGURE 3.10
Stacked percentage bar
chart of the
Embarked attribute

The following snippet creates an equivalent chart using Pandas plotting functions:

```
# a stacked percentage bar chart for the Embarked attribute
# showing the number of survivors in each category
survived_df = df_titanic[df_titanic['Survived']==1]
not_survived_df = df_titanic[df_titanic['Survived']==0]

values = df_titanic['Embarked'].dropna().unique()
counts = df_titanic['Embarked'].value_counts(dropna=True)

embarked_counts_survived = survived_df['Embarked'].value_counts(dropna=True)
embarked_counts_not_survived =
not_survived_df['Embarked'].value_counts(dropna=True)

embarked_counts_survived_percent = embarked_counts_survived / counts * 100
embarked_counts_not_survived_percent = embarked_counts_not_survived / counts *
100

embarked_counts_survived_percent.name = 'Survived'
embarked_counts_not_survived_percent.name = 'Not Survived'
df = pd.concat([embarked_counts_survived_percent,
embarked_counts_not_survived_percent], axis=1)

fig, axes = plt.subplots(figsize=(9,9))
plt.xlabel('Embarkation Point')
plt.ylabel('% Survived ')

df.plot.bar(stacked=True, grid=True, ax=axes, color=['#009bdb', '#00974d'])
```

Pie Charts

Pie charts are an alternative to bar charts and can be used to plot the proportion of unique values in a categorical attribute. The pyplot module provides the pie() function that can be used to create a pie chart. The pie function of the pyplot module uses the underlying pie() method of the axes class. You can access the documentation for the pyplot pie() function at https://matplotlib.org/api/_as_gen/matplotlib.pyplot.pie.html.

The following snippet uses the pyplot pie() function on the contents of the Embarked column of the Titanic dataset to create a pie chart that depicts the percentage of passengers boarding from each embarkation point. Figure 3.11 depicts the resulting pie chart.

```
# use pyplot functions to plot a pie chart of the 'Embarked' attribute
fig = plt.figure(figsize=(9,9))

embarkation_ports = df_titanic['Embarked'].dropna().unique()
counts = df_titanic['Embarked'].value_counts(dropna=True)

total_embarked = counts.values.sum()
counts_percentage = counts / total_embarked * 100

counts_percentage.values
plt.pie(counts_percentage.values,
        labels=embarkation_ports,
        autopct='%1.1f%%', shadow=True, startangle=90)
```

FIGURE 3.11

Pie chart of proportion of passengers embarking from different ports

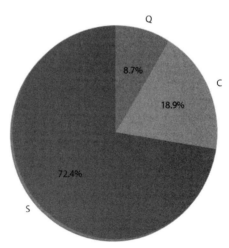

You can also use the Pandas dataframe plot.pie() function to create pie charts. If your data is already in a Pandas dataframe, this approach will require significantly less code. The downside to using the Pandas plotting function is the reduced level of options to customize the pie chart. The following snippet uses Pandas plotting functions to make the same pie chart:

```
# use Pandas functions to plot a pie chart of the 'Embarked' attribute
fig = plt.figure(figsize=(7,7))
df_titanic['Embarked'].value_counts(dropna=True).plot.pie()
```

When the target attribute of a dataset is binary, a pie chart can help convey the distribution of values in each categorical attribute, grouped by the target binary attribute. The following snippet uses Matplotlib's Axes.pie() method to create three pie charts showing the percentage of survivors from the three embarkation ports in the Titanic dataset. Figure 3.12 depicts the resulting pie charts.

```
# three pie charts, showing the proportion
# of survivors for each embarkation point
# S = Southampton
# C = Cherbourg
# Q = Queenstown
S_df = df_titanic[df_titanic['Embarked'] == 'S']
C_df = df_titanic[df_titanic['Embarked'] == 'C']
Q_df = df_titanic[df_titanic['Embarked'] == 'Q']

S_Total_Embarked = S_df['Embarked'].count()
S_Survived_Count = S_df[S_df['Survived']==1].Embarked.count()
S_Survived_Percentage = S_Survived_Count / S_Total_Embarked * 100
S_Not_Survived_Percentage = 100.0 - S_Survived_Percentage

C_Total_Embarked = C_df['Embarked'].count()
C_Survived_Count = C_df[C_df['Survived']==1].Embarked.count()
C_Survived_Percentage = C_Survived_Count / C_Total_Embarked * 100
C_Not_Survived_Percentage = 100.0 - C_Survived_Percentage

Q_Total_Embarked = Q_df['Embarked'].count()
Q_Survived_Count = Q_df[Q_df['Survived']==1].Embarked.count()
Q_Survived_Percentage = Q_Survived_Count / Q_Total_Embarked * 100
Q_Not_Survived_Percentage = 100.0 - Q_Survived_Percentage


fig, axes = plt.subplots(1, 3, figsize=(16,4))

Wedge_Labels = ['Survived', 'Not Survived']
S_Wedge_Sizes = [S_Survived_Percentage, S_Not_Survived_Percentage]
C_Wedge_Sizes = [C_Survived_Percentage, C_Not_Survived_Percentage]
Q_Wedge_Sizes = [Q_Survived_Percentage, Q_Not_Survived_Percentage]

axes[0].pie(S_Wedge_Sizes, labels=Wedge_Labels, autopct='%1.1f%%', shadow=True,
startangle=90)
axes[0].set_title('Southampton')

axes[1].pie(C_Wedge_Sizes, labels=Wedge_Labels, autopct='%1.1f%%', shadow=True,
startangle=90)
axes[1].set_title('Cherbourg')

axes[2].pie(Q_Wedge_Sizes, labels=Wedge_Labels, autopct='%1.1f%%', shadow=True,
startangle=90)
axes[2].set_title('Queenstown')
```

FIGURE 3.12
Pie charts showing the
proportion of
survivors from each
embarkation point

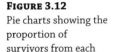

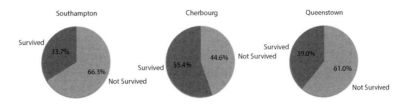

FIGURE 3.12
Pie charts showing the
proportion of
survivors from each
embarkation point

The same pie charts can be created using far less code if you were to use the Pandas plotting functions, at the expense of loss in customizability. The following snippet will generate the same chart using Pandas plotting functions:

```
# three pie charts, showing the proportion
# of survivors for each embarkation point
# S = Southampton
# C = Cherbourg
# Q = Queenstown

survived_df = df_titanic[df_titanic['Survived']==1]
not_survived_df = df_titanic[df_titanic['Survived']==0]

values = df_titanic['Embarked'].dropna().unique()
counts = df_titanic['Embarked'].value_counts(dropna=True)

embarked_counts_survived = survived_df['Embarked'].value_counts(dropna=True)
embarked_counts_not_survived =
not_survived_df['Embarked'].value_counts(dropna=True)

embarked_counts_survived_percent = embarked_counts_survived / counts * 100
embarked_counts_not_survived_percent = embarked_counts_not_survived / counts *
100

embarked_counts_survived_percent.name = 'Survived'
embarked_counts_not_survived_percent.name = 'Not Survived'
df = pd.concat([embarked_counts_survived_percent,
embarked_counts_not_survived_percent], axis=1)

df.T.plot.pie(sharex=True, subplots=True, figsize=(16, 4))
```

Box Plot

A box plot provides a way to view the distribution of a numerical attribute. It was created in 1969 by John Tukey. A box plot is used to find out if the values of the attribute are symmetrically distributed, the overall spread of the values, and information on outliers. A box plot provides information on five statistical qualities of the attribute values:

◆ *First quartile:* 25% of the values of the attribute are less than this number. This is also known as the 25th percentile.

◆ *Second quartile:* 50% of the values of the attribute are less than this number. This is also known as the 50th percentile, or the median value.

◆ *Third quartile:* 75% of the values of the attribute are less than this number. This is also known as the 75th percentile.

◆ *Minimum:* This value is computed using the formula Min = Q1 − 1.5 * IQR, where IQR is the inter-quartile range, defined as Q3 − Q2. Any attribute values that are lower than this minimum will be treated as outliers in the plot.

◆ *Maximum:* This value is computed using the formula Min = Q3 + 1.5 * IQR, where IQR is the inter-quartile range, defined as Q3 − Q2. Any attribute values that are greater than this maximum will be treated as outliers in the plot.

The pyplot module provides the boxplot() function that can be used to create a box plot. The boxplot() function of the pyplot module uses the underlying boxplot() method of the axes class. You can access the documentation for the pyplot boxplot() function at https://matplotlib.org/api/_as_gen/matplotlib.pyplot.boxplot.html.

The following snippet uses the pyplot boxplot() function on the contents of the Age column of the Titanic dataset to create a box plot that depicts the spreads of the values of the attribute. Figure 3.13 depicts the resulting box plot.

```
# use pyplot functions to create a box plot of the 'Embarked' attribute
fig , axes = plt.subplots(figsize=(9,9))
box_plot = plt.boxplot(df_titanic['Age'].dropna())
axes.set_xticklabels(['Age'])
```

FIGURE 3.13
Box plot showing the distribution of the Age attribute

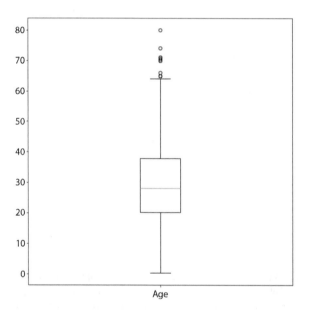

The following snippet will generate the same box plot using Pandas plotting functions:

```
df_titanic.boxplot(column = 'Age', figsize=(9,9), grid=False);
```

The compact nature of box plots makes them extremely useful to compare the distributions of different numerical attributes, or the distributions of subgroups within a numerical attribute. The following snippet uses `pyplot` functions to create two box plots of the Age attribute, one for those that survived the Titanic disaster, and the other for those that did not. Figure 3.14 depicts the resulting box plots.

```
# compare box plots of the Age attribute for those who survived
# against those that did not.
survived_df = df_titanic[df_titanic['Survived']==1].dropna()
not_survived_df = df_titanic[df_titanic['Survived']==0].dropna()

fig , axes = plt.subplots(figsize=(9,9))
box_plot = plt.boxplot([survived_df['Age'], not_survived_df['Age']],
                        labels=['Survived', 'Not Survived'])
```

FIGURE 3.14
Box plots of the Age attribute comparing the distribution of survivors with those who did not survive the Titanic disaster

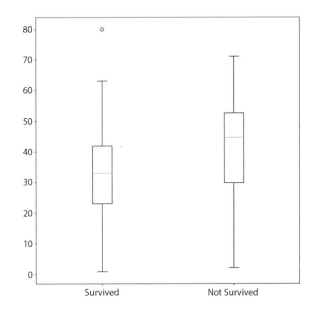

The following snippet will generate the same box plot using Pandas plotting functions:

```
df_titanic.boxplot(column = 'Age', by = 'Survived', figsize=(9,9), grid=False);
```

Scatter Plots

A scatter plot is a 2D plot that plots two continuous numeric attributes against each other. One attribute is plotted along the x-axis and the other is plotted along the y-axis. Scatter plots are a collection of points and are typically used to plot the correlation between variables, with each point of the scatter plot representing the value of two variables. Scatter plots can also be used to visualize the grouping of data. The following snippet creates a scatter plot of the Age and Fare attributes from the Titanic dataset after normalizing the values and imputing missing values with the mean of the attribute. Figure 3.15 depicts the resulting scatter plot.

```
# impute missing values:
# Age with the median age
# Fare with the mean fare
median_age = df_titanic['Age'].median()
df_titanic["Age"].fillna(median_age, inplace=True)

mean_fare = df_titanic['Fare'].mean()
df_titanic["Fare"].fillna(mean_fare, inplace=True)

# use pyplot functions to create a scatter plot of the 'Age' and 'Fare' attribute
fig , axes = plt.subplots(figsize=(9,9))
plt.xlabel('Age')
plt.ylabel('Fare')
plt.grid()

plt.scatter(df_titanic['Age'], df_titanic['Fare'])
```

FIGURE 3.15

Scatter plot of the Age attribute against the Fare attribute

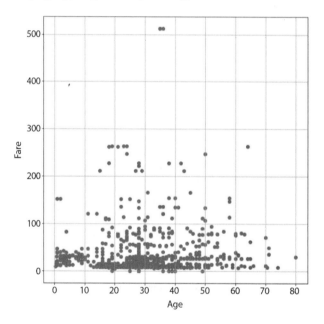

The Pandas dataframe contains the plot.scatter() function that can be used to create a scatter plot. The following snippet demonstrates the use of this function to create an equivalent scatter plot:

```
df_titanic.plot.scatter(x='Age', y='Fare', figsize=(9,9))
```

You can use a scatter plot to get a visual indicator of the degree of correlation between two attributes. It is common to create a matrix of scatter plots of each attribute in the dataset against every other attribute; this, however, is only practical for a small number of attributes. Figure 3.16 shows the scatter plot of attributes that have the ideal strong positive and strong negative correlation. The ideal strong positive correlation would occur when most of the points lie along a straight line from the bottom-left corner to the top-right corner of the plot. The ideal strong negative correlation would occur when most of the points lie along a straight line from the top-left corner to the bottom-right corner of the plot.

FIGURE 3.16
Scatter plots depicting the ideal strong positive and strong negative correlation

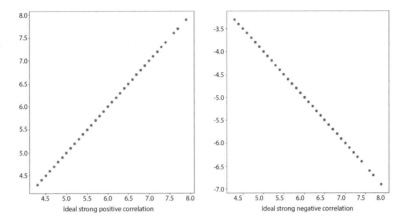

The following snippet presents a function that can be used to generate a scatter plot matrix out of the contents of a Pandas dataframe. The function takes three arguments. The first is the dataframe object, the second is the height of the figure (in inches), and the third is the width of the figure (in inches):

```
# Generates a M X M scatterplot matrix of subplots.
def generate_scatterplot_matrix(df_input, size_h, size_w):
    num_points, num_attributes = df_input.shape
    fig, axes = plt.subplots(num_attributes, num_attributes, figsize=(size_h,
size_w))

    column_names = df_input.columns.values

    for x in range(0, num_attributes):
        for y in range(0, num_attributes):
            axes[x , y].scatter(df_input.iloc[:,x], df_input.iloc[:,y])

            # configure the ticks
            axes[x , y].xaxis.set_visible(False)
            axes[x , y].yaxis.set_visible(False)

            # Set up ticks only on one side for the "edge" subplots...
            if axes[x , y].is_first_col():
                axes[x , y].yaxis.set_ticks_position('left')
                axes[x , y].yaxis.set_visible(True)
                axes[x , y].set_ylabel(column_names[x])

            if axes[x , y].is_last_col():
                axes[x , y].yaxis.set_ticks_position('right')
                axes[x , y].yaxis.set_visible(True)
```

```
                if axes[x , y].is_first_row():
                    axes[x , y].xaxis.set_ticks_position('top')
                    axes[x , y].xaxis.set_visible(True)

                if axes[x , y].is_last_row():
                    axes[x , y].xaxis.set_ticks_position('bottom')
                    axes[x , y].xaxis.set_visible(True)
                    axes[x , y].set_xlabel(column_names[y])


        return fig, axes
```

To see a scatter plot matrix, let's use the generate_scatter_plot function on the popular Iris dataset. Recall from Chapter 2 that Scikit-learn contains a toy version of the Iris dataset. The dataset contains the heights and widths of the sepals and petals of iris flowers. The following snippet loads the Iris dataset into a dataframe and uses the generate_scatter_plot function to create a scatter plot matrix. The resulting figure is depicted in Figure 3.17.

```
import sklearn
iris = sklearn.datasets.load_iris()
df_iris = pd.DataFrame(iris.data, columns = iris.feature_names)
generate_scatterplot_matrix (df_iris, 20, 20)
```

FIGURE 3.17

Scatter plot matrix of the features of the Iris dataset

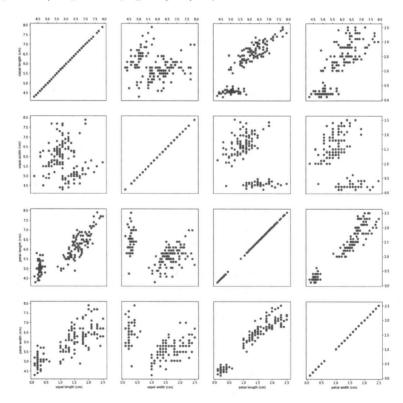

As you can see, Matplotlib does not have a built-in function to create a scatter plot matrix. The Pandas plotting module has a function called `scatter_matrix()` that can be used to generate a scatter plot matrix from a dataframe. The following snippet demonstrates the use of the `scatter_matrix()` function:

```
import sklearn.datasets
import pandas.plotting

iris = sklearn.datasets.load_iris()
df_iris = pd.DataFrame(iris.data, columns = iris.feature_names)

pandas.plotting.scatter_matrix(df_iris, figsize=(12, 12))
```

Scatter plots can also be used to visualize clusters within data. The following snippet creates a synthetic dataset of x, y values in four clusters and plots all the values in a scatter plot. The synthetic data is created using Scikit-learn's `make_blobs()` function. You can learn more about this function at `https://scikit-learn.org/stable/modules/generated/sklearn.datasets.make_blobs.html`. Figure 3.18 depicts the resulting scatter plot.

```
# scatter plots can also be used to visualize
# groups within data. This is illustrated below
# using a synthetic dataset

from sklearn.datasets import make_blobs
coordinates, clusters = make_blobs(n_samples = 500, n_features = 2, centers=4,
random_state=12)

coordinates_cluster1 = coordinates[clusters==0]
coordinates_cluster2 = coordinates[clusters==1]
coordinates_cluster3 = coordinates[clusters==2]
coordinates_cluster4 = coordinates[clusters==3]

fig , axes = plt.subplots(figsize=(9,9))
plt.xlabel('X Values')
plt.ylabel('Y Values')
plt.grid()

plt.scatter(coordinates_cluster1[:,0], coordinates_cluster1[:,1])
plt.scatter(coordinates_cluster2[:,0], coordinates_cluster2[:,1])
plt.scatter(coordinates_cluster3[:,0], coordinates_cluster3[:,1])
plt.scatter(coordinates_cluster4[:,0], coordinates_cluster4[:,1])
```

NOTE To follow along with this chapter ensure you have installed Anaconda Navigator and Jupyter Notebook as described in Appendix A.

You can download the code files for this chapter from `www.wiley.com/go/machinelearningawscloud` or from GitHub using the following URL:

`https://github.com/asmtechnology/awsmlbook-chapter3.git`

FIGURE 3.18
Scatter plot of four
clusters of data

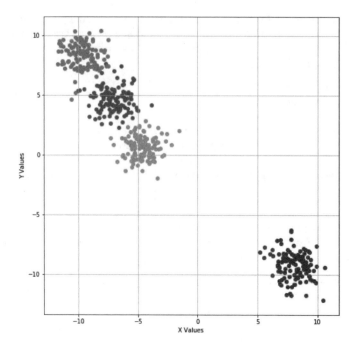

Summary

- Matplotlib is a plotting library for Python that offers functionality to generate numerous types of plots and the ability to customize these plots.

- The `pyplot` module within Matplotlib provides a high-level functional plotting interface.

- Matplotlib also provides a lower-level object-oriented API that can be used on its own, or in conjunction with the `pyplot` module.

- Seaborn is another Python plotting package that builds on top of Matplotlib.

- A histogram is commonly used to visualize the distribution of a numeric variable. Histograms are not applicable when dealing with categorical variables.

- The binning strategy significantly affects the appearance of a histogram.

- Bar charts are commonly used when you are dealing with categorical variables. Bar charts can be used with both nominal and ordinal categorical data.

- A stacked bar chart uses one bar per categorical value and splits the bar to depict the distribution of subgroups within the category.

- A box plot provides a way to view the distribution of a numerical attribute.

Chapter 4

Creating Machine Learning Models with Scikit-learn

WHAT'S IN THIS CHAPTER

◆ Introduction to Scikit-learn

◆ Learn to split your training data into training and testing sets

◆ Learn to use k-fold cross validation

◆ Learn to create different types of machine learning models

In Chapter 2, you learned about techniques to explore data and perform feature engineering. In this chapter you will learn to use Scikit-learn to split your training data into training and test sets, and to create different types of machine learning models. This chapter will use the Titanic and Iris datasets to illustrate different types of model-building techniques. A copy of these datasets is included with the files that accompany this chapter.

NOTE   To follow along with this chapter ensure you have installed Anaconda Navigator and Jupyter Notebook as described in Appendix A.

You can download the code files for this chapter from www.wiley.com/go/machinelearningawscloud or from GitHub using the following URL:

```
https://github.com/asmtechnology/awsmlbook-chapter4.git
```

Introducing Scikit-learn

Scikit-learn is a Python library that provides a number of features that are suitable for machine learning engineers and data scientists. It was developed by David Cournapeau in 2007 and today provides ready-to-use implementations of several popular machine learning algorithms such as linear regression, logistic regression, support vector machines, clustering, and random forests. In addition to providing ready-to-use implementations of popular machine learning algorithms, Scikit-learn also provides tools to split datasets into test-train subsets, implement k-fold cross validation, evaluate model performance using popular metrics, and detect outliers, and includes algorithms to aid with feature selection. Scikit-learn builds upon several other libraries such as NumPy, Pandas, and Matplotlib, and at its core is focused on model-building and -evaluation tasks, and not tasks such as data loading and visualization.

Scikit-learn is one of the reasons for the rise in number of real-world applications of machine learning. Scikit-learn's vast collection of algorithms allow you to get started with machine learning without a significant background in mathematics and statistics.

In order to use your data with Scikit-learn, it must be loaded into NumPy arrays or Pandas dataframes. You can get more information on the capabilities of Scikit-learn at `https://scikit-learn.org/stable/`.

Creating a Training and Test Dataset

At its heart, building a machine learning model involves creating a computer program that can draw inferences from the features during the training phase and then testing the quality of the model by making predictions. A common practice involves setting aside some of the labeled training data before the model-building phase and testing the model using this data that the model has not previously encountered. The performance of the model on this unseen data is used to determine if the model is good enough, or if improvements are needed. The benefit of having a separate training and testing set is that it ensures the model has not memorized the training examples (a phenomenon known as overfitting). It is important to note that in the case of supervised learning, both the training and test sets are labeled and the original dataset must be evenly shuffled before the subsets are created.

Scikit-learn provides a function called `train_test_split()` in the `model_selection` submodule that can be used to split a Pandas dataframe into two dataframes, one for model building and the other for model evaluation. The `test_train_split()` function has several parameters, most of which have default values. The most commonly used parameters are:

♦ `test_size`: This value can be an integer or floating-point number. When the value is an integer, it specifies the number of elements that should be retained for the test set. When the value is a floating-point number, it specifies the percentage of the original dataset to include in the test set.

♦ `random_state`: This is an integer value that is used to seed the random-number generator used to shuffle the samples.

The output of the `train_test_split()` function is a list of four arrays in the following order:

♦ The first item of the list is an array that contains the training set features.

♦ The second item of the list is an array that contains the test set features.

♦ The third item of the list is an array that contains the training set labels (target variable).

♦ The fourth item of the list is an array that contains the test set labels.

You can find detailed information on the parameters of the `train_test_split()` function at `https://scikit-learn.org/stable/modules/generated/sklearn.model_selection.train_test_split.html`.

The following snippet demonstrates the use of this function to split the Iris flowers dataset into a training and test set, with 25% of the data reserved for the test set:

```
import numpy as np
import pandas as pd
# load iris data set
```

```
from sklearn.datasets import load_iris
iris_dataset = load_iris()
df_iris_features = pd.DataFrame(data = iris_dataset.data,
columns=iris_dataset.feature_names)
df_iris_target = pd.DataFrame(data = iris_dataset.target, columns=['class'])
# split iris dataset
iris_split = train_test_split(df_iris_features, df_iris_target,
                test_size=0.25, random_state=17)
df_iris_features_train = iris_split[0]
df_iris_features_test = iris_split[1]
df_iris_target_train = iris_split[2]
df_iris_target_test = iris_split[3]
```

You can use the dataframe's shape property to inspect the size of the training and test datasets created by the `train_test_split()` function:

```
df_iris_features.shape, df_iris_target.shape
((150, 4), (150, 1))
df_iris_features_train.shape, df_iris_target_train.shape
((112, 4), (112, 1))
df_iris_features_test.shape, df_iris_target_test.shape
((38, 4), (38, 1))
```

If you use the dataframe's head() method to inspect the first five rows of the original df_iris_features dataset and compare it with the first five rows of the df_iris_features_train dataset, you will notice that the train_test_split() function has automatically shuffled the data before splitting. This is illustrated in Figure 4.1.

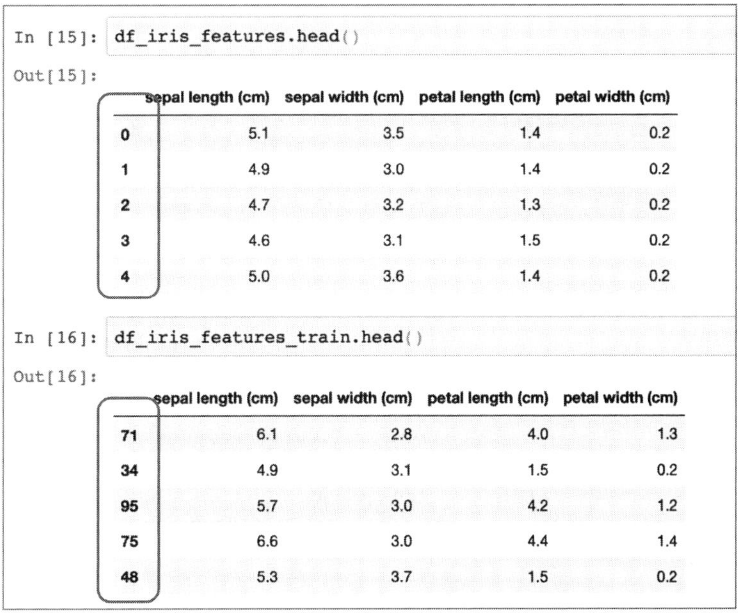

FIGURE 4.1
Scikit-learn's train_test_split() method automatically shuffles the data prior to splitting.

In [15]: `df_iris_features.head()`

Out[15]:

	sepal length (cm)	sepal width (cm)	petal length (cm)	petal width (cm)
0	5.1	3.5	1.4	0.2
1	4.9	3.0	1.4	0.2
2	4.7	3.2	1.3	0.2
3	4.6	3.1	1.5	0.2
4	5.0	3.6	1.4	0.2

In [16]: `df_iris_features_train.head()`

Out[16]:

	sepal length (cm)	sepal width (cm)	petal length (cm)	petal width (cm)
71	6.1	2.8	4.0	1.3
34	4.9	3.1	1.5	0.2
95	5.7	3.0	4.2	1.2
75	6.6	3.0	4.4	1.4
48	5.3	3.7	1.5	0.2

The default behavior of the `train_test_split()` function is to shuffle the data, then determine the boundary observation where the training set should end and prepare two datasets by splitting at this boundary position. If the problem you are trying to solve is one of multi-class classification and your original data has a disproportionate number of samples from one category over the other, then it is important to ensure that the split datasets also have similar proportions. The `train_test_split()` function has a parameter called `stratify` that can be used to achieve a stratified split, maintaining the proportions of categorical observations before and after the split. The following snippet demonstrates the use of the `stratify` parameter:

```
# iris dataset, with stratified sampling
iris_split_strat = train_test_split(df_iris_features, df_iris_target,
                                    test_size=0.25, random_state=17,
stratify=df_iris_target)
df_iris_features_train2 = iris_split_strat[0]
df_iris_features_test2 = iris_split_strat[1]
df_iris_target_train2 = iris_split_strat[2]
df_iris_target_test2 = iris_split_strat[3]
```

The following snippet uses Pandas' plotting functions to create a bar chart of the distribution of categories in the original dataset, the unstratified training set, and the stratified training set. Note that the distribution in the stratified set is closer to the original, though not identical. The resulting plots are depicted in Figure 4.2.

```
# visualize the distribution of target values in the
# original dataset and the training sets created by the train_test_split
# function, with and without stratification
# use Pandas dataframe functions to plot a bar chart of the 'Embarked' attribute
fig, axes = plt.subplots(1, 3, figsize=(15,5))
axes[0].set_title('df_iris_target')
df_iris_target['class'].value_counts(dropna=False).plot.bar(grid=True,
ax=axes[0])
axes[1].set_title('df_iris_target_train')
df_iris_target_train['class'].value_counts(dropna=False).plot.bar(grid=True,
ax=axes[1])
axes[2].set_title('df_iris_target_train2')
df_iris_target_train2['class'].value_counts(dropna=False).plot.bar(grid=True,
ax=axes[2])
```

The distribution of target values between the three categories of flowers is identical in the Iris flowers dataset. This can be seen in the first histogram in Figure 4.2, with each category having 50 values. To better illustrate the use of stratified sampling, the following snippet loads the toy version of the UCI ML wines dataset and plots the difference between stratified and unstratified splits. The UI ML wines dataset is another popular dataset used by beginners for multi-class classification problems. It contains a number of numeric features that contain the results of chemical analysis on wines grown in four different regions of Italy, and a categorical target that indicates the overall quality of the wine. You can find information on the attributes of this dataset at `https://scikit-learn.org/stable/datasets/index.html`. The resulting plots are depicted in Figure 4.3.

FIGURE 4.2
Comparison of the distribution of target variables in the original and split datasets, with and without stratified sampling

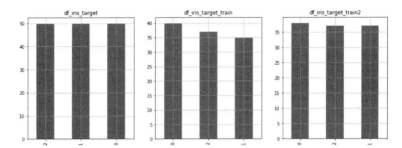

```
# Load the UCI ML Wines dataset
from sklearn.datasets import load_wine
wine_dataset = load_wine()
df_wine_features = pd.DataFrame(data = wine_dataset.data,
columns=wine_dataset.feature_names)
df_wine_target = pd.DataFrame(data = wine_dataset.target, columns=['class'])
#wines dataset
wines_split = train_test_split(df_wine_features, df_wine_target,
                               test_size=0.25, random_state=17)
df_wine_features_train = wines_split[0]
df_wine_features_test = wines_split[1]
df_wine_target_train = wines_split[2]
df_wine_target_test = wines_split[3]
# wines dataset, with stratified sampling
wines_split_strat = train_test_split(df_wine_features, df_wine_target,
                                     test_size=0.25, random_state=17,
stratify=df_wine_target)
df_wine_features_train2 = wines_split_strat[0]
df_wine_features_test2 = wines_split_strat[1]
df_wine_target_train2 = wines_split_strat[2]
df_wine_target_test2 = wines_split_strat[3]

# visualize the distribution of target values in the
# original wines dataset and the training sets created by the train_test_split
# function, with and without stratification
# use Pandas dataframe functions to plot a bar chart of the 'Embarked' attribute
fig, axes = plt.subplots(1, 3, figsize=(15,5))
axes[0].set_title('df_wine_target')
df_wine_target['class'].value_counts(dropna=False).plot.bar(grid=True,
ax=axes[0])
axes[1].set_title('df_wine_target_train')
df_wine_target_train['class'].value_counts(dropna=False).plot.bar(grid=True,
ax=axes[1])
axes[2].set_title('df_wine_target_train2')
df_wine_target_train2['class'].value_counts(dropna=False).plot.bar(grid=True,
ax=axes[2])
```

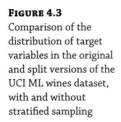

FIGURE 4.3
Comparison of the
distribution of target
variables in the original
and split versions of the
UCI ML wines dataset,
with and without
stratified sampling

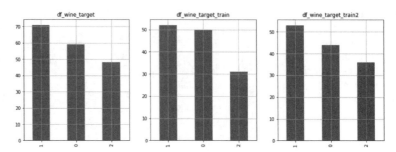

K-Fold Cross Validation

The main drawback with the idea of splitting the training dataset into a training and validation set is that it is possible for the samples in the training set to exhibit characteristics that may not be found in any of the samples in the test set. While shuffling the data can help mitigate this, the extent of the mitigation depends on various factors such as the size of the original dataset, and the proportion of samples that exhibit a particular characteristic. The solution to avoid creating a model that is susceptible to characteristics only found in the training set is embodied in a technique called k-fold cross validation. At a very high level, the k-fold cross validation technique works as follows:

1. Choose a value of k.

2. Shuffle the data.

3. Split the data into k equal subsets.

4. For each value of k:

   a. Train a model that uses the kth subset as the test set and the samples of the k-1 subsets as the training set.

   b. Record the performance of the model when making predictions on the kth subset.

5. Compute the mean performance of the individual models to work out the overall performance.

K-fold cross validation can help minimize the possibility of the model picking up on unexpected bias in the training set. The idea behind k-fold cross validation is to shuffle the entire dataset randomly and divide it into a number of smaller sets (known as folds) and train multiple models (or the same model multiple times). During each training and evaluation cycle, one of the folds will be held out as the test set and the remaining will make the training set. This is illustrated in Figure 4.4.

If k=1, then the k-fold cross validation approach becomes similar to the train/test split method discussed earlier in this chapter. If k=n, the number of samples in the training set, then in effect the test set contains only one sample, and each sample will get to be part of the test set during one of the iterations. This technique is also known as leave-one-out cross validation. Many academic research papers use k=5 or k=10; however, there is no hard-and-fast rule governing the value of k.

FIGURE 4.4
Cross-validation
using k-folds

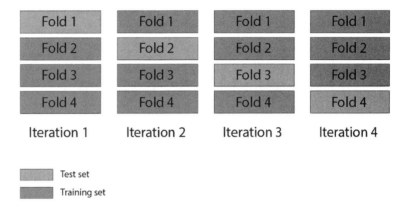

Scikit-learn provides a class called KFold as part of the model-building module that can be used to create the folds and enumerate through the folds. The constructor for the KFold class takes three parameters:

◆ n_splits: An integer that represents the number of folds required.

◆ shuffle: An optional Boolean value that indicates whether the data should be shuffled before the folds are created.

◆ random_state: An optional integer that is used to seed the random-number generator used to shuffle the data.

The KFold class provides two methods:

◆ get_n_splits(): Returns the number of folds

◆ split(): Gets the indices of the training and test set members for each fold.

You can find more information on the KFold class at https://scikit-learn.org/stable/modules/generated/sklearn.model_selection.KFold.html. The following snippet demonstrates the use of the KFold class to split the contents of the Iris dataset into 10 folds and generate the test and training sets:

```
# perform 10-fold split on the Iris dataset
from sklearn.model_selection import KFold
kf = KFold(n_splits=10, shuffle=True)
fold_number = 1
for train_indices, test_indices in kf.split(df_iris_features):

    print("Fold number:", fold_number)
    print("Training indices:", train_indices)
    print("Testing indices::", test_indices)

    fold_number = fold_number + 1

    df_iris_features_train = df_iris_features.iloc[train_index]
    df_iris_target_train = df_iris_target.iloc[train_index]
```

```
df_iris_features_test = df_iris_features.iloc[test_index]
df_iris_target_test = df_iris_target.iloc[test_index]
```

You can inspect the index positions that constitute the training and test sets for each iteration. The indices for the first two iterations are presented here:

```
Fold number: 1
Training indices: [  0   1   2   3   4   5   6   7   8   9  10  11  12  13  14
 15  16  18
 19  20  21  22  23  26  27  28  29  31  32  33  34  35  36  38  39  41
 42  43  44  46  47  48  49  50  51  52  53  54  55  56  57  58  59  60
 61  62  63  64  65  66  68  69  70  71  72  73  74  75  76  77  78  79
 80  82  83  84  85  86  87  88  89  90  91  94  95  96  97  98  99 100
101 102 103 104 105 106 107 108 109 110 111 112 113 114 115 116 117 118
120 121 122 123 124 125 127 128 129 130 131 132 133 134 135 136 137 138
139 140 141 142 143 145 146 147 148]
Testing indices:: [ 17  24  25  30  37  40  45  67  81  92  93 119 126 144 149]

Fold number: 2
Training indices: [  1   2   3   4   5   6   7   8   9  10  12  13  14  16  17
 18  19  20
 21  22  23  24  25  26  27  28  29  30  31  32  34  35  36  37  39  40
 41  42  43  44  45  46  47  48  50  51  52  53  55  56  57  58  59  60
 61  62  63  64  65  67  68  69  70  71  73  74  75  76  77  78  80  81
 83  84  85  86  87  88  89  91  92  93  94  95  96  97  98  99 100 101
102 103 104 105 106 107 109 110 111 112 113 114 115 116 117 118 119 120
121 122 123 124 125 126 128 130 131 132 133 134 135 136 137 138 139 140
141 142 143 144 145 146 147 148 149]
Testing indices:: [  0  11  15  33  38  49  54  66  72  79  82  90 108 127 129]
```

Creating Machine Learning Models

In this section you will learn to create models that can be used to both predict the value of the target variable from the feature variables and classify data. A selection of models will be looked at, some of which assume a linear relationship between the target and the features, as well as models that can be used when the relationship is nonlinear.

Linear Regression

Linear regression is a statistical technique that aims to find the equation of a line (or hyperplane) that is closest to all the points in the dataset. To understand how linear regression works, let's assume you have a training dataset of 100 rows, and each row consists of three features, Y1, Y2, and Y3, and a known target value X. Linear regression will assume that the relationship between the target variable X and input features Y1, Y2, and Y3 is linear, and can be expressed by this equation:

$$X_i = \alpha Y1_i + \beta Y2_i + \gamma Y3_i + \varepsilon.$$

where:

♦ X_i is the predicted value of the ith target variable.

♦ $Y1_i$ is the ith value of feature Y1.

- ◆ Y2$_i$ is the ith value of feature Y2.

- ◆ Y3$_i$ is the ith value of feature Y3.

- ◆ α, β, γ are the coefficients of the features Y1, Y2, Y3.

- ◆ ε is a constant term, also known as the bias term or intercept.

The training process will iterate over the entire training set multiple times and calculate the best values of α, β, γ, and ε. A set of values is considered better if they minimize an error function. An error function is a mathematical function that captures the difference between the predicted and actual values of X$_i$. Root mean square error (RMSE) is a commonly used error function and is expressed mathematically as:

$$RMSE = \sqrt{\frac{\sum_{i=1}^{N}\left(X_i' - X_i\right)^2}{N}}$$

In effect, linear regression attempts to find the best line (or hyperplane in higher dimensions) that fits all the data points. The output of linear regression is a continuous, unbounded value. It can be a positive number or a negative number, and it can have any value, depending on the inputs with which the model was trained. Therefore, linear regression models are commonly used to predict a continuous numeric value.

Scikit-learn implements linear regression in a class called `LinearRegression`, which is part of the `linear_model` module. We will now use this class to implement a linear regression model on the popular Boston housing dataset. The dataset consists of 506 rows, and each row consists of 13 continuous numeric features that contain information such as the per-capita crime rate, average number of rooms per house, rate of property tax, and pupil-teacher ratio. The target value contains the median house price of owner-occupied homes in various parts of Boston.

The dataset does not contain any missing values, and Scikit-learn includes the entire dataset as part of its `datasets` module. You can find more information on the attributes of this dataset at `https://scikit-learn.org/stable/datasets/index.html`. Recall from Chapter 2 that Scikit-learn provides a function called `DESCR` that can be used to print the description of a toy dataset. The following snippet loads the Boston housing dataset and uses the `DESCR` function to print the description of the dataset:

```
# load boston house dataset
from sklearn.datasets import load_boston
boston_dataset = load_boston()
df_boston_features = pd.DataFrame(data = boston_dataset.data,
columns=boston_dataset.feature_names)
df_boston_target = pd.DataFrame(data = boston_dataset.target, columns=['price'])
# print a description of the dataset.
print(boston_dataset.DESCR)
Boston house prices dataset
---------------------------

**Data Set Characteristics:**
    :Number of Instances: 506
    :Number of Attributes: 13 numeric/categorical predictive. Median Value
(attribute 14) is usually the target.
```

```
:Attribute Information (in order):
    - CRIM      per capita crime rate by town
    - ZN        proportion of residential land zoned for lots over 25,000 sq.ft.
    - INDUS     proportion of non-retail business acres per town
    - CHAS      Charles River dummy variable (= 1 if tract bounds river; 0
otherwise)
    - NOX       nitric oxides concentration (parts per 10 million)
    - RM        average number of rooms per dwelling
    - AGE       proportion of owner-occupied units built prior to 1940
    - DIS       weighted distances to five Boston employment centres
    - RAD       index of accessibility to radial highways
    - TAX       full-value property-tax rate per $10,000
    - PTRATIO   pupil-teacher ratio by town
    - B         1000(Bk - 0.63)^2 where Bk is the proportion of blacks by town
    - LSTAT     % lower status of the population
    - MEDV      Median value of owner-occupied homes in $1000's
:Missing Attribute Values: None
:Creator: Harrison, D. and Rubinfeld, D.L.
This is a copy of UCI ML housing dataset.
https://archive.ics.uci.edu/ml/machine-learning-databases/housing/


This dataset was taken from the StatLib library which is maintained at Carnegie
Mellon University.
The Boston house-price data of Harrison, D. and Rubinfeld, D.L. 'Hedonic
prices and the demand for clean air', J. Environ. Economics & Management,
vol.5, 81-102, 1978.   Used in Belsley, Kuh & Welsch, 'Regression diagnostics
...', Wiley, 1980.   N.B. Various transformations are used in the table on
pages 244-261 of the latter.
The Boston house-price data has been used in many machine learning papers that
address regression
problems.

.. topic:: References
   - Belsley, Kuh & Welsch, 'Regression diagnostics: Identifying Influential
Data and Sources of Collinearity', Wiley, 1980. 244-261.
   - Quinlan,R. (1993). Combining Instance-Based and Model-Based Learning. In
Proceedings on the Tenth International Conference of Machine Learning, 236-243,
University of Massachusetts, Amherst. Morgan Kaufmann.
```

Creating the linear model involves splitting the 506 rows of the Boston housing dataset into a training set and a validation set, and using the training set to train the model. The following code snippet creates a 75/25 split of the 506 rows and uses 75% of the original data to train a linear regression model:

```
# create a training dataset and a test dataset using a 75/25 split.
from sklearn.model_selection import train_test_split
boston_split = train_test_split(df_boston_features, df_boston_target,
```

```
                              test_size=0.25, random_state=17)
df_boston_features_train = boston_split[0]
df_boston_features_test = boston_split[1]
df_boston_target_train = boston_split[2]
df_boston_target_test = boston_split[3]
# train a linear model
from sklearn.linear_model import LinearRegression
linear_regression_model = LinearRegression(fit_intercept=True)
linear_regression_model.fit(df_boston_features_train, df_boston_target_train)
```

You can instantiate a linear regression model by using the class constructor. The constructor has four parameters, all of which are optional. In most cases, you will instantiate a LinearRegression instance using the default zero-parameter constructor:

```
linear_regression_model = LinearRegression()
```

In the preceding snippet, the fit_intercept constructor parameter is set to True. The fit_intercept parameter is used to indicate that the samples are not zero-centered and that the model should calculate the intercept term. If fit_intercept is False, then the model will assume the y-axis intercept is 0 and will only attempt to fit lines (or hyperplanes) that satisfy this constraint. You can find more information on the constructor parameters at https://scikit-learn.org/stable/modules/generated/sklearn.linear_model.LinearRegression.html.

Once you have created a LinearRegression instance, training the model is a simple matter of calling the fit() method, and passing in a dataframe that contains the features and a dataframe that contains the known target values. Once training is complete, you can access the coefficients and intercept terms of the linear model using the coef_ and intercept_ attributes of the LinearRegression instance. The following snippet lists the coefficients and intercept terms after training a linear regression model using the Boston house prices dataset. Note there are 13 coefficients, corresponding to the 13 feature variables:

```
print (linear_regression_model.coef_)
[[-1.12960344e-01  5.48578928e-02  6.71605489e-02  3.26195457e+00
  -1.70702665e+01  3.49123817e+00  7.03121906e-05 -1.37355630e+00
   3.12880217e-01 -1.32867294e-02 -9.57749225e-01  7.70369247e-03
  -5.59461017e-01]]
print (linear_regression_model.intercept_)
[38.51522467]
```

Once you have the trained model, you can use the model to make predictions. The following snippet uses the linear_regression_model object to make predictions on the test set (25% of the original 506 samples):

```
# use the linear model to create predictions on the test set.
predicted_median_house_prices =
linear_regression_model.predict(df_boston_features_test)
```

You will learn about ways to evaluate machine learning models in Chapter 5, but in this case you could get an idea of the quality of predictions created by this model by creating a scatter plot of the predictions made by the model on the test set against the actual house prices in the test set. The following snippet uses functions from Matplotlib's pyplot module to create a scatter plot. The resulting plot is depicted in Figure 4.5.

```
%matplotlib inline
import matplotlib.pyplot as plt
# use pyplot module to create a scatter plot of predicted vs expected values
fig, axes = plt.subplots(1, 1, figsize=(9,9))
plt.scatter(df_boston_target_test, predicted_median_house_prices)
plt.xlabel("Expected Prices")
plt.ylabel("Predicted prices")
plt.title("Expected vs Predicted prices")
```

FIGURE 4.5

Scatter plot of expected
vs. predicted
house prices

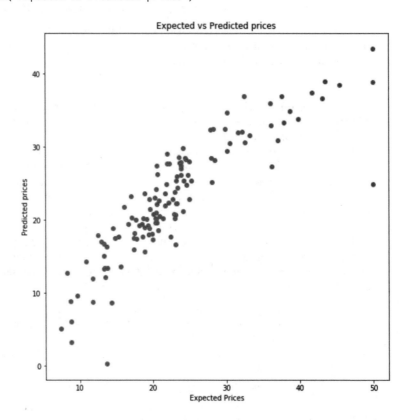

In the ideal case, the scatter plot of the expected house prices against the values predicted by your model should be close to a straight line.

To better understand the result of changing the fit_intercept parameter while creating the LinearRegression instance, the following snippet creates a synthetic dataset of 50 random two-dimensional points and attempts to create two linear regression models on the data. The first model is created with fit_intercept = False, and the second model is created with fit_intercept = True. Both models are presented the X and Y coordinates of the 50 points as training data, with the X coordinate values representing the feature variable and the Y coordinate values representing the target.

In effect, after training, the models will be able to predict the Y coordinate from the X coordinate. Since the X coordinate is the only input feature of this model, the model will contain only one coefficient term. The snippet then creates a scatter plot of the 50 points and overlays the regression line generated by each model. The resulting plot is depicted in Figure 4.6.

```python
# create a synthetic regression dataset of X, Y values.
from sklearn.datasets import make_regression
from sklearn.preprocessing import MinMaxScaler
SyntheticX, SyntheticY = make_regression(n_samples=50, n_features=1, noise=35.0,
random_state=17)
x_scaler = MinMaxScaler()
x_scaler.fit(SyntheticX.reshape(-1,1))
SyntheticX = x_scaler.transform(SyntheticX.reshape(-1,1))
y_scaler = MinMaxScaler()
y_scaler.fit(SyntheticY.reshape(-1,1))
SyntheticY = y_scaler.transform(SyntheticY.reshape(-1,1))

# demonstrate effect of fit_intercept parameter on a simple synthetic dataset.
linear_regression_model_synthetic1 = LinearRegression(fit_intercept=True)
linear_regression_model_synthetic1.fit(SyntheticX, SyntheticY)
linear_regression_model_synthetic2 = LinearRegression(fit_intercept=False)
linear_regression_model_synthetic2.fit(SyntheticX, SyntheticY)
c1 = linear_regression_model_synthetic1.coef_
i1 = linear_regression_model_synthetic1.intercept_
YPredicted1 = np.dot(SyntheticX, c1) + i1
c2 = linear_regression_model_synthetic2.coef_
i2 = linear_regression_model_synthetic2.intercept_
YPredicted2 = np.dot(SyntheticX, c2) + i2
# use pyplot module to create a scatter plot of synthetic dataset
# and overlay the regression line from the two models.
fig, axes = plt.subplots(1, 1, figsize=(9,9))
axes.axhline(y=0, color='k')
axes.axvline(x=0, color='k')
plt.scatter(SyntheticX, SyntheticY)
plt.plot(SyntheticX, YPredicted1, color='#042fed', label='fit_intercept=True')
plt.plot(SyntheticX, YPredicted2, color='#d02fed', label='fit_intercept=False')
plt.legend()
plt.xlabel("X")
plt.ylabel("Y")
```

In Figure 4.6, you can see that the regression line generated by the model with fit_intercept = False is anchored at Y = 0. The model is therefore constrained in terms of the lines it can generate. On the other hand, the line generated by the model with fit_intercept = True is not anchored at Y = 0, and therefore the model is able to determine the best value for the Y intercept as a result of the training process.

FIGURE 4.6
Scatter plot of synthetic
dataset along with
regression lines

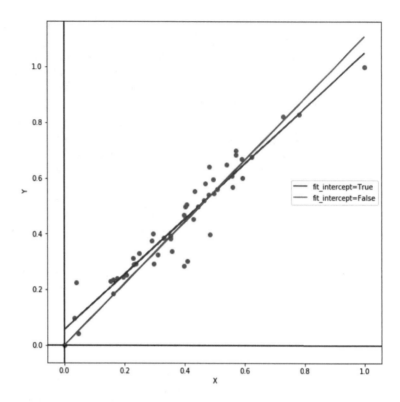

Support Vector Machines

A support vector machine (SVM) is a versatile model that can be used for a variety of tasks, including classification, regression, and outlier detection. The original algorithm was invented in 1963 by Vladimir Vapnik and Alexey Chervonenkis as a binary classification algorithm. During the training process, support vector machine models aim to create a decision boundary that can partition the data points into classes. If the dataset has just two features, then this decision boundary is two-dimensional and can be conveniently represented in a scatter plot. If the decision boundary is linear, it will take the form of a straight line in two dimensions, a plane in three dimensions, and a hyperplane in n-dimensions. As humans, we cannot visualize more than three dimensions, which is why in order to understand how SVMs work, we'll consider a two-dimensional example with a fictional dataset with two features, and each point belonging to one of two classes. Let's also assume that the data is linearly separable—that is, you can draw a line that can separate them. Figure 4.7 depicts a scatter plot of feature values of points from this fictional dataset, with one class of observations represented as circles and the other as stars. The figure also presents three possible linear decision boundaries, each capable of separating the observations into two different sets.

The decision boundary to the left is too close to the first set of observations and there is a risk that a model with that decision boundary could misclassify real-world observations were they only slightly different from the training set. The decision boundary to the right has a similar problem in that it is too close to the second set of observations. The decision boundary in the middle is optimal because it is as far away as possible from both classes

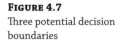

FIGURE 4.7

Three potential decision boundaries

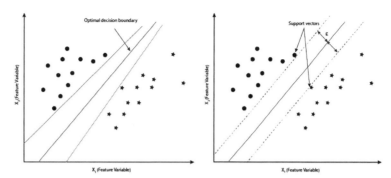

and at the same time clearly separates both classes. SVM models aim to find this middle (optimal), or to put it in another way, aim to find the decision boundary that maximizes the distance between the two classes of observations on either side. The half-width of the margin is denoted by the Greek letter ε (epsilon). The points on the edges of the margin are called support vectors (the vector is assumed to originate at the origin and terminate at these points). In effect one could say these vectors are supporting the margins—hence the name support vectors.

Most real-world data is not linearly separable as the dataset depicted in Figure 4.7, and therefore linear decision boundaries are unable to clearly separate the classes. Furthermore, even when the data is linearly separable, there is a possibility that the margin of separation is not as wide as the fictional example in Figure 4.7. Data points are often too close together to allow for wide, clear margins between the decision boundary and the support vectors on either side, and to handle this, SVM implementations include the concept of a tolerance parameter that controls the number of support vectors that can be inside the margins, which in turn has an impact on the width of the margin. Setting a large tolerance value results in a wider margin with more samples in the margin, whereas setting a small tolerance value will result in a narrow margin. Having a wide margin is not necessarily a bad thing, as long as most of the points in the margin are on the correct side of the decision boundary.

Scikit-learn provides an implementation of support vector machine–based classifiers in the SVC class, which is part of the `sklearn.svm` module. We will now use this class to implement an SVM-based classification model on the popular Pima Indians diabetes dataset. The database consists of eight feature variables that represent various medical measurements such as blood pressure, plasma glucose concentration, BMI, and insulin levels, and contains a binary target variable called Outcome, which indicates whether the individual in question has diabetes. The dataset was originally created by the National Institute of Diabetes and Digestive and Kidney Diseases, and you can find the Kaggle version of the dataset at `https://www.kaggle.com/uciml/pima-indians-diabetes-database`. A copy of the dataset has been included with the resources that accompany this chapter.

The following snippet can be used to load the dataset from a CSV file, create Pandas dataframes with the feature and target data, normalize the feature data, and create a 75/25 test-train split:

```
# load Pima Indians Diabetes dataset
diabetes_dataset_file = './datasets/diabetes_dataset/diabetes.csv'
df_diabetes = pd.read_csv(diabetes_dataset_file)
df_diabetes_target = df_diabetes.loc[:,['Outcome']]
```

```
df_diabetes_features = df_diabetes.drop(['Outcome'], axis=1)
# normalize attribute values
from sklearn.preprocessing import MinMaxScaler
diabetes_scaler = MinMaxScaler()
diabetes_scaler.fit(df_diabetes_features)
nd_diabetes_features = diabetes_scaler.transform(df_diabetes_features)
df_diabetes_features_normalized = pd.DataFrame(data=nd_diabetes_features,
columns=df_diabetes_features.columns)
# create a training dataset and a test dataset using a 75/25 split.
diabetes_split = train_test_split(df_diabetes_features_normalized,
df_diabetes_target,
                            test_size=0.25, random_state=17)
df_diabetes_features_train = diabetes_split[0]
df_diabetes_features_test = diabetes_split[1]
df_diabetes_target_train = diabetes_split[2]
df_diabetes_target_test = diabetes_split[3]
```

The following snippet creates an instance of the SVC class that attempts to find a linear decision boundary, trains the SVC instance using the training set (75% of the samples), and uses the predict() method to make predictions on the test set. You can learn more about instantiating an SVC instance at https://scikit-learn.org/stable/modules/generated/sklearn.svm.SVC.html.

```
# create an SVM classifier for the features of the diabetes dataset using a
linear kernel
from sklearn.svm import SVC
svc_model = SVC(kernel='linear', C=1)
svc_model.fit(df_diabetes_features_train, df_diabetes_target_train)
# use the SVC model to create predictions on the test set.
predicted_diabetes = svc_model.predict(df_diabetes_features_test)
```

Chapter 5 covers techniques to evaluate the performance of classification models, but for now you can examine the predictions themselves using the Python print() function:

```
print (predicted_diabetes)
[0 0 0 0 1 0 0 1 1 0 1 0 0 0 0 0 0 0 0 1 0 0 1 0 0 1 0 1 0 0 0 0 0 0 0 1
 0 0 0 0 0 0 0 0 1 0 1 0 0 0 0 0 0 0 0 0 0 0 0 1 0 0 0 0 0 1 0 0 0
 0 0 0 0 0 0 1 0 0 0 1 1 0 0 0 0 0 0 0 0 0 0 0 0 0 1 1 1 0 0 1 0 0 1 0
 1 0 0 0 0 0 0 0 0 0 0 0 0 0 0 0 0 1 0 0 0 1 0 0 0 0 1 0 1 0 1 0 0 0
 0 0 0 1 0 0 0 0 0 0 0 0 1 0 1 1 0 0 0 1 0 0 0 1 1 0 0 0 1 0 0 0 0 0 1 0
 0 0 0 0 1 0 0]
```

The real power of SVM-based classifiers is their ability to create nonlinear decision boundaries. Support vector models use a mathematical function called a kernel that is used to transform each input point into a higher-dimensional space where a linear decision boundary can be found. This will be easier to understand with an example. Figure 4.8 shows a scatter plot of another fictional dataset with two features per data point, and each data point belonging to one of two classes. In this case, it is quite clear that there is no linear decision boundary (straight line) that can classify all data points correctly—no matter which way you draw a straight line you will always end up with some samples on the wrong side of the line.

FIGURE 4.8
Data that cannot be classified using a linear decision boundary in two-dimensional space

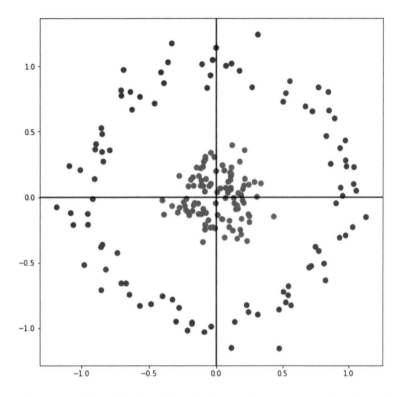

If, however, you add an extra dimension (z-axis) to the data, and compute z values for each point using the equation z = x² + y², then the data becomes linearly separable along the z-axis using a plane at z = 0.3. This is depicted in Figure 4.9.

FIGURE 4.9
Data that cannot be classified using a linear decision boundary in two-dimensional space can be classified in three-dimensional space.

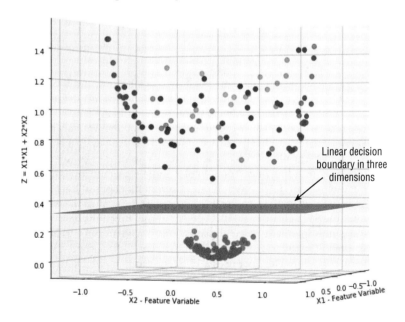

Since z was computed as $x^2 + y^2$, the decision plane at $z = 0.3$ implies $x^2 + y^2 = 0.3$, which is nothing but the equation of a circle in two dimensions. Therefore, the linear decision boundary in three-dimensional space has become a nonlinear decision boundary in two-dimensional space. This is illustrated in Figure 4.10.

FIGURE 4.10

Nonlinear decision boundary in two-dimensional space

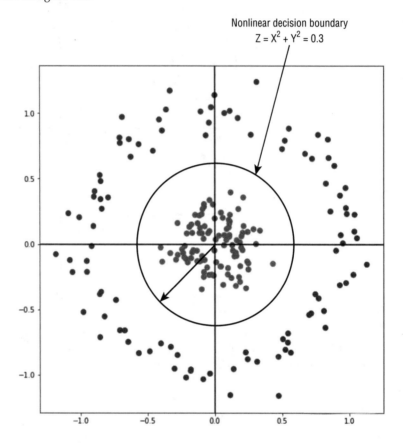

This is an oversimplification of how kernels work, and if you are interested in learning more about SVM kernels you should read *An Introduction to Support Vector Machines and Other Kernel-based Learning Methods* by Nello Cristianini and John Shawe-Taylor (`https://www.cambridge.org/core/books/an-introduction-to-support-vector-machines-and-other-kernelbased-learning-methods/A6A6F4084056A4B23F88648DDBFDD6FC`).

Scikit-learn allows you to choose from a number of common kernels when creating the SVC instance, including linear, polynomial, radial basis functions, and custom kernels. You can find out more about the different types of kernel functions at `https://scikit-learn.org/stable/modules/svm.html#svm-kernels`. In order to visualize the effect of different kernels, let's train multiple SVM classifiers with different kernel functions on a dataset. The following snippet trains multiple SVM-based classifiers on a synthetic binary classification dataset with two features. The first classifier uses a linear kernel, the second classifier uses a 2nd-degree polynomial kernel, the third classifier uses a 15th-degree polynomial kernel, and the fourth kernel uses a radial basis function (RBF) kernel:

```
# create a synthetic binary classification dataset with 2 features.
from sklearn.datasets import make_classification
Synthetic_BinaryClassX, Synthetic_BinaryClassY =
make_classification(n_samples=50, n_features=2, n_redundant=0, n_classes=2)

# scale synthetic dataset between -3, 3
from sklearn.preprocessing import MinMaxScaler
scaler = MinMaxScaler(feature_range=(-3,3))
scaler.fit(Synthetic_BinaryClassX.reshape(-1,1))
Synthetic_BinaryClassX = scaler.transform(Synthetic_BinaryClassX)
# create multiple SVM classifiers
from sklearn.svm import SVC
svc_model_linear = SVC(kernel='linear', C=1, gamma='auto')
svc_model_polynomial2 = SVC(kernel='poly', degree=2, C=1, gamma='auto')
svc_model_polynomial15 = SVC(kernel='poly', degree=15, C=1, gamma='auto')
svc_model_rbf = SVC(kernel='rbf', C=1, gamma='auto')
svc_model_linear.fit(Synthetic_BinaryClassX, Synthetic_BinaryClassY)
svc_model_polynomial2.fit(Synthetic_BinaryClassX, Synthetic_BinaryClassY)
svc_model_polynomial15.fit(Synthetic_BinaryClassX, Synthetic_BinaryClassY)
svc_model_rbf.fit(Synthetic_BinaryClassX, Synthetic_BinaryClassY)
```

With the models created, we can use Matplotlib functions to plot the data points as well as decision boundaries of each classifier. The following snippet shows how to visualize the decision boundary of an SVM classifier (portions of the code are taken from https://scikit-learn. org/stable/auto_examples/exercises/plot_iris_exercise.html). The resulting plots are depicted in Figure 4.11.

```
#
# portions of this code are from
# source: https://scikit-learn.org/stable/auto_examples/svm/plot_iris.html
#
%matplotlib inline
import matplotlib.pyplot as plt
def plot_contours(ax, clf, xx, yy, **params):
    """Plot the decision boundaries for a classifier.
    Parameters
    ----------
    ax: matplotlib axes object
    clf: a classifier
    xx: meshgrid ndarray
    yy: meshgrid ndarray
    params: dictionary of params to pass to contourf, optional
    """
    Z = clf.predict(np.c_[xx.ravel(), yy.ravel()])
    Z = Z.reshape(xx.shape)
    out = ax.contourf(xx, yy, Z, **params)
    return out
def make_meshgrid(x, y, h=.02):
```

```python
    """Create a mesh of points to plot in
    Parameters
    ----------
    x: data to base x-axis meshgrid on
    y: data to base y-axis meshgrid on
    h: stepsize for meshgrid, optional
    Returns
    -------
    xx, yy : ndarray
    """
    x_min, x_max = x.min() - 1, x.max() + 1
    y_min, y_max = y.min() - 1, y.max() + 1
    xx, yy = np.meshgrid(np.arange(x_min, x_max, h),
                         np.arange(y_min, y_max, h))
    return xx, yy
# pick out 2 features X0 and X1
X0 = Synthetic_BinaryClassX[:,0]
X1 = Synthetic_BinaryClassX[:,1]
xx, yy = make_meshgrid(X0, X1, 0.02)#np.meshgrid(np.arange(-3, 3, 0.002),
np.arange(-3, 3, 0.002))

fig, axes = plt.subplots(2, 2, figsize=(16,16))
# plot linear kernel
plot_contours(axes[0,0], svc_model_linear,
              xx, yy, cmap=plt.cm.coolwarm, alpha=0.8)
axes[0,0].scatter(X0, X1, s=30,  c=Synthetic_BinaryClassY)
axes[0,0].set_xlim(xx.min(), xx.max())
axes[0,0].set_ylim(yy.min(), yy.max())
axes[0,0].set_title('Linear Kernel')

# plot 2nd degree polynomial kernel
plot_contours(axes[0,1], svc_model_polynomial2, xx, yy,
              cmap=plt.cm.coolwarm, alpha=0.8)
axes[0,1].scatter(X0, X1, s=30, c=Synthetic_BinaryClassY)
axes[0,1].set_xlim(xx.min(), xx.max())
axes[0,1].set_ylim(yy.min(), yy.max())
axes[0,1].set_title('2nd Degree Polynomial Kernel')
# plot 15 degree polynomial kernel
plot_contours(axes[1,0], svc_model_polynomial15, xx, yy,
              cmap=plt.cm.coolwarm, alpha=0.8)
axes[1,0].scatter(X0, X1, s=30, c=Synthetic_BinaryClassY)
axes[1,0].set_xlim(xx.min(), xx.max())
axes[1,0].set_ylim(yy.min(), yy.max())
axes[1,0].set_title('5th Degree Polynomial Kernel')
# plot RBF kernel
plot_contours(axes[1,1], svc_model_rbf, xx, yy,
              cmap=plt.cm.coolwarm, alpha=0.8)
```

```
axes[1,1].scatter(X0, X1, s=30, c=Synthetic_BinaryClassY)
axes[1,1].set_xlim(xx.min(), xx.max())
axes[1,1].set_ylim(yy.min(), yy.max())
axes[1,1].set_title('RBF Kernel')
plt.show()
```

FIGURE 4.11

Effect of kernel choice
on decision boundaries

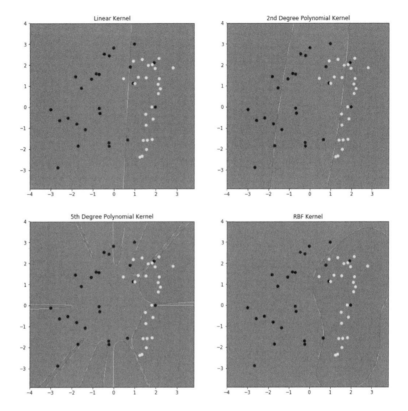

Support vector machine–based models can also be used for linear regression tasks. When used for linear regression tasks, you are no longer looking for a decision boundary that can spilt the points between classes, but instead the line (or hyperplane) that best fits the samples. Support vector regression (SVR) is a technique that attempts to find the best line, or hyperplane, that fits the training variables. The difference between linear regression and SVR is the manner in which this hyperplane is determined. Linear regression in two dimensions fundamentally attempts to find the line that minimizes the sum of the distances of the data points from the line. SVR, on the other hand, attempts to find the line that contains the largest number of data points within a fixed distance from the hyperplane. Figure 4.12 illustrates the difference between linear regression and SVR in a two-dimensional scenario.

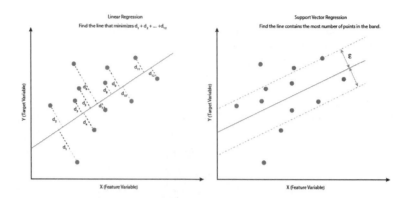

Scikit-learn provides an implementation of support vector machine–based regressors in the SVR class, which is part of the `sklearn.svm` module. The following snippet will use the SVR class to implement an SVM-based regression model on the Boston housing prices dataset to predict the median house price. A scatter plot of the predicted vs. actual house prices is presented in Figure 4.13.

FIGURE 4.13
SVR predictions on
Boston housing dataset

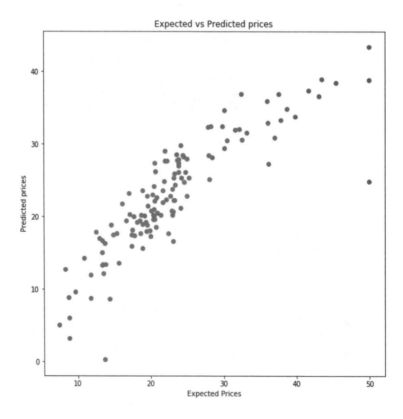

```
# train a linear model on the Boston house prices dataset.
from sklearn.svm import SVR
svr_model = SVR(kernel='linear', C=1.5, gamma='auto', epsilon=1.5)
svr_model.fit(df_boston_features_train, df_boston_target_train.values.ravel())
# use the SVR model to create predictions on the test set.
svr_predicted_prices = svr_model.predict(df_boston_features_test)
%matplotlib inline
import matplotlib.pyplot as plt
# use pyplot module to create a scatter plot of predicted vs expected values
fig, axes = plt.subplots(1, 1, figsize=(9,9))
plt.scatter(df_boston_target_test, predicted_median_house_prices)
plt.xlabel("Expected Prices")
plt.ylabel("Predicted prices")
plt.title("Expected vs Predicted prices")
```

Logistic Regression

Logistic regression, despite having the word *regression* in its name, is a technique that can be used to build binary and multi-class classifiers. Logistic regression (also known as logit regression) builds upon the output of linear regression and returns a probability that the data point is of one class or another. Recall that the output of linear regression is a continuous unbounded value, whereas probabilities are continuous bounded values—bounded between 0.0 and 1.0.

In order to use a continuous value for binary classification, logistic regression converts it into a probability value between 0.0 and 1.0 by feeding the output of linear regression into a logistic function. In statistics a logistic function is a type of function that converts values from [–infinity, + infinity] to [0, 1]. In the case of logistic regression, the logistic function is the sigmoid function, which is defined as:

$$\text{Sigmoid}(x) = \frac{1}{1+e^{-x}}$$

FIGURE 4.14
The sigmoid function

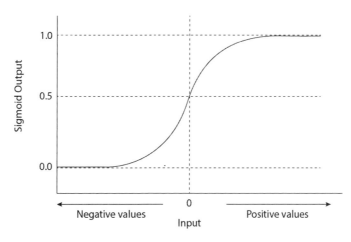

The graph of the sigmoid function is presented in Figure 4.14. The output of the sigmoid function will never go below 0.0 or above 1.0, regardless of the value of the input.

The output of the sigmoid function can be used for binary classification by setting a threshold value and treating all values below that as class A and everything above the threshold as class B (Figure 4.15).

FIGURE 4.15
Using the sigmoid
function for binary
classification

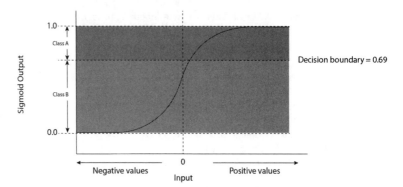

Scikit-learn provides the LogisticRegression class as part of the linear_model module. We will now use this class to implement a logistic regression–based binary classification model on the popular Pima Indians diabetes dataset:

```
# load Pima Indians Diabetes dataset
diabetes_dataset_file = './datasets/diabetes_dataset/diabetes.csv'
df_diabetes = pd.read_csv(diabetes_dataset_file)
df_diabetes_target = df_diabetes.loc[:,['Outcome']]
df_diabetes_features = df_diabetes.drop(['Outcome'], axis=1)
# normalize attribute values
from sklearn.preprocessing import MinMaxScaler
diabetes_scaler = MinMaxScaler()
diabetes_scaler.fit(df_diabetes_features)
nd_diabetes_features = diabetes_scaler.transform(df_diabetes_features)
df_diabetes_features_normalized = pd.DataFrame(data=nd_diabetes_features,
columns=df_diabetes_features.columns)
# create a training dataset and a test dataset using a 75/25 split.
diabetes_split = train_test_split(df_diabetes_features_normalized,
df_diabetes_target,
                          test_size=0.25, random_state=17)
df_diabetes_features_train = diabetes_split[0]
df_diabetes_features_test = diabetes_split[1]
df_diabetes_target_train = diabetes_split[2]
df_diabetes_target_test = diabetes_split[3]
# train a logistic regression model on the diabetes dataset.
from sklearn.linear_model import LogisticRegression
logistic_regression_model = LogisticRegression(penalty='l2', fit_intercept=True,
solver='liblinear')
logistic_regression_model.fit(df_diabetes_features_train, df_diabetes_target_
train.values.ravel())
# use the  model to create predictions on the test set, with a threshold of 0.5
logistic_regression_predictions =
logistic_regression_model.predict(df_diabetes_features_test)
```

The constructor of the `LogisticRegression` class takes several parameters, some of which are common with the `LinearRegression` class. You can find out more about these parameters at `https://scikit-learn.org/stable/modules/generated/sklearn.linear_model .LogisticRegression.html`. The predictions made by the model can be examined using the Python `print()` function:

```
print (logistic_regression_predictions)
[0 1 0 0 0 0 0 1 1 1 1 1 0 0 0 0 1 0 0 0 1 0 0 1 0 0 1 0 1 0 1 0 1 0 0 0 0 0 1
 0 0 0 0 0 0 1 0 0 1 0 1 0 0 0 0 0 1 0 0 0 0 0 0 1 0 0 0 0 0 1 0 0 0
 0 0 0 0 0 0 1 0 0 0 1 1 0 0 0 0 0 0 0 0 0 0 1 0 0 1 1 1 0 0 1 0 0 1 0
 1 0 0 1 0 0 0 0 0 0 0 0 0 0 0 0 0 0 1 0 0 0 0 0 0 0 1 0 0 0 1 0 0 0
 0 0 0 1 0 0 0 0 0 0 0 0 1 0 0 1 0 0 0 1 0 0 0 1 1 0 0 0 0 0 0 0 1 0 1
 0 0 0 0 1 0 0]]
```

The binary predictions are made using a probability cut-off of 0.5. If the probability value estimated by the underlying linear regression model is > 0.5, the output class will be 0. Scikit-learn does not allow you to change this probability cut-off; however, you can use the `predict_proba()` method of the `LogisticRegression` instance to access the prediction probabilities before the thresholding operation was applied:

```
# access class-wise probabilities
logistic_regression_probabilities =
logistic_regression_model.predict_proba(df_diabetes_features_test)
```

Since there are two output classes, the `predict_proba()` method will give you two probabilities per data point. The first column contains the probability that the point will be labeled 0, and the second column contains the probability that the point will be labeled 1:

```
print (logistic_regression_probabilities)
[[0.85694005 0.14305995]
 [0.37165061 0.62834939]
 [0.73695232 0.26304768]
 [0.880803   0.119197  ]
 ...
 ...
 [0.41292724 0.58707276]
 [0.63547121 0.36452879]
 [0.52728275 0.47271725]]]
```

Because these numbers represent probabilities, the sum of the prediction probabilities for any data point will be 1.0. Furthermore, since there are only two classes, you can use the information in any one column to work out the value of the other column by subtracting from 1.0. The following snippet uses the information in the first column (probability that the output class is 0) and implements custom thresholding logic at 0.8. Any probabilities greater than 0.8 will be labeled 0:

```
# implement custom thresholding logic
dfProbabilities = pd.DataFrame(logistic_regression_probabilities[:,0])
predictions = dfProbabilities.applymap(lambda x: 0 if x > 0.8 else 1)
```

You can examine the predictions with this new threshold of 0.8 by printing the contents of predictions. Compare these predictions with the predictions made by the model with Scikit-learn's default cut-off threshold of 0.5:

```
print (predictions.values.ravel())
[0 1 1 0 1 1 1 1 1 1 1 1 1 1 1 0 1 0 1 1 1 0 1 1 1 0 1 1 1 0 0 1 0 1
 1 0 1 0 0 1 1 0 1 1 1 1 1 0 1 1 1 1 1 1 0 1 1 0 1 1 0 1 1 1 1 1 1 0
 0 1 0 1 1 1 1 1 0 1 1 1 0 0 0 0 1 0 0 1 1 1 1 1 1 1 1 0 1 1 1 0 1 0
 1 1 1 1 1 0 1 1 1 0 1 1 0 1 0 1 1 1 0 1 1 1 0 1 1 1 1 0 1 0 0 1
 1 1 1 0 1 0 0 1 1 1 0 1 1 1 0 1 1 1 1 0 1 1 0 1 1 1 1 1 0 1 1 1
 1 1 1 1 1 1]
```

As mentioned earlier, logistic regression builds upon the output of linear regression. You can inspect the coefficients and intercept of the underlying linear model through the coef_ and intercept_ attributes of the model:

```
print (logistic_regression_model.coef_)
[[ 1.48972976  3.4891602  -0.7344297  -0.07461329  0.16776565  1.81409369
   1.39383873  1.03554067]]
print (logistic_regression_model.intercept_)
[-4.06714158]
```

Logistic regression is inherently a binary classifier, but it can be used as a multi-class classifier for datasets where the target variable can belong to more than two classes. There are two fundamental approaches that can be used to use a binary classifier for multi-class problems:

- *One-versus-rest approach:* This is also known as the OVR approach, and it involves creating a number of binary classification models, with each model predicting the probability that the output is one of the subclasses. This approach will create N models for N classes, and the final class output by the multi-class classifier corresponds to the model that predicted the highest probability. Consider the popular Iris flowers dataset, where the target variable can have one of three values [0, 1, 2], corresponding to the type of Iris flower. In this case, the OVR approach would involve training three logistic regression models. The first model would predict the probability that the output class is 0 or not 0. Likewise, the second model would only predict the probability that the output class is 1 or not 1, and so on. The one-versus-rest approach is sometimes also referred to as the one-versus-all (OVA) approach

- *One-versus-one approach:* This is known as the OVO approach, and it also involves creating a number of binary classification models and picking the class that corresponds to the model that outputs the largest probability value. The difference between the OVO approach and the OVR approach is in the number of models created. The OVO approach creates one model for each pairwise combination of output classes. In the case of the Iris flowers dataset, the OVO approach would also create three models:

  - Logistic regression model that predicts output class as 0 or 1
  - Logistic regression model that predicts output class as 0 or 2
  - Logistic regression model that predicts output class as 1 or 2

As you can see, the number of models generated increases with the number of features.

Scikit-learn provides the `OneVsOneClassifier` and the `OneVsRestClassifier` classes in the `multiclass` module that encapsulate the complexity of creating multiple binary classification models and training them. The constructor for these classes takes a binary classification model as input. Some model classes within Scikit-learn are inherently capable of multi-class classification, and you may be surprised to learn that `LogisticRegression` is one of them. However, before we discuss the implementation of inherent multi-class classification in the LogisticRegression class, let's examine how we can use the OneVsRestClassifier to create an ensemble of binary LogisticRegression models and use the ensemble as a multi-class classifier. You can learn more about the classes in the `multiclass` package at `https://scikit-learn.org/stable/modules/multiclass.html`.

The following snippet demonstrates using the `OneVsRestClassifier` class to create a multi-class classifier from an ensemble of binary `LogisticRegression` models on the Iris flowers dataset:

```
# load Iris flowers dataset
from sklearn.datasets import load_iris
iris_dataset = load_iris()
df_iris_features = pd.DataFrame(data = iris_dataset.data,
columns=iris_dataset.feature_names)
df_iris_target = pd.DataFrame(data = iris_dataset.target, columns=['class'])
# normalize attribute values
from sklearn.preprocessing import MinMaxScaler
iris_scaler = MinMaxScaler()
iris_scaler.fit(df_iris_features)
nd_iris_features = iris_scaler.transform(df_iris_features)
df_iris_features_normalized = pd.DataFrame(data=nd_iris_features, columns=df_
iris_features.columns)
# create a training dataset and a test dataset using a 75/25 split.
from sklearn.model_selection import train_test_split
iris_split = train_test_split(df_iris_features_normalized, df_iris_target,
                              test_size=0.25, random_state=17)
df_iris_features_train = iris_split[0]
df_iris_features_test = iris_split[1]
df_iris_target_train = iris_split[2]
df_iris_target_test = iris_split[3]
# implement multi-class classification using
# OVA (a.ka. OVR) approach and LogisticRegression
from sklearn.multiclass import OneVsRestClassifier
from sklearn.linear_model import LogisticRegression
logit_model = LogisticRegression(penalty='l2', fit_intercept=True,
solver='liblinear')
ovr_logit_model = OneVsRestClassifier(logit_model)
ovr_logit_model.fit(df_iris_features_train, df_iris_target_train.values.ravel())
# use the  model to create predictions on the test set, with a threshold of 0.5
ovr_logit_predictions = ovr_logit_model.predict(df_iris_features_test)
```

You can inspect the classes predicted by the OVR logistic regression model by using the Python print() function. As you can see, the output classes predicted for the members of the test set are one of three values—0, 1, or 2:

```
print (ovr_logit_predictions)
[0 2 2 1 2 2 2 2 1 2 2 0 1 0 2 0 0 2 2 2 2 0 2 1 2 2 1 1 0 1 0 1 0 0 0 1 2 1
 2]
```

You can inspect the class-wise probabilities from the OneVsRestClassifier instance by using the predict_proba() method, just as you did earlier with the LogisticRegression instance. This time, though, the result will have three values for each member of the test set. The first number is the probability that the output class is 0, the second number is the probability that the output class is 1, and so on:

```
# access class-wise probabilities
ovr_logit_probs = ovr_logit_model.predict_proba(df_iris_features_test)
print(ovr_logit_probs)
[[0.82272514 0.12785864 0.04941622]
 [0.12044579 0.40056122 0.47899299]
 [0.02542865 0.32329645 0.6512749 ]
 [0.18305903 0.42111625 0.39582472]
 [0.05944138 0.38763397 0.55292465]
 [0.07236737 0.36312485 0.56450777]
 [0.16344427 0.37963956 0.45691617]
 [0.01998424 0.24601841 0.73399734]
 [0.18950936 0.48395363 0.32653701]
 [0.03663432 0.40209894 0.56126674]
 [0.02062532 0.27783051 0.70154417]
 [0.73577162 0.22066942 0.04355896]
 [0.15270279 0.42746281 0.41983439]
 [0.77216659 0.18251154 0.04532187]
 [0.05309898 0.32231709 0.62458393]
 [0.815817   0.13825926 0.04592374]
 [0.73489217 0.22191513 0.0431927 ]
 [0.04491288 0.36458749 0.59049964]
 [0.02065056 0.27871118 0.70063826]
 [0.02127991 0.35388486 0.62483523]
 [0.07152985 0.41695375 0.5115164 ]
 [0.7706894  0.18349734 0.04581325]
 [0.07040028 0.36307885 0.56652087]
 [0.19267192 0.4727485  0.33457958]
 [0.15280003 0.38212573 0.46507424]
 [0.17395557 0.31901921 0.50702523]
 [0.12736739 0.48820204 0.38443056]
 [0.13568065 0.44198711 0.42233224]
 [0.7867313  0.16963785 0.04363084]
 [0.17115366 0.45770086 0.37114548]
 [0.74540203 0.20735953 0.04723843]
 [0.31041971 0.43132172 0.25825857]
```

```
[0.80839308 0.15516489 0.03644203]
[0.80848648 0.13549109 0.05602242]
[0.21762134 0.48521286 0.29716579]
[0.15584948 0.41625218 0.42789834]
[0.19201639 0.40706352 0.4009201 ]
[0.03199536 0.34175085 0.62625378]]
```

While training an ensemble of binary models is one way to build models capable of multi-class classification, some algorithms like logistic regression can be modified to inherently support multi-class classification. In the case of logistic regression, the modification involves training multiple linear regression models internally, and replacing the sigmoid function with another function—the softmax function. The softmax function is capable of receiving inputs from multiple linear regression models and outputting class-wise probabilities. The softmax function is also known as the normalized exponential function, and its equation is illustrated in Figure 4.16.

To understand how this function works, let's consider the Iris flowers dataset. Each row of the dataset contains four continuous numeric attributes and a multi-class target with three possible output classes: 0, 1, 2. When a softmax logistic regression model is trained on this dataset, it will contain three linear regression models within it, one for each target class. When the model is used for making predictions, each linear regression model will output a continuous numeric value that will be fed into the softmax function, which will in turn output three class-wise probabilities.

Scikit-learn's implementation of the LogisticRegression class is inherently capable of multinomial classification; all you need to do is include the multi_class = 'multinomial' and solver = 'lbfgs' constructor arguments while instantiating the class. The following snippet uses Scikit-learn's LogisticRegression class on a multi-class classification problem with softmax regression:

```
# implement multi-class classification using
# softmax (a.k.a multinomial regression) classifier
from sklearn.linear_model import LogisticRegression
softmax_logit_model = LogisticRegression(penalty='l2', fit_intercept=True,
solver='lbfgs', multi_class='multinomial')
softmax_logit_model.fit(df_iris_features_train,
df_iris_target_train.values.ravel())
# use the  model to create predictions on the test set
softmax_logit_predictions = softmax_logit_model.predict(df_iris_features_test)
```

You can inspect the classes predicted by the softmax logistic regression model by using the Python print() function. As you can see, the output classes predicted for the members of the test set are one of three values—0, 1, or 2:

```
print (softmax_logit_predictions)
[0 1 2 1 2 2 1 2 1 2 2 0 1 0 2 0 0 2 2 2 1 0 2 1 1 2 1 1 0 1 0 1 0 0 1 1 1
2]
```

You can inspect the class-wise probabilities by calling the predict_proba() method on the LogisticRegression instance. As you would expect, the result has three values for each member of the test set. The first number is the probability that the output class is 0, the second number is the probability that the output class is 1, and so on (see the code example on page 109).

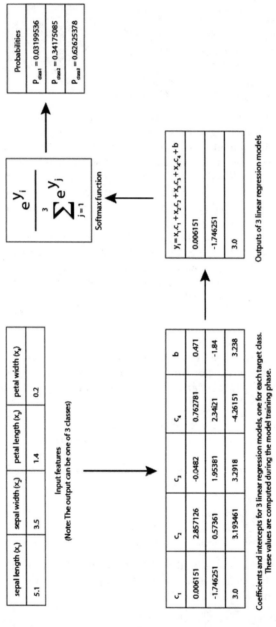

FIGURE 4.16
Softmax logistic regression

```
# access class-wise probabilities
softmax_logit_probs = softmax_logit_model.predict_proba(df_iris_features_test)
print(softmax_logit_probs)
[[0.89582633 0.09444564 0.00972803]
 [0.09889138 0.50828121 0.39282741]
 [0.01311439 0.23998685 0.74689876]
 [0.1645445  0.56290434 0.27255115]
 [0.04525701 0.42873174 0.52601125]
 [0.05219811 0.40090084 0.54690105]
 [0.1412285  0.49318467 0.36558684]
 [0.00512255 0.1226479  0.87222954]
 [0.18517246 0.6381944  0.17663314]
 [0.0301524  0.40920296 0.56064464]
 [0.00767857 0.15588852 0.83643291]
 [0.85228205 0.14095824 0.00675971]
 [0.1344201  0.56001268 0.30556722]
 [0.87716333 0.11550045 0.00733622]
 [0.03095013 0.30494959 0.66410028]
 [0.89925442 0.09260716 0.00813842]
 [0.86906457 0.12521241 0.00572302]
 [0.0286017  0.35588746 0.61551083]
 [0.00777372 0.15176958 0.84045669]
 [0.01219112 0.26741715 0.72039173]
 [0.05557848 0.49114599 0.45327553]
 [0.86733298 0.12475638 0.00791064]
 [0.05107527 0.39427714 0.55464759]
 [0.18367433 0.62661521 0.18971046]
 [0.1288656  0.49409071 0.37704369]
 [0.12588161 0.41550633 0.45861205]
 [0.12692498 0.64014023 0.23293479]
 [0.11348037 0.57595155 0.31056808]
 [0.85890116 0.13346798 0.00763086]
 [0.32189697 0.55802372 0.12007931]
 [0.91075124 0.08432501 0.00492375]
 [0.87466417 0.11230055 0.01303528]
 [0.21216432 0.63742445 0.15041124]
 [0.12872766 0.55202598 0.31924635]
 [0.16895463 0.54601673 0.28502864]
 [0.01604996 0.28654283 0.69740721]]
```

Decision Trees

Decision trees are, as their name suggests, tree-like structures where each parent node represents a decision boundary and child nodes represent outcomes of the decision. The topmost node of the tree is known as the root node. Building a decision tree model involves picking a suitable attribute for the decision at the root node, and then recursively partitioning the tree into nodes until some optimal criteria are met.

Decision trees are very versatile and can be used for both classification and regression tasks. When used for classification tasks, they are inherently capable of handling multi-class problems and are not affected by the scale of individual features. Predictions made by decision trees also have the advantage of being easy to explain—all you need to do is traverse the nodes of the decision tree and you will be able to explain the prediction. This is not the case for models such as neural networks, where it is not possible to explain why the model predicts something. Models such as decision trees that allow you to easily understand the reasoning behind a prediction are called white-box models, whereas models such as neural networks that do not provide the ability to explain a prediction are called black-box models.

Scikit-learn provides the DecisionTreeClassifier class as part of the tree package. We will now use this class to implement a decision tree–based multi-class classification model on the popular Iris flowers dataset:

```
from sklearn.datasets import load_iris
iris_dataset = load_iris()
df_iris_features = pd.DataFrame(data = iris_dataset.data,
columns=iris_dataset.feature_names)
df_iris_target = pd.DataFrame(data = iris_dataset.target, columns=['class'])
# normalize attribute values
from sklearn.preprocessing import MinMaxScaler
iris_scaler = MinMaxScaler()
iris_scaler.fit(df_iris_features)
nd_iris_features = iris_scaler.transform(df_iris_features)
df_iris_features_normalized = pd.DataFrame(data=nd_iris_features,
columns=df_iris_features.columns)
# create a training dataset and a test dataset using a 75/25 split.
from sklearn.model_selection import train_test_split
iris_split = train_test_split(df_iris_features_normalized, df_iris_target,
                              test_size=0.25, random_state=17)
df_iris_features_train = iris_split[0]
df_iris_features_test = iris_split[1]
df_iris target_train = iris_split[2]
df_iris_target_test = iris_split[3]
# create a decision tree based multi-class classifier.
from sklearn.tree import DecisionTreeClassifier
dtree_model = DecisionTreeClassifier(max_depth=4)
dtree_model.fit(df_iris_features_train, df_iris_target_train.values.ravel())
# use the  model to create predictions on the test set
dtree_predictions = dtree_model.predict(df_iris_features_test)
```

The constructor of the DecisionTreeClassifier class takes several parameters, most of which begin with max_ or min_ and are used to enforce constraints on the decision tree. Unlike other model types, decision trees do not have any inherent form of regularization and will aim to fit the training data near-perfectly. The problem with this is that decision tree models are likely to overfit the training data, and the way to prevent overfitting is to enforce constraints on the tree-building process such as the maximum depth of the tree, minimum number of samples in a leaf node, etc. You can find out more about the constructor parameters at https://scikit-learn.org/stable/modules/generated/sklearn.tree.DecisionTreeClassifier.html. The predictions made by the model can be examined using the Python print() function:

```
print (dtree_predictions)
[0 1 2 1 2 2 1 2 1 2 2 0 1 0 2 0 0 2 2 2 1 0 2 1 1 1 1 1 0 1 0 1 0 0 1 1 1
2]
```

To visualize the decision tree you will first need to use the `sklearn.tree.export_graphviz()` function to export the nodes of the tree into the Graphviz DOT file format, and then use Graphviz functions to convert the DOT file into an image. You can learn more about Graphviz at `https://pydotplus.readthedocs.io/reference.html`. The following snippet can be used to create a graph from a decision tree classifier. The resulting graph is depicted in Figure 4.17.

```
from sklearn.externals.six import StringIO
from IPython.display import Image
from sklearn.tree import export_graphviz
import pydotplus
dot_data = StringIO()
export_graphviz(dtree_model, out_file=dot_data,
                filled=True, rounded=True,
                special_characters=True)
graph = pydotplus.graph_from_dot_data(dot_data.getvalue())
Image(graph.create_png())
```

FIGURE 4.17

Decision tree
visualization

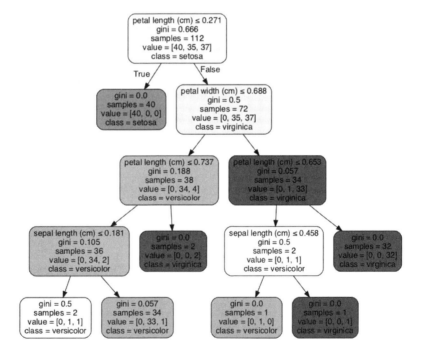

To make predictions with this decision tree, you start with the condition on the root node: `petal length <= 0.271`. There are two branches from this node—the branch on the left should be traversed if the condition is met, and the branch on the right is traversed if the condition is not met. You then repeat this process until you reach a leaf node, and the class associated with the leaf node will be the prediction.

The root node also contains some additional information: `samples=112` implies that there are 112 samples in the dataset that this condition applies to. The value array implies that out of 112 samples, 40 belong to the first class, 35 to the second class, and 37 to the third class. The `gini=0.666` value represents the Gini score associated with the node. A Gini score is a measure of impurity and is one of two impurity measures that Scikit-learn's implementation of decision trees provides, the other one being Entropy. A pure node is one which has elements that all belong to the same class, and a Gini score of 0.0. During the model-building process, the decisions that form the nodes (such as `petal_length <= 0.271`) are chosen so as to create the purest subsets on both child nodes. Tree building is a recursive process and stops when either the Gini score associated with a node is 0.0 or a criterion such as maximum permissible depth of the tree has been reached. You can learn more about Gini scores in *The Gini Methodology: A Primer on Statistical Methodology* by Shlomo Yitzhaki and Edna Schechtman (`https://www.springer.com/gb/book/9781461447191`).

A decision tree can also be used for regression problems, and Scikit-learn provides the `DecisionTreeRegressor` class to create decision trees for regression. A decision tree for regression is very similar to a tree used for classification, with the key difference being that each node predicts a numeric value instead of a class. The following snippet uses the `DecisionTreeRegressor` class to create a decision tree on the Boston housing dataset and uses the model to predict median house prices for the members of the test set. Figure 4.18 contains the decision tree generated by the model.

```
# create a decision tree based regressor on the Boston housing dataset.
from sklearn.tree import DecisionTreeRegressor
dtree_reg_model = DecisionTreeRegressor(max_depth=4)
dtree_reg_model.fit(df_boston_features_train,
df_boston_target_train.values.ravel())
# use the  model to create predictions on the test set
dtree_reg_predictions = dtree_reg_model.predict(df_boston_features_test)
```

NOTE   To follow along with this chapter ensure you have installed Anaconda Navigator and Jupyter Notebook as described in Appendix A.

You can download the code files for this chapter from www.wiley.com/go/ machinelearningawscloud or from GitHub using the following URL:

https://github.com/asmtechnology/awsmlbook-chapter4.git

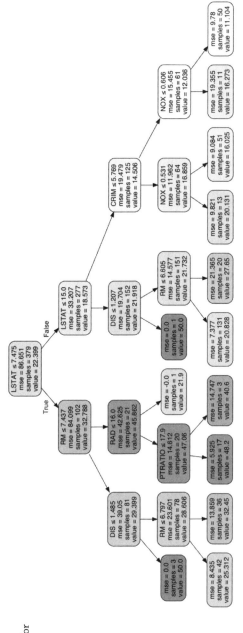

FIGURE 4.18
Decision tree for regression

Summary

- Scikit-learn is a Python library that provides a number of features that are suitable for machine learning engineers and data scientists.

- Scikit-learn provides a function called `train_test_split()` in the `model_selection` module that can be used to split a Pandas dataframe into two dataframes, one for model building and the other for model evaluation.

- K-fold cross validation can help minimize the possibility of the model picking up on unexpected bias in the training set.

- Linear regression is a statistical technique that aims to find the equation of a line (or hyperplane) that is closest to all the points in the dataset.

- Scikit-learn implements linear regression in a class called `LinearRegression`, which is part of the `linear_model` module.

- A support vector machine (SVM) is a versatile model that can be used for a variety of tasks, including classification, regression, and outlier detection.

- Scikit-learn provides an implementation of support vector machine–based classifiers in the, SVC class, which is part of the `sklearn.svm` module.

- Support vector models use a mathematical function called a kernel that is used to transform each input point into a higher-dimensional space where a linear decision boundary can be found.

- Logistic regression, despite having the word *regression* in its name, is a technique that can be used to build binary and multi-class classifiers.

- Scikit-learn provides the `LogisticRegression` class as part of the `linear_model` module.

- Logistic regression is inherently a binary classifier, but it can be used as a multi-class classifier for datasets where the target variable can belong to more than two classes.

- Decision trees are very versatile and can be used for both classification and regression tasks. When used for classification tasks they are inherently capable of handling multi-class problems and are not affected by the scale of individual features.

Chapter 5

Evaluating Machine Learning Models

WHAT'S IN THIS CHAPTER

◆ Learn how to evaluate the performance of regression models

◆ Learn how to evaluate the performance of classification models

◆ Learn to use the grid-search technique to choose the optimal set of hyperparameters for your model

In the previous chapter, you learned how to use Scikit-learn to create different types of machine learning models. In this chapter you will learn to use Scikit-learn to evaluate the performance of the models you have trained and techniques to select the values of hyperparameters that will result in an optimal model.

Since the purpose of a machine learning model is to predict something correctly, you will want to ensure that the predictive accuracy of your model is good enough for you to deploy it into production. It is therefore important to evaluate the performance of the model on data that the model has not seen previously, so as to get an accurate picture of how the model is likely to perform on real-world data (which it will also not have seen previously). Techniques such as creating test-train splits and k-fold cross validation, both of which have been discussed in Chapter 4, allow you to keep aside some of the training data for evaluation.

NOTE   To follow along with this chapter ensure you have installed Anaconda Navigator and Jupyter Notebook as described in Appendix A.

You can download the code files for this chapter from www.wiley.com/go/machinelearning-awscloud or from GitHub using the following URL:

https://github.com/asmtechnology/awsmlbook-chapter5.git

Evaluating Regression Models

The purpose of a linear regression model is to predict a continuous numeric value, such as a house price. There are two types of techniques that can be used to evaluate the predictive accuracy of a regression model: creating a scatter plot of the true and predicted values and computing a statistical metric that captures the total prediction error across members of the test set. The visual results obtained from a 2D scatter plot are simple to understand: the x-axis contains the actual values, and the y-axis contains the predicted values. The closer the points are to a 45-degree line anchored at the origin, the better the prediction will be.

The following snippet uses Scikit-learn to load the Boston housing prices dataset and train a linear regression model and a decision tree–based model on the data. A scatter plot of the actual vs. predicted value for both models is presented side-by-side in Figure 5.1.

```python
import numpy as np
import pandas as pd

# load boston house prices dataset
from sklearn.datasets import load_boston
boston_dataset = load_boston()
df_boston_features = pd.DataFrame(data = boston_dataset.data, columns=boston_
dataset.feature_names)
df_boston_target = pd.DataFrame(data = boston_dataset.target, columns=['price'])

# create a training dataset and a test dataset using a 75/25 split.
from sklearn.model_selection import train_test_split

boston_split = train_test_split(df_boston_features, df_boston_target,
                                test_size=0.25, random_state=17)
df_boston_features_train = boston_split[0]
df_boston_features_test = boston_split[1]
df_boston_target_train = boston_split[2]
df_boston_target_test = boston_split[3]

# train a linear model on the Boston house prices dataset.
from sklearn.linear_model import LinearRegression
linear_reg_model = LinearRegression(fit_intercept=True)
linear_reg_model.fit(df_boston_features_train, df_boston_target_train)

# create a decision tree based regressor on the Boston house prices dataset.
from sklearn.tree import DecisionTreeRegressor
dtree_reg_model = DecisionTreeRegressor(max_depth=10)
dtree_reg_model.fit(df_boston_features_train, df_boston_target_train.
values.ravel())

# use the  models to create predictions on the test set
linear_reg_predictions = linear_reg_model.predict(df_boston_features_test)
dtree_reg_predictions = dtree_reg_model.predict(df_boston_features_test)

# create a scatter plot of predicted vs actual values

%matplotlib inline
import matplotlib.pyplot as plt

fig, axes = plt.subplots(1, 2, figsize=(18,9))
axes[0].scatter(df_boston_target_test, linear_reg_predictions)
```

```
axes[0].set_xlabel("Expected Prices")
axes[0].set_ylabel("Predicted prices")
axes[0].set_title("Linear Regression Model")

axes[1].scatter(df_boston_target_test, dtree_reg_predictions)
axes[1].set_xlabel("Expected Prices")
axes[1].set_ylabel("Predicted prices")
axes[1].set_title("Decision Tree Model")

# plot the ideal prediction line
IdealPrices = np.linspace(0.0, df_boston_target_test.values.max(), 50)
IdealPredictions = IdealPrices
axes[0].plot(IdealPrices, IdealPredictions, color='#ff0000', label='ideal
prediction line')
axes[1].plot(IdealPrices, IdealPredictions, color='#ff0000', label='ideal
prediction line')

axes[0].legend()
axes[1].legend()
```

FIGURE 5.1

Comparison of predictive accuracies of a linear regression model and decision tree model on the Boston housing data

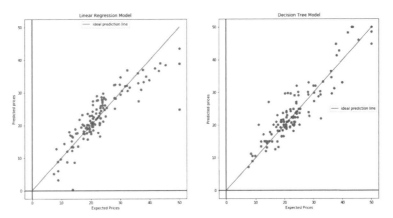

In addition to obtaining visual measures of accuracy, you can also use statistical techniques to evaluate the quality of a regression model. We will look at some of the commonly used metrics next.

RMSE Metric

The root mean squared error (RMSE) metric is popular when it comes to evaluating the performance of a regression model. As the name suggests, root mean square is the square root of the mean squared error (MSE). For a given item in the test set, the error in prediction is the difference between the predicted value and the actual value; this error can be either positive or negative, and squaring it ensures that the direction of the error does not matter (as squared numbers are always positive). The mean squared error is the mean of the squared prediction errors of all the items in the training set. This is illustrated in Figure 5.2.

FIGURE 5.2
Mean squared error and
root mean
squared error

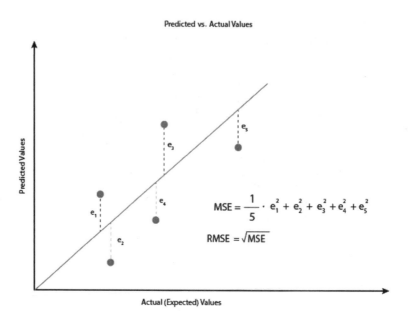

Scikit-learn encapsulates the computation of the mean squared error in the `sklearn`
`.metrics.mean_squared_error()` function. The following snippet uses this function to compute the MSE and RMSE of the predictions made by the linear regression model and the decision
tree regression model on the Boston housing prices dataset:

```
# compute MSE , RMSE, using Scikit-learn

from sklearn.metrics import mean_squared_error
mse_linear_reg_model = mean_squared_error(df_boston_target_test,
linear_reg_predictions)
mse_dtree_reg_model = mean_squared_error(df_boston_target_test, dtree_reg_
predictions)

from math import sqrt
rmse_linear_reg_model = sqrt(mse_linear_reg_model)
rmse_dtree_reg_model = sqrt(mse_dtree_reg_model)
```

You can examine the RMSE values using the Python `print()` function. As you can see, the
RMSE for the decision tree–based model is lower than the RMSE for the linear regression model,
which implies the decision tree–based model is the better of the two:

```
print (rmse_linear_reg_model, rmse_dtree_reg_model)
4.256139223131222 3.502392685222358
```

The benefit of root mean squared error is that its value is in the same units as the variable you
are trying to predict. For example, the house prices in the Boston housing prices dataset are
expressed in units of $1,000.00. An RMSE of 3.502 implies that on an average the house prices
predicted by this model will be off from the true house price by $3502.00. Since the value of the
RMSE is in the units of the target variable, it is easy to understand.

Unfortunately, the drawback of RMSE is that its value is sensitive to the magnitude of the target variable. If the target variables are larger numbers, the value of the RMSE will be a larger number, and therefore the RMSE cannot be used to compare models trained on different datasets.

R² Metric

The R² metric is another statistical metric that can be used to get an idea of the quality of the model. However, unlike RMSE, the value of the R² metric always lies between 0.0 and 1.0. The R² metric is also known as the coefficient of determination, and is a measure of the distance of the predicted values from the regression line.

Scikit-learn encapsulates the computation of the coefficient of determination in the `sklearn.metrics.mean_r2_score()` function. The following snippet uses this function to compute the R² score of the predictions made by the linear regression model and the decision tree regression model on the Boston housing prices dataset:

```
# compute coefficient of determination (r2 score)

from sklearn.metrics import r2_score
r2_linear_reg_model = r2_score(df_boston_target_test, linear_reg_predictions)
r2_dtree_reg_model = r2_score(df_boston_target_test, dtree_reg_predictions)
```

You can examine the R2 values using the Python `print()` function. As you can see, the R2 for the decision tree–based model is higher than the R2 score for the linear regression model, which implies the decision tree–based model is, once again, the better of the two:

```
print (r2_linear_reg_model, r2_dtree_reg_model)

0.7663974484228384 0.8418112461085272
```

Evaluating Classification Models

There are two types of classification models: binary and multi-class. Binary classification models are used when the target attribute can have only two discrete values (or classes). Multi-class classification models are used when the target attribute can have more than one discrete value. Let's consider binary classification models first.

Binary Classification Models

One of the simplest metrics that can be used to gauge the quality of the model is to simply count the number of times the model predicts the correct class. Whether or not this value has any meaning would depend on the proportion of samples that belong to each class, and the significance of the classes themselves. For instance, if a test set contains 100 samples, 50 of which are from class A and the other 50 from class B, with neither class being more significant to the problem domain than the other, then a model that predicts the correct class 80% of the time is straightforward to understand. If, however, 95 items in the test set were from class A and only 5 were from class B, the model that predicts the correct class 80% of the time is not so good after all. The problem can be significantly worse if the model was meant to predict whether an individual had a deadly illness, and the five samples from class B were the only ones that indicated presence of the illness. This is not an impossible situation; there is a very high possibility that a random sample of the general population will have very few individuals with a specific illness.

Before we look at better measures of a binary classification model's performance, let's first see how we can compute this simple metric. The following snippet trains a logistic regression, support vector machine (SVM), and decision tree classifier on the Pima Indians diabetes dataset and computes the percentage of correct predictions:

```python
import numpy as np
import pandas as pd
import os

# load Pima Indians Diabetes dataset
diabetes_dataset_file = './datasets/diabetes_dataset/diabetes.csv'
df_diabetes = pd.read_csv(diabetes_dataset_file)
df_diabetes_target = df_diabetes.loc[:,['Outcome']]
df_diabetes_features = df_diabetes.drop(['Outcome'], axis=1)

# normalize attribute values
from sklearn.preprocessing import MinMaxScaler

diabetes_scaler = MinMaxScaler()
diabetes_scaler.fit(df_diabetes_features)
nd_diabetes_features = diabetes_scaler.transform(df_diabetes_features)
df_diabetes_features_normalized = pd.DataFrame(data=nd_diabetes_features,
columns=df_diabetes_features.columns)

# create a training dataset and a test dataset using a 75/25 split.
from sklearn.model_selection import train_test_split

diabetes_split = train_test_split(df_diabetes_features_normalized,
df_diabetes_target,
                                  test_size=0.25, random_state=17)
df_diabetes_features_train = diabetes_split[0]
df_diabetes_features_test = diabetes_split[1]
df_diabetes_target_train = diabetes_split[2]
df_diabetes_target_test = diabetes_split[3]

# train an SVM classifier for the features of the diabetes dataset using an RBF
kernel from sklearn.svm import SVC
svc_model = SVC(kernel='rbf', C=1, gamma='auto')
svc_model.fit(df_diabetes_features_train,
df_diabetes_target_train.values.ravel())

# train a logistic regression model on the diabetes dataset
from sklearn.linear_model import LogisticRegression
logit_model = LogisticRegression(penalty='l2', fit_intercept=True,
solver='liblinear')
logit_model.fit(df_diabetes_features_train,
df_diabetes_target_train.values.ravel())

# train a decision tree based binary classifier.
from sklearn.tree import DecisionTreeClassifier
```

```
dtree_model = DecisionTreeClassifier(max_depth=4)
dtree_model.fit(df_diabetes_features_train,
df_diabetes_target_train.values.ravel())

# use the models to create predictions on the diabetes test set
svc_predictions = svc_model.predict(df_diabetes_features_test)
logit_predictions = logit_model.predict(df_diabetes_features_test)
dtree_predictions = dtree_model.predict(df_diabetes_features_test)

# simplistic metric - the percentage of correct predictions
svc_correct = svc_predictions == df_diabetes_target_test.values.ravel()
svc_correct_percent = np.count_nonzero(svc_correct) / svc_predictions.size * 100

logit_correct = logit_predictions == df_diabetes_target_test.values.ravel()
logit_correct_percent = np.count_nonzero(logit_correct) /
logit_predictions.size * 100

dtree_correct = dtree_predictions == df_diabetes_target_test.values.ravel()
dtree_correct_percent = np.count_nonzero(dtree_correct) / dtree_predictions.
size * 100
```

Using the Python print() function, the results indicate that the logistic regression model and the decision tree model perform about the same, but the logistic regression model has the edge:

```
print (svc_correct_percent, logit_correct_percent, dtree_correct_percent)

73.95833333333334 76.5625 75.52083333333334
```

Now let's look at other performance metrics that could be used in binary classification problems. Some of the problems with simply counting the number of times a model predicts the correct answer were introduced earlier in this chapter. To get a better idea of the model's performance, what you need is a set of metrics that capture the class-wise performance of the model. The most commonly used primary metrics for binary classification are listed next. These metrics assume one of the two target classes represents a positive outcome, whereas the other represents a negative outcome:

◆ *True positive (TP) count:* The number of times the model predicted a positive outcome, and the prediction was correct.

◆ *False positive (FP) count:* The number of times the model predicted a positive outcome, and the prediction was incorrect.

◆ *True negative (TN) count:* The number of times the model predicted a negative outcome, and the prediction was correct.

◆ *False negative (FN) count:* The number of times the model predicted a negative outcome, and the prediction was incorrect.

This class-wise prediction accuracy is also sometimes referred to as the class-wise confusion, and when these four primary metrics are placed in a 2 × 2 matrix, the resulting matrix is called the confusion matrix. Figure 5.3 depicts a confusion matrix and explains what the individual numbers mean.

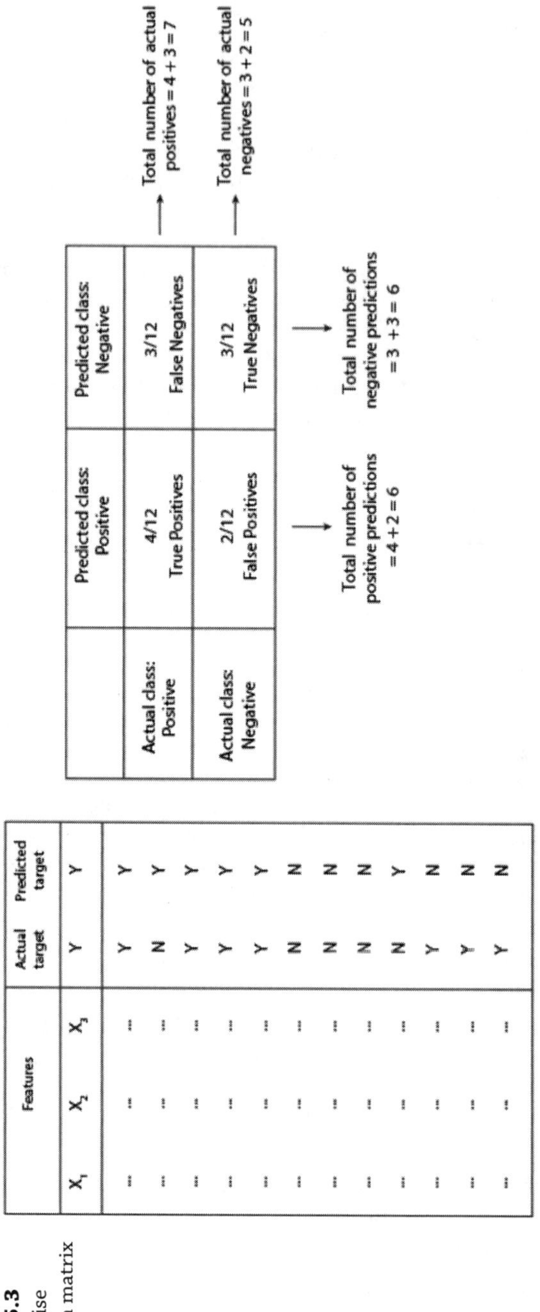

FIGURE 5.3
A class-wise confusion matrix

	Features		Actual target	Predicted target
X_1	X_2	X_3	Y	Y
...	...	...	Y	Y
...	...	...	N	Y
...	...	...	Y	Y
...	...	...	Y	Y
...	...	...	Y	Y
...	...	...	N	N
...	...	...	N	N
...	...	...	N	N
...	...	...	N	Y
...	...	...	Y	N
...	...	...	Y	N
...	...	...	Y	N

	Predicted class: Positive	Predicted class: Negative	
Actual class: Positive	4/12 True Positives	3/12 False Negatives	Total number of actual positives = 4 + 3 = 7
Actual class: Negative	2/12 False Positives	3/12 True Negatives	Total number of actual negatives = 3 + 2 = 5
	Total number of positive predictions = 4 + 2 = 6	Total number of negative predictions = 3 + 3 = 6	

Scikit-learn provides a function called `confusion_matrix()` in the `metrics` submodule that can be used to compute the confusion matrix for a classification model. You can find detailed information on the parameters of the `confusion_matrix()` function at `https://scikit-learn.org/stable/modules/generated/sklearn.metrics.confusion_matrix.html`.

The following snippet demonstrates the use of this function to compute the confusion matrix for the three binary classification models created earlier in this section:

```
# compute confusion matrix
from sklearn.metrics import confusion_matrix

cm_svc = confusion_matrix(df_diabetes_target_test.values.ravel(), svc_predictions)
cm_logit = confusion_matrix(df_diabetes_target_test.values.ravel(),
logit_predictions)
cm_dtree = confusion_matrix(df_diabetes_target_test.values.ravel(),
dtree_predictions)

# extract true negative , false positive, false negative, true positive.
#
# the sklearn confusion_matrix() function returns in the following matrix
#
#       TN      FP
#       FN      TP

tn_svc, fp_svc, fn_svc, tp_svc = cm_svc.ravel()
tn_logit, fp_logit, fn_logit, tp_logit = cm_logit.ravel()
tn_dtree, fp_dtree, fn_dtree, tp_dtree = cm_dtree.ravel()
```

You can now examine the values of the primary metrics for the three models using the Python `print()` function:

```
print (tn_svc, fp_svc, fn_svc, tp_svc)
>> 113 8 42 29

print (tn_logit, fp_logit, fn_logit, tp_logit)
>> 113 8 37 34

print (tn_dtree, fp_dtree, fn_dtree, tp_dtree)
>> 103 18 29 42
```

In addition to these primary statistical metrics, data scientists use the following secondary metrics. The values of these metrics are computed from the primary metrics:

◆ *Accuracy:* This is defined as (TP + TN) / (Total number of predictions). This is basically the same as counting the number of times the model predicted the correct value.

◆ *Precision:* This is defined as TP / (TP + FP). If you look at Figure 5.3, you will notice that the denominator is the total number of positive predictions made by the model. Therefore, precision can also be written as TP / (Total number of positive prediction), and it measures how precise your model is. Precision is a good measure to use when there is a high cost associated with a false positive. The closer the value is to 1.0, the more precise are the positive predictions.

◆ *Recall:* This is defined as TP / (TP + FN). Looking at Figure 5.3, you will notice that the denominator of this expression is the actual number of positive samples in the dataset. Therefore, the expression to compute recall can be rewritten as TP / (Total number of positive samples in the evaluation set). Recall is a good measure to use when there is a high cost associated with false negatives.

The following snippet computes the accuracy, precision, and recall values for the three models, using the information obtained from the confusion matrix:

```
# compute accuracy, precision, and recall

accuracy_svc = (tp_svc + tn_svc) / (tn_svc + fp_svc + fn_svc + tp_svc)
accuracy_logit = (tp_logit + tn_logit) / (tn_logit + fp_logit + fn_logit + tp_logit)
accuracy_dtree = (tp_dtree + tn_dtree) / (tn_dtree + fp_dtree + fn_dtree + tp_dtree)

precision_svc = tp_svc / (tp_svc + fp_svc)
precision_logit = tp_logit / (tp_logit + fp_logit)
precision_dtree = tp_dtree / (tp_dtree + fp_dtree)

recall_svc = tp_svc / (tp_svc + fn_svc)
recall_logit = tp_logit / (tp_svc + fn_logit)
recall_dtree = tp_dtree / (tp_dtree + fn_dtree)
```

Using the Python `print()` function, you can examine the accuracy, precision, and recall:

```
print (accuracy_svc, accuracy_logit, accuracy_dtree)
>> 0.7395833333333334   0.765625   0.7552083333333334

print (precision_svc, precision_logit, precision_dtree)
>> 0.7837837837837838   0.8095238095238095   0.7

print (recall_svc, recall_logit, recall_dtree)
0.4084507042253521   0.5151515151515151   0.5915492957746479
```

The logistic regression model has the highest precision of 80.95%, whereas the decision tree has the highest recall of 59.14%. Your choice of model will be influenced by the problem domain. What matters more: precision or recall?

It is important to note that all three classification models trained in this section compute class-wise prediction probabilities, and then threshold the probabilities to arrive at the binary output class. Scikit-learn uses a threshold of 0.5, and while it does not allow you to change this threshold, it does provide access to the underlying probabilities so that you can implement your own threshold if you want to. This means that the performance metrics discussed in this section will change for different values of the threshold. One possibility is to compute the confusion matrix for 100 thresholds between 0.0 and 1.0 and pick the threshold value that provides the best balance between accuracy, precision, and recall.

Data scientists often use a visualization tool called the ROC (receiver operating characteristics) curve, and a metric called AUC (area under ROC curve) to evaluate the quality of a classification model. The ROC curve is computed by plotting the rate of true positives on the y-axis, against the rate of false positives on the x-axis for a number of different confusion matrices, computed for threshold values between 0.0 and 0.1.

Scikit-learn provides a function called `roc_curve()` in the `metrics` submodule that can be used to compute the true and false positive rates (TPR and FPR) for a number of different threshold values. You can find detailed information on the parameters of the `roc_curve()` function at https://scikit-learn.org/stable/modules/generated/sklearn.metrics. roc_curve.html.

The following snippet demonstrates the use of the `roc_curve()` function to compute the true and false positive rates for the three binary classification models created earlier in this section, and plots the ROC curves using Matplotlib's pyplot module. The resulting ROC curves are depicted in Figure 5.4.

```
# plot ROC curves for the three classifiers.

# compute prediction probabilities
svc_probabilities = svc_model.predict_proba(df_diabetes_features_test)
logit_probabilities = logit_model.predict_proba(df_diabetes_features_test)
dtree_probabilities = dtree_model.predict_proba(df_diabetes_features_test)

# calculate the FPR and TPR for all thresholds of the SVC model
import sklearn.metrics as metrics
svc_fpr, svc_tpr, svc_thresholds =
metrics.roc_curve(df_diabetes_target_test.values.ravel(),
                                              svc_probabilities[:,1],
                                              pos_label=1,
                                              drop_intermediate=False)

# calculate the FPR and TPR for all thresholds of the logistic regression model
logit_fpr, logit_tpr, logit_thresholds =
metrics.roc_curve(df_diabetes_target_test.values.ravel(),

logit_probabilities[:,1],
                                              pos_label=1,

drop_intermediate=False)

# calculate the FPR and TPR for all thresholds of the decision tree model
dtree_fpr, dtree_tpr, dtree_thresholds = metrics.roc_curve(df_diabetes_target_
test.values.ravel(),

dtree_probabilities[:,1],
                                              pos_label=1,

drop_intermediate=False)



# plot ROC curves
%matplotlib inline
import matplotlib.pyplot as plt

fig, axes = plt.subplots(1, 3, figsize=(18,6))

axes[0].set_title('ROC curve: SVC model')
axes[0].set_xlabel("True Positive Rate")
axes[0].set_ylabel("False Positive Rate")
axes[0].plot(svc_fpr, svc_tpr)
axes[0].axhline(y=0, color='k')
axes[0].axvline(x=0, color='k')
```

```
axes[1].set_title('ROC curve: Logit model')
axes[1].set_xlabel("True Positive Rate")
axes[1].set_ylabel("False Positive Rate")
axes[1].plot(logit_fpr, logit_tpr)
axes[1].axhline(y=0, color='k')
axes[1].axvline(x=0, color='k')

axes[2].set_title('ROC curve: Tree model')
axes[2].set_xlabel("True Positive Rate")
axes[2].set_ylabel("False Positive Rate")
axes[2].plot(dtree_fpr, dtree_tpr)
axes[2].axhline(y=0, color='k')
axes[2].axvline(x=0, color='k')
```

FIGURE 5.4
ROC curves for three
binary classifica-
tion models

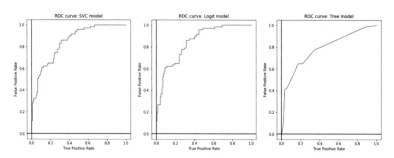

Scikit-learn also provides the auc() function in the metrics module that can compute the area under the ROC curve from the true and false positive rates returned by the roc_curve() function. The following snippet computes the AUC metric for the three classification models:

```
# compute AUC metrics for the three models
svc_auc = metrics.auc(svc_fpr, svc_tpr)
logit_auc = metrics.auc(logit_fpr, logit_tpr)
dtree_auc = metrics.auc(dtree_fpr, dtree_tpr)
```

Using the Python print() function to examine the values of the AUC metrics for the three models, the logistic regression model provides the highest AUC value:

```
print (svc_auc, logit_auc, dtree_auc)
0.845186823419858    0.8467000349202654    0.7846001629612384
```

Multi-Class Classification Models

Multi-class classification models are used when the target variable can belong to more than two classes. Fortunately, most of the techniques used to evaluate the performance of binary classification models can be applied to their multi-class counterparts. The concept of the confusion matrix can easily be extended to multi-class classification. The confusion matrix for an n-class classification would be represented as an n × n matrix where the rows represent the actual classes, and the columns represent the predicted classes. Figure 5.5 depicts a multi-class confusion matrix for a five-class problem.

FIGURE 5.5
Multi-class confusion matrix for a five-class dataset

	Predicted class: Apple	Predicted class: Banana	Predicted class: Mango	Predicted class: Pineapple	Predicted class: Orange	
Actual class: Apple	4	2	1	1	1	→ Total number of Apples = 4 + 2 + 1 + 1 + 1 = 9
Actual class: Banana	2	3	1	2	2	→ Total number of Bananas = 2 + 3 + 1 + 2 + 2 = 10
Actual class: Mango	1	0	6	2	0	→ Total number of Mangoes = 1 + 0 + 6 + 2 + 0 = 9
Actual class: Pineapple	0	0	3	8	1	→ Total number of Pineapples = 0 + 0 + 3 + 8 + 1 = 12
Actual class: Orange	1	2	1	0	5	→ Total number of Oranges = 1 + 2 + 1 + 0 + 5 = 9
	↓ Total number of predicted Apples = 8	↓ Total number of predicted Bananas = 7	↓ Total number of predicted Mangoes = 12	↓ Total number of predicted Pineapples = 13	↓ Total number of predicted Oranges = 9	

Scikit-learn's `confusion_matrix()` function can also be used to compute the confusion matrix for multi-class classification models. The following code snippet trains a softmax logistic and decision tree model on the Iris flowers training dataset, uses the models to make predictions, and computes the confusion matrix:

```python
# load Iris flowers dataset
from sklearn.datasets import load_iris
iris_dataset = load_iris()
df_iris_features = pd.DataFrame(data = iris_dataset.data, columns=iris_dataset.
feature_names)
df_iris_target = pd.DataFrame(data = iris_dataset.target, columns=['class'])

# normalize attribute values
from sklearn.preprocessing import MinMaxScaler
iris_scaler = MinMaxScaler()
iris_scaler.fit(df_iris_features)
nd_iris_features = iris_scaler.transform(df_iris_features)
df_iris_features_normalized = pd.DataFrame(data=nd_iris_features,
columns=df_iris_features.columns)

# create a training dataset and a test dataset using a 75/25 split.
from sklearn.model_selection import train_test_split
iris_split = train_test_split(df_iris_features_normalized, df_iris_target,
                              test_size=0.25, random_state=17)
df_iris_features_train = iris_split[0]
df_iris_features_test = iris_split[1]
df_iris_target_train = iris_split[2]
df_iris_target_test = iris_split[3]

# softmax (a.k.a multinomial regression) classifier
from sklearn.linear_model import LogisticRegression
softmax_logit_model = LogisticRegression(penalty='l2', fit_intercept=True,
solver='lbfgs', multi_class='multinomial')
softmax_logit_model.fit(df_iris_features_train, df_iris_target_train.
values.ravel())

# create a decision tree based multi-class classifier.
from sklearn.tree import DecisionTreeClassifier
mc_dtree_model = DecisionTreeClassifier(max_depth=4)
mc_dtree_model.fit(df_iris_features_train, df_iris_target_train.values.ravel())

# use the  model to create predictions on the test set
softmax_logit_predictions = softmax_logit_model.predict(df_iris_features_test)
mc_predictions = mc_dtree_model.predict(df_iris_features_test)

# compute confusion matrix
from sklearn.metrics import confusion_matrix

cm_softmax = confusion_matrix(df_iris_target_test.values.ravel(), softmax_logit_
predictions)
```

```
cm_mc_dtree = confusion_matrix(df_iris_target_test.values.ravel(), mc_
predictions)
```

You can inspect the confusion matrices generated by the two classifiers by using the Python print() function:

```
print(cm_softmax)

[[10  0  0]
 [ 0 14  1]
 [ 0  1 12]]


print(cm_mc_dtree)

[[10  0  0]
 [ 0 15  0]
 [ 0  1 12]]
```

Multi-class confusion matrices are often visualized as heat maps. The following snippet visualizes the two confusion matrices as heat maps side by side. Portions of the snippet have been adapted from https://scikit-learn.org/stable/auto_examples/model_selection/plot_confusion_matrix.html. The resulting heatmaps are depicted in Figure 5.6.

```
# plot confusion matrices as heatmaps
%matplotlib inline
import matplotlib.pyplot as plt

# plot the confusion matrix as a heat map using Matplotlib functions.
#
# portions of this code have been adapted from
# https://scikit-learn.org/stable/auto_examples/model_selection/plot_confusion_
matrix.html
def plot_confusion_matrix(cmatrix, class_labels, axes, title, cmap):

    heatmap_image = axes.imshow(cmatrix, interpolation='nearest', cmap=cmap)
    axes.figure.colorbar(heatmap_image, ax=axes)

    num_rows = cmatrix.shape[0]
    num_cols = cmatrix.shape[1]

    axes.set_title(title)
    axes.set_xlabel('Predicted')
    axes.set_ylabel('True')

    axes.set_xticks(np.arange(num_cols))
    axes.set_yticks(np.arange(num_rows))
    axes.set_xticklabels(class_labels)
    axes.set_yticklabels(class_labels)

    # Loop over data dimensions and create text annotations.
    #fmt = '.2f' if normalize else 'd'
```

```
        thresh = cmatrix.max() / 2.
        for y in range(num_rows):
            for x in range(num_cols):
                axes.text(x, y, format(cmatrix[y, x], '.0f'),
                        ha="center", va="center",
                        color="white" if cmatrix[y, x] > thresh else "black")

fig, axes = plt.subplots(1, 2, figsize=(18,6))

plot_confusion_matrix(cm_softmax,
                        iris_dataset.target_names, axes[0],
                        "Softmax Regression",
                        plt.cm.Greens)

plot_confusion_matrix(cm_mc_dtree,
                        iris_dataset.target_names, axes[1],
                        "Decision Tree Regression",
                        plt.cm.Greens)
```

FIGURE 5.6
Multi-class confusion
matrix for two models
trained on the Iris
flowers dataset

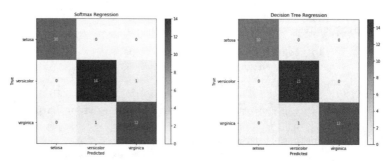

For a multi-class classification model, you can compute the overall accuracy metric, and the class-wise precision, and the recall. These metrics would be defined as follows:

◆ *Accuracy:* In a multi-class classification model, the overall accuracy of the model is the number of times the model predicted the correct answer. Using a confusion matrix, accuracy can be represented as the Sum of the diagonal elements / Total number of predictions. In the case of the confusion matrix for the decision tree model depicted in Figure 5.6, the overall accuracy is 37/38.

◆ *Precision:* In a multi-class classification problem, the class-wise precision for a given class would be defined as the Number of times the model predicted the class correctly / Total number of predictions made for that class. Using a confusion matrix, precision can be represented graphically as the ratio of the number in the diagonal element to the column total. In the case of the confusion matrix for the decision tree model depicted in Figure 5.6, the class-wise precision for the Setosa class is 10/10, Versicolor is 15/16, and Virginica is 12/12.

◆ *Recall:* In a multi-class classification problem, the class-wise recall for a given class would be defined as the Number of times the model predicted the class correctly / Total number of elements of that class. Using a confusion matrix, recall can be represented graphically as the ratio of the number in the diagonal element to the row total. In the case of the confusion matrix for the decision tree model depicted in Figure 5.6, the class-wise recall for the Setosa class is 10/10, the Versicolor class is 15/15, and Virginica is 12/13.

Choosing Hyperparameter Values

During a machine learning project, creating a single model and computing metrics is not enough. As you have learned in this chapter and the previous ones, there are a number of factors that could influence the performance of the model, from feature engineering to the choice of model and hyperparameters used during the model building. In order to automate the process of finding the optimal model, data scientists often use the grid search technique to try various combinations of hyperparameters and pick the model that appears to perform best. Scikit-learn provides the GridSearchCV class in the model_selection module that can be used to perform an exhaustive search over a set of parameter values. You can learn more about the GridSearchCV class at https://scikit-learn.org/stable/modules/generated/sklearn.model_selection.GridSearchCV.html.

The following code snippet uses the GridSearchCV class to try different hyperparameter combinations for a multi-class decision tree classifier on the Iris flowers dataset and returns the hyperparameters that result in the best precision score:

```
# use grid search to find the hyperparameters that result
# in the best accuracy score for a decision tree
# based classifier on the Iris Flowers dataset
from sklearn.model_selection import GridSearchCV
from sklearn.tree import DecisionTreeClassifier

grid_params = {
    'criterion': ['gini', 'entropy'],
    'splitter': ['best', 'random'],
    'max_depth': [2, 3, 4, 5, 6, 7, 8, 9, 10, 11, 12],
    'min_samples_split': [2, 3, 4, 5, 6, 7, 8, 9, 10, 11, 12],
    'max_features': ['auto', 'sqrt', 'log2'],
    'presort': [True, False]
}

grid_search = GridSearchCV(estimator=DecisionTreeClassifier(),
                           param_grid=grid_params, scoring='accuracy',
                           cv=10, n_jobs=-1)

grid_search.fit(df_iris_features.values, df_iris_target)
```

In this snippet, grid_params is a dictionary of hyperparameters and the values for each parameter that you want to try. The elements of the dictionary will depend on the model that you want to train. This example uses a decision tree classification model and the dictionary has six entries that correspond to some of the hyperparameters of the DecisionTreeClassifier class. The grid search process will build a model with each combination of hyperparameters, which in this case will be $2 \times 2 \times 11 \times 11 \times 3 \times 2 = 15{,}488$ models.

The cv=10 parameter in the constructor of the GridSearchCV class is used to control the number of folds, which in this case is set to 10 and therefore each of the 15,488 models will be trained using 10-fold cross validation. Depending on the speed of your computer, this code can take a significant amount of time to execute. Once the grid search is complete, you can inspect the value of the hyperparameters that resulted in the best model, and the accuracy of that model, using the following statements:

```
best_parameters = grid_search.best_params_
print(best_parameters)

{'criterion': 'entropy', 'max_depth': 7, 'max_features': 'sqrt', 'min_samples_
split': 12, 'presort': False, 'splitter': 'random'}

best_accuracy = grid_search.best_score_
print(best_accuracy)

0.98
```

NOTE   To follow along with this chapter ensure you have installed Anaconda Navigator and Jupyter Notebook as described in Appendix A.

You can download the code files for this chapter from `www.wiley.com/go/machinelearning-awscloud` or from GitHub using the following URL:

`https://github.com/asmtechnology/awsmlbook-chapter5.git`

Summary

♦ There are two types of techniques that can be used to evaluate the predictive accuracy of a regression model: creating a scatter plot of the true and predicted values, and computing a statistical metric that captures the total prediction error across members of the test set.

♦ The root mean squared error (RMSE) metric is popular when it comes to evaluating the performance of a regression model. As the name suggests, root mean square is the square root of the mean squared error (MSE).

♦ The R^2 metric is another statistical metric that can be used to get an idea of the quality of the model.

♦ The R^2 metric is also known as the coefficient of determination. It is a measure of the distance of the predicted values from the regression line.

♦ The true positive count for a binary classification model is defined as the number of times the model predicted a positive outcome, and the prediction was correct.

♦ The false positive count for a binary classification model is defined as the number of times the model predicted a positive outcome, and the prediction was incorrect.

♦ The true negative count for a binary classification model is defined as the number of times the model predicted a negative outcome, and the prediction was correct.

♦ The false negative count for a binary classification model is defined as the number of times the model predicted a negative outcome, and the prediction was incorrect.

♦ Accuracy, precision, and recall are additional metrics that can be used to evaluate a binary classification model.

Part 2

Machine Learning with Amazon Web Services

Chapter 6

Introduction to Amazon Web Services

WHAT'S IN THIS CHAPTER

- ◆ Introduction to the basics of cloud computing

- ◆ Introduction to the AWS ecosystem and key services used to build machine learning solutions

- ◆ Signing up for an account under the AWS free tier

In this chapter, you learn about what cloud computing is, read about common models of abstraction used when discussing cloud-based services, and discover a high-level overview of Amazon's offerings in the cloud-computing space, with emphasis on services that help build machine learning solutions. The chapter wraps up by walking you through signing up for an AWS account.

What Is Cloud Computing?

Cloud computing is defined by the U.S. National Institute of Standards and Technology (NIST) as "a model for enabling ubiquitous, convenient, on-demand network access to a shared pool of configurable computing resources (such as networks, servers, storage, applications and services) that can be rapidly provisioned and released with minimal management effort or service provider interaction."[1]

NIST defines five essential characteristics in this model. Each of these is briefly examined next:

- ◆ *Broad network access:* A consumer should be able to access services from anywhere.

- ◆ *Resource pooling:* A provider's computing resources are pooled to support multiple customers.

- ◆ *On-demand self-service:* A consumer should be able to provision computing resources (such as virtual servers) as needed, with minimal human interaction.

- ◆ *Measured service:* A consumer should be able to use computing resources on a pay-as-you-use basis.

---

[1] Peter Mell and Timothy Grance, "The NIST Definition of Cloud Computing," NIST Special Publication 800-145. September 2011. (http://nvlpubs.nist.gov/nistpubs/Legacy/SP/nistspecialpublication800-145.pdf)

◆ *Elasticity:* A consumer should be able to provision additional resources automatically and on demand. To ensure this, the provider pools computing resources to provide horizontal scalability to the consumer.

Cloud-computing solutions provide two major advantages to businesses:

◆ *Costs:* The cloud-computing paradigm is based on sharing and optimal utilization of hardware resources. A business need only pay for the time during which it utilizes a resource. When a resource is not needed, the business can relinquish it and make it available for someone else to use. This reduces both the upfront hardware investment cost for a business as well as ongoing maintenance costs. The cloud service provider, not the consumer, handles the maintenance of the underlying hardware.

◆ *Availability:* The time to provision a ready-to-use resource in the cloud is significantly lower than having to set up a similar resource in-house. For instance, a business could provision a virtual server with a cloud provider within seconds, whereas the actual process of procuring new server hardware and software usually takes a few months in most medium to large organizations.

Cloud Service Models

Cloud computing is built on virtualization technology. Fundamentally, there are two types of virtualization:

◆ *Application virtualization:* A single machine hosts one or more applications that are delivered to one or more users over the Internet.

◆ *Hardware virtualization:* Also known as server virtualization, in this model a single physical machine hosts multiple virtual machines. Each virtual machine can have its own operating system (different from the operating system of the underlying physical machine) and its own unique set of applications.

As an end user, you expect to consume one or more services from your cloud-computing provider over the Internet. These services can range from bare-bones virtual machines with a basic operating system to entire suites of applications. Five common models for cloud services are shown in Figure 6.1. These can be conceptualized using a layered model, with higher layers building upon the services offered by lower layers.

◆ *Infrastructure as a service (IaaS):* You specify the low-level details of the virtual server you require, including the number of CPUs, RAM, hard disk space, networking capabilities, and operating system. The cloud provider offers a virtual machine to match these requirements. In addition to virtual servers, the definition of IaaS includes networking peripherals such as firewalls, load balancers, and storage. Therefore provisioning multiple load-balanced Java application servers on the cloud as well as storing your files on a cloud-based disk would both come under the IaaS model.

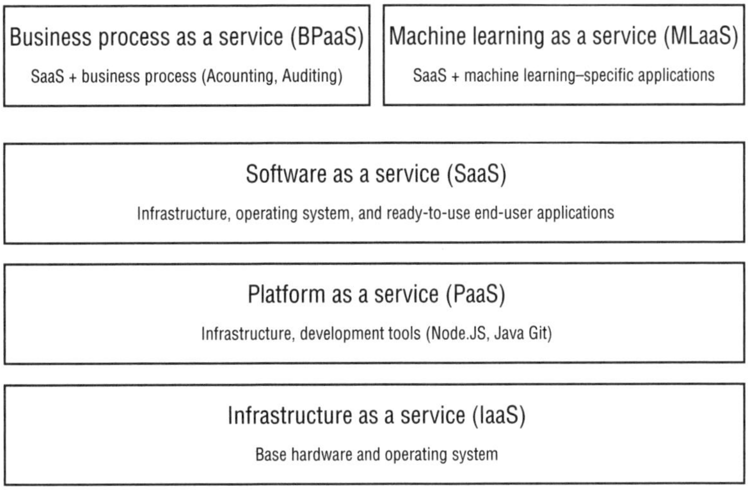

FIGURE 6.1
Common cloud
service models

Business process as a service (BPaaS)	Machine learning as a service (MLaaS)
SaaS + business process (Acounting, Auditing)	SaaS + machine learning–specific applications

Software as a service (SaaS)
Infrastructure, operating system, and ready-to-use end-user applications

Platform as a service (PaaS)
Infrastructure, development tools (Node.JS, Java Git)

Infrastructure as a service (IaaS)
Base hardware and operating system

◆ *Platform as a service (PaaS):* You choose between combinations of infrastructure and preconfigured software that best suits your needs. The cloud provider offers a virtual machine with preconfigured internal applications to match your requirements. The PaaS model is generally easier to use as you do not have to set up the underlying hardware and software; however, this can also be restrictive as your level of control on the underlying systems is significantly reduced compared to the IaaS model. The choice of infrastructure and pre-installed software differs between cloud providers, and if a cloud vendor does not provide something off the shelf that meets your needs, you are out of luck.

◆ *Software as a service (SaaS):* You specify the kind of software application you want to use, such as a word processor. The cloud provider provisions the required infrastructure, operating system, and applications to match your requirement. Most SaaS cloud providers include a limited choice of the hardware characteristics that run the application and as a user you usually have no direct access to the underlying hardware that runs your application. You are also tied to the limitations of the hardware and software chosen by your cloud provider. If, for instance, a cinema chain is using a SaaS cloud-based booking system to manage ticket sales and the system is unavailable due to an internal error with the hardware used by the cloud provider, there is little the cinema chain can do but wait until the cloud provider has fixed the issue.

◆ *Business process as a service (BPaaS):* You specify a business process that you want to outsource to a cloud provider. The cloud service provider provisions the hardware, operating system, support software, and web applications to provide the required service. A good example of BPaaS would be a cloud-based service to compute quarterly value-added tax (VAT) returns and submit these returns to the relevant tax authority on your behalf. Such a service could present you with a browser-based front end in which you upload your invoices and business bank statements. The service could then extract relevant information from the uploaded documents (using OCR, perhaps), fill out the relevant tax authority's forms, ask you to review the results, and submit the return on your behalf once you are happy with the numbers.

◆ *Machine learning as a service (MLaaS):* The cloud provider provides a number of services to assist with data modeling, machine learning model building, data transformation, data visualization, natural language processing, facial recognition, prediction, and deep learning. The services themselves may be classed as either software/application-level or platform-level services. The classification depends on how much control and flexibility is provided to the end user. The cloud provider automatically provisions the underlying infrastructure with sufficient capacity to scale up with demand.

Cloud Deployment Models

A deployment model answers the following questions:

◆ Who can access a computing resource?

◆ How can a user access a computing resource?

◆ Where is the physical hardware?

Cloud-computing solutions have four distinct deployment models:

◆ *Public cloud:* A public cloud provides services over the Internet to a consumer located anywhere in the world. The physical resources utilized by the provider to supply these services can also be anywhere in the world. This type of service could represent potential challenges to organizations such as banks that are prevented by regulatory requirements from storing confidential data on external systems. The cloud provider is generally responsible for procurement, setup, physical security, and maintenance of the physical infrastructure. To an extent the cloud provider is also responsible for the security of the application and data; this would depend on the service model (IaaS/PaaS/SaaS).

◆ *Private cloud:* A private cloud offers services to a single organization. Services are provided over a secure internal network and are not accessible to the general public over the Internet. The organization owns the physical hardware that supplies underlying services and is responsible for setup, maintenance, and security of both the infrastructure and all the software that runs on the infrastructure. Because of the large infrastructure costs associated with this model, only very large corporations can afford to have their own private clouds. A private cloud is commonly referred to as an on-premises cloud, and can offer any combination of IaaS/SaaS/PaaS to the organization.

◆ *Community cloud:* A community cloud provides services to a small group of entities (individuals, universities, or corporations) over a secure network. The underlying resources used to supply the services are owned by the entities that the community cloud serves. In essence, this type of cloud service can be thought of as something between a public cloud and a private cloud. The service is not accessible to members of the general public and does not put a significant drain on any one entity's finances. The entities involved usually share a common goal or provide services in a common industry sector.

◆ *Hybrid cloud:* A hybrid cloud is essentially a cloud service that is composed of other types of cloud services. For example, a hybrid cloud could consist of both public and private clouds. The public subcloud could provide services that are intended for consumption by any user over the Internet. A private cloud could offer services that are sensitive to the business. Most large organizations use a hybrid cloud model. It lets them provision public cloud resources when needed for a specific business case, while continuing to enjoy the security and control that a private cloud allows for all their existing processes.

The AWS Ecosystem

Amazon Web Services is the most rapidly evolving cloud-computing service in the market. The current AWS offering consists of over a hundred services offered in locations around the world, with new services being added every year.

New additions to AWS are announced at AWS re:Invent, which is the official annual AWS conference. You can find more information on AWS re:Invent at `https://reinvent.awsevents.com`.

Figure 6.2 describes a brief timeline of AWS. AWS was born in a paper presented by Chris Pinkham and Benjamin Black to Jeff Bezos in 2003.

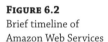

FIGURE 6.2

Brief timeline of
Amazon Web Services

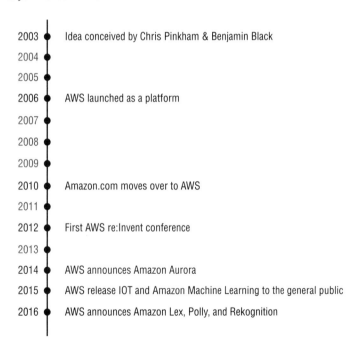

This paper suggested selling Amazon's internal infrastructure as a service to the world. In 2006 AWS was officially launched as a platform with a few key services, including EC2 and S3.

In November 2010, Amazon announced that all of Amazon.com had migrated to AWS. The first AWS re:Invent conference took place from November 27 to November 29, 2012, at the Venetian Hotel in Las Vegas. In 2015, Amazon launched its own machine learning platform called

Amazon Machine Learning, and in 2016 announced three new API-based services specifically geared toward machine learning applications: Amazon Rekognition, Amazon Polly, and Amazon Lex.

At the time this book was written, AWS offered 130 services, each of which resided in one of 20 different service categories. The service categories are as follows:

◆ Compute

◆ Storage

◆ Database

◆ Migration

◆ Networking & Content Delivery

◆ Developer Tools

◆ Management Tools

◆ Media Services

◆ Machine Learning

◆ Analytics

◆ Security, Identity & Compliance

◆ Mobile Services

◆ AR & VR

◆ Application Integration

◆ AWS Cost Management

◆ Customer Engagement

◆ Business Productivity

◆ Desktop & App Streaming

◆ Internet of Things

◆ Game Development

You can find details on all AWS services within these categories at https://aws.amazon.com/products/.

Amazon's offerings in the machine learning space are grouped into two categories: application services and platform services.

Machine Learning Application Services

These services are designed to solve specific machine learning problems out of the box and can be integrated into your own applications via APIs. Some of the services in this category are listed here:

◆ *Amazon Comprehend:* This is a service that allows you to build applications that need to understand the structure and content of text. Amazon Comprehend uses Natural

Language Processing (NLP) to extract insights into the content of documents. The insights can be entities (people, places), key phrases, sentiment (positive, neutral, mixed, or negative), and syntax. Amazon Comprehend is applicable across a variety of use cases; for example, an application that can examine the contents of forums to understand topics that your customers are interested in. Amazon Comprehend is covered in Chapter 13.

◆ *Amazon Lex:* This is a service that allows you to build conversational interfaces (chatbots) that support both text and voice. Amazon Lex uses deep learning to implement Natural Language Understanding (NLU) and Automatic Speech Recognition (ASR) and is the same engine that is used in Amazon Alexa. Amazon Lex is covered in Chapter 14.

◆ *Amazon Polly:* This is a text-to-speech service that you can use in your application. It supports multiple languages and a selection of voices. Amazon Polly can be used in several real-world applications, including newsreaders, games, and eLearning platforms. Amazon Polly is not covered in this book. You can learn more about Amazon Polly at `https://aws.amazon.com/polly`.

◆ *Amazon Rekognition:* This is a service that provides APIs for deep learning–based object detection and recognition in images and videos. Amazon Rekognition can be used in a variety of real-world applications, including content-based search in images and videos, facial biometric verification, and inappropriate-content detection. Amazon Rekognition is covered in Chapter 18.

◆ *Amazon Translate:* This is a document-translation service that can be used to translate text between a variety of languages. You can use it to translate unstructured text or build applications that support multiple languages. Amazon Translate is not covered in this book. You can find more information on Amazon Translate at `https://aws.amazon.com/translate/`.

◆ *Amazon Transcribe:* This is a speech-to-text service that can transcribe speech in audio files into text. It can be used for a variety of applications, including generating closed-caption text for a video. Amazon Transcribe is not covered in this book. You can find more information on Amazon Transcribe at `https://aws.amazon.com/transcribe/`.

Machine Learning Platform Services

These services provide you with tools to build, train, and evaluate machine learning models. Platform services do not address any specific machine learning problem out of the box; instead, you need to use them to build a machine learning solution from scratch to address the problem you are working on. Some of the services in this category are listed here:

◆ *Amazon Machine Learning*: This is a cloud-based service that lets you quickly build machine learning models using a wizard-based interface. Amazon Machine Learning is intended for simpler applications that can be solved using linear and logarithmic regression models and does not require the user to write any code. You can set up APIs to expose your Amazon Machine Learning models with minimal effort. Amazon Machine Learning is covered in Chapter 15.

◆ *Amazon SageMaker*: This is a fully managed service that lets you build, train, and deploy your own machine learning models using a variety of algorithms and frameworks on dedicated machine learning–optimized compute infrastructure. Amazon SageMaker also allows you to create notebook instances that can be used for data visualization, exploration, and analysis. These notebook instances come pre-installed with a Jupyter Notebook server, a number of popular Python machine learning libraries, and a number of conda kernels. Amazon SageMaker is covered in Chapters 16 and 17.

◆ *AWS DeepLens:* This is a wireless video camera and an integrated cloud-based development platform. You can train Convolutional Neural Networks (CNNs) on the development platform and deploy the models to the wireless video cameras. AWS DeepLens is not covered in this book. You can get more information on AWS DeepLens at `https://aws.amazon.com/deeplens/`.

Support Services

In the previous sections you learned about Amazon's machine learning application and platform services. These services do not operate in isolation—often you will find yourself using a number of other AWS services during the build and deployment phases of your machine learning application. In this section you will look at a few AWS services that you are likely to encounter while building and deploying machine learning solutions:

◆ *AWS IAM:* Amazon Identity and Access Management (IAM) lets you securely control who can access your AWS resources, what resources they can access, and what they can do with these resources. IAM is covered in Chapter 8.

◆ *AWS Lambda:* AWS Lambda lets users run snippets of code without provisioning an infrastructure. This service is billed on a pay-as-you-go model, with users only paying for the execution time of their lambda code. There is no charge when code is not running. Lambda code can be set up to automatically trigger from other AWS services or called directly from any web or mobile app. AWS Lambda is covered in Chapter 12.

◆ *Amazon S3:* Amazon Simple Storage Service (S3) is a secure, durable, and scalable cloud-based object store. Using this service, you can store your files in the cloud. Amazon S3 is covered in Chapter 9.

◆ *Amazon DynamoDB:* Amazon DynamoDB is a high-performance, scalable cloud-based NoSQL database service. Amazon DynamoDB is covered in Chapter 11.

◆ *Amazon Cognito:* Amazon Cognito allows you to create identity profiles for your app's users and allow them to sign in to the app with their Amazon, Facebook, Twitter, or Google accounts. Once users have authenticated from the app, the app is given a token that can be used to access AWS cloud resources securely. Amazon Cognito also offers a service that allows authenticated users to sync their app data on different devices. Amazon Cognito is covered in Chapter 10.

Sign Up for an AWS Free-Tier Account

To use AWS, you need to sign up for an AWS account. If you do not already have one, you can sign up for an account under the AWS free tier. An AWS account under the free tier is designed to enable you to try some of the AWS offerings free for 12 months, subject to certain usage limits. Go to `https://aws.amazon.com/free/` to obtain information on what is included in an AWS free-tier account. Amazon Machine Learning is not available under an AWS free-tier account.

To create an AWS account under the free tier, you need to go through a five-step process. Some of the steps have multiple substeps:

1. Contact Information

2. Payment Information

3. Identity Verification

4. Support Plan Selection

5. Confirmation

Step 1: Contact Information

To start the sign-up process for an AWS account under the free tier, visit aws.amazon.com and click the Create an AWS Account link on the top-right corner of the page (see Figure 6.3).

FIGURE 6.3
Amazon Web
Services home page

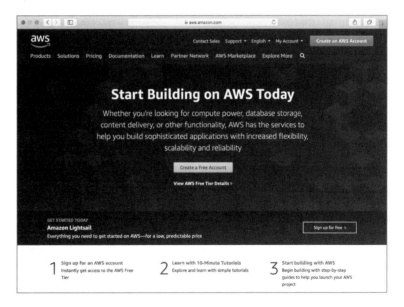

Amazon frequently tries out new user experiences with its customers, so this page may look different from the screenshot. However, you should still be able to find the relevant option to create an AWS account on the page.

Type in a valid email address, password, and account name on the Create an AWS Account screen (see Figure 6.4) and click the Continue button. The account name is a personal identifier you can use for this account.

You will be asked to indicate if the account is for an individual or a company (Figure 6.5). Select the option appropriate to your situation. This chapter assumes you have opted to create a Personal (individual) account.

FIGURE 6.4
AWS sign-in screen

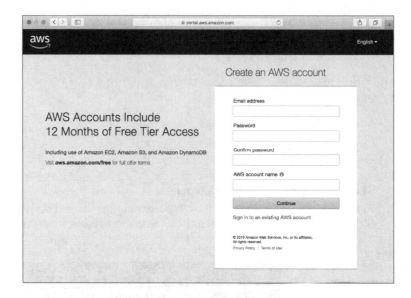

FIGURE 6.5
Contact
Information screen

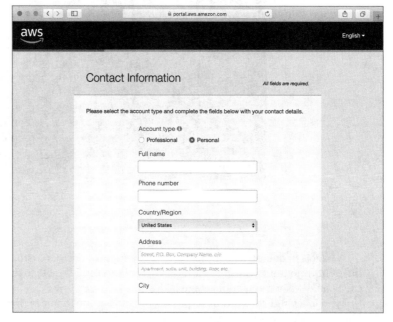

You will be asked to provide contact information (including a phone number) on the Contact Information screen. You must provide a phone number that you have immediate access to and can receive a call on. Scroll down to the bottom of the page if necessary, read and accept the terms and conditions of the AWS customer agreement, and click Create Account and Continue to move to the next step.

Step 2: Payment Information

You need to provide credit/debit card details (see Figure 6.6). Although an account under the free tier provides access to some AWS services for free, not all services are included in the free tier. If you use services not included under the free-tier account or exceed the usage limits of services under the free tier, the card you provide is charged.

FIGURE 6.6

Payment
Information screen

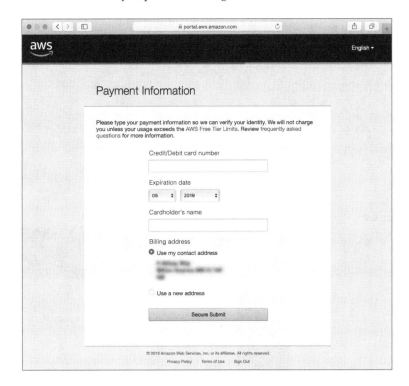

The precise services and options that are available under the free tier can change from time to time. Every effort will be made in this book to inform you whether an example utilizes AWS features outside those available in the free tier. To get up-to-date information on what is included in the free tier, visit `https://aws.amazon.com/free/`.

Type your credit/debit card details and click the Secure Submit button to move on to the identity verification step.

Step 3: Identity Verification

The identity verification process involves receiving a call from an automated system on a number you provide and entering a four-digit PIN into your phone when prompted. Type a telephone number and click Call Me Now (see Figure 6.7).

A four-digit PIN then appears on the web page (see Figure 6.8). You receive a call on the telephone number you have provided and are asked to enter the four-digit PIN you see on the web page.

FIGURE 6.7
Phone
Verification screen

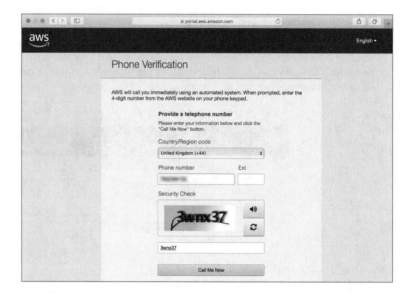

FIGURE 6.8
Phone verification PIN

The identity verification process completes once you key in the four-digit PIN over the phone. The web page refreshes to reflect this (see Figure 6.9).

Click Continue to move on to the next step of the account creation process.

FIGURE 6.9
Completing the identity
verification process

Step 4: Support Plan Selection

Select a support plan from the list of options available (see Figure 6.10). The options are:

- Basic
- Developer
- Business
- Enterprise

FIGURE 6.10
Support plan selection

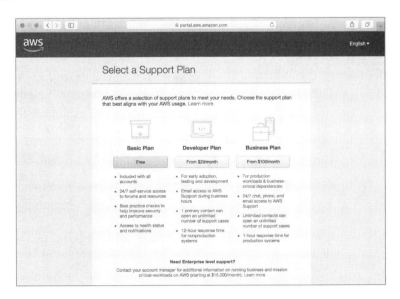

The support plans are cumulative and differ in the level of support that you receive, with the more expensive options giving you access to an Amazon employee to answer your questions. The default, selected option is Basic, and it is free. For the purposes of this book, the Basic support plan suffices. Select the default Basic support plan and click Continue.

Step 5: Confirmation

You receive confirmation that your AWS free-tier account is now set up (see Figure 6.11).

FIGURE 6.11
Completing the
sign-up process

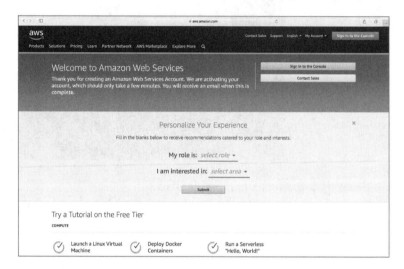

You also receive a confirmation message by email to the address you used during the sign-up process. In the next chapter you learn different ways you can access AWS and how to secure the account you have just created.

Summary

◆ Cloud computing is defined by the U.S. National Institute of Standards and Technology (NIST) as "a model for enabling ubiquitous, convenient, on-demand network access to a shared pool of configurable computing resources (e.g., networks, servers, storage, applications and services) that can be rapidly provisioned and released with minimal management effort or service provider interaction."

◆ Cloud computing provides both cost and availability benefits to businesses.

◆ Common cloud-computing service models include infrastructure as a service (IaaS), platform as a service (PaaS), software as a service (SaaS), business process as a service (BPaaS), and machine learning as a service (MLaaS).

◆ Cloud solutions are deployed using standard deployment models. A deployment model defines how a computing resource can be accessed, who can access the resource, and where the physical hardware is located.

◆ There are four distinct deployment models that are commonly used for cloud solutions: private cloud, public cloud, community cloud, and hybrid cloud.

◆ AWS offers over 100 different cloud services, grouped into 20 different service categories. Amazon is continuously adding to the services that are available.

◆ An AWS account under the free tier is designed to enable you to try some of the AWS offerings free for 12 months, subject to certain usage limits.

◆ Amazon's cloud-based machine learning services can be classified into two categories: application services and platform services.

Chapter 7

AWS Global Infrastructure

WHAT'S IN THIS CHAPTER

◆ Introduction to the AWS global infrastructure

◆ A tour of the AWS management console

In the previous chapter, you got an overview of the cloud services offered by Amazon, with emphasis on services for machine learning applications. In this chapter you will learn about the AWS global infrastructure. AWS physical infrastructure consists of a system of geographical regions, Availability Zones, and content distribution edge locations. Not all AWS services are available in every region.

Regions and Availability Zones

An AWS region is a physical location in the world from which cloud-based services are offered. Amazon ensures that you get to choose the region in which your data is physically located, making it easy for you to meet regional regulatory requirements.

An AWS region is divided into multiple Availability Zones (AZs) (see Figure 7.1).

FIGURE 7.1
Multiple Availability
Zones in a single region

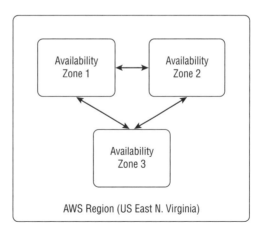

An Availability Zone consists of one or more data centers, housed in separate facilities, each with redundant power, networking, and connectivity. These data centers are connected to each other with private fiber-optic networking and enable you to build and operate scalable and fault-tolerant applications that are not possible from a single data center.

Availability Zones let you architect applications that automatically fail over between the AZs in a region without interruption. As of this writing, nineteen regions are spread throughout the world. Additionally, Amazon has announced that it is planning new regions in Bahrain, SAR China, and Sweden. You can find a complete list of regions and Availability Zones at https://aws.amazon.com/about-aws/global-infrastructure/.

Table 7.1 lists the current AWS regions and AZs within each region.

TABLE 7.1:   AWS Regions and Availability Zones

REGION	AVAILABILITY ZONES	COMMENTS
U.S. West (Oregon)	3	Launched in 2011.
U.S. West (Northern California)	3	Launched in 2009.
U.S. East (Northern Virginia)	6	Launched in 2006.
U.S. East (Ohio)	3	Launched in 2016.
AWS GovCloud	3	Launched in 2011. Only accessible to U.S. government employees.
Canada (Central)	2	Launched in 2016.
EU (Ireland)	3	Launched in 2007.
EU (Frankfurt)	3	Launched in 2014.
EU (London)	3	Launched in 2016.
EU (Paris)	3	Launched in 2017.
Asia Pacific (Singapore)	2	Launched in 2010.
Asia Pacific (Tokyo)	4	Launched in 2011.
Asia Pacific (Osaka)	1	Launched in 2018.
Asia Pacific (Sydney)	3	Launched in 2012.
Asia Pacific (Seoul)	2	Launched in 2016.
Asia Pacific (Mumbai)	2	Launched in 2016.

TABLE 7.1:   AWS Regions and Availability Zones   *(CONTINUED)*

REGION	AVAILABILITY ZONES	COMMENTS
China (Beijing)	2	Launched in 2014 in partnership with Beijing Sinnet Technology Co., Ltd. ("Sinnet"), the service operator and provider for AWS China (Beijing) Region.
China (Ningxia)	3	Launched in 2014 in partnership with Ningxia Western Cloud Data Technology Co., Ltd. ("NWCD"), the service operator and provider for AWS China (Ningxia) Region.
South America (São Paulo)	3	Launched in 2011.
Canada	2	Launched in 2016

NOTE   Not all cloud-based services are available in every region. To get a comprehensive list of services available in each region, visit `https://aws.amazon.com/about-aws/global-infrastructure/regional-product-services/`.

When you start out using AWS, you will most likely base all your cloud-based applications in a single region. The default region applied to new AWS account sign-ups from the UK and the United States is U.S. East (Northern Virginia).

At some point in the future, you may want to base some of your cloud services in different regions to serve customers there more quickly. Cross-region replication is not automatically applied and usually involves additional effort and costs.

Edge Locations

An edge location is a content-distribution end point for CloudFront. Amazon CloudFront is a secure content delivery service that integrates with Amazon's S3 and allows caching of frequently used media files closer to the point of consumption. More than 50 edge locations are found around the world. You can get a complete list of edge locations at `https://aws.amazon.com/about-aws/global-infrastructure/`.

To understand how edge locations work, let's assume you have a video file in an S3 bucket in the Asia Pacific (Tokyo) region that your users want to access. This video file has a URL that your users can employ to download the video.

Every time a user decides to download your video, no matter where he is, he needs to connect across the Internet to a data center in Tokyo. This can involve significant delays depending on how far your users are from the data center (see Figure 7.2).

You can place copies of this video file in S3 buckets in additional AWS regions like Beijing and Singapore to mitigate the problem to an extent.

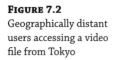

FIGURE 7.2
Geographically distant users accessing a video file from Tokyo

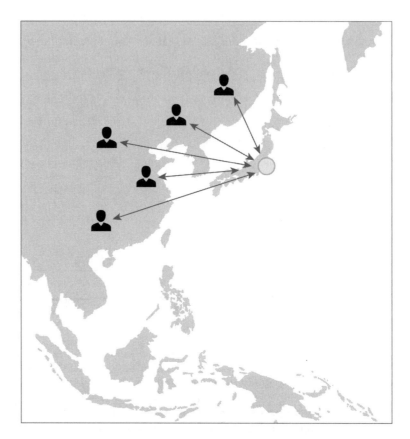

If you decided to use CloudFront to distribute this video file, give your users a new CloudFront URL for the video, not the original S3 URL. The first user who accesses your video still ends up connecting to a data center in Tokyo. When CloudFront receives the first request, it automatically caches this video at an edge location, closer to the user, for subsequent access. If another user in the same geographical area as the first user were to request the same file, CloudFront would use the cached copy from the edge location, resulting in significantly lower latency for the second user (see Figure 7.3).

Using CloudFront with S3 involves additional costs and setup, but if your application requires your user to download large files frequently, CloudFront can result in a significantly improved experience for your users.

Accessing AWS

In this section you learn about the different means by which you (or your application) can connect to AWS. An individual or application can connect to AWS in four ways:

◆ Using the AWS management console

◆ Using the command-line interface

◆ Using platform-specific developer SDKs

◆ Using RESTful web services

FIGURE 7.3
Edge locations can be used to cache frequently used content

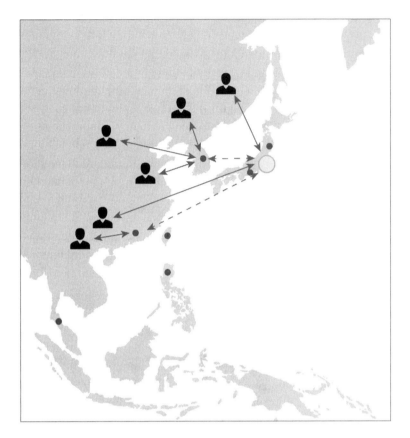

Beneath its surface and true to its name, AWS is a collection of RESTful web services. You can access every service AWS offers via a RESTful web service. The management console, command-line interface, and platform-specific SDKs build upon the underlying RESTful web service API. The manner in which you choose to access AWS depends on your job function.

If you are managing or administering services, you are likely to prefer the management console's web-based, user-friendly interface. If you are a DevOps person who frequently executes scripts, you are likely to prefer the command-line interface. And if you are an app developer, you are likely to use an SDK specific to your platform if one is available.

As of this writing, developer SDKs are available for the following platforms:

◆ Python

◆ Ruby

◆ C++

◆ iOS

- ◆ Android
- ◆ Java
- ◆ .NET
- ◆ Node.js
- ◆ PHP
- ◆ Go

You can get an up-to-date list of platform-specific developer SDKs along with installation instructions and SDK documentation at `https://aws.amazon.com/tools/`. The lessons in this book primarily utilize the AWS management console and occasionally the AWS SDK for Python.

The AWS Management Console

The AWS management console is a web-based application that permits you to manage your AWS account and configure cloud-based services. Log in to the AWS management console at `https://aws.amazon.com`.

Click the Sign in to The Console link located at the upper-right corner of the website (see Figure 7.4). You are asked to provide your AWS account username and password.

FIGURE 7.4
AWS home page

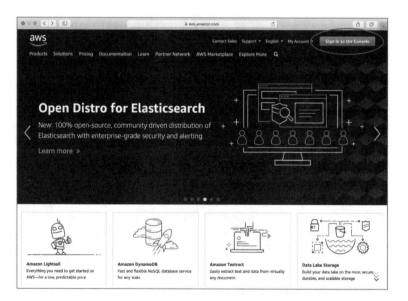

The landing page of the management console provides quick links to configuration pages for various AWS services, as well as links to training videos (see Figure 7.5). The look and feel of the landing page is constantly updated; therefore, the appearance of the landing page may differ from the screenshots.

FIGURE 7.5

AWS management
console home page

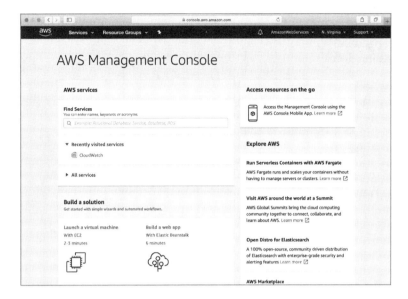

The menu bar at the top of the management console offers several useful options (see Figure 7.6). This navigation menu does not change when you move to different pages within the management console.

FIGURE 7.6

AWS management
console menu bar

HOME MENU

The leftmost icon in the menu bar is the home icon. This menu item can be used to access the home screen of the management console from any page.

SERVICES MENU

The Services menu (see Figure 7.7) contains links to all AWS services and can be used to quickly jump to the relevant subsection within the management console for any service.

RESOURCE GROUPS MENU

The Resource Groups menu allows you to access a subset of your own AWS resources (such as EC2 instances, load balancers, and databases) that have been tagged. A new AWS account has no resource groups configured; in such a case, the Resource Groups menu resembles Figure 7.8.

FIGURE 7.7
Accessing the Services
menu in the AWS
management console

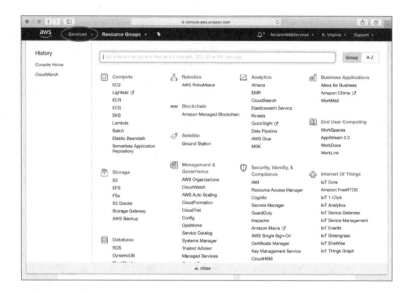

FIGURE 7.8
Resource Groups menu

Let's assume that you have created a Java-based application called *CustomerAPI* and are using a number of EC2 instances to support the application in the AWS EU (London) region. If all the EC2 instances that support the application have been assigned a tag called Name with value CustomerAPI, you could then create a resource group to logically group all the EC2 instances and view all these grouped resources on one screen (see Figure 7.9).

Existing resource groups can be accessed by clicking the Saved Groups menu item under the Resource Groups menu (see Figure 7.10).

Clicking the CustomerAPI-Infrastructure resource group takes you a screen where you can see all AWS resources that are included in the group (see Figure 7.11).

Resource groups provide a convenient means to access resources quickly. Membership of a resource in a resource group is based on the value assigned to a few tags, the type of the resource, and the region in which it resides. Membership of a resource in a resource group does not mean individual resources automatically belong to a virtual network, have restricted IP addresses, or are assigned security permissions.

ACCOUNT MENU

You can use the Account menu to configure account settings, access contact information and billing reports, and update security credentials. Unlike other menus discussed so far, the Account menu appears with the name used when creating the AWS account and not the name Account (see Figure 7.12).

FIGURE 7.9
Creating a
resource group

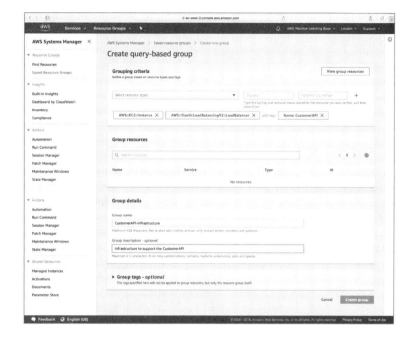

FIGURE 7.10
Tagged resources are
visible in the Resource
Groups menu.

FIGURE 7.11
Resources in the
CustomerAPI-
Infrastructure
resource group

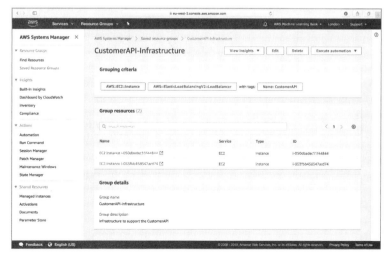

FIGURE 7.12
Account menu

REGIONS MENU

With the Regions menu, you can select the AWS region to which the management console is attached. By default, the management console is set to use the U.S. East (Northern Virginia) region, and any resources you allocate will be built there. To change regions, simply click the menu and select a different region (see Figure 7.13).

FIGURE 7.13
Regions menu

SUPPORT MENU

The Support menu is the rightmost option in the menu bar. You can use the options under this menu to contact AWS customer support and access documentation.

Summary

- ◆ Amazon uses a system of geographical regions to provide cloud-based services to end users. Not all AWS services are available in every region.

- ◆ An AWS region is a physical location in the world from which cloud-based services are offered.

- ◆ A region is divided into multiple Availability Zones. An Availability Zone consists of one or more data centers.

- ◆ An edge location is a content-distribution end point for CloudFront. Amazon CloudFront is a secure content delivery service that integrates with Amazon's S3 and allows caching of frequently used media files closer to the point of consumption.

- ◆ You can access AWS services using the AWS management console, the command-line interface, platform-specific developer SDKs, and a set of RESTful web services.

Chapter 8

Identity and Access Management

WHAT'S IN THIS CHAPTER

- ◆ Introduction to the basic concepts of Identity and Access Management (IAM)
- ◆ Creating users, groups, and roles
- ◆ Securing the root account with multifactor authentication
- ◆ Setting up a password rotation policy

Identity and Access Management (IAM) is a web service that allows you to securely manage users, configure security credentials, set up password rotation policies, configure multifactor authentication, and control which AWS resources users can access. Using IAM, you can control who can access your AWS resources, what resources they can access, and what they can do with those resources.

IAM is commonly accessed using the AWS management console, or the AWS command-line tools. In this chapter, you learn how to use the management console to set up users, groups, roles, and policies, and secure your root account.

Key Concepts

In this section, you learn some of the key concepts you will encounter when working with IAM.

Root Account

When you sign up to use AWS, you are asked to provide an e-mail address and a password as part of the sign-up process. The end of a successful sign-up journey creates a root identity using the e-mail address and password you provided. This root account has unrestricted access to all resources in your AWS account, including billing and the ability to change your password.

When you log in to the AWS management console using the e-mail address and password that were used during the sign-up process, you are, in effect, logging in as the root user.

Amazon recommends that you do not use your root account for everyday access and that you never share your root account credentials with anyone. For an additional layer of security, it is highly recommended that you enable multifactor authentication (MFA) on the root account.

For everyday use, the recommended practice is to use IAM to create separate users and employ groups and policies to set up the appropriate levels of access for these users. You learn about configuring MFA in the "Securing the Root Account with MFA" section and creating users in the "Creating a User" section later in this chapter.

User

An IAM user corresponds to a user or application in your organization. Each IAM user has a dedicated sign-in link, password, and access keys. However, IAM users are not separate AWS accounts; they live within the root AWS account (see Figure 8.1).

FIGURE 8.1
IAM users exist under the root AWS account.

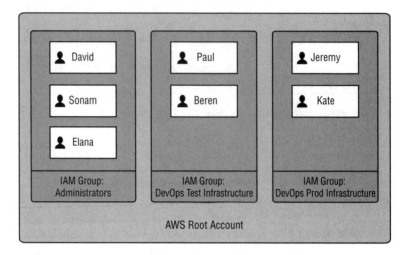

IAM users are provided a dedicated sign-in link and password to log in to the AWS management console and a set of access keys to programmatically access AWS services. The permissions associated with an IAM user dictate which sections of the AWS management console can be accessed by the IAM user.

Because IAM users can have their own access keys, you can create IAM users for applications that need to access AWS programmatically. Therefore, an IAM user does not necessarily represent an actual individual.

Amazon recommends that you create an IAM user account with administrative privileges and utilize that user to create other IAM users for individuals/applications in your company.

Identity Federation

Identity federation allows individuals/applications who are authenticated through other means (such as Active Directory, SAML (Security Assertion Markup Language) token, Facebook) to receive a temporary IAM user account that can programmatically access AWS services. Identity federation requires the user to first sign in to the external identity provider, retrieve a token from the external identity provider, and finally present the token to IAM to receive a temporary set of credentials for AWS resources (see Figure 8.2).

Identity federation can be helpful when your users have existing identities in a corporate directory or Internet identities. IAM supports two types of identity federation. The distinction is made on the basis of where the external identity is stored:

◆ Enterprise identity federation

◆ Web identity federation

FIGURE 8.2
Obtaining temporary
credentials

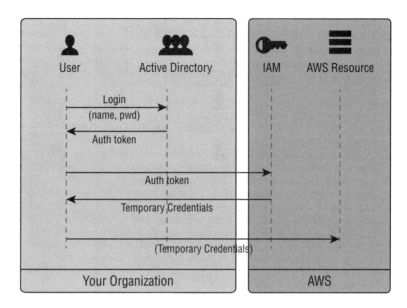

ENTERPRISE IDENTITY FEDERATION

In enterprise identity federation, the identity is stored outside AWS, in your own enterprise directory. Users who are already authenticated in your organization's network do not need to sign in with a new set of credentials to access AWS.

Users with identities in Microsoft Active Directory (AD) can employ AWS Directory Service to establish trust between their AD accounts and your AWS account.

Users with identities in a SAML 2.0–compatible corporate directory can configure the directory to provide single sign-on (SSO) access to the AWS management console.

WEB IDENTITY FEDERATION

In web identity federation, the identity is stored with a well-known third-party provider such as Facebook, Google, or Amazon. This is ideal if you are developing a web/mobile app that allows your users to log in using their existing Facebook, Amazon, or Google accounts. Using web identity federation in a web/mobile app does not require you to distribute long-term security credentials, or create a custom sign-in and identity management code within the app. Amazon recommends that you use Amazon Cognito Identity to manage identity federation.

NOTE   For more information on identity federation, visit `http://docs.aws.amazon.com/IAM/latest/UserGuide/introduction_identity-management.html`.

Group

A group is a logical entity that can organize IAM users. Groups can have attached policies that apply to all members of the group. Groups simplify permissions management instead of managing permissions for every user of your organization; you can attach sets of users to groups and administer permissions at the group level (see Figure 8.3).

FIGURE 8.3
IAM groups contain
users and permissions.

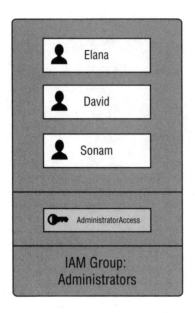
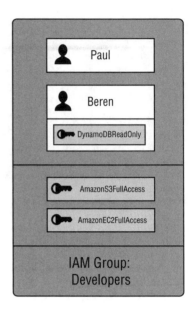

In larger organizations, it is quite common to have groups aligned with the departments and job roles associated within the company.

Policy

A policy is a JSON document that grants permissions and can be associated with a user, group, or role. A policy document lists the actions that can be performed and the resources that can be affected. When utilizing groups for user management, both users and groups can have policies attached to them. In such a case, the net set of actions a user can perform is the result of the combination of the policies applied to the user and those inherited via group membership. Policies can be one of two types:

- *User-based policy:* A user-based policy is attached to a user. It describes the actions the user can perform and the resources the user can access.

- *Resource-based policy:* A resource-based policy is attached to a resource. It describes the users who can access the resource and the actions they can perform on the resource. Not all AWS services support resource-based policies. The main use of a resource-based policy is to allow cross-account access to your AWS resources. Cross-account access occurs when IAM users from another AWS account access resources from your AWS account.

Role

A role is an identity object similar to a user that can have policies attached to it. However, unlike a user, a role does not have credentials associated with it and is not uniquely associated with a single person. A role can be assumed by a person or a service.

Roles are primarily for providing an AWS service access to another AWS service in your account, such as to allow an EC2 instance access to an S3 bucket. Roles are also involved when IAM users created in another organization's AWS account, or users authenticated with other identity providers, want to access your AWS services.

When a user assumes a role, the permissions associated with the role temporarily supersede his existing permissions. When the user stops using the role, the user's original permissions are restored.

When a role is assumed by a service (such as EC2), the service is given a temporary set of access credentials for the role. Thus, if you wanted your EC2 instance to access objects from a DynamoDB database, you would not create a username/password for the EC2 instance. Instead, you would create a role with the correct permissions and assign the EC2 instance to the role.

A role has two separate policies associated with it:

◆ *Trust policy:* This policy specifies who is allowed to assume the role.

◆ *Permissions policy:* This policy specifies what actions and resources the person who assumes the role is allowed to use.

Common Tasks

In this section, you learn to manage users, groups, roles, and permissions using IAM and the AWS management console. The topics in this section require access to the AWS management console. If you have not created users under your root account, you need to log in to the AWS management console with your root account credentials (see Figure 8.4).

FIGURE 8.4
Root account
login screen

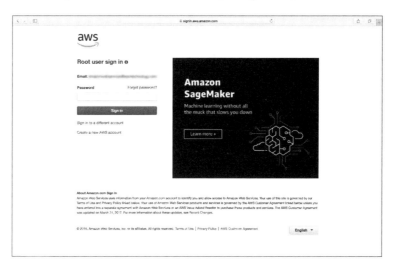

If you have already created an IAM user account for day-to-day administrative tasks, you should use the dedicated sign-in link for the user account to access the AWS management console (see Figure 8.5).

You cannot use your root account credentials to sign in through a dedicated sign-in link. IAM accounts are not restricted to the region that is currently set up in the management console (see Figure 8.6); they apply across all AWS regions. While employing the management console to configure IAM, it is good practice to select a region that is physically closest to you. Doing so ensures you experience the least latency while using the management console.

FIGURE 8.5
IAM user-specific
login screen

FIGURE 8.6
AWS management
console region selector

Once you have logged in to the AWS management console, select the IAM link from the Services drop-down menu (see Figure 8.7).

FIGURE 8.7
Accessing the IAM
management console

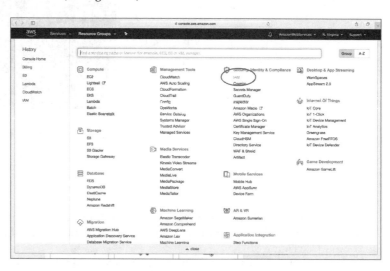

The IAM dashboard appears. At the top of the dashboard, you see the IAM users sign-in link. This is the dedicated sign-in link that you should give your users (see Figure 8.8).

FIGURE 8.8
User-specific IAM
sign-in link

Below the IAM users sign-in link, you are presented with a summary of the number of IAM resources that have been created, as well as a checklist of common tasks you need to perform to secure your IAM account (see Figure 8.9).

FIGURE 8.9
IAM resource dashboard

Creating a User

Follow these steps to create a user:

1. Click the Users link in the IAM dashboard to load the user management page. Click the Add User button to start the process of creating a user under your root account (see Figure 8.10).

FIGURE 8.10
Creating an IAM user

2. Specify a username as well as the access type for the new user (see Figure 8.11).

FIGURE 8.11
User details screen

The access type has two options. A user can have either one or both access types enabled:

◆ *Programmatic access:* Checking this option generates a set of credentials (access key ID, secret access key) that can connect to AWS services from the command-line tools, device-specific SDKs, or RESTful API.

◆ *AWS Management Console access:* Checking this option generates a password that enables you to log in to the AWS management console using the dedicated users sign-in link.

If you allow access to the AWS management console, you have the option to provide a custom password as well as require the user to change the password on first login. Click Next to proceed to the next step.

3. Once you have specified a username and access type, you are asked to configure permissions for the user (see Figure 8.12).

FIGURE 8.12
Configuring user permissions

Permissions are represented by JSON documents called policies. You can assign permissions to a user in three ways:

◆ *Adding the user to a group:* You can add the user to a group and assign permissions to the group. Permissions set on a group apply to the users within the group.

◆ *Directly attaching policies:* You can attach one or more policies directly to a user.

◆ *Copy permissions from an existing user:* You can copy the policies associated with an existing user.

Using groups to manage permissions is the recommended approach. Ensure the option labeled Add User To Group is selected, and click the Create Group button.

4. Type a name for the new group and select one or more policies to associate with the group. Click the Create Group button to finish creating the group. In this example the name of the group is DevOps_Engineers with a single policy called EC2FullAccess (Figure 8.13).

FIGURE 8.13
Creating a new group

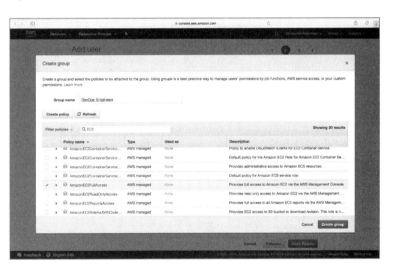

5. On clicking the Create Group button, you will be taken back to the previous screen and will see your new group listed alongside existing groups (Figure 8.14).

You can select multiple groups from the list, in which case the combined effect of the policies across the selected groups will apply to the user.

The list of groups also contains information on the policies associated with the group. Clicking a policy name will load the policy editor in a new window (Figure 8.15).

A policy is expressed as a JSON document, formatted according to the rules of the IAM Policy Language. You can learn more about the IAM Policy Language at `http://docs.aws.amazon.com/IAM/latest/UserGuide/reference_policies.html`.

FIGURE 8.14
The new group appears
alongside existing
groups.

FIGURE 8.15
The EC2FullAccess policy
loaded in the
policy editor

The JSON document for the EC2FullAccess policy contains the following:

```
{
    "Version": "2012-10-17",
    "Statement": [
        {
            "Action": "ec2:*",
            "Effect": "Allow",
            "Resource": "*"
        },
        {

            "Effect": "Allow",
            "Action": "elasticloadbalancing:*",
            "Resource": "*"
        },
```

```
{
    "Effect": "Allow",
    "Action": "cloudwatch:*",
    "Resource": "*"
},
{
    "Effect": "Allow",
    "Action": "autoscaling:*",
    "Resource": "*"
},
{
    "Effect": "Allow",
    "Action": "iam:CreateServiceLinkedRole",
    "Resource": "*",
    "Condition": {
        "StringEquals": {
            "iam:AWSServiceName": [
                "autoscaling.amazonaws.com",
                "ec2scheduled.amazonaws.com",
                "elasticloadbalancing.amazonaws.com",
                "spot.amazonaws.com",
                "spotfleet.amazonaws.com"
            ]
        }
    }
}
        ]
}
```

Each policy document begins with a string key called "Version", which in this case is the date this AWS-provided policy was created.

A policy also always has an array of statements. Each element of this array describes the ability (or inability) to perform an action on a resource. In case of the EC2FullAccess policy, there are several statements. One such statement allows access to all Elastic Load Balancer (ELB) resources:

6. After you have selected the groups to which you want the user to belong, click the Next button to display the screen shown in Figure 8.16, where you review the settings for the new user you are about create.

7. Click the Create User button to finish creating the user.

You are presented with a confirmation screen like the one in Figure 8.17 that contains the name of the user just created as well as access credentials.

This is the only opportunity to record these access credentials somewhere safely and share them with the user for whom you have created the user account.

8. Use the Download .csv button to download the full set of credentials for the user, and click the Close button to go back to the IAM home screen.

FIGURE 8.16
Review user settings screen

FIGURE 8.17
User confirmation screen

Modifying Permissions Associated with an Existing Group

To modify the permissions that apply to an existing group, click the Groups link on the IAM home screen and select the name of the group from the list of existing groups (Figure 8.18).

You are presented with a summary page that provides options to modify the permissions that apply to the group (see Figure 8.19).

FIGURE 8.18
List of groups

FIGURE 8.19
Group permissions summary

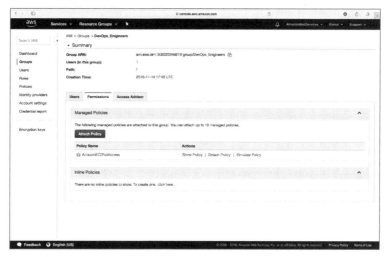

Creating a Role

To create a new role, complete the steps in this section:

1. Click the Roles link on the IAM home screen and click the Create Role button (see Figure 8.20).

2. Select the type of entity that will assume this role. Recall that a role has two policies attached to it: a trust policy and a permissions policy. A trust policy defines who can assume the role. IAM allows you to select from one of four types of entities:

   ◆ *AWS Service:* Select this option if the role is to be used by an AWS service, such as Amazon EC2. Roles that are used by AWS services are also known as service roles.

FIGURE 8.20
Creating a new role
using the IAM console

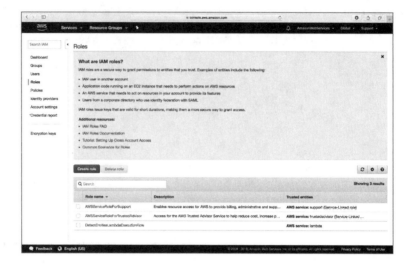

◆ *Another AWS Account:* Select this option if the role is to be used for IAM users who belong to a different AWS account.

◆ *Web Identity:* Select this option if the role is to be assumed by users who have been authenticated using an OIDC provider.

◆ *SAML 2.0 Federation:* Select this option if the role is to be assumed by users who have been authenticated using SAML 2.0.

The example in this section creates an AWS service role that will be assumed by EC2 instances, and will allow access to Amazon DynamoDB resources in the same account. Select AWS Service as the entity type and click EC2 from the list of available AWS service names (Figure 8.21). Click the Next button to proceed.

FIGURE 8.21
Creating a service role
for EC2 instances

3. Configure the permissions policy of the role. The permissions policy defines what actions a user or service can perform once it has assumed this role. You can attach up to 10 permissions to a single role.

Type the word **Dynamo** in the search field, select the policy called AmazonDynamoDBFullAccess, and click the Next button (Figure 8.22).

FIGURE 8.22
Attaching a policy to a role

4. The next screen allows you to create optional tags and associate them with the role (Figure 8.23). Tags are optional key-value pairs that can be associated with a role; a role can have up to 50 tags. The role that is being created in this section does not have any tags associated with it; however, you are free to add tags if you wish. Click the Next button to move to the next step.

FIGURE 8.23
You can associate up to 50 optional tags with a role.

5. The next screen provides a summary of the new role and allows you to provide a name for the role. Role names can be up to 64 characters in length and cannot be edited once the role is created. When you have finished typing the name of the role, click the Create Role button to finish creating the role (see Figure 8.24).

FIGURE 8.24
Review new role screen

Securing the Root Account with MFA

In this section, you learn to secure your root AWS account using multifactor authentication (MFA). The concept of MFA involves using at least two factors to authenticate a user. The factors are:

◆ Something you know (such as a password)

◆ Something you have (such as a hardware token, or a smartphone app)

◆ Something you are (such as a biometric fingerprint, or voice)

MFA is commonly used to secure sensitive resources and is increasingly being adopted by systems that you use as part of your day-to-day life, including Internet banking. It is highly recommended that you enable MFA where possible. When enabled, MFA adds an additional security step when someone attempts to use root account credentials to log in to the AWS management console. In this additional step, the individual is asked to provide a temporary and unique six-digit numeric code that an authentication device generates.

1. To configure MFA on your root account, log in to the AWS management console using your root account credentials and navigate to the IAM dashboard. Click the chevron beside the Activate MFA row under the Security Status dashboard (Figure 8.25).

The Activate MFA row will expand to reveal the Manage MFA button. When you click this button, a dialog box may appear reminding you that it is best practice to use a dedicated IAM user with administrative privileges as opposed to the root account (Figure 8.26). Click the Continue To Security Credentials button to proceed.

FIGURE 8.25
Accessing MFA settings

FIGURE 8.26
Configure security
credentials warning

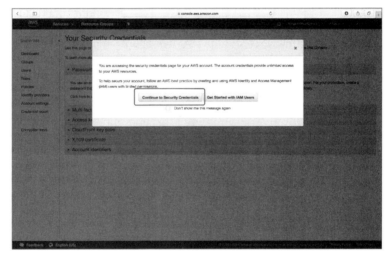

2. You will be taken to the security credentials page. Expand the multifactor authentication chevron to reveal the Activate MFA button (which will be in blue now) and click the Activate MFA button (Figure 8.27).

3. When you click this button, a dialog box will appear asking you to choose the type of MFA device you want to activate. You can use one of two types of MFA devices:

   ◆ *Virtual MFA Device:* A virtual MFA device is a software application like Google Authenticator that runs on smartphones. Google Authenticator is available for both iOS and Android devices.

   ◆ *U2F Key:* U2F is an open authentication standard created by the FIDO alliance. A U2F key is a USB key that you attach to your computer and physically interact with (instead of entering a code).

FIGURE 8.27
The Activate MFA
button is enabled.

◆ *Hardware MFA Device:* This is a physical authentication device you need to have purchased before activation. As of this writing, the device must be provided by Gemalto—a third-party MFA device manufacturer whose devices are compatible with AWS MFA.

NOTE Because Google Authenticator runs on a smartphone that you will probably carry around with you every day, there is always the possibility of the phone being stolen and the MFA authenticator being compromised.

A hardware MFA device (or U2F key) that is locked away is always more secure than a virtual MFA device on a smartphone that you carry with you.

To find out more about purchasing a hardware MFA device and other compatible virtual MFA apps, visit `https://aws.amazon.com/iam/details/mfa/`.

In this example, we are going to use the Google Authenticator app. Select the Virtual MFA Device option and click the Continue button (see Figure 8.28).

4. The next screen contains a QR code and two text fields. Launch the Google Authenticator app on your smartphone and scan the QR code. If the QR code is not visible on the web page, click the Show QR Code link to reveal it (Figure 8.29).

5. A six-digit code appears on the app. Type this code into the Authentication Code 1 field below the QR code. Wait for a minute, and a new code appears in the app. Type the new code into the Authentication Code 2 field and click the Assign MFA button to finish enabling MFA on the root account.

Multifactor authentication is not a feature that is exclusive to the root account. Any IAM user can choose to enable MFA on his own user accounts, and enabling MFA on the root account does not automatically enable MFA for IAM user accounts under the root account.

FIGURE 8.28
Choosing the MFA
device type

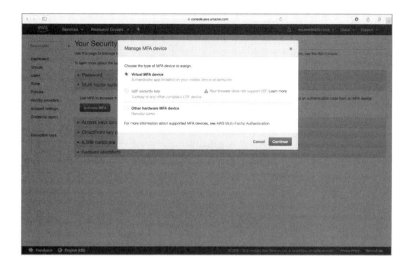

FIGURE 8.29
Configuring a step-up
authenticator

Now that you have enabled MFA on the root account, if you log out of the AWS management console and try to sign in again, you will be asked to provide an authentication code after you have entered your root account credentials. Launch Google Authenticator on your smartphone and type the six-digit authentication code from Google Authenticator into the text field on the web page.

Setting Up an IAM Password Rotation Policy

In the following steps, you configure a password rotation policy for your IAM users:

1. Log in to the AWS management console using your root account credentials and navigate to the IAM dashboard. Expand the Apply An IAM Password Policy menu item and click the Manage Password Policy button.

2. Select from the available options to create a suitable IAM password rotation policy and click the Apply Password Policy button (Figure 8.30).

FIGURE 8.30
IAM password pol-
icy settings

Summary

◆ Identity and Access Management (IAM) is a service that allows you to manage users and what resources they can access.

◆ The IAM service is typically accessed using the AWS management console.

◆ When you sign up to AWS you receive a root identity using the e-mail address and password you provided.

◆ Your root AWS account has unrestricted access to all resources in your account and must not be used for everyday use.

◆ For everyday use, you should set up IAM users, groups, and policies to set up appropriate access levels for these users.

◆ An IAM user can represent an individual or application.

◆ Identity federation allows individuals/applications who are authenticated through other means (such as Active Directory, Facebook) to receive a temporary IAM user account that can be used to programmatically access AWS services.

◆ A group is a logical entity that can organize IAM users. Groups can have attached policies that apply to all members of the group.

◆ A policy is a JSON document that grants permissions to a user, group, or role.

◆ A role is an identity object similar to a user but does not have credentials associated with it. A role has a set of permissions associated with it.

◆ Roles are primarily for providing an AWS service access to another AWS service in your account.

Chapter 9

Amazon S3

WHAT'S IN THIS CHAPTER

- ◆ Introduction to the basic concepts of Amazon S3
- ◆ Learn to create Amazon S3 buckets
- ◆ Learn to upload objects into Amazon S3 buckets
- ◆ Learn to download objects from Amazon S3 buckets
- ◆ Learn to interact with Amazon S3 using the AWS CLI tools

NOTE   Amazon occasionally updates the user interface of the Amazon S3 management console. As a result, some of the screenshots in this chapter may not match what you see in your web browser. However, the general concepts that you will learn in this chapter will still be applicable.

Amazon Simple Storage Service (S3) is a highly reliable web service that allows you to securely store and retrieve object data in the AWS cloud. After Amazon EC2, Amazon S3 is one of the most commonly used services. Data on Amazon S3 is spread across multiple devices and availability zones within a region automatically.

Amazon S3 is an object-based storage service (not block-based). It is ideal for storing files but cannot be used to install an operating system; thus, it cannot provide the storage for an EC2 instance.

Data within Amazon S3 is stored using a key-value system, with keys being globally unique. There is no limit to how much data can be stored on Amazon S3; however, the maximum size of a single file cannot exceed 5 TB.

Key Concepts

In this section, you learn some of the key concepts you will encounter when working with Amazon S3.

Bucket

A bucket is a folder on Amazon S3 where you can store your files. Bucket names are globally unique; therefore, no two users can own a bucket with the same name. Amazon S3 does not internally implement a hierarchical file system similar to what you encounter on your computer's operating system. All files across all Amazon S3 buckets are stored within a global flat file system. However, your bucket names can contain the forward path delimiter character (/). Therefore, you can name your buckets in such a way so as to create the appearance of a nested folder structure.

For each bucket you create, you can set up permissions that control who can access the bucket and what they can do with the bucket. Each object you store in an Amazon S3 bucket has an object key and metadata associated with it.

Object Key

An object key is a sequence of UTF-8 characters that identifies an object in an Amazon S3 bucket. The key is assigned to the object when it is first uploaded into an Amazon S3 bucket and can be up to 1024 bytes long.

The key name is basically the name of the file you have uploaded to the bucket. Amazon S3 internally stores data alphabetically, which means files with similar names are stored next to each other on the same physical disks. This can be an important factor to consider if the files you are planning on storing in Amazon S3 are going to have some kind of sequential naming scheme, or share a common prefix with each other. If this is the case, you could encounter performance bottlenecks when reading the data out of Amazon S3; you may want to consider naming the files differently or adding a short random string, or a timestamp to the start of the filename.

Object Value

The object value is the data that you are storing. It is a sequence of bytes and can be up to 5 TB in length.

Version ID

The version ID is a string value that identifies the version of the object. Amazon S3 assigns a version ID when you upload an object to a bucket. If object versioning is subsequently enabled, every update to the object creates a new version ID. Together, the object key and the version ID uniquely identify an object.

Storage Class

Each object in Amazon S3 has a storage class associated with it. The storage class determines how Amazon S3 stores the data for the object and if you will be charged additional costs to read the data. Amazon S3 offers the following storage classes:

◆ *Standard:* This is the default storage class for objects when they are uploaded to Amazon S3. It is ideal if your use case requires high reliability, durability, and quick access times. This storage class has been designed for 99.99% availability, 99.999999999% durability. Data is stored redundantly across devices and facilities and can withstand the loss of two facilities simultaneously.

◆ *Standard - IA:* IA is an acronym for *infrequently accessed.* This storage class is designed for long-lived objects that are accessed less frequently, costs less to use than the Standard storage class, and is designed to provide the same availability and durability as the Standard storage class. You can access your objects in real time, but each retrieval has an additional charge associated with it.

◆ *Reduced Redundancy Storage (RRS):* This storage class is designed for noncritical objects that can easily be reproduced. The objects cost less to store than the Standard storage class but are stored at lower levels of redundancy. This storage class is designed for 99.99% availability and 99.99% durability.

◆ *Glacier:* Amazon Glacier is an independent, low-cost cloud-based archival solution. This storage class uses Amazon Glacier to store your objects and is suitable for data-archiving tasks. Storage costs are extremely low, but it can take up to 5 hours to read the data.

Costs

Amazon charges you for the following aspects when you use Amazon S3. The specific costs differ between regions.

◆ *Storage:* You are charged for the objects you store in your Amazon S3 buckets.

◆ *Requests:* You are charged for the number of requests being made for objects in your Amazon S3 buckets.

◆ *Storage Management Pricing:* In November 2016, Amazon announced a new feature called Amazon S3 Object Tagging. Amazon S3 allows you to create object-based tags, and these tags can be created, updated, and deleted at any time during the life of the object. These tags can be used to get information on which objects are being accessed more than others. Amazon charges you a small fee per tag. For more information on Amazon S3 Object Tagging, visit `https://aws.amazon.com/about-aws/whats-new/2016/11/revolutionizing-s3-storage-management-with-4-new-features/`.

◆ *Data Transfer Pricing:* Additional costs are involved if you want to replicate your Amazon S3 buckets across different regions.

◆ *Transfer Acceleration:* Amazon S3 Transfer Acceleration is a feature that allows you to leverage Amazon CloudFront's CDN endpoints to offer your users access to the content of your Amazon S3 buckets. For instance, if your bucket were located in Tokyo, without Transfer Acceleration your users from around the world would have to make requests to Tokyo. With Transfer Acceleration enabled, they would only have to make requests to the nearest CloudFront CDN endpoint, which in many cases would be located much closer to them than the Amazon S3 bucket.

You can visit the following site to get an idea of the difference in access times with and without Amazon S3 Transfer Acceleration:

`http://s3-accelerate-speedtest.s3-accelerate.amazonaws.com/en/accelerate-speed-comparsion.html`

To get an updated list of charges, visit `https://aws.amazon.com/s3/pricing/`.

Subresources

Every bucket and object in Amazon S3 has a set of subordinate objects associated with it. These subordinate objects are called subresources of the object. Subresources cannot exist on their own; they are always associated with a bucket or an object. When this chapter was written, two subresources were associated with Amazon S3 objects:

◆ *acl:* This is an access control list that defines the list of people who have access to the resource as well as what they can do with the resource.

◆ *torrent:* You can use this to retrieve a `.torrent` file associated with the specific resource.

Object Metadata

Two kinds of metadata are associated with each object in Amazon S3: system-defined and user-defined.

SYSTEM-DEFINED METADATA

As the name suggests, system-defined metadata is automatically maintained by Amazon S3 and includes information such as object creation date, object size, and more. Users cannot edit all system-defined metadata fields. Table 9.1 lists the system-defined metadata fields associated with an object.

TABLE 9.1:   Amazon S3 System-Defined Metadata

NAME	DESCRIPTION	USER EDITABLE
Date	Date when the object was created.	No
Content-Length	Size of the object in bytes.	No
Last-Modified	Date when the object was last modified (or created if the object has never been modified).	No
Content-MD5	MD5 hash of the object.	No
x-amz-server-side-encryption	Indicates whether server-side encryption is enabled for the object and which service is providing the encryption.	No
x-amz-version-id	The version number of the object, only applicable to objects that have versioning enabled.	No
x-amz-delete-marker	Only applicable to objects that have versioning enabled; for such objects this field indicates whether the object is a delete marker.	No
x-amz-storage-class	Storage class used for storing the object.	Yes
x-amz-website-redirect-location	If configured, allows you to redirect requests for the object to another object or external URL.	Yes
x-amz-server-side-encryption-aws-kms-key-id	Applicable only if server-side encryption is enabled on the object. Contains the ID of the encryption key that encrypted the object.	Yes
x-amz-server-side-encryption-customer-algorithm	Indicates if server-side encryption is enabled on the object using customer-provided keys.	Yes

USER-DEFINED METADATA

User-defined metadata is any additional key-value metadata provided by the user when the object was created.

Common Tasks

In this section, you learn to use the AWS management console to create Amazon S3 buckets and manage the content in these buckets. Log in to the IAM console using your dedicated IAM user-specific sign-in link and navigate to the Amazon S3 service home page (Figure 9.1).

FIGURE 9.1
Accessing the Amazon
S3 management console

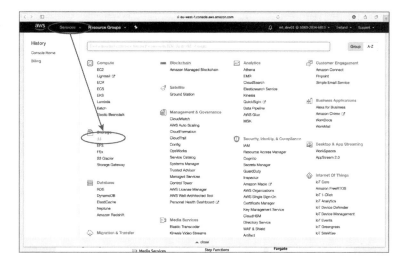

Creating a Bucket

To create a new Amazon S3 bucket, follow these steps.

1. Click the Create Bucket button. The Amazon S3 service is available in all regions, so you do not need to select a region in the management console. If you have never created an Amazon S3 bucket you will be presented with the S3 management console welcome page (see Figure 9.2).

   If you have existing buckets in your Amazon S3 account, you will be presented with a page that lists them (Figure 9.3).

2. A bucket, on the other hand, is region-specific, and you will need to provide a unique name for your bucket as well as select the region in which you want to create it (Figure 9.4). Click Next to proceed to the next screen once you have specified the bucket name and region.

   In this section, the name of the bucket being created is `com.asmtechnology.samplebucket` and is located in the EU (Ireland) region. The name you choose for your bucket must be globally unique, and prefixing a reverse domain name is a common practice to ensure unique naming.

FIGURE 9.2
Amazon S3 management
console welcome page

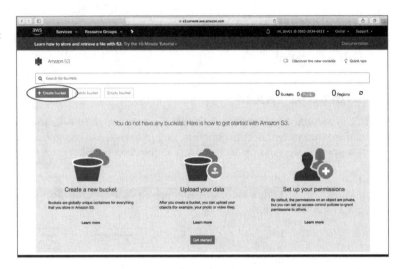

FIGURE 9.3
List of Amazon
S3 buckets

3. You are presented with a screen that will let you configure bucket versioning, logging, and cost allocation tags (Figure 9.5). You do not need to set up these options at this stage; click Next.

4. You are presented with a screen that will let you configure permissions for the new bucket (Figure 9.6). By default, a new bucket is not accessible publicly, and can only be accessed by the user who created it via the AWS CLI or the AWS management console.

Access to Amazon S3 resources are controlled using resource-based IAM policies. A resource-based IAM policy is a JSON document that describes which IAM users have access to a resource, and what they can do with the resource. Amazon S3 buckets and objects within the buckets have independent resource-based policies, and objects do not inherit permissions from a bucket.

FIGURE 9.4
Specifying the bucket
name and region

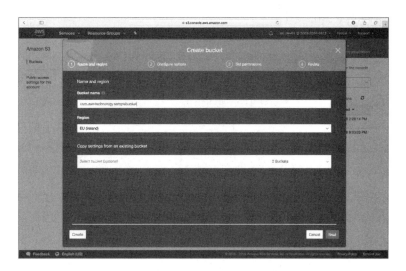

FIGURE 9.5
Configuring versioning,
logging, and cost
allocation tags

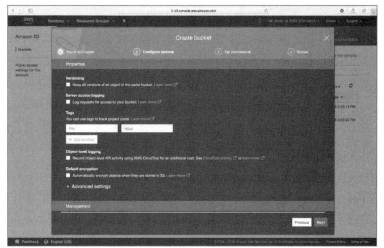

Each bucket also has an XML document associated with it, called an access control list (ACL). The ACL is used to control access to the bucket from other AWS accounts, and the general public.

It is highly recommended to leave the default options unchanged on this screen, and change them (if needed) at a later point in time. Click Next to proceed.

5. You are presented with a screen that summarizes the options and settings for the bucket that will be created (Figure 9.7). Click the Create Bucket button to create the bucket.

FIGURE 9.6
Configuring bucket permissions

FIGURE 9.7
Bucket summary page

6. The bucket will be created, and you will be taken to a page that lists all your Amazon S3 buckets. When you click the icon beside the name of a bucket from the list, a pop-up window will appear with shortcuts to options that allow you to configure bucket-specific settings (Figure 9.8).

If you have one or more buckets, this screen becomes the home screen presented to you whenever you visit the Amazon S3 console.

FIGURE 9.8
List of Amazon S3
buckets in your account

Uploading an Object

Complete these steps to upload an object to an existing bucket.

1. Click the name of the bucket in the list of buckets to access its contents (Figure 9.9).

FIGURE 9.9
Contents of an
Amazon S3 bucket

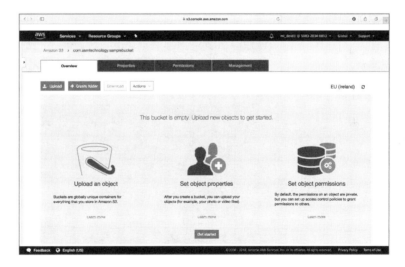

2. Click the Upload button to bring up the File Upload dialog box (Figure 9.10). Use the options in the File Upload dialog box to select one or more files from your computer; then click the Next button.

3. You are presented with a screen that will let you configure permissions for the new object (Figure 9.11). By default, a new object can only be accessed by the user who created it via the AWS CLI or the AWS management console. If you want the object to be accessible to

other AWS accounts, you can add the accounts to the ACL for the bucket. If you would like the object to be accessible to users on the Internet via a URL, ensure you change the value in the Manage Public Permissions drop-down menu from Do Not Grant Public Read Access To This Object(s) to Grant Public Read Access To This Object in the Manage Permissions drop-down menu.

FIGURE 9.10
Selecting files in the File Upload dialog box

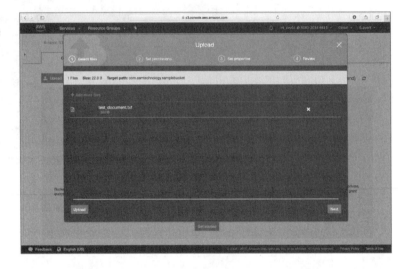

FIGURE 9.11
Configuring object permissions

4. You are presented with a screen that will let you select a storage class and an encryption setting, and specify any user-defined metadata for the new file (Figure 9.12). By default, a new file uses the Standard storage class and no encryption. User-defined metadata is a set of key-value pairs that can only be specified at the point when an object is created. Accept the default options and click Next.

FIGURE 9.12
Configuring file storage
class and encryption

5. You are presented with a screen that summarizes the options and settings for the file that will be uploaded (Figure 9.13). Click the Upload button to upload the file to the bucket.

FIGURE 9.13
File summary page

Once the file has finished uploading, it appears in your bucket (Figure 9.14).

Accessing an Object

To download an object from your Amazon S3 bucket onto your computer, follow these steps:

1. Navigate to the bucket using the Amazon S3 management console, select the icon beside the name of the bucket, and click the Download button in the pop-up dialog that appears on the screen (Figure 9.15).

FIGURE 9.14
Amazon S3 bucket
showing a file

FIGURE 9.15
Downloading a file
from a bucket

If you do not want to use the management console, you can also access any object in Amazon S3 using a URL.

2. To find the URL for an object in an Amazon S3 bucket, navigate to the bucket in the management console and select the object within the bucket. Copy the value of the Object URL field in the pop-up dialog (Figure 9.16).

The value within the Object URL field is a URL that follows this naming convention:

```
https://s3.<region name>.amazonaws.com/<bucket name> /<file name>
```

FIGURE 9.16
Locating the Amazon S3
Object URL

For example, a file called `sunset.jpg`, in a bucket called `com.asmtechnology.awsbook`
`.testbucket1`, in the eu-west-2 region can be accessed using the following URL:

`https://s3.eu-west-2.amazonaws.com/com.asmtechnology.awsbook.testbucket1/`
`sunset.jpg`

If both the bucket and the file you are accessing are not publicly accessible, you will
receive an access denied error when you try the URL in a web browser (Figure 9.17).

FIGURE 9.17
Non-public buckets and
files are not accessible
using a URL.

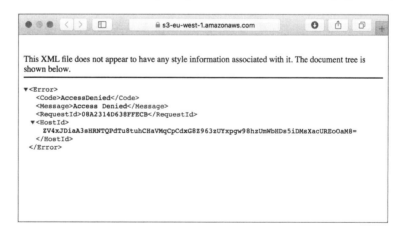

3. Before you can make the object publicly accessible, you will need to change the public
access settings for the bucket. Select the bucket and switch to the Permissions tab
(Figure 9.18).

FIGURE 9.18
Accessing Amazon S3
bucket permissions

4. Click the Edit button and uncheck all four options (Figure 9.19).

FIGURE 9.19
Configuring Amazon S3
bucket permissions

5. Click the Save button.

6. Switch to the Overview tab and select the object in the Amazon S3 bucket. Click the Make Public menu item under the Actions drop-down menu (Figure 9.20).

7. Click the Make Public button in the pop-up dialog that appears on the screen (Figure 9.21).

If you retry the URL in a web browser, you will be able to access the file. You can either set permissions at an individual object level, or you can set up permissions for the entire bucket.

FIGURE 9.20
Accessing the Make
Public option

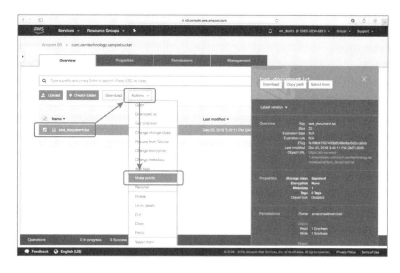

FIGURE 9.21
Making a file publicly
accessible

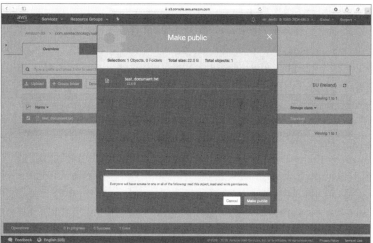

Changing the Storage Class of an Object

The default storage class of objects on Amazon S3 is Standard. To change the storage class of an object:

1. Navigate to the bucket using the Amazon S3 management console and select the object from the contents of the bucket.

2. Select the Change Storage Class menu item under the Actions drop-down menu (Figure 9.22).

3. Select an option for the storage class and click the Save button.

FIGURE 9.22
Changing the storage
class of an object

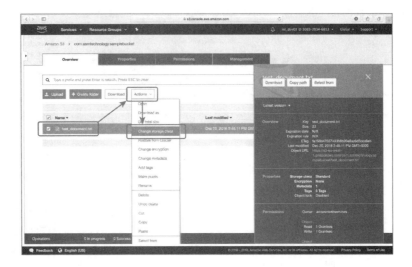

Deleting an Object

To delete an object from an Amazon S3 bucket:

1. Navigate to the bucket using the Amazon S3 management console and select the object from the contents of the bucket.

2. Select the Delete menu item under the Actions drop-down menu (Figure 9.23).

FIGURE 9.23
Deleting an object from
an Amazon S3 bucket

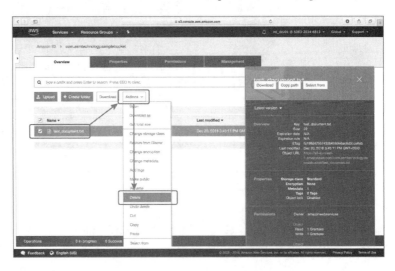

Once you delete an object, it is permanently removed from Amazon S3. The only exception to this rule occurs when versioning has been enabled on a bucket, in which case an object that has been deleted from a bucket can be restored.

Amazon S3 Bucket Versioning

Versioning is a bucket-level concept that, when enabled, stores all versions of an object. You can download an older version of an object, and you can even recover an object after it has been deleted. Once versioning is enabled on a bucket, you cannot remove it. You can, however, temporarily suspend versioning.

To enable versioning on a bucket:

1. Navigate to the bucket in the management console and click the Properties tab.

2. Expand the Versioning section, select the Enable Versioning option, and click the Save button (Figure 9.24).

FIGURE 9.24
Enabling bucket versioning

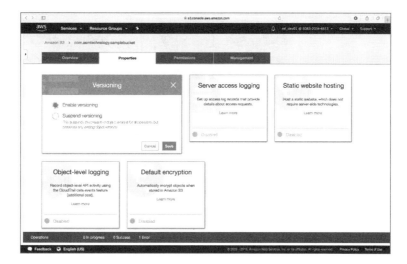

To understand how versioning works:

1. Create a new text document on your computer called welcome_letter.txt and in that document type the following line:

   ```
   Welcome to the world of Amazon Web Services.
   ```

2. Save the document on your computer and upload it to a bucket that has versioning enabled. To make the document accessible to the public you can select Grant Public Read Access To This Object(s) in the Manage Public Permissions drop-down (Figure 9.25). This will ensure you can access the document from a web browser.

3. Obtain the URL for the document and open the document in a web browser. Your web browser should render the contents of the text document.

4. Open the welcome_letter.txt file that you had previously saved on your computer, and edit its contents to resemble the following:

   ```
   Welcome to the world of Amazon Web Services.
   Amazon S3 versioning allows you to access older versions of documents.
   ```

FIGURE 9.25
Making an object
publicly accessible while
uploading it

5. Save the file and upload it again to the same bucket.

6. Once the document has finished uploading, click the row titled `welcome_letter.txt` to reveal a pop-up dialog with options. Expand the versions drop-down menu in the pop-up dialog to reveal links to the different versions of the document (Figure 9.26).

FIGURE 9.26
Accessing docu-
ment versions

The newest version of the document is always listed at the top. It is important to remember that you are charged for the combined space occupied by all versions of a document.

7. If you want to delete a version of the document that you do not need, click the trash can icon beside a document version in the versions drop-down menu. When you delete a version of a document (and not the entire document itself), the version you are deleting is permanently lost.

8. If instead you want to delete the document, select the document, and use the Delete menu item under the Actions menu.

When versioning is enabled on a bucket, you will see an additional selector that allows you to view all versions of the objects in your bucket (Figure 9.27).

FIGURE 9.27
Version selector switch

When the selector switch is set up to show versioned objects, you can see not only object versions, but also delete markers, which are special entries used to indicate that an object has been deleted. Restoring a deleted object is simply a matter of deleting the delete marker.

Accessing Amazon S3 Using the AWS CLI

You can use the AWS CLI to interact with Amazon S3 over the command line. Setup and configuration of the CLI client for Mac OS X and Windows is covered in Appendix C.

The general syntax of the aws command follows:

```
$ aws <service identifier > <service instructions>
```

The service identifier is a string that identifies an AWS service you want to interact with. The service identifier for Amazon S3 is s3 (in lowercase). Each service supports a different list of instructions. For a complete list of s3 instructions that are available within the CLI, visit http://docs.aws.amazon.com/cli/latest/userguide/using-s3-commands.html.

As an example, the ls instruction retrieves a list of all buckets in the user account that have been configured into the CLI. If you type the following instruction at the command prompt:

```
$ aws s3 ls
```

you receive a list of buckets:

```
Abhisheks-MacBook:~ abhishekmishra$ aws s3 ls
2017-01-15 16:52:59 com.asmtechnology.awsbook.testbucket1
Abhisheks-MacBook:~ abhishekmishra$
```

In addition to the high-level operations that can be performed using the s3 service identifier, Amazon also provides access to lower-level operations using the s3api service identifier. For more information on lower-level operations that can be performed on Amazon S3 buckets using the s3api service identifier, visit http://docs.aws.amazon.com/cli/latest/userguide/using-s3api-commands.html.

Summary

◆ Amazon S3 is a key-value, object-based storage service.

◆ Amazon S3 organizes objects into buckets; bucket names must be globally unique.

◆ Objects can be uploaded to Amazon S3 buckets using the AWS management console or the AWS CLI.

◆ You can control access to both buckets and the objects in buckets.

◆ Each object in Amazon S3 has a storage class associated with it. The storage class determines how Amazon S3 stores the data for the object and if you will be charged additional costs to read the data.

◆ Amazon S3 versioning allows you to save multiple versions of an object. You are charged for the combined space occupied by all versions of a document.

## Chapter 10

Amazon Cognito

- Introduction to the basic concepts of Amazon Cognito
- Learn to create a user pool
- Learn to create an identity pool
- Learn when to use user pools and identity pools

Amazon Cognito is Amazon's cloud-based, OAuth 2.0–compliant identity management solution. You can use Amazon Cognito to manage a database of users, allow external web and mobile applications to authenticate users against this database, and authorize access to external APIs and AWS resources.

Amazon Cognito consists of two different components:

- Amazon Cognito user pools
- Amazon Cognito identity pools

In this chapter you will learn about these components and how to use them together to provide secure access to your AWS resources.

Key Concepts

In this section, you learn some of the key concepts you will encounter when working with Amazon Cognito.

Authentication

Authentication refers to the concept of determining who a user is. This can be achieved in various ways, but the most common method is to ask a user for a username and password and compare the values provided by the user against a user database. The user database contains not just the username and password, but also other attributes such as a phone number and email address.

Authorization

Authorization refers to the concept of determining what systems an authenticated user can access, and what actions they can take on the system.

Identity Provider

An *identity provider* is a RESTful API service that is compliant with a well-known standard such as OAuth 2.0, OpenID Connect (OIDC), or SAML, and either includes a user database or is integrated with an external user database. Identity providers allow users to provide their credentials (such as username and password). The identity provider validates these credentials against a database, and issues a token that stands as proof of authentication.

Client

In the context of an authentication flow, a *client* is an external (third-party) application that your users want to use to access their information, which is held in your systems. The client application can also be your own application, in which case the authentication flow can be simplified.

OAuth 2.0

OAuth 2.0 is an authorization framework that allows external client applications to obtain limited access to a user's resources, on behalf of the user, without the user having to divulge their credentials to the client application. Here is the formal definition of OAuth 2.0 from the Internet Engineering Task Force in RFC 6749 (IETF: https://tools.ietf.org/html/rfc6749):

> *The OAuth 2.0 authorization framework enables a third-party application to obtain limited access to an HTTP service, either on behalf of a resource owner by orchestrating an approval interaction between the resource owner and the HTTP service, or by allowing the third-party application to obtain access on its own behalf.*

Depending on the capabilities of the client application, and the level of trust the user is willing to place in the client application, OAuth 2.0 defines four different types of flows (also known as grant types):

- Authorization Code Grant
- Implicit Grant
- Resource Owner Password Credentials Grant
- Client Credentials Grant

OpenID Connect

OpenID Connect is an authentication protocol, built on top of OAuth 2.0. OAuth 2.0 is a loosely defined authorization framework; it does not define details such as the technical format of the access token, or how the access token can be verified by the server. OIDC builds upon these shortcomings and adds the concept of a Jason Web Token (JWT)-based identity token on top of the access token. The attributes of the identity token are referred to as *claims* and are defined in RFC 7519.

Amazon Cognito User Pool

An Amazon Cognito user pool is a database of users and a set of services that allow creating user records into the database (sign up) and authenticating users against this database. Unlike IAM users, users in an Amazon Cognito user pool cannot log in to the AWS management console or access AWS services such as Amazon S3, AWS Lambda, and so on.

Each user in a user pool has a set of configurable attributes associated with a user record such as name, email address, and phone number, some of which are optional. Amazon Cognito user pools provide the necessary server-side APIs to create users in a user pool, provide security features such as multifactor authentication and email verification, and also allow you to invoke AWS Lambda functions at different points of the user registration and authentication process.

Amazon Cognito user pools are fully OAuth 2.0–compliant and support the Auth Code, Implicit, and Client Credentials flows. The result of authentication against an Amazon Cognito user pool is an access token and a signed JWT identity token. The access token can be used with any REST API that is designed to accept bearer access tokens, and the identity token can be used by a REST API to get additional information on the authenticated user (such as address, phone number, and so on). The additional user information available in the identity token is expressed as a set of JWT claims.

The identity token can also be used with an Amazon Cognito identity pool to obtain a temporary set of credentials that can be used to access AWS services such as S3 and DynamoDB. Amazon Cognito signs the identity token, and the signature of the token can be validated against a well-known certificate that Amazon publishes on the Internet.

Identity Pool

An *identity pool* is a collection of Amazon Cognito federated identity objects, which are associated with authenticated users. A federated identity object consists of a set of credentials that can be used to access services such as Amazon S3 and Amazon DynamoDB. A federated identity object is short-lived, and only issued to a requesting party that can provide a valid OIDC-compliant identity token or SAML token. Each federated identity object has an IAM policy document that controls what AWS resources can be accessed.

Amazon Cognito Federated Identities

Amazon Cognito Federated Identities is a service that provides the mechanism to exchange a valid OIDC-compliant identity token or SAML token for a federated identity object. If you are using Amazon Cognito user pools as your OAuth 2.0 identity provider, you can easily integrate the user pool with an identity pool to seamlessly exchange the JWT identity token you receive from the user pool for a federated identity object.

User pools and identity pools are used together to form a complete authentication and authorization solution to allow access to your AWS resources to non-IAM users using your web or mobile apps.

Besides Amazon Cognito user pools, identity pools can be used to provide temporary AWS credentials for users who have authenticated with the following additional mechanisms:

♦ Facebook login

♦ Google login

♦ Amazon login

♦ Other OIDC providers such as Auth0, Ping, etc.

♦ SAML providers

Common Tasks

In this section, you learn to use the Amazon Cognito management console to create S3 user pools and identity pools, and configure identity pools to issue federated identities for users who present a valid access token issued by an Amazon Cognito user pool. Log in to the IAM console using your dedicated IAM user-specific sign-in link and navigate to the Amazon Cognito service home page (Figure 10.1).

FIGURE 10.1
Accessing the S3 management console

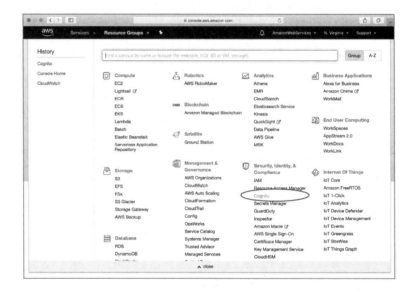

Creating a User Pool

To create a new Amazon Cognito user pool, follow these steps.

1. Click the Manage User Pools button on the Cognito splash screen to access a list of existing user pools (Figure 10.2).

2. To add a new user pool, click the Create A User Pool button on the top-right corner of the screen (Figure 10.3). User pools are specific to AWS regions. Make sure you have set up the AWS management console to use the correct region before creating the user pool.

3. Type a name for the new user pool and click the Step Through Settings button (Figure 10.4). The user pool name must be between 1 and 128 characters long and cannot be changed after the user pool is created. Pool names can contain uppercase and lowercase letters (a–z, A–Z), numbers (0–9), and the following special characters: + = , . @ and -.

4. The Attributes screen allows you to specify how you want users to sign in, and what information they need to provide during the sign-up process. You can configure a user pool to require users to set up a unique username to identify themselves, which is different from their email address, or allow users to use their email address/phone number as the username.

FIGURE 10.2
Amazon Cognito
splash screen

FIGURE 10.3
Creating a new user pool

FIGURE 10.4
Specifying the name of
the new user pool

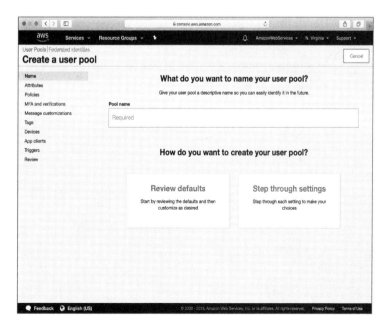

During the sign-up process, a profile is generated for the user. At the very least, the profile will consist of the username and the password, but it can also contain other attributes such as birthdate and address. Select the attributes that you require from users when they sign up for your app (Figure 10.5).

FIGURE 10.5
User pool attributes

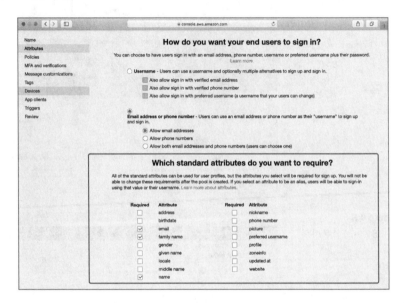

Attributes can be thought of as fields in a table that contain information on registered users. Every user can have one or more of the following standard attributes:

◆   address

◆   birthdate

◆   email_address

◆   family_name

◆   gender

◆   given_name

◆   locale

◆   middle_name

◆   name

◆   nickname

◆   phone_number

◆   picture

◆   preferred_username

- profile
- timezone
- updated_at
- website

Most of these attributes are optional. Place checkmarks next to attributes that you want to make mandatory. Attributes cannot be switched between required and nonrequired once you create the user pool. When a user is authenticated against a user pool, the JWT identity token that is returned by Amazon Cognito can contain these attributes as claims.

In case you are wondering, the attribute names available to choose from while creating a username are standard attribute names, as described in the OpenID Connect specification available at `http://openid.net/specs/openid-connect-core-1_0.html#StandardClaims`.

If you need additional attributes beyond those available in the standard list, you can create custom attributes on the same screen (Figure 10.6).

FIGURE 10.6
Adding a custom attribute to a user pool

Click the Next Step button when you are ready to proceed.

5. The Policies screen allows you to set a password security policy, set up whether users can sign up without the help of an administrator, and indicate the number of days until an unused administrator-created account expires.

   Using the options on the screen, select the security requirements that you want passwords to adhere to (Figure 10.7).

FIGURE 10.7
Setting up user
pool policies

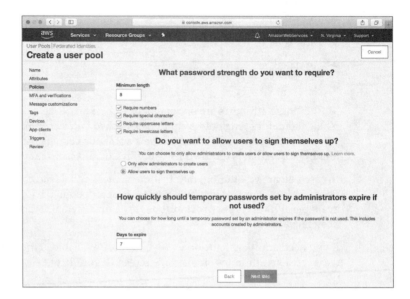

Ensure the Allow Users To Sign Themselves Up option is selected. If it is not, users cannot sign up using your app; you have to manually create accounts for them in the user pool using the Amazon Cognito management console. You can also specify the number of days that must elapse before any unused user accounts that were created through the management console expire. The default value is 7 days.

Click the Next Step button to proceed.

6. The MFA and Verifications screen allows you to enable multi-factor authentication and email/phone number verification for user accounts (Figure 10.8).

FIGURE 10.8
Multifactor authentica-
tion settings for
the user pool

When enabled, MFA adds an additional security step when someone attempts to log in to your mobile app. In this additional step, the individual is asked to provide a temporary and unique six-digit numeric code that an authentication device generates.

You can also select whether users need to verify their email address or phone number as part of the sign-up process. If you disable both email address and phone number verification, users are unable to reset forgotten passwords.

If you decide to enable phone number verification, Cognito needs to use Amazon SNS to send SMS messages to a user's devices. For Cognito to be able to access Amazon SNS, you are prompted to create a new IAM role that can be assumed by Cognito when communicating with Amazon SNS.

7. The Message Customizations screen allows you to customize the text of the email and SMS verification message (Figure 10.9).

FIGURE 10.9
Customizing email and SMS verification messages

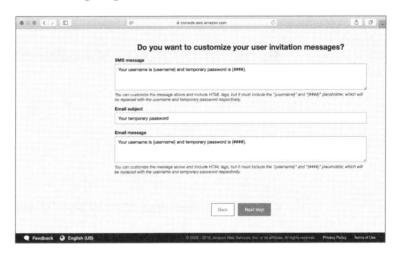

You do not need to change the default messages. However, if you do choose to do so, ensure that your messages contain the {####} placeholder string. Cognito replaces the placeholder string with a four-digit verification code that the user must enter into your app as part of the sign-up process.

Click the Next Step button to proceed.

8. The Tags screen allows you to add cost allocation tags that can be used to track your AWS costs (Figure 10.10).

If you add cost allocation tags to a user pool, your AWS cost allocation report includes costs and usage aggregated using these tags. If you would like to learn more about using cost allocation tags with your AWS resources, visit `http://docs.aws.amazon.com/awsaccountbilling/latest/aboutv2/cost-alloc-tags.html`.

Click the Next Step button to proceed.

9. The Devices screen gives you options to decide if you would like the user pool to remember the devices used by your users to log in to your app (Figure 10.11).

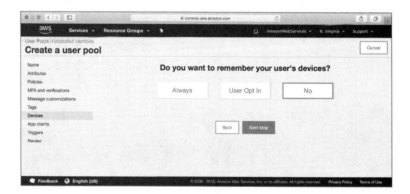

You can choose between three options:

◆ *No:* This is the default option. Devices are not remembered.

◆ *Always:* Every device used by users of your app is remembered.

◆ *User Opt In:* Your users are given an option to remember the device that they are using. You must create the user interface in your app to allow the user to opt in.

If you choose to have Cognito remember a user's devices, a device identifier (key and secret) is assigned to each device the first time a user signs in with that device. This key is not used for anything other than identifying the device, but Cognito tracks it. You also have the option of suppressing MFA challenges for devices that Cognito tracks.

Click the Next Step button to proceed.

10. The App Clients screen allows you to configure external applications that can connect to the user pool to authenticate users (Figure 10.12). Each application defined in this screen is issued a client ID, and sometimes a client secret. You will need to provide these values to the app developer. The client secret should not be shared publicly, and the external application must have a secure mechanism to store this client secret.

FIGURE 10.12
Configuring applications that can use the user pool to authenticate users

In the case of mobile and web applications that have access to a trusted server, a common practice is to have the application retrieve the client secret from its own trusted server before connecting to Amazon Cognito to authenticate the user. If the application is not capable of storing the client secret securely (such as a JavaScript application), you need to ensure that you do not generate a client secret while configuring the app entry in the user pool.

You can add apps to the user pool after it has been created, in which case you can skip to the next step. If you would like to add an application at this stage, click the Add An App Client link on the page, and remember to uncheck the Generate Client Secret option if the app is unable to secure the client secret (Figure 10.13).

FIGURE 10.13
Create Application screen

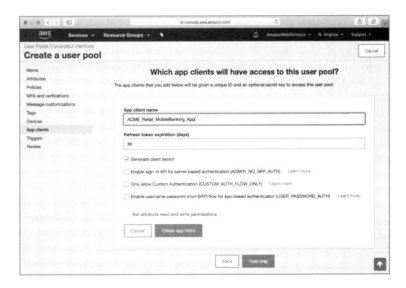

While creating the application, you can also choose which of the user pool attributes will be present as claims in the JWT identity token that is generated after the user successfully authenticates. Click the Create App Client button under the fields to finish creating the app. Your new app is listed (Figure 10.14), and you have the option to create additional apps within the user pool.

FIGURE 10.14
List of client applications in the user pool

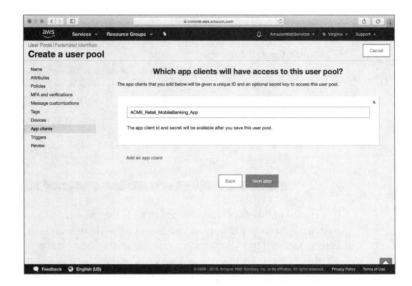

If you are creating the app client entry during the process of creating the user pool, the client ID and client secret will not be available to view until after the pool has been created.

Click the Triggers menu on the left-side menu to proceed to the next step.

11. The Triggers screen lets you associate AWS Lambda functions with specific user pool triggers (Figure 10.15).

FIGURE 10.15
Use triggers to call AWS Lambda functions at specific points in the user authentication process.

As of when this book was written, the following triggers are available:

◆ *Pre Sign-Up:* Invoked when users submit all their details to create a new account in the user pool. Your AWS Lambda function can validate the information submitted by the user and accept or decline the sign-up request.

◆ *Pre Authentication:* Invoked when users submit their details to authenticate against the user pool. Your AWS Lambda function can validate the information submitted by the user and accept or decline the authentication request.

◆ *Post Authentication:* Invoked after a user is authenticated. Your AWS Lambda function can be used to generate appropriate analytic messages or send an email message to the user's account.

◆ *Custom Message:* Invoked before an email/SMS verification message is sent and before an MFA message is sent. Your AWS Lambda function can customize the content of the message that is sent.

◆ *Post Confirmation:* Invoked after the user has successfully completed email/SMS verification. Your AWS Lambda function can be used to generate appropriate analytic messages or send an email message to the user's account.

◆ *Define Auth Challenge:* Invoked at the start of a custom authentication flow. Your AWS Lambda function can define the authentication challenge that the user will need to satisfy as part of the custom authentication flow.

◆ *Create Auth Challenge:* Invoked after a custom authentication flow has begun. Your AWS Lambda function is called to create the challenge that was defined in the AWS Lambda function executed for the Define Auth Challenge trigger.

◆ *Verify Auth Challenge Response*: Invoked to verify the validity of the user's response to a custom authentication challenge.

◆ *Pre Token Generation:* Invoked before the JWT identity token is generated. Your AWS Lambda function can customize the claims in the JWT token.

◆ *User Migration:* Invoked when users are migrated from an existing directory service to your user pool.

12. The Review screen allows you to review the options you have specified so far (Figure 10.16).

When you have finished reviewing the settings for the user pool, click the Create Pool button to create the user pool.

Retrieving the App Client Secret

While configuring the list of client apps that have access to unauthenticated APIs in the user pool, you have the option of generating a client ID and a client secret for each app. The client secret is only available after the user pool has been created.

FIGURE 10.16
User pool Review screen

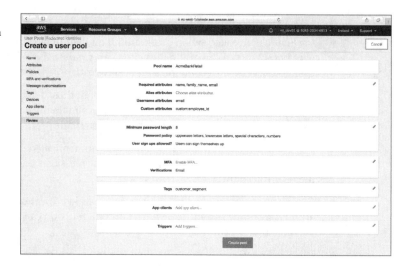

FIGURE 10.17
Click the Show Details
button to reveal the
app client ID and the
app client secret.

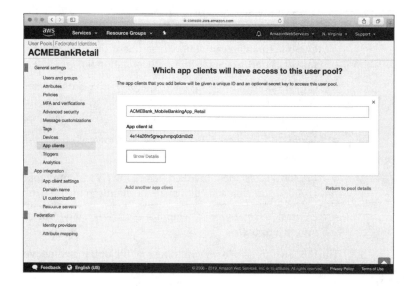

Once you have finished creating the user pool, your new user pool is listed alongside any existing user pools in the Cognito user pool management console.

Click your user pool and navigate to the App Clients section of the user pool to view a list of app clients. Click the Show Details button to view the client ID and client secret (Figure 10.17).

It is your responsibility to safely distribute and store the client secret within your application.

Creating an Identity Pool

An identity pool is a database of federated identities that can be used to obtain a set of temporary credentials to access other AWS services such as S3 and DynamoDB. These federated identities are unique within an identity pool and are linked to identities from identity providers such as Amazon Cognito user pools, Facebook, Google, and Amazon.com.

Identity pools are specific to AWS regions. Make sure you have set up the AWS management console to use the correct region before creating the identity pool. To create a new Amazon Cognito identity pool, follow these steps:

1. Click the Manage Identity Pools button on the Cognito splash screen (Figure 10.18).

FIGURE 10.18
Amazon Cognito
splash screen

2. If you do not have any identity pools in the AWS region, you will be taken to the first step of the Create Identity Pool wizard (Figure 10.19).

FIGURE 10.19
Creating a new
identity pool

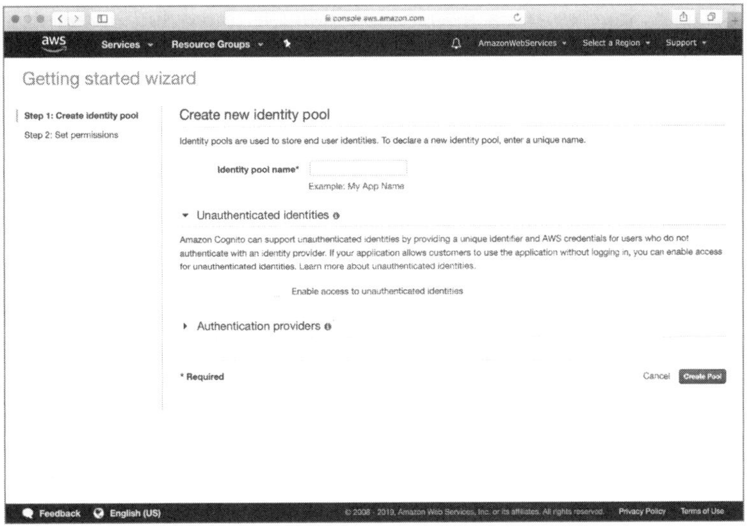

If you have one or more existing identity pools in the AWS region, you will be taken to a screen that lists the identity pools. Locate the Create New Identity Pool button in the top-left corner of the screen (Figure 10.20).

FIGURE 10.20
List of existing
identity pools

3. Specify a name for your identity pool. It is a good idea to uncheck the Enable Access To Unauthenticated Identities check box. Enabling this check box will generate a set of AWS credentials for users who have not authenticated with an identity provider.

   One scenario where you may want to enable access through unauthenticated identities is if the external application is your own, and your app is built in such a way that users do not have to authenticate on the first screen of the app. In such a case, your app may need to access some of your AWS resources to provide the functionality that is not dependent on knowing who is using the app. For example, a recent announcements screen in your app could be powered by an Amazon DynamoDB table in your AWS account. For your app to read items from this Amazon DynamoDB table, it would have to use the set of unauthenticated credentials.

4. Expand the Authentication Provider's section of the page and configure the identity providers whose identity tokens you wish to accept. If you are using Amazon Cognito user pools as your identity provider, enter the user pool ID and the app client ID (Figure 10.21).

   If you have multiple app clients defined in your user pool, you will need to create multiple identity pools, as an identity pool can only be linked to a single app client in your user pool.

   Click the Create Pool button at the bottom of the page to proceed.

5. The next screen lets you create new roles for authenticated and unauthenticated identities (Figure 10.22). You also have the option to select an existing role.

FIGURE 10.21
Specifying the Amazon
Cognito user pool ID and
app client ID

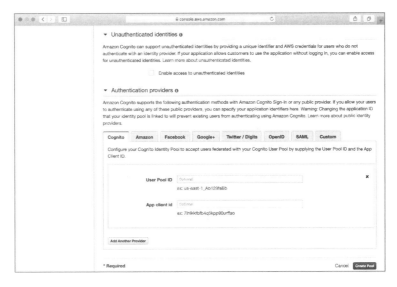

FIGURE 10.22
Cognito, by default,
creates new roles for
authenticated and
unauthenticated
identities.

The authenticated role decides what services from your account can be accessed by an external application provided the user of the app has successfully authenticated with an identity provider. The unauthenticated role controls what services can be accessed by an external app without an authenticated user. The app will need to provide a set of credentials to prove it is a trusted application, even though the user who is using the app is unauthenticated.

You can update the policies using the IAM management console to exercise fine-grained control over your AWS resources.

6. Click the Allow button at the bottom of the screen to finish creating the new identity pool.

User Pools or Identity Pools: Which One Should You Use?

If you are new to Amazon Cognito, and API authentication in general, it can be difficult to understand the differences between user pools and identity pools and when to use what.

Underneath the hood, AWS is a set of REST web services; however, not all of these web services accept OIDC access and identity tokens. In fact, the only web service that directly supports OIDC tokens is Amazon API Gateway. What this means is that you cannot access your Amazon S3 resources using OIDC tokens unless you expose the Amazon S3 resources to the outside world via an Amazon API Gateway.

The native AWS REST APIs that power services like Amazon S3, Amazon Dynamo DB, and AWS Lambda all work using a set of credentials consisting of an access key ID and a secret access key. When you create IAM users, you have the option of generating these keys (Figure 10.23).

FIGURE 10.23

Accessing the credentials needed to access AWS services

When you configure the AWS CLI, you are asked to provide these credentials as part of the configuration process:

```
Microsoft Windows [Version 10.0.16299.785]
(c) 2017 Microsoft Corporation. All rights reserved.

C:\Users\mishr>aws configure
AWS Access Key ID [None]: AKIAIR...VCOFA
AWS Secret Access Key [None]: dpk52etGa....U9H0f5ouPcqG
Default region name [None]:
Default output format [None]:
```

IAM allows you to issue access key IDs and secret access keys on a per-IAM user basis. You create IAM users manually using the IAM management console, and share the access key ID and secret access key with the user securely, asking the user to keep them safe. The access key ID and secret access key are bearer credentials—there is no way for the AWS CLI to know that the person typing those values is not the user for whom they were created—which is why you ask your IAM users to keep these values safe and never include them in your apps.

An Amazon Cognito identity pool issues temporary access key IDs and secret access keys and, therefore, identity pools should be used only when you want to access your AWS resources, without using an API gateway. But the question is, who should the identity pool issue these keys to? This is where linking the identity pool to an identity provider comes in. Once an identity pool is linked to an identity provider, temporary AWS credentials will only be issued to those requests that present a signed identity token issued by the identity provider.

An Amazon Cognito user pool is an identity provider much like Auth0 or Ping. It allows users to authenticate themselves and receive an access token and an identity token. These tokens can be used with any REST API that can accept OIDC tokens. Therefore, if you need to access some existing, non-AWS, REST APIs that can accept OIDC tokens, then you should only use Amazon Cognito user pools.

Summary

- ◆ Amazon Cognito is Amazon's cloud-based, OAuth 2.0-compliant identity management solution.

- ◆ An Amazon Cognito user pool is a database of users and a set of services that allow creating user records into the database (sign-up) and authenticating users against this database.

- ◆ Amazon Cognito user pools are fully OAuth 2.0–compliant and support the Auth Code, Implicit, and Client Credentials flows.

- ◆ An identity pool is a collection of Amazon Cognito federated identity objects, which are associated with authenticated users.

- ◆ A federated identity object consists of a set of credentials that can be used to access AWS services such as Amazon S3 and Amazon DynamoDB.

- ◆ User pools and identity pools are used together to form a complete authentication and authorization solution to allow access to your AWS resources to non-IAM users using your web or mobile apps.

Chapter 11

Amazon DynamoDB

- ◆ Introduction to DynamoDB—Amazon's NoSQL database

- ◆ Create a DynamoDB table

- ◆ Use the Amazon Comprehend management console to analyze text

- ◆ Adding items to a DynamoDB table

- ◆ Performing scans and queries on a DynamoDB table

NOTE   Amazon occasionally updates the user interface of the Amazon DynamoDB management console. As a result, some of the screenshots in this chapter may not match what you see in your web browser. However, the general concepts that you will learn in this chapter will still be applicable.

DynamoDB is Amazon's cloud-based, highly scalable, redundant NoSQL database service. Amazon removes the hassle involved in building and maintaining a redundant scalable database service by taking care of administrative tasks such as hardware procurement, setup, replication, and scaling for you.

Using Amazon DynamoDB, you can create database tables in the AWS cloud and read/write to these tables using a web-based management console or the AWS CLI, or directly from your projects using one of the AWS SDKs. Amazon DynamoDB stores your data on fast SSD storage and spreads the data in your tables across a number of servers to allow for fast and consistent access times. All the data in your tables is also automatically replicated across all the availability zones (AZs) in your chosen region.

In addition to a cloud-based DynamoDB service, Amazon provides a downloadable version of DynamoDB that you can run locally on your computer. For more information on the download-able version of DynamoDB, visit https://docs.aws.amazon.com/amazondynamodb/latest/developerguide/DynamoDBLocal.html.

Key Concepts

In this section you will learn some of the key concepts you will encounter while working with Amazon DynamoDB.

Tables

DynamoDB stores your data in tables, which are just collections of data. The concept of a table is present in virtually every database management system.

Unlike traditional relational database management systems (RDBMSs), DynamoDB does not require tables to have a predefined schema or any kind of predefined relationships between tables. Behind the scenes, data in a DynamoDB table is stored in JSON files.

DynamoDB tables are AWS region–specific, and are automatically replicated across all AZs within the region.

Global Tables

A global table is a collection of one or more identical replica tables spread across different AWS regions. Each replica table stores the same set of items. Global tables allow changes to be propagated across the underlying region-specific replica tables automatically.

Items

A DynamoDB table is a collection of objects called items. An item is a group of attributes and can be thought of as rows within a table. For example, each item within a table called BankAccounts would correspond to a bank account. There is no limit to the number of items that can exist within a table.

Attributes

An attribute is a fundamental unit of data within an item and is not broken down further. You can think of attributes as columns within a table. For example, attributes in a table called BankAccounts could be AccountNumber, AccountType, and CurrentBalance.

There is no restriction on the number of attributes that an item can contain. items within the same table can contain different attributes. This is quite different from tables in relational databases where the schema for the table is predefined and each row within the table contains the same number of columns.

An attribute can be one of the following data types:

◆ *Scalar types:* Number, String, Binary, Boolean

◆ *Document types:* List (Array), Map (Dictionary)

◆ *Set types:* String Set, Number Set, Binary Set

For more information on attribute data types, visit http://docs.aws.amazon.com/amazondynamodb/latest/developerguide/HowItWorks.NamingRulesDataTypes.html.

Primary Keys

Every table in DynamoDB has a primary key that identifies items within. The primary key is an attribute defined when the table is created and every item (row) must have a unique value for the primary key. The primary key attribute must be a scalar of type Number, String, or Binary. There are two types of primary keys in a DynamoDB table:

◆ *Partition key:* This is a simple primary key; it is a single attribute that must be unique across all items in the table. DynamoDB uses the value of this key to work out the partition (physical storage volume) on which to store the item.

◆ *Partition key and sort key:* This is a composite primary key composed of two attributes. The first attribute of the composite key is a partition key used by DynamoDB to determine the physical storage volume on which the item will be stored. The second part of the composite key is the sort key, which sorts values that are stored together on the same storage volume. Items in a table with a composite primary key can have the same value for the partition key, which means those items are stored together. However, the combination of partition key and sort key must be unique for each item in the table.

The partition key is also known as the hash key as its value is used as an input to a hash function to determine the storage volume where the item will be stored. The sort key is also known as the range key.

Secondary Indexes

When you create a table in DynamoDB, you are asked to provide a primary key (simple or composite). DynamoDB allows you to read data from the table by providing the values of the primary key attributes.

If, however, you want to read the data using other non-key attributes, you need to create a secondary index on the table. A secondary index is created using a combination of two attributes, the first attribute is known as the partition key and the second is known as the sort key.

There are two types of secondary indexes:

◆ *Global secondary index:* The partition key and sort key portions of the index can be any two attributes in the table, different from the attributes that make up the primary key.

◆ *Local secondary index:* The partition key of the index is the same as the partition key of the table; the sort key portion of the index can be any other attribute in the table.

Once you have created a secondary index on the table, you can use the index in queries and scans.

Queries

A query is an operation that searches for data in a DynamoDB table based on the value of the primary key attribute. You must provide the value of the partition key and the sort key (if using a composite primary key) and a comparison operator. The query returns a set with all the items in the table that match the query. By default, the query includes the value of all the attributes for each item in the set. You can provide an additional expression called a projection expression into a query to return fewer attributes for an item.

The projection expression is applied to filter the results of the query before presenting the results to you. Amazon charges you for the amount of data you read from DynamoDB and in the case of queries, the charges are calculated before the projection expression is applied. You can only build queries on the value of attributes that are part of the primary key or one of the secondary indexes on the table.

Scans

A scan is an operation that returns all the items in the table. Unlike a query, a scan does not retrieve specific items based on the value of a key or index; it provides all the data in the table.

You can provide an additional expression called a projection expression into a scan to return fewer attributes for an item. The projection expression is applied to filter the results of the scan before presenting the results to you.

Amazon charges you for the amount of data you read from DynamoDB, and since a scan will read the entire table you will be charged for all the data in the table—even if you filter the results to return a single item. In case of large tables this can quickly become an expensive proposition. Whenever possible, opt for a query instead of a scan.

Read Consistency

DynamoDB tables are scoped at the region level. It is possible to have two tables with the same name in different regions, and these tables will have no relationship with each other. When you create a table, it is created in the region you have selected in the management console.

Within a region, AWS stores redundant copies of the data in your DynamoDB tables across multiple AZs. When you write data to a DynamoDB table, AWS updates all copies of the data. However, it can take a small amount of time before all copies of your data have been updated.

When you read data from a DynamoDB table, you can choose from one of two different consistency models:

◆ *Eventually consistent reads:* The response may not reflect the results of the most recent write operation and may contain stale data. It takes about a second for AWS to update all copies of the table across multiple AZs within a region; however, the delay can be significant if you are using global tables.

◆ *Strongly consistent reads:* The response contains the data from all prior writes that were successful. The response is likely to take more time because DynamoDB has to wait for all prior update operations to conclude.

The default read consistency model for DynamoDB is eventual consistency, which can be interpreted to mean, "read operations will eventually be consistent." DynamoDB queries and scans have an additional optional parameter that allows you to specify the read consistency model that you want to use.

Read/Write Capacity Modes

Amazon charges you for reading and writing data to DynamoDB and provides two options that allow you to control how these charges will be calculated:

◆ *On Demand Mode:* This is a flexible pay-per-request model for read and write requests and you only pay for what you use. This is a good option if your application has unpredictable usage patterns. The amount you are billed will depend on the number of read and write request units you have consumed.

One read request unit represents one strongly consistent read request, or two eventually consistent read requests for an item up to 4 KB in size. If the item being read is larger than 4 KB, additional read request units are required. For example, each time your application reads a 5 KB item with strongly consistent reads, it will consume two read request units.

One write request unit represents one write operation for an item 1 KB in size. If the item being written is larger than 1 KB, additional write request units will be consumed.

◆ *Provisioned Mode:* This mode allows you to specify, in advance, the I/O capacity for your table. If your application exceeds these limits, requests will be subject to throttling and will fail with an HTTP 400 error. DynamoDB allows you to set up an auto scaling rule when using provisioned mode. Auto scaling when used with a DynamoDB table will provide a margin by which the provisioned I/O capacity for a table can grow before throttling occurs. Provisioned throughput is specified in terms of read and write capacity units.

One read capacity unit represents one strongly consistent read per second, or two eventually consistent reads per second for items up to 4 KB in size. If the item being read is larger than 4 KB, additional read capacity units are required. For example, if your application requires reading 100 items per second, with each item being 2 KB in size, and you want strongly consistent reads, you need to provision 100 read capacity units. Even though each item is 2 KB in size, Amazon rounds up the item size to the nearest 4 KB boundary when calculating throughput capacity for reads. This means that if your items were 5 KB in size, you would need to provision twice the number of read capacity units (200 read capacity units).

One write capacity unit represents one write per second for items up to 1 KB in size. For example, if your application requires writing 100 items per second, with each item being 2 KB in size, you need to provision 200 write capacity units.

You are billed for the I/O units that you have reserved (or consumed) as well as an additional flat fee for data storage costs. For more information on the costs involved with DynamoDB, visit `https://aws.amazon.com/dynamodb/pricing/`.

When creating a table, you are asked to specify the read and write capacity mode. Once the table has been created, you can switch between read and write modes once every 24 hours.

Common Tasks

In this section you learn to use the AWS management console to create DynamoDB tables and manage the data in these buckets.

Log in to the AWS management console using the dedicated sign-in link for your development IAM user account. Use the region selector to select a region where the Amazon DynamoDB service is available. Click the Services menu and access the Amazon DynamoDB service home page (Figure 11.1).

DynamoDB tables are scoped at the region level, so make sure you have set up the management console to use the appropriate region. The screenshots in this section assume that the console is connected to the EU (Ireland) region.

Creating a Table

If you have never used DynamoDB, you are presented with the splash screen (Figure 11.2).

If you have used DynamoDB in the past, you arrive at the DynamoDB dashboard (Figure 11.3). Follow the steps outlined below to create a table.

1. Regardless of which screen you arrive at, click the Create Table button to get started with creating a DynamoDB table. On the Create DynamoDB Table screen (Figure 11.4), provide a table name between 3 and 255 characters in length. Unlike S3 buckets, DynamoDB table names are not globally unique; they only need to be unique for your account, within the selected region.

FIGURE 11.1
Accessing the Amazon
DynamoDB service
home page

FIGURE 11.2
Amazon DynamoDB
splash screen

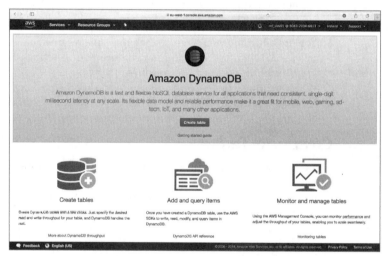

2. If you would like to follow along with the exercises in this chapter, call the table **customer**. Specify the name of the primary key attribute to be **customerID**. By default, the Create Table screen is configured to create a simple primary key. If you want to use a composite (partition + sort) key, check the Add Sort Key check box (Figure 11.5).

3. The default Create Table screen is also configured to not create secondary indexes, to reserve a provisioned throughput capacity of 5 read units and 5 write units, and to enable capacity auto scaling. Not having a secondary index at this point is not a problem because we don't have data in the table. However, as you are billed for provisioned throughput capacity you reserve, you should start with the smallest number of read and write units and increase these if needed in the future.

FIGURE 11.3
Amazon
DynamoDB dashboard

FIGURE 11.4
Specifying a table name

FIGURE 11.5
Specifying a composite
key for a table

4. Uncheck the Use Default Settings check box and scroll down to the bottom of the page to locate the Provisioned Capacity section. Disable auto scaling and change the number of read and write units to 1 each (Figure 11.6).

FIGURE 11.6
Changing the provisioned I/O capacity

5. Click the Create button to create the table. The table takes a few minutes to form. Once it is created, your screen should resemble Figure 11.7.

FIGURE 11.7
Amazon DynamoDB table overview

Adding Items to a Table

This section assumes you have created the customer table as described in the previous section.

1. In the DynamoDB dashboard, select the `customer` table, switch to the Items tab, and click the Create Item button (Figure 11.8).

FIGURE 11.8
Creating a new item in
the customer table

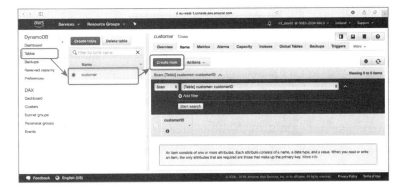

You are presented with a dialog box that lets you add attributes for the new item. The only attribute that is available by default is the primary key attribute of the table (Figure 11.9).

FIGURE 11.9
Item attributes dialog
showing default primary
key attribute

You can add attributes by clicking the Add (+) button beside an existing attribute and selecting Append or Insert from the context menu. Append adds a new attribute after the selected attribute, whereas Insert adds the new attribute before the selected attribute (Figure 11.10).

FIGURE 11.10
Adding item attributes

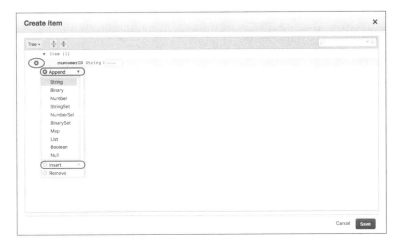

2. Set the value of `customerID` to **1** and use the Add (+) button to create the following string attributes with the specified values (Figure 11.11):

◆ `firstName`: John

◆ `lastName`: Woods

◆ `address`: 17 Hollow Road, Bromley

◆ `postcode`: BR34 980

◆ `country`: United Kingdom

FIGURE 11.11
Specifying multiple attributes

3. If you prefer to work directly with the JSON representation of the new item, select the Text option in the view mode drop-down combo box (Figure 11.12).

FIGURE 11.12
Viewing item attributes as JSON

4. Click the Save button to add the new item to the table. You should see the new item listed in the table (Figure 11.13).

FIGURE 11.13
Amazon DynamoDB table with one item

5. Add another item to the table with the following attributes:

customerID: 2

firstName: Sonam

lastName: Mishra

isHomeOwner: True

As you can see in Figure 11.14, items in a table can have different attributes. This is unlike a table in a traditional RDBMS system in which each row has to have the same columns.

FIGURE 11.14
Each item in an Amazon DynamoDB table can have different attributes.

Creating an Index

This section assumes you have created the customer table as described in the "Creating a Table" section.

1. In the DynamoDB dashboard, select the customer table, switch to the Indexes tab, and click the Create Index button (Figure 11.15).

FIGURE 11.15
Creating an index

You are presented with a dialog box that lets you set up the properties of the new index (Figure 11.16).

2. Use the following properties to create the index:

Primary Key: firstName

Sort Key: lastName

Index Name: Use default settings

Projected Attributes: All

Read Capacity Units: 1

Write Capacity Units: 1

FIGURE 11.16
Index properties dialog

3. Click the Create Index button to finish creating the index. Your index may take a few minutes to create. Once the index is created, you see it listed under the Indexes tab (Figure 11.17).

FIGURE 11.17
Amazon DynamoDB
table index list

Once you have created this index, every new item you add to the table has three mandatory fields: customerID, firstName, and lastName (Figure 11.18).

FIGURE 11.18
Mandatory fields
for new items

Even though you have created an index on firstName and lastName, you can still create a new item with the same values as the firstName and lastName attributes of an existing item. However, the value of the customerID attribute must be unique because it is the primary key attribute.

4. Add another item to the table with the following attributes:

customerID:3

firstName: Sonam

lastName: Mishra

The list of items in your table should resemble Figure 11.19. You should see two items having the same values for the firstName and lastName attributes.

FIGURE 11.19
Multiple items in an
Amazon
DynamoDB table

Performing a Scan

This section assumes you have created the customer table as described in the "Creating a Table" section.

1. In the DynamoDB dashboard, select the customer table, and switch to the Items tab. The default view that you see with all the items in the table listed is the result of a scan on the primary key customerID. You can verify this by looking at the dark gray area on top of the first item of the table (Figure 11.20).

FIGURE 11.20
List of items returned as
a result of a
scan operation

2. You can use the Add Filter button to add a filter expression that trims the results in the set. Figure 11.21 shows the results of the scan after a filter expression has been applied on the firstName attribute.

FIGURE 11.21
Adding a filter expres-
sion to a scan

3. If you have an index defined on the table, you can select it from the drop-down combo box (see Figure 11.22) and click the Start Search button to perform a scan based on the index.

FIGURE 11.22
Indexes can be used
while performing a scan.

The difference between a scan on an index and a scan on the primary key is that the latter returns every item in the table (because all items, by definition, have a value for the primary key attribute). An index, on the other hand, is defined on a selection of attributes, and a scan on an index only returns the items in the table that have values for the attributes defined in the index.

It is important to keep in mind that a scan returns all the elements in a table based on a primary key or index and then applies optional filter expressions to trim down the result set. On a large table, a single scan operation could easily consume all the provisioned read capacity, even though the filter expression may trim the result set to a single row.

Performing a Query

This section assumes you have created the `customer` table as described in the "Creating a Table" section.

In the DynamoDB dashboard, select the `customer` table and switch to the Items tab. Switch from Scan mode to Query mode using the drop-down combo box (Figure 11.23).

FIGURE 11.23

Switching from Scan mode to Query mode

A query is similar to a scan in many respects, with one important difference: unlike a scan, a query only returns those items that match the criteria specified by query. Figure 11.24 depicts the results of a query that matches an item with customerId = 1.

FIGURE 11.24

Querying a DynamoDB table based on the partition key

You can choose to perform a query on the primary key or an index defined on the table. You can use filter expressions to trim the result set returned by a query.

Summary

♦ DynamoDB is Amazon's cloud-based, highly scalable, redundant NoSQL database service.

♦ DynamoDB stores your data on fast SSD storage and spreads the data in your tables across a number of servers to allow for fast and consistent access times.

♦ All the data in your tables is also automatically replicated across all the availability zones (AZs) in your chosen region.

♦ A global table is a collection of one or more identical replica tables spread across different AWS regions. Each replica table stores the same set of items. Global tables allow changes to be propagated across the underlying region-specific replica tables automatically.

♦ In addition to a cloud-based DynamoDB service, Amazon provides a downloadable version of DynamoDB that you can run locally on your computer.

♦ DynamoDB does not require tables to have a predefined schema or any kind of predefined relationships between tables.

♦ Behind the scenes, data in a DynamoDB table is stored in JSON files.

♦ A partition key is used to work out the partition (physical storage volume) on which to store the item.

♦ A composite primary key consists of both a partition key as well as a sort key. The sort key is used to sort values that are stored on the same storage volume.

♦ A secondary key can be thought of as an additional composite primary key.

♦ A query is an operation that searches for data in a DynamoDB table based on the value of the primary key attribute.

♦ A scan is an operation that returns all the items in the table. Unlike a query, a scan does not retrieve specific items based on the value of a key or index; it provides all the data in the table.

♦ DynamoDB streams allow tables to generate events when the table is modified.

Chapter 12

AWS Lambda

WHAT'S IN THIS CHAPTER

◆ Introduction to AWS Lambda

◆ Creating a Python Lambda function

◆ Testing an AWS Lambda function

◆ Viewing execution logs

◆ Deleting AWS Lambda functions and Amazon CloudWatch log groups

AWS Lambda is a service that lets you run code on the Amazon cloud without provisioning servers. Amazon manages the infrastructure needed to run your code, and you are billed for the time when your code is running.

AWS Lambda code is triggered in response to events. AWS can trigger events for a variety of scenarios, such as a file being uploaded to an Amazon S3 bucket, a change in an Amazon DynamoDB table, arrival of data on an Amazon Kinesis stream, and so on. With AWS Lambda, you can provide some code that can be triggered when one of these events occurs with very low (millisecond) latency.

AWS Lambda is highly scalable and is capable of running parallel instances of your code in response to concurrent events with AWS managing the provisioning of resources in the background. You can also use Amazon API Gateway to build RESTful APIs that run AWS Lambda code in response to HTTP events. Entire application back-end systems can be built in this way, without provisioning a single server.

Common Use Cases for Lambda

AWS Lambda is extremely powerful, but it only works for you if your code is in one of the supported languages and you do not need access to the underlying hardware that is executing the code. Some of the common use cases for AWS Lambda follow:

◆ *Serverless back end:* Using a combination of API Gateway and AWS Lambda, you can build a complete, highly scalable, OAuth2.0-compliant RESTful API to support an external application without provisioning a single server.

◆ *Triggers:* You can use AWS Lambda to run code in response to changes in Amazon S3 buckets and Amazon DynamoDB tables. The code could perform a variety of tasks such as enforcing data integrity checks, firing emails, writing to queues, and interacting with other AWS services such as Amazon Machine Learning and AWS Rekognition, to name a few.

◆ *Maintenance:* You can use AWS Lambda to run code in response to scheduled events. Such code could perform essential maintenance and cleanup of content in databases.

◆ *Streams:* You can configure AWS Lambda code to run in response to new data arriving on Kinesis streams. Amazon Kinesis streams allow you to build applications that process streaming data from several sources such as social media streams, financial transactions, and IOT hardware.

Key Concepts

In this section you will learn some of the key concepts you will encounter while working with AWS Lambda.

Supported Languages

AWS Lambda supports the following languages:

◆ Node.js

◆ Ruby

◆ Java

◆ C#

◆ Python

◆ Go

You can author your code using a variety of IDEs, such as Eclipse and Visual Studio. Amazon provides a web-based IDE as part of the AWS Lambda console. The web-based IDE provided by Amazon has limited features when compared against Eclipse or Visual Studio, but is very useful if you want to quickly put together a function in Node.js or Python. For a complete list of IDEs and tools available to create your Lambda code, visit `http://docs.aws.amazon.com/lambda/latest/dg/lambda-app.html`.

The examples in this chapter are presented in Python. Visit `http://docs.aws.amazon.com/lambda/latest/dg/lambda-introduction-function.html` for information on the other supported languages.

Lambda Functions

To create an AWS Lambda function, you first create a deployment package that contains the code you want to execute along with any dependencies. When you use the AWS Lambda console to create your function, the deployment package is created for you. If you are using your own IDE, you will need to create the deployment package yourself and then upload this deployment package and configuration information to AWS Lambda to create the Lambda function.

The deployment package in most cases is a `.zip` file that is uploaded to AWS Lambda using either the command-line tools or the AWS Lambda management console. You do not need to create the deployment package manually; you can use tools such as Jenkins and Maven. For more information on creating a deployment package for one of the supported languages, visit `http://docs.aws.amazon.com/lambda/latest/dg/deployment-package-v2.html`.

The configuration information that accompanies the deployment package provides the following key information:

◆ *Compute requirements:* You specify the amount of memory you want to allocate to your Lambda function. AWS Lambda allocates CPU resources in proportion to the amount of memory you have requested. The ratio of the CPU to memory allocation is the same as that of an M3 EC2 instance. If you would like to know the precise hardware that you will get for a particular instance type, visit https://aws.amazon.com/ec2/instance-types/.

◆ *Execution timeout:* This is a number in seconds that determines the maximum amount of time the function is allowed to execute. Once this time limit is reached, the Lambda function is terminated.

◆ *Execution role:* This is an IAM role that AWS Lambda assumes when it executes your function.

◆ *Handler name:* This is the name of the method in your code where AWS Lambda begins execution.

Programming Model

Regardless of the language you choose to write your Lambda function, a few core concepts are common to all Lambda functions: handlers, events, context, logging, and exceptions.

HANDLERS

The handler is the entry point in your Lambda function. It is a method that AWS Lambda calls to start execution of your function. The handler method can subsequently invoke other methods in the code that make up the Lambda function.

When your handler method is invoked, AWS Lambda injects data about the event that triggered your Lambda function, as well as a context object. You can access this event data through the first parameter of the handler method.

The name of the handler method is identified in the configuration information you supply when creating the Lambda function. The syntax of the handler method for a Lambda function written in Python is as follows:

```
def lambda_handler(event, context):
    return a_value
```

A handler can return a value. If the lambda function was invoked synchronously, the caller will receive the return value serialized as a JSON object. An example of how to use the `return` statement is provided in the following snippet:

```
def lambda_handler(event, context):

    # return the account details that were detected.
    return {
      'bankAccountNumber': '57478289274' ,
      'accountName': 'Mr. Chris Woods'
    }
```

EVENTS

The event is the first parameter of the handler method. It is a standard JSON dictionary with the following general syntax:

```
{
    "key3": "value3",
    "key2": "value2",
    "key1": "value1"
}
```

Events are generated by event sources. An event source is an AWS service or custom application that publishes an event. Table 12.1 lists some of the commonly used event sources and the type of events they generate.

TABLE 12.1:   Common Event Sources for AWS Lambda

SERVICE	EVENTS	DESCRIPTION
Amazon S3	S3 Put, S3 Delete	The S3 Put and S3 Delete events are fired when a new object is created or deleted in an S3 bucket.
Amazon DynamoDB	DynamoDB Update	The DynamoDB Update event is fired when any kind of update is made to a DynamoDB table. To use Lambda with DynamoDB, you need to enable a DynamoDB stream for the table. DynamoDB writes an entry for each update to the stream. Lambda polls this stream and invokes your function for each entry in the stream.

You can find a complete list of AWS services that can act as event sources at `http://docs.aws.amazon.com/lambda/latest/dg/invoking-lambda-function.html`.

Although the body of each event is a JSON dictionary, the entries within the dictionary are specific to the event. For instance, the payload for an S3 PUT event is as follows:

```
{
    "Records": [
    {
    "eventVersion": "2.0",
    "eventTime": "1970-01-01T00:00:00.000Z",
    "requestParameters": {
        "sourceIPAddress": "127.0.0.1"
    },
    "s3": {
        "configurationId": "testConfigRule",
        "object": {
            "eTag": "0123456789abcdef0123456789abcdef",
            "sequencer": "0A1B2C3D4E5F678901",
            "key": "HappyFace.jpg",
            "size": 1024
```

```
        },
        "bucket": {
            "arn": bucketarn,
            "name": "sourcebucket",
            "ownerIdentity": {
            "principalId": "EXAMPLE"
            }
        },
        "s3SchemaVersion": "1.0"
    },
    "responseElements": {
        "x-amz-id-2": "EXAMPLE123/5678abcdee/mnopFGH",
        "x-amz-request-id": "EXAMPLE123456789"
    },
    "awsRegion": "us-east-1",
    "eventName": "ObjectCreated:Put",
    "userIdentity": {
        "principalId": "EXAMPLE"
    },
    "eventSource": "aws:s3"
    }]
}
```

The payload of a DynamoDB Update event is as follows:

```
{
    "Records": [
    {
    "eventID": "1",
    "eventVersion": "1.0",
    "dynamodb": {
        "Keys": {
            "Id": {
                "N": "101"
            }
        },
        "NewImage": {
            "Message": {
                "S": "New item!"
            },
            "Id": {
                "N": "101"
            }
        },
        "StreamViewType": "NEW_AND_OLD_IMAGES",
        "SequenceNumber": "111",
        "SizeBytes": 26
    },
```

```
        "awsRegion": "us-west-2",
        "eventName": "INSERT",
        "eventSourceARN": eventsourcearn,
        "eventSource": "aws:dynamodb"
        }]
}
```

You can find sample event data for different types of AWS events at https://docs.aws .amazon.com/lambda/latest/dg/lambda-services.html.

CONTEXT

This is the second parameter of a handler method. Using this object, your code can interact with AWS Lambda to get useful information about the execution environment. Here is some of the information you can obtain from the context object:

♦   The number of seconds remaining before Lambda terminates the function.

♦   The CloudWatch log group stream associated with the function.

♦   The AWS request ID that was returned to the client when the function was invoked. This ID can be used for follow-up inquiries with AWS support.

♦   The name of the mobile app, and the device invoking the function, if the function is invoked using the AWS Mobile SDK.

LOGGING

Any logging statements in your Lambda function are written out to CloudWatch logs. The precise statements you use in your code to generate these logs depend on the programming language you are using. If you are creating your function using Python, you can use the following statements to create log entries:

♦   `print()`

♦   `logging.Logger.info()`

♦   `logging.Logger.error()`

If you use the Logger module, your log entries will contain additional information such as time stamp and log level.

EXCEPTIONS

Your function can create an exception to notify AWS Lambda that an error had occurred while executing the function code. The manner in which exceptions are created depends on the programming language you are using.

In case of Lambda functions written in Python, you can use the `raise` statement to raise an exception, as illustrated in the following handler:

```
def lambda_handler(event, context):

        raise AnException('Something went wrong!')
```

When this handler is invoked, AWS Lambda will return the following error message:

```
{
    "errorMessage": "Something went wrong!",
    "stackTrace": [
      [
        "/var/task/some_function.py",
        3,
        "lambda_handler",
        "raise AnException('Something went wrong!')"
      ]
    ],
    "errorType": "AnException"
}
```

If the client that invoked the AWS Lambda function has invoked it synchronously, the client will receive the error message and AWS Lambda will write a copy of the error message to the Amazon CloudWatch log. If the client invoked the AWS Lambda function asynchronously, the error message will only be written to the Amazon CloudWatch log.

Execution Environment

When an AWS Lambda function is invoked in response to an event, AWS Lambda launches an execution environment (container) for the function based on the configuration settings provided when the function was created. The underlying operating system for a container is Amazon Linux. Each container comes preinstalled with a number of libraries and provides some disk space in the `/tmp` directory.

For more information on the standard libraries that come with a container, refer to `https://docs.aws.amazon.com/lambda/latest/dg/lambda-runtimes.html`.

Lambda needs a little time to create a new container and bootstrap it before passing control to your handler method. To increase efficiency, Lambda keeps the container around for a short while after your function has finished executing. If another copy of your function is executed within this short time, Lambda reuses the container.

You cannot assume that a container will be reused. It is entirely up to AWS Lambda to make that decision. However, if an execution container is reused, it has the following implications for your code:

- ◆ Variable declarations in your Lambda function code, outside the handler method, remain initialized. This could be useful if your code was establishing a database connection and storing the connection in a variable. You could add logic in your code that checks whether the connection variable is already initialized and only create a new connection if it is not.

- ◆ The contents of the `/tmp` directory of the container are not deleted.

- ◆ Any background processes (or callbacks in the case of Node.js) initiated by the previous instance of your function, that did not complete when the previous instance of your function ended, are resumed. You must ensure any such processes are complete before your Lambda function exits.

Service Limitations

AWS Lambda places limits on the size of your Lambda function as well as the runtime compute resources they can utilize. The maximum number of concurrent executions is capped at 1000 and the total storage that can be used by the Lambda function and its components is capped at 75 GB. You can request an increase to these limits.

However, there are other limits for which you cannot request an increase. Some of these limits are:

◆ The memory allocated to your function at runtime must lie between 128 MB and 3008 MB, allocated in 64 MB increments.

◆ The maximum timeout interval for the function is 900 seconds.

◆ For synchronous invocations, the size of the request and response payloads must not exceed 6 MB.

◆ For asynchronous invocations, the size of the request and response payloads must not exceed 256 KB.

You can find out more about these limits, including how to request an increase to the number of concurrent executions and file size, at `https://docs.aws.amazon.com/lambda/latest/dg/limits.html`.

Pricing and Availability

AWS Lambda is available on a pay-per-use model. You will be charged based on the number of requests for your function and the duration for which the function code executes. Duration is rounded up to the nearest 100ms boundary. This service is included in the AWS free-tier account. You can get more details on the pricing model at `https://aws.amazon.com/lambda/pricing/`.

Common Tasks

In this section, you learn to create and test Python AWS Lambda functions using the AWS Lambda console and the AWS CLI tools.

To create and configure AWS Lambda functions, you should use an IAM user with suitable privileges. Log in to the AWS management console using the dedicated sign-in link for your development IAM user account. The screenshots in this section assume that the console is connected to the EU (Ireland) region. Click the Services menu and navigate to the AWS Lambda service home page (Figure 12.1).

Creating a Simple Python Lambda Function Using the AWS Management Console

If you are using Lambda for the first time, you are presented with the AWS Lambda splash screen (Figure 12.2).

Follow the instructions listed below to create a Lambda function with Python 3.6 code.

FIGURE 12.1
AWS Lambda service home page

FIGURE 12.2
AWS Lambda splash screen

1. Expand the menu on the left side of the page and click the Dashboard link to access the AWS Lambda dashboard. If you have used Lambda in the past, you arrive at the AWS Lambda dashboard (Figure 12.3).

2. Click the Create Function button on the AWS Lambda dashboard screen to start the process of creating a new Lambda function.

3. If you want to view a list of existing Lambda functions, click the Functions menu item in the menu on the left side of the page (Figure 12.4). You can also create a Lambda function from the Functions page by clicking the Create Function button on the page.

FIGURE 12.3

AWS Lambda dashboard

FIGURE 12.4

List of existing AWS
Lambda functions

NOTE You can use the management console to create Lambda functions using Ruby, Node.js, or Python. For Java and C#, you need to use the AWS command-line tools and dedicated IDE plug-ins to package the Lambda function.

After clicking the Create Function button, you are taken to the Create Function screen where you have three choices (Figure 12.5):

◆ Create a function from scratch

◆ Select a blueprint as a starting point

◆ Look up the AWS Serverless Application repository for a function created by someone else that does what you need

A blueprint is a template for building a Lambda function. AWS Lambda offers several blueprints for Lambda functions written in Node.js and Python. Blueprints make it easy to configure event sources for your Lambda function code.

4. Since we are going to create a function from scratch. Ensure the Author From Scratch option is selected.

5. Name the function **TestFunction**, use the Runtime drop-down to select the Python 3.6 runtime, and select the Create A New Role With Basic Permissions option in the Execution Role drop-down (Figure 12.6).

FIGURE 12.5
AWS Lambda Create
Function screen

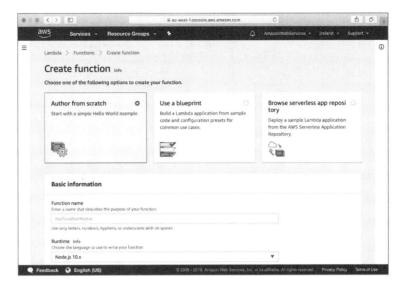

FIGURE 12.6
Lambda function Name
and Runtime settings

6. Click on the Create Function button to finish creating the function. While creating the new function, AWS Lambda will also create a new service role for your function that will allow access to Amazon Cloudwatch logs. The name of the role will begin with the name of the function, which in this case is `TestFunction`.

The function that we are creating in this section does not need access to any additional AWS resources and therefore, we will not update the policy document associated with the role. If, however, you want your function to access other AWS resources in addition to Amazon CloudWatch, you can use the IAM management console (Figure 12.7) to modify the permissions policy document associated with the role.

FIGURE 12.7
Inspecting the permissions policy document associated with the IAM role created by AWS Lambda

7. When the Lambda function has been created, you will be taken to the function configuration page (Figure 12.8) where you can configure triggers and the code for the function.

FIGURE 12.8
Lambda function configuration page

The Lambda function configuration page can also be accessed by selecting the Functions menu item from the menu on the left-hand side of the AWS Lambda management console page and selecting the TestFunction from the list of available Lambda functions (Figure 12.9).

FIGURE 12.9
List of AWS
Lambda functions

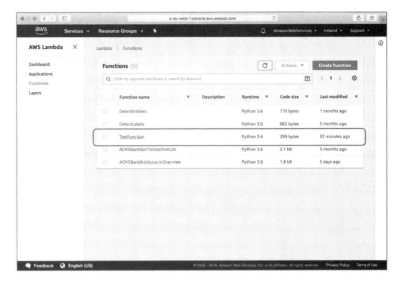

In Chapters 13 and 18 you create Lambda functions that are triggered when items are uploaded to an S3 bucket, and use AWS Comprehend and Rekognition to detect and process the content of the uploaded item. The Lambda function being built in this section is not going to be associated with AWS event sources and therefore has no triggers. This function is tested by manually triggering it with a JSON document in place of an event.

8. Scroll down to the Function Code section of the page and replace the existing sample Lambda function code with the following (Figure 12.10):

```python
import json
import logging

def lambda_handler(event, context):

    logger = logging.getLogger()
    logger.setLevel(logging.INFO)

    logger.info('Found event{}'.format(event))

    accountName = event['accountName']
    accountNumber = event['accountNumber']
    sortCode = event['sortCode']

    logger.info('AccountName:' + accountName)
    logger.info('AccountNumber:' + accountNumber)
    logger.info('Sort Code:' + sortCode)

    if accountNumber == '1234' and sortCode == '5678':
        return {
```

```
        'statusCode': 200,
        'body': json.dumps('This is the correct account!')
        }
    else:
        return {
        'statusCode': 200,
        'body': json.dumps('This is not the correct account!')
        }
```

FIGURE 12.10
Updating the code for the AWS Lambda function

9. Click the Save button to save these changes.

Testing a Lambda Function Using the AWS Management Console

You can use the management console to test the Lambda function. In the previous section, you created a Python Lambda function. In this section, you test it using a dummy event.

1. Click the Functions menu item in the Lambda dashboard to access a list of Lambda functions (Figure 12.11).

FIGURE 12.11
List of AWS Lambda functions

2. Click the function called TestLambdaFunction to access the function's code and settings.

3. Click the Test button located at the top-right corner of the page. You are presented with a dialog box that lets you provide a test event in JSON format. Name the event **TestJSONEvent**, replace the default JSON content of the event with the following JSON code, and click the Save and Test button (Figure 12.12):

```
{
    "accountName": "Abhishek Mishra",
    "accountNumber": "1234",
    "sortCode": "5678"
}
```

FIGURE 12.12

Configuring a test event

You will see your test event listed in a drop-down menu beside the Test button. If you have defined multiple test events, the drop-down menu allows you to select a test event. The Configure Test Events menu item allows you to edit existing test events as well as create additional test events (Figure 12.13).

FIGURE 12.13

Configuring a test event

4. Ensure the TestJSONEvent event is selected from the available test events and click the Test button to execute the AWS Lambda function. Your function code will be executed and the results will be presented to you (Figure 12.14).

FIGURE 12.14
AWS Lambda function execution results

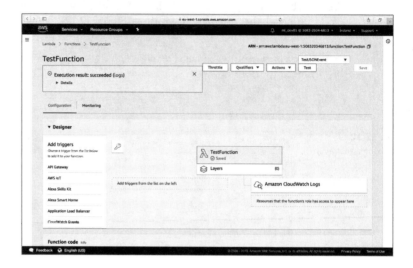

You should see that the function succeeded with the following output message:

```
{
    "statusCode": 200,
    "body": "\"This is the correct account!\""
}
```

5. Expand the chevron beside the function execution result to get more detailed information, including the time taken to execute the function, the cost of execution, and the logs (Figure 12.15).

FIGURE 12.15
Accessing AWS Lambda function execution statistics and logs

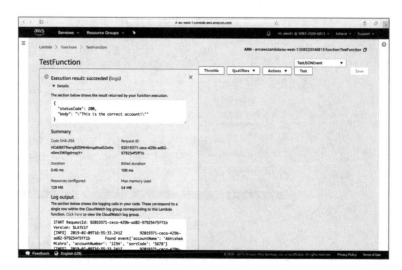

The console log resembles the following:

```
START RequestId: 92019371-ceca-429b-ad82-979254f5ff1b Version: $LATEST
[INFO]. 2019-02-09T16:55:33.241Z. 92019371-ceca-429b-ad82-
979254f5ff1b Found event{'accountName': 'Abhishek Mishra',
'accountNumber': '1234', 'sortCode': '5678'}
[INFO] 2019-02-09T16:55:33.241Z 92019371-ceca-429b-ad82-
979254f5ff1b AccountName:Abhishek Mishra
[INFO] 2019-02-09T16:55:33.241Z 92019371-ceca-429b-ad82-
979254f5ff1b AccountNumber:1234
[INFO] 2019-02-09T16:55:33.241Z 92019371-ceca-429b-ad82-
979254f5ff1b Sort Code:5678
END RequestId: 92019371-ceca-429b-ad82-979254f5ff1b
REPORT RequestId: 92019371-ceca-429b-ad82-979254f5ff1b Duration:
0.46 ms Billed Duration: 100 ms Memory Size: 128 MB Max
Memory Used: 54 MB
```

The logs generated by your function are enclosed between START and END elements. The console log also contains a REPORT object that has information on the execution time, memory footprint, and billed duration.

Deleting an AWS Lambda Function Using the AWS Management Console

You can use the AWS management console to delete a Lambda function. Deleting an AWS Lambda function does not automatically delete the execution role or the Amazon CloudWatch log for the function.

1. To delete an AWS Lambda function, click the Functions menu item in the AWS Lambda dashboard to access a list of functions. Select the function you want to delete and select the Actions ➤ Delete function menu item (Figure 12.16).

FIGURE 12.16
Accessing the Delete function menu item

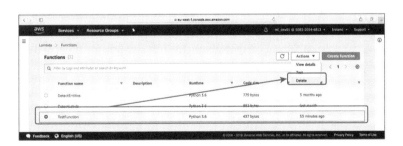

You do not need to delete the execution role if you plan to use it for another function. You can delete the Amazon CloudWatch log for the function by accessing the Amazon CloudWatch service from the Services drop-down (Figure 12.17).

FIGURE 12.17

Accessing the Amazon
CloudWatch dashboard

2. Once you are in the CloudWatch dashboard, click the Logs menu item to access a list of logs (Figure 12.18).

FIGURE 12.18

List of Amazon
CloudWatch log groups

3. Select the log corresponding to your Lambda function, and select the Actions ➤ Delete Log Group menu item (Figure 12.19).

FIGURE 12.19

Accessing the Delete Log
Group menu item

Summary

◆ AWS Lambda is a service that lets you run code on the Amazon cloud without provisioning servers.

◆ AWS Lambda code is triggered in response to events.

◆ AWS Lambda is highly scalable and is capable of running millions of parallel instances of your code in response to concurrent events.

◆ You can also use Amazon API Gateway to build RESTful APIs that run AWS Lambda code in response to HTTP events.

◆ You can use AWS Lambda to run code in response to changes in Amazon S3 buckets, Amazon DynamoDB tables, and other AWS resources.

◆ AWS Lambda supports Node.js, Java, C#, Ruby, Go, and Python.

◆ A deployment package is usually a `.zip` file that contains your function code along with any dependencies.

◆ A deployment package can be uploaded using either the command-line tools or the AWS Lambda management console.

◆ You specify the amount of memory you want to allocate to your Lambda function. AWS Lambda allocates CPU resources in proportion to the amount of memory you have requested.

◆ AWS Lambda functions must execute within a fixed amount of time, capped at 900 seconds. Once this time limit is reached, the Lambda function is terminated.

◆ You need to set up an IAM role that will be assumed by AWS Lambda when it executes your function. This IAM role should contain relevant policies that will allow your code to access other AWS resources such as Amazon S3 buckets.

Chapter 13

Amazon Comprehend

♦ Introduction to Natural Language Processing (NLP) concepts

♦ Introduction to the Amazon Comprehend NLP service

♦ Use the Amazon Comprehend management console to analyze text

♦ Use the AWS CLI to analyze text

♦ Call Amazon Comprehend APIs from AWS Lambda

Amazon Comprehend is a fully managed web service that provides access to a deep-learning–based Natural Language Processing (NLP) and topic-modeling engine that you can use in your projects to analyze the content of text documents and implement features such as topic-based classification, content-based search, and customer sentiment analysis.

The machine learning models used by Amazon Comprehend are pre-trained and continually improved by Amazon using inputs from a variety of real-world sources, including Amazon product reviews. Training a deep-learning model is a complex and lengthy task. Using Amazon Comprehend for NLP tasks lets you focus on solving a business problem without having to worry about building, deploying, and maintaining a complex machine learning model.

Key Concepts

In this section you will learn some of the key concepts you will encounter while working with Amazon Comprehend.

Natural Language Processing

Natural Language Processing (NLP) is a discipline within artificial intelligence that focuses on creating algorithms that allow computers to analyze, understand, and derive meaning from text. NLP algorithms can be used to extract meaningful and useful information from text such as:

♦ *Entities:* Amazon Comprehend can analyze text and return a list of named entities such as people and places, along with a confidence score. Each entity has an associated type. Amazon Comprehend supports the following entity types:

COMMERCIAL_PRODUCT

DATE

EVENT

> LOCATION
>
> ORGANIZATION
>
> PERSON
>
> QUANTITY
>
> TITLE
>
> OTHER

◆ *Key phrases:* Amazon Comprehend can analyze text and return a list of key phrases (or talking points) as well as confidence scores. A key phrase is defined as a noun phrase that talks about a particular thing—such as "my new camera." This could be useful if you were using Amazon Comprehend to analyze blog posts and wanted information on what people were talking about.

◆ *Sentiment:* Amazon Comprehend can analyze text and return an indicator of the overall sentiment (Positive, Negative, Neutral, or Mixed) along with confidence scores for each sentiment. This could be useful if you were using Amazon Comprehend to analyze customer comments and product reviews.

◆ *Syntax:* Amazon Comprehend can be used to analyze text and identify word boundaries and labels such as nouns, pronouns, adjectives, and verbs. Amazon Comprehend can identify the following syntax elements:

> Nouns
>
> Verbs
>
> Numerals
>
> Particles
>
> Pronouns
>
> Proper nouns
>
> Punctuation
>
> Symbols
>
> Subordinating conjunctions
>
> Adjectives
>
> Adpositions
>
> Adverbs
>
> Auxiliaries
>
> Coordinating conjunctions
>
> Determiners
>
> Interjections

♦ *Dominant language:* Amazon Comprehend can be used to identify the dominant language in a document. The identified language is represented using codes described in RFC 5646. Amazon Comprehend also provides a confidence score that indicates the level of confidence in the analysis. The confidence score does not indicate the percentage of the language that makes up the document.

Topic Modeling

Topic modeling uses NLP algorithms to examine the content of a text document and determine a set of topics (such as entertainment, sports, politics, etc.) that best describe the content. Early attempts at topic modeling were based purely on using preset dictionaries of keywords associated with each topic. Topic modeling is generally used to organize a collection of documents. A database table could be populated using the results of topic modeling and used by an application to retrieve documents.

Amazon Comprehend uses a Latent Dirichlet Allocation (LDA)–based model and is able to infer the context behind the occurrence of a keyword. LDA is a statistical topic modeling approach and assumes that a document is a mixture of a small set of topics and that each topic contains a small set of keywords that are frequently associated with it.

Keywords can be associated with different topics in different documents. For example, the use of the word "drill" in a document that is talking about dentistry will result in the word being associated with the topics of "dentistry" or "medicine." The use of the same word in a document about offshore oil rigs will result in the word being associated with topics such as "energy," "petroleum," and so on.

Language Support

Amazon Comprehend's text analysis features support six languages at the time this book was written:

♦ English

♦ French

♦ German

♦ Italian

♦ Portuguese

♦ Spanish

Amazon Comprehend's language detection feature supports over a hundred languages (but you can only use the text analysis features on six languages). You can get information on the list of languages supported by the language detection APIs at https://docs.aws.amazon.com/comprehend/latest/dg/how-languages.html.

Pricing and Availability

Amazon Comprehend is available on a pay-per-use model. You will be charged based on the amount of text you process on a monthly basis. This service is included in the AWS free-tier account. You can get more details on the pricing model at https://aws.amazon.com/comprehend/pricing/.

Amazon Comprehend is not available in all regions. You can get information on the regions in which it is available from the following URL: https://aws.amazon.com/about-aws/global-infrastructure/regional-product-services/.

Text Analysis Using the Amazon Comprehend Management Console

In this section you will use the Amazon Comprehend management console to perform entity, key phrase, dominant language, syntax, and sentiment analysis on a short text document.

Amazon Comprehend can be used in both interactive and asynchronous mode. In interactive mode, you paste a small amount of text on a web page, click a button to begin the analysis, and view the results of the analysis on the same page within a few seconds.

Using Amazon Comprehend in asynchronous mode involves creating analysis jobs that run asynchronously, reading documents from an S3 bucket, and writing the results of the analysis to a text file in another bucket. Asynchronous mode is not covered in this book. You can find more information on using Amazon Comprehend in asynchronous mode at https://docs.aws.amazon.com/comprehend/latest/dg/how-async.html.

Log in to the AWS management console using the dedicated sign-in link for your development IAM user account. Use the region selector to select a region where the Amazon Comprehend service is available. The screenshots in this section assume that the console is connected to the EU (Ireland) region. Click the Services menu and access the Amazon Comprehend service home page (Figure 13.1).

FIGURE 13.1

Accessing the Amazon Comprehend service home page

Click the Try Amazon Comprehend link on the page (Figure 13.2).

FIGURE 13.2
Testing the capabilities
of Amazon Comprehend

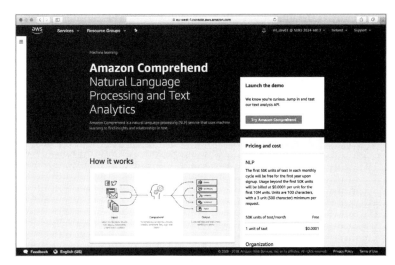

Replace the contents of the Input text field with the following paragraph and click the Analyze button (Figure 13.3):

> *Machine Learning is a discipline within Artificial Intelligence that deals with creating algorithms that learn from data. Machine learning traces its roots to a computer program created in 1959 by a computer scientist Arthur Samuel while working for IBM. Samuel's program could play a game of checkers and was based on assigning each position on the board a score that indicated the likelihood of leading towards winning the game. The positional scores were refined by having the program play against itself, and with each iteration the performance of the program improved. The program was in effect, learning from experience, and the field of machine learning was born.*
>
> *Machine learning specifically deals with the problem of creating computer programs that can generalize and predict information reliably, quickly, and with accuracy resembling what a human would do with similar information. Machine learning algorithms require a lot of processing and storage space, and until recently were only possible to deploy in very large companies, or in academic institutions. Recent advances in storage, processor, GPU technology and the ability to rapidly create new virtual computing resources in the cloud have finally provided the processing power required to build and deploy machine learning systems at scale, and get results in real-time.*

FIGURE 13.3
Analyzing text with
Amazon Comprehend

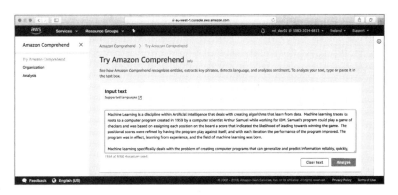

Amazon Comprehend will take a few seconds to analyze the text. The results of the analysis will be provided as insights on the same page, below the original text that was analyzed. Scroll down to locate the Insights section of the page. The Insights section will list the results of entity, key phrase, language, sentiment, and syntax analysis (Figure 13.4).

FIGURE 13.4
Amazon Comprehend presents analysis results as insights.

Behind the scenes, the user-friendly web-based management console makes use of AWS APIs for the analysis. The following APIs are used to provide the results that you see listed in the Insights section:

- Entity detection: DetectEntities
- Key phrase detection: DetectKeyPhrases
- Language detection: DetectDominantLanguage
- Sentiment analysis: DetectSentiment
- Syntax analysis: DetectSyntax

You can find more information on these APIs at the following URL: `https://docs.aws.amazon.com/comprehend/latest/dg/API_Operations.html`.

Interactive Text Analysis with the AWS CLI

You can use the AWS CLI to access the underlying Amazon Comprehend APIs and perform text analysis over the command line. This section assumes you have installed and configured the AWS CLI to use your development IAM credentials.

Entity Detection with the AWS CLI

To perform entity detection using the AWS CLI, launch a Terminal window on your Mac or a Command Prompt window on Windows, and type the following command:

```
$ aws comprehend detect-entities \
      --region "eu-west-1" \
      --language-code "en" \
      --text "Machine learning traces its roots to a computer program created in
1959 by a computer scientist Arthur Samuel while working for IBM"
```

This command uses the DetectEntities API (identified on the command line using the `detect-entities` identifier), and specifies the AWS region to be used, as well as the text to be analyzed.

Press the Enter key on your keyboard to execute the command. After a few seconds, the output on your computer should resemble the following:

```
{
    "Entities": [
        {
            "Score": 0.9976276755332947,
            "Type": "DATE",
            "Text": "1959",
            "BeginOffset": 67,
            "EndOffset": 71
        },
        {
            "Score": 0.9960350394248962,
            "Type": "PERSON",
            "Text": "Arthur Samuel",
            "BeginOffset": 96,
            "EndOffset": 109
        },
        {
            "Score": 0.9668458700180054,
            "Type": "ORGANIZATION",
            "Text": "IBM",
            "BeginOffset": 128,
            "EndOffset": 131
        }
    ]
}
```

Amazon Comprehend has found three entities in the text and the result of the DetectEntities API is a JSON document containing details on the entities. The details include the type of entity, the value of the entity, the character position within the text where the entity was first located, and the confidence score. A confidence score is a number between 0.0 and 1.0. Higher numbers imply that Amazon Comprehend has more confidence in its analysis.

If no entities are found, the DetectEntities API returns a JSON object with an empty `Entities` array. This can be observed if you type the following command on your Terminal window and press the Enter key:

```
$ aws comprehend detect-entities \
    --region "eu-west-1" \
    --language-code "en" \
    --text "Machine learning specifically deals with the problem of creating
computer programs that can generalize and predict information reliably, quickly,
and with accuracy resembling what a human would do with similar information."
```

The result of executing the command should contain an empty Entities array implying that Amazon Comprehend could not find any entities:

```
{
    "Entities": []
}
```

Key Phrase Detection with the AWS CLI

To detect key phrases in a snippet of text, you will make use of the DetectKeyPhrases API. Type the following command in your Terminal window (or Command Prompt window):

```
$ aws comprehend detect-key-phrases \
--region "eu-west-1" \
--language-code "en" \
--text "Machine learning traces its roots to a computer program created in 1959
by a computer scientist Arthur Samuel while working for IBM"
```

This command uses the DetectKeyPhrases API (identified on the command line using the detect-key-phrases identifier), and specifies the AWS region to be used, as well as the text to be analyzed.

Press the Enter key on your keyboard to execute the command. After a few seconds, the output on your computer should resemble the following:

```
{
    "KeyPhrases": [
        {
            "Score": 0.5423930883407593,
            "Text": "Machine",
            "BeginOffset": 0,
            "EndOffset": 7
        },
        {
            "Score": 0.6729782819747925,
            "Text": "traces",
            "BeginOffset": 17,
            "EndOffset": 23
        },
        {
            "Score": 0.9950423836708069,
            "Text": "its roots",
            "BeginOffset": 24,
            "EndOffset": 33
        },
```

```
    {
        "Score": 0.9978877902030945,
        "Text": "a computer program",
        "BeginOffset": 37,
        "EndOffset": 55
    },
    {
        "Score": 0.9986926913261414,
        "Text": "1959",
        "BeginOffset": 67,
        "EndOffset": 71
    },
    {
        "Score": 0.9789828062057495,
        "Text": "a computer scientist Arthur Samuel",
        "BeginOffset": 75,
        "EndOffset": 109
    }
    ]
}
```

Sentiment Analysis with the AWS CLI

To get an indication of the overall sentiment of a snippet of text, you will make use of the DetectSentiment API. Type the following command in your Terminal window (or Command Prompt window):

```
$ aws comprehend detect-sentiment \
    --region "eu-west-1" \
    --language-code "en" \
    --text "Machine learning traces its roots to a computer program created in
1959 by a computer scientist Arthur Samuel while working for IBM"
```

This command uses the DetectSentiment API (identified on the command line using the detect-sentiment identifier), and specifies the AWS region to be used, as well as the text to be analyzed.

Press the Enter key on your keyboard to execute the command. After a few seconds, the output on your computer should resemble the following:

```
{
    "Sentiment": "NEUTRAL",
    "SentimentScore": {
        "Positive": 0.0015290803276002407,
        "Negative": 0.0024455683305859566,
        "Neutral": 0.9954049587249756,
        "Mixed": 0.0006204072269611061
    }
}
```

Using Amazon Comprehend with AWS Lambda

In the previous sections of this chapter you have learned to use Amazon Comprehend using the management console and the AWS CLI. While using these APIs interactively certainly provides results, you cannot integrate AWS Comprehend with your own projects in this way.

To integrate AWS in a real-world project, you will most likely pick one of two approaches:

◆ Use one of the language-specific AWS SDKs and call the Amazon Comprehend APIs directly from your code.

◆ Create an AWS Lambda function that will call the Amazon Comprehend APIs when triggered.

In this section you will create an AWS Lambda function that will be triggered when a document is uploaded to an S3 bucket. Once triggered, the AWS Lambda function will read the uploaded document from S3 and use Amazon Comprehend's entity detection APIs to create a file in a different S3 bucket that contains a list of entities discovered in the document.

In real-world scenarios, there may be several other events that you could use to trigger the AWS Lambda function, such as a message being posted to an SNS topic or an HTTP request being received by an API Gateway. Triggering an AWS Lambda function in the scenarios just described is not covered in this book.

NOTE   To follow along with this section ensure you have created the S3 buckets listed in Appendix B.

You can download the code files for this chapter from www.wiley.com/go/machinelearning-awscloud or from GitHub using the following URL:

https://github.com/asmtechnology/awsmlbook-chapter13.git

To get started, log in to the AWS management console using the dedicated sign-in link for your development IAM user account and use the region selector to select a region where the Amazon Comprehend service is available. The screenshots in this section assume that the console is connected to the EU (Ireland) region. Click the Services menu and access the AWS Lambda service home page.

If you are using Lambda for the first time, you will be presented with the AWS Lambda splash screen (Figure 13.5). Expand the menu on the left side of the page and click the Dashboard menu item to access the AWS Lambda dashboard.

FIGURE 13.5
AWS Lambda
splash screen

If you have used Lambda in the past, you will arrive at the AWS Lambda dashboard (Figure 13.6). You can click the Create Function button to start the process of creating a new AWS Lambda function.

FIGURE 13.6
AWS Lambda dashboard

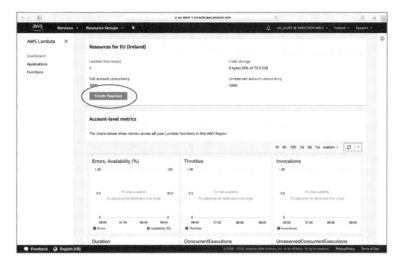

After clicking the Create function button, you will be asked to select a template for the function (Figure 13.7). You can either create a Lambda function from scratch, use a predefined template (known as a blueprint) as a starting point, or create a ready-to-use function by picking code from the AWS Serverless Application Repository. Select the Author From Scratch option.

FIGURE 13.7
Creating an AWS
Lambda function
from scratch

Name the function **DetectEntities**, use the Runtime drop-down to select the Python 3.6 runtime, and select the Create A New Role With Basic Lambda Permissions from the Execution Role drop-down (Figure 13.8).

FIGURE 13.8
Lambda Function Name
and Runtime settings

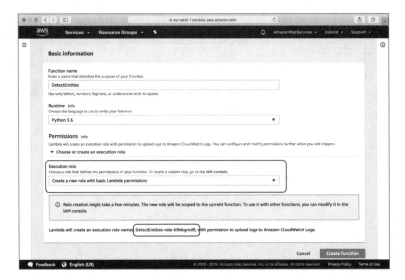

AWS will create a new IAM role for your function with a minimal set of permissions that will allow your function to write logs to AWS CloudWatch. The name of this IAM role is displayed below the Execution Role drop down in Figure 13.8 and will be similar to `DetectEntities-role-xxxxx`. Make a note of this name as you will need to modify the role to allow access to Amazon S3 and Amazon Comprehend. Click on the Create Function button at the bottom of the page to create the AWS Lambda function and the IAM role.

After the AWS Lambda function is created, use the services menu to switch to the IAM management console and navigate to the new IAM role that was just created for you when you created the lambda function. Locate the permissions policy document associated with the role and click on the Edit Policy button (Figure 13.9).

FIGURE 13.9
Viewing the default
policy document
associated with the IAM
role created by
AWS Lambda

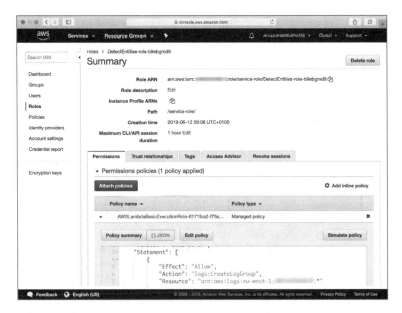

You will be taken to the policy editor screen; click on the JSON tab to view the policy document as a JSON file (Figure 13.10).

FIGURE 13.10
Updating the default
policy document
associated with the IAM
role created by
AWS Lambda

Add the following objects to the Statement array:

```
{
    "Action": [
        "comprehend:DetectEntities"
    ],
    "Effect": "Allow",
    "Resource": "*"
},
{
    "Action": [
        "s3:GetObject",
        "s3:PutObject"
    ],
    "Effect": "Allow",
    "Resource": "arn:aws:s3:::*"
}
```

Your final policy document should resemble this snippet:

```
{
    "Version": "2012-10-17",
    "Statement": [
        {
            "Effect": "Allow",
            "Action": "logs:CreateLogGroup",
            "Resource": "arn:aws:logs:eu-west-1:5083XXXX:*"
        },
```

```
      {
          "Effect": "Allow",
          "Action": [
              "logs:CreateLogStream",
              "logs:PutLogEvents"
          ],
          "Resource": [
              "arn:aws:logs:eu-west-1:508XXXX13:log-group:/aws/lambda/
DetectEntities:*"
          ]
      },
      {

          "Action": [
              "comprehend:DetectEntities"
          ],
          "Effect": "Allow",
          "Resource": "*"
      },
      {
          "Action": [
              "s3:GetObject",
              "s3:PutObject"
          ],
          "Effect": "Allow",
          "Resource": "arn:aws:s3:::*"
      }
  ]
}
```

This policy document allows AWS Lambda to write logs to CloudWatch, call the AWS Comprehend DetectEntities API, and read/write objects from any S3 bucket in your account. You can allow access to additional Amazon Comprehend APIs by adding the relevant actions after "comprehend:DetectEntities". You can get a list of available Amazon Comprehend actions that can be used in policy documents at https://docs.aws.amazon.com/comprehend/latest/dg/comprehend-api-permissions-ref.html.

Click on the Review Policy button at the bottom of the page to go to the Review Policy screen (Figure 13.11).

Click on the Save changes button to finish updating the IAM policy. After the policy changes have been saved, use the Services menu to switch back to the AWS Lambda management console and navigate to the DetectEntities lambda function (Figure 13.12). The function designer section of the page should now list Amazon CloudWatch Logs, Amazon S3, and Amazon Comprehend as the resources that can be accessed by the function.

Locate the function designer section of the page and add the Amazon S3 trigger to the function (Figure 13.13).

FIGURE 13.11
Review Policy screen

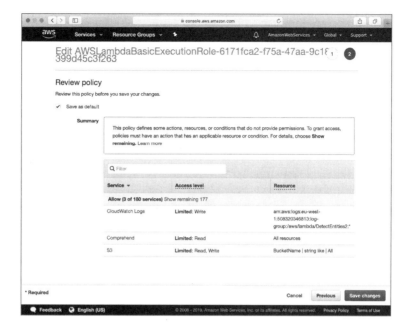

FIGURE 13.12
AWS Lambda function designer

Scroll down to the Configure Triggers section and choose an S3 bucket that will serve as the event source. In this example, the source bucket is called `awsml-comprehend-entitydetection-source`. Ensure the Event Type is set to Object Created (All) and click the Add button to finish configuring the S3 event trigger (Figure 13.14).

FIGURE 13.13
Adding the Amazon S3
trigger to the AWS
Lambda function

FIGURE 13.14
Configuring the Amazon
S3 event trigger

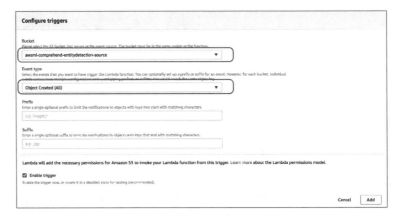

Click the Save button at the top of the page to save your changes. By creating the trigger, you have set up the Lambda function to be executed every time a new file is uploaded to the source S3 bucket.

To update the Lambda function code, scroll down to the function designer and click the function name to reveal the code editor (Figure 13.15).

FIGURE 13.15
Accessing the function
code editor

Replace the boilerplate code in the code editor with the contents of Listing 13.1.

LISTING 13.1: Python 3.6 AWS Lambda function code to perform entity analysis with Amazon Comprehend

```python
import json
import boto3
import os
import sys
import uuid
import logging

def lambda_handler(event, context):

    logger = logging.getLogger()
    logger.setLevel(logging.INFO)

    comprehend_client = boto3.client('comprehend')

    logger.info('Found event{}'.format(event))

    for record in event['Records']:
        # Read the value of the eventSource attribute.
        #
        # You can use this to conditionally handle events
        # from different triggers in the same lambda function.
        event_source = record['eventSource']
        logger.info(event_source)

        # read S3 bucket and object key
        bucket = record['s3']['bucket']['name']
        key = record['s3']['object']['key']

        # read the contents of the document uploaded to S3
        obj = boto3.resource('s3').Object(bucket, key)
        data = obj.get()['Body'].read().decode('utf-8')

        # use Amazon comprehend to detect entities in the text
        entities = comprehend_client.detect_entities(Text=data,
        LanguageCode='en')

        #write results of entity analysis
        output_bucket = 'awsml-comprehend-entitydetection-result'
        output_key = 'entityanalysis-' + key
        output_obj = boto3.resource('s3').Object(output_bucket,output_key)
        output_obj.put(Body=json.dumps(entities))
```

```
# return the entities that were detected.
return {
'statusCode': 200,
'outputBucket': output_bucket
}
```

Click the Save button below the function editor to finish creating your Lambda function. To test this function, use the Services drop-down menu to switch to Amazon S3 and navigate to the bucket that you have associated with the AWS Lambda function trigger. Upload a UTF-8 text file into the bucket. In a few seconds, you should see a new file created in the output bucket with the results of the entity analysis.

The output bucket is hardcoded in Listing 13.1. You should change it to the appropriate value if you are using a different bucket name. The bucket names and files used in this example are:

- *Source bucket:* awsml-comprehend-entitydetection-source

- *Destination bucket:* awsml-comprehend-entitydetection-result

- *Input file:* comprehend_entitydetection_input1.txt

- *Output file:* entityresult-comprehend_entitydetection_input1.txt

NOTE You can download the code files for this chapter from www.wiley.com/go/ machinelearningawscloud or from GitHub using the following URL:

https://github.com/asmtechnology/awsmlbook-chapter13.git

Summary

- Amazon Comprehend is a fully managed web service that provides access to a deep-learning–based Natural Language Processing (NLP) and topic modeling engine.

- Amazon Comprehend can be used to detect entities, key phrases, syntax, and the dominant language of a document.

- Amazon Comprehend can be used to analyze a set of documents and create a list of topics associated with each document.

- Amazon Comprehend can be used interactively through the management console as well as the AWS CLI.

- The underlying Amazon Comprehend APIs can be used from a number of SDKs for popular programming languages.

- You can create AWS Lambda functions that make use of Amazon Comprehend APIs and trigger the AWS Lambda function from a variety of events.

Chapter 14

Amazon Lex

WHAT'S IN THIS CHAPTER

◆ Introduction to the Amazon Lex service

◆ Use the Amazon Lex management console to create a chatbot

◆ Use the Amazon Lex management console to test a chatbot

◆ Create Amazon DynamoDB tables and AWS Lambda functions to support the chatbot

Amazon Lex is a fully managed web service that allows you to create conversation interfaces that can support both voice and text. Using Amazon Lex you can leverage the power of the conversational engine that is used by Amazon Alexa to create chatbots in your own applications.

You can integrate your chatbot into mobile applications using the AWS Mobile SDK, with web applications using the AWS JavaScript SDK, and into common messaging platforms such as Facebook Messenger, Slack, and Twilio. You do not need to worry about provisioning and maintaining infrastructure to support your chatbot.

NOTE   You can download the code files for this chapter from www.wiley.com/go/
machinelearningawscloud or from GitHub using the following URL:

https://github.com/asmtechnology/awsmlbook-chapter14.git

Key Concepts

In this section you learn some of the key concepts you will encounter while working with Amazon Lex.

Bot

A *bot* (also known as a chatbot) is a program that can accept natural-language input and is designed to simulate human conversation. Chatbots are generally accessed over the internet and used to provide some kind of commercial service to customers, such as order fulfillment, technical support, etc. Used properly, chatbots can support conversational interfaces within desktop, mobile, and web applications and can cut the cost of maintaining a large team of support personnel in a call center. Chatbots also incorporate an element of NLP to understand the input provided by a customer and work out what action to take. In order for chatbots to provide business services, they are usually integrated with a variety of business back-end systems such as order processing, customer management, etc.

Client Application

Amazon Lex chatbots are server-side applications that expose their functionality using REST APIs. While these APIs can work with both text and voice, Amazon Lex does not include a front-end interface. The front-end user interface is something that the customer directly interacts with, and in the case of text-only chatbots it looks like a chat window where the customer can type something. You can either create your own desktop, web, or mobile client application and integrate with the Amazon Lex chatbot via an API, or use an existing messaging platform such as Slack, Facebook Messenger, or Twilio to act as the front-end interface for your Amazon Lex chatbot.

Intent

An *intent* is an object that represents an action that a user of your chatbot can perform. When creating an intent, you provide the following information:

- A descriptive intent name.

- A set of sample phrases that a customer can use to invoke the functionality provided by the intent.

- One or more optional placeholders for the customer to provide inputs. This would depend on the functionality encapsulated within the intent. For example, an intent that allows a customer to order shoes will require the customer to provide information such as shoe size, color, and material.

- A mechanism by which Amazon Lex can fulfill the customer's request. The recommended fulfillment mechanism is an AWS Lambda function; however, you can configure the chatbot to return a JSON object to the front-end application so that the client can handle the fulfillment of the customer's request through other means.

An Amazon Lex chatbot can support multiple intents. The intent selected by the chatbot will depend on a phrase typed or spoken by the user. For example, a chatbot that allows a customer to order a new pair of shoes and track the status of an order could have two intents. The first intent could handle the scenario where the customer wants to order a new pair of shoes and could be invoked when the customer types (or speaks) a phrase similar to "Hi, I would like to order a pair of shoes." The second intent could handle order tracking and could be invoked when the customer types a question similar to "Where is my order?"

Slot

A *slot* is a parameter within an intent that the customer must provide a value for. For instance, an intent that allows a customer to order a pair of shoes could require the user to provide a number of parameters such as the color, size, and material. Since chatbots aim to provide conversational interfaces, they need to be fairly robust to minor input variations. These variations could arise from a number of factors, including typographical errors and use of synonyms. For example, a chatbot that asks the customer to specify a date should be able to handle a range of values including words like *today, tomorrow,* and *next Friday,* and date formats in different locales. In order to build this kind of robustness, Amazon Lex requires that each slot is assigned a slot type.

A slot type is conceptually similar to an enumerated data type, except that Amazon Lex uses the list of enumerated values that the slot type can accept to train a machine learning model that provides the robustness needed to handle subtle variances. There are two kinds of slot types:

◆ *Built-in slot types*: Amazon Lex supports some of the built-in slot types from the Amazon Alexa Skills kit as well as additional slot types that are not included in the Amazon Alexa Skills kit. These built-in slot types can handle common inputs like email addresses, date, time, and location. You can find more information on built-in slot types at `https://docs` `.aws.amazon.com/lex/latest/dg/howitworks-builtins-slots.html`.

◆ *Custom slot types*: A custom slot type is an enumeration that you define. For each element of the enumeration, you can also define a number of synonyms. Custom slot types also let you define how Amazon Lex should resolve the values provided by the customer. You can choose to configure the slot type to accept the user's input only if the value is an exact match with one of the enumerated values or synonyms. When configured in this manner, the output of the user-input resolution process will be a single value.

Alternatively, you can configure a slot type to accept free-form input and then resolve it to the closest matching element of the enumeration or synonym. When configured in this manner, a machine learning model is used to assist with the matching process and the user input will be used to continuously train the machine learning model so that it performs better over time. The output of the resolution process in this case is a list of possible enumeration values, each with a probability value.

Utterance

An *utterance* is a phrase associated with an intent. When a user of your chatbot types (or speaks) that phrase, Amazon Lex will initialize the intent that is preconfigured to handle the phrase. When you create intents, you specify a list of utterances. Amazon Lex uses the list of utterances to train a machine learning model that is used to resolve similar phrases. This approach provides a layer of robustness so that your users do not have to type the same phrases word for word that the bot developer defined while building the chatbot.

Programming Model

Amazon Lex provides two sets of APIs: the model-building API and the runtime API. The model-building API can be used to create, build, and deploy a chatbot application on the AWS cloud. The Amazon Lex runtime API can be used to interact with a chatbot that is deployed.

Amazon Lex also provides a web-based management console that can be used to create, deploy, and test chatbots. The web-based management console includes an embedded test harness, which appears like a chat window and can be used as a test client for the chatbot. Behind the scenes, the web-based management console uses the model-building and runtime APIs. To integrate a chatbot with a client application, you are unlikely to use the runtime APIs directly; instead, you will use one of the AWS SDKs for the programming language of your choice. The AWS SDK will then use the Amazon Lex runtime API to interact with your server-side chatbot.

Inputs and outputs to the Amazon Lex APIs are JSON objects. The web-based management console provides tools to inspect the underlying API calls to the chatbot generated by the embedded test harness.

Each intent in the chatbot can have an AWS Lambda function that can be used for initialization, slot validation, and fulfillment. Fulfillment need not be handled by an AWS Lambda function; you can configure your chatbot to return to the client a JSON object that contains all the relevant details needed to fulfill the intent. You can learn more about the Amazon Lex model-building and runtime API operations at `https://docs.aws.amazon.com/lex/latest/dg/programming-model.html`.

Pricing and Availability

Amazon Lex is available on a pay-per-use model. You will be charged based on the number of text or voice requests processed by your bots at the end of each month. This service is not included in the AWS free-tier account; however, you can try Amazon Lex free for a year as long as you process fewer than 10,000 text requests and 5,000 speech requests in a month. You can get more details on the pricing model at `https://aws.amazon.com/lex/pricing/`.

Amazon Lex is not available in all regions. You can get information on the regions in which it is available at `https://aws.amazon.com/about-aws/global-infrastructure/regional-product-services/`.

Creating an Amazon Lex Bot

In this section you will use the Amazon Lex management console to create a bot called `ACMEBankBot`, which can be used by customers of a fictional bank called ACMEBank to perform simple account operations through a conversational interface. The bot will be text-only, and support the following customer actions through the use of intents:

◆ *Account overview:* Returns a JSON object that contains information on the accounts held by the customer and the balance in each account. The customer will be asked to provide a four-digit numeric customer identifier, which will be used by the bot to retrieve a list of accounts for the customer from a database.

◆ *View recent transactions:* Returns a JSON object that contains information on five recent transactions in an account. The customer will be asked to provide a customer identifier and an account identifier, which will be used by the bot to retrieve a list of transactions in the account from a database.

The data for the customers and accounts of the fictional bank will be held in DynamoDB tables, which will also be created in this section. We will start by creating the DynamoDB tables that hold account and transactional data, followed by AWS Lambda functions that will be used by the two intents listed above. With the DynamoDB tables and AWS Lambda functions in place, you will then proceed to build, deploy, and test the chatbot using the web-based management console.

Creating Amazon DynamoDB Tables

Log in to the AWS management console using the dedicated sign-in link for your development IAM user account. Use the region selector to select a region where both the Amazon DynamoDB service and Amazon Lex are available. Click the Services menu and access the Amazon DynamoDB service home page (Figure 14.1).

FIGURE 14.1

Accessing the Amazon
DynamoDB service
home page

The screenshots in this section assume that the console is connected to the EU (Ireland) region.
If you have never used DynamoDB, you will be presented with the splash screen (Figure 14.2).

FIGURE 14.2

Amazon DynamoDB
splash screen

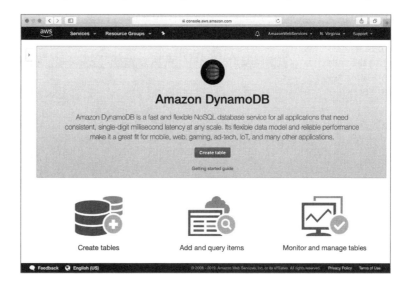

If you have used DynamoDB in the past, you will arrive at the DynamoDB dashboard
(Figure 14.3).

FIGURE 14.3
Amazon
DynamoDB dashboard

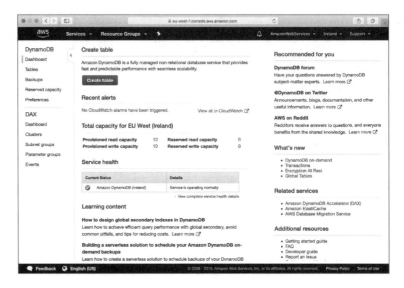

FIGURE 14.3
Amazon
DynamoDB dashboard

Regardless of which screen you arrive at, click the Create Table button to get started with creating a DynamoDB table. On the Create DynamoDB Table screen (Figure 14.4), name the new table `ACMEBankAccount` and specify the name of the partition key attribute to be a string called `CustomerIdentifier`, and the sort key attribute to be a string called `AccountIdentifier`.

FIGURE 14.4
Specifying the table
name, partition key,
and sort key

Uncheck the Use Default Settings check box and scroll down to the bottom of the page to locate the Provisioned Capacity section. Disable auto scaling and change the number of read and write units to 1 each (Figure 14.5).

FIGURE 14.5
Changing the provisioned I/O capacity

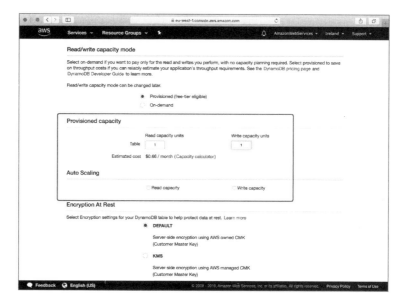

Click the Create button to create the table. The table takes a few minutes to form. Once it is created, your screen should resemble Figure 14.6.

FIGURE 14.6
Amazon DynamoDB table overview

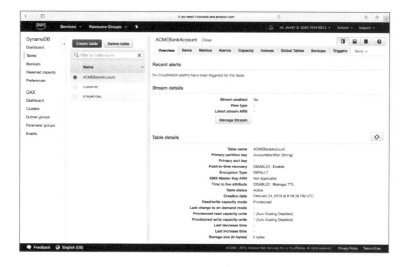

Follow the same steps to create another table with the following settings (see Figure 14.7):

◆ *Table Name:* ACMEAccountTransaction

◆ *Partition Key:* AccountIdentifier

◆ *SortKey:* TransactionIdentifier

FIGURE 14.7
Settings for the
ACMEAccount
Transaction table

Ensure you uncheck the Use Default Settings check box, and scroll down to the bottom of the page to disable auto scaling and change the number of read and write units to 1 each.

Create another table with the following settings:

◆ *Table Name:* ACMEBankCustomer

◆ *Partition Key:* CustomerIdentifier

After creating the ACMEBankCustomer, ACMEBankAccount, and ACMEAccountTransaction tables, your Amazon DynamoDB dashboard should list all three tables (see Figure 14.8).

FIGURE 14.8
Amazon DynamoDB
table overview

Now that you have created the tables, in order for the bot to function correctly, the tables will need some data. The ACMEBankCustomer table will hold details on the bank's customers, and for the purposes of this chatbot, a couple of customer records in this table will be sufficient. Click on the `ACMEBankCustomer` table in the Amazon DynamoDB dashboard, switch to the Items tab, and click the Create Item button (Figure 14.9).

You will be presented with a dialog box that lets you specify the attributes for the new item.

FIGURE 14.9
Creating a new item in the ACMEBank Customer table

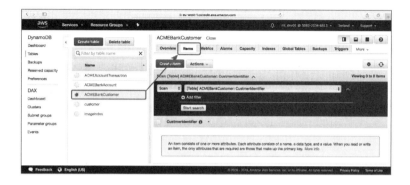

Create an item using the following information:

◆ *CustomerIdentifier:* 1000

◆ *FirstName:* John

◆ *LastName:* Woods

Create a second item using the following information:

◆ *CustomerIdentifier:* 2000

◆ *FirstName:* Sonam

◆ *LastName:* Mishra

After creating the two items, your screen should resemble Figure 14.10.

FIGURE 14.10
ACMEBankCustomer table with two items

After creating a couple of customer records in the ACMEBankCustomer table, you need to create accounts for these customers. Account data will be held in the ACMEBankAccount table, so for the purposes of this chatbot, add five entries to the ACMEBankAccount table using the information in Table 14.1.

TABLE 14.1:   ACMEBankAccount Table Items

CUSTOMERIDENTIFIER	ACCOUNTIDENTIFIER	ACCOUNTTYPE	ACCOUNTBALANCE
1000	1001	Saving	5000
1000	1002	Current	10000
2000	2001	Saving	50000
2000	2002	HighInterestSaver	275000
2000	2003	Current	10000

These entries ensure that two accounts belong to the customer with identifier 1000, and three accounts to the customer with identifier 2000. The customer identifier can be used with the ACMEBankCustomer table you created earlier to obtain the name of customer. After creating these five entries in the ACMEBankAccount table, your screen should resemble Figure 14.11.

FIGURE 14.11
ACMEBankAccount
table with five items

After creating five accounts in the ACMEBankAccount table, you need to create a few transactions in these accounts. Add items to the ACMEAccountTransaction table using the information in Table 14.2.

TABLE 14.2: ACMEAccountTransaction Table Items

ACCOUNTIDENTIFIER	TRANSACTIONIDENTIFIER	DATE	TYPE	AMOUNT
1001	1	02.28.2019	CR	5500
1001	2	03.01.2019	CW	200
1001	3	03.01.2019	TFR	300
1002	1	02.28.2019	CR	10000
2001	1	02.28.2019	CR	52000
2001	2	03.06.2019	TFR	2000
2002	1	02.28.2019	CR	275000
2003	1	02.28.2019	CR	10000

The `ACMEAccountTransaction` table contains details of all transactions across all accounts. Each transaction has the following attributes:

◆ *AccountIdentifier:* Identifies an account held by the customer.

◆ *TransactionIdentifier:* Uniquely identifies a given transaction.

◆ *Date*: The date of the transaction in mm.dd.yyyy format. For simplicity this table does not store the time of the transaction.

◆ *Type*: The type of transaction. For simplicity, this attribute will only have one of three possible values: CR – Credit, CW – Cash Withdrawal, TFR – Account Transfer.

◆ *Amount:* The amount of the transaction.

With these changes in place, you have built the table structure needed to store data on ACMEBank's customers, accounts, and transactions. You have also loaded these tables with some data. The chatbot that is built later in this chapter will use AWS Lambda functions to access the data you have loaded into these tables.

Creating AWS Lambda Functions

In this section you will create two AWS Lambda functions, which will be used by the chatbot. The chatbot will consist of two intents. While creating an intent, Amazon Lex allows you to specify a validation function and a fulfillment function. The validation function is used to validate the input provided by the user; the fulfillment function is called by the chatbot to fulfill the intent. While it is possible to use separate AWS Lambda functions for validation and fulfillment, the approach taken in this chapter is to use the same function for both validation and fulfillment—which is why you will make only two functions and not four.

To better understand the how AWS Lambda functions are used with chatbot intents, consider the example of a chatbot that helps a customer order a pizza. Such a chatbot may include an intent called `OrderPizza` that will be invoked when a user types (or speaks) a phrase similar to

"I want to order a pizza." The intent will then ask the user for the toppings, type of crust, and the size of the pizza. The first time the validation function is invoked is when the intent is loaded. The validation function is subsequently invoked each time the user provides information for one of the intent's slots. Once the customer provides values for all the slots, the fulfillment function will be invoked to place the order with the local pizza store.

The AWS Lambda functions that will be created in this section are briefly described here:

♦ *ACMEBankBotAccountOverview:* Used to validate the four-character numeric customer identifier slot and retrieve information on the accounts held by the customer.

♦ *ACMEBankBotTransactionList:* Used to validate the four-character numeric customer identifier slot and the four-character numeric account identifier slot, and retrieve a list of transactions from the specified account.

CREATING THE ACMEBankBotAccountOverview AWS LAMBDA FUNCTION

Click the Services menu and access the AWS Lambda service home page. Ensure the management console is configured to use the same region in which your Amazon DynamoDB tables have been created. Click the Create Function button to start the process of creating a new AWS Lambda function. If you are new to AWS Lambda, or would like to refresh your knowledge, refer to Chapter 12 before continuing with the rest of this section.

After clicking the Create Function button, you will be asked to select a template for the function (Figure 14.12). Select the Author From Scratch option.

FIGURE 14.12
Creating an AWS Lambda function from scratch

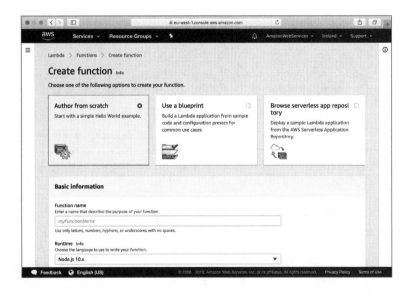

Name the function `ACMEBankBotAccountOverview`, use the Runtime drop-down to select the Python 3.6 runtime, and select the Create A New Role With Basic Lambda Permissions option in the Execution Role drop-down (Figure 14.13).

FIGURE 14.13
Lambda function name
and runtime settings

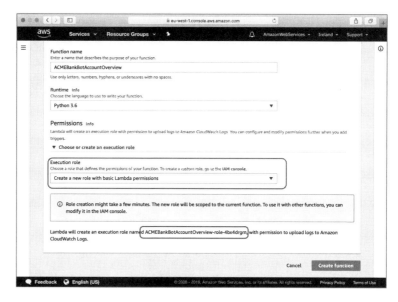

AWS will create a new IAM role for your function with a minimal set of permissions that will allow your function to write logs to AWS CloudWatch. The name of this IAM role is displayed below the Execution Role drop-down in Figure 14.13 and will be similar to `ACMEBankBotAccountOverview-role-xxxxx`. Make a note of this name as you will need to modify the role to allow access to Amazon DynamoDB. Click the Create Function button at the bottom of the page to create the AWS Lambda function and the IAM role.

After the AWS Lambda function is created, use the Services menu to switch to the IAM management console and navigate to the new IAM role that was just created for you when you created the Lambda function. Locate the permissions policy document associated with the role and click the Edit Policy button (Figure 14.14).

You will be taken to the policy editor screen. Click the JSON tab to view the policy document as a JSON file (Figure 14.15).

Add the following object to the `Statement` array:

```
{
    "Effect": "Allow",
    "Action": "dynamodb:*",
    "Resource": "*"
},
```

Your final policy document should resemble this:

```
{
    "Version": "2012-10-17",
    "Statement": [
        {
            "Effect": "Allow",
```

```
        "Action": [
            "logs:CreateLogStream",
            "logs:PutLogEvents"
        ],
        "Resource": "arn:aws:logs:eu-west-1:xxxxx:log-
group:/aws/lambda/ACMEBankBotAccountOverview:*"
    },
    {

        "Effect": "Allow",
        "Action": "dynamodb:*",
        "Resource": "*"
    },
    {

        "Effect": "Allow",
        "Action": "logs:CreateLogGroup",
        "Resource": "arn:aws:logs:eu-west-1:xxxx:*"
    }
]
}
```

FIGURE 14.14
Viewing the default
policy document
associated with the IAM
role created by
AWS Lambda

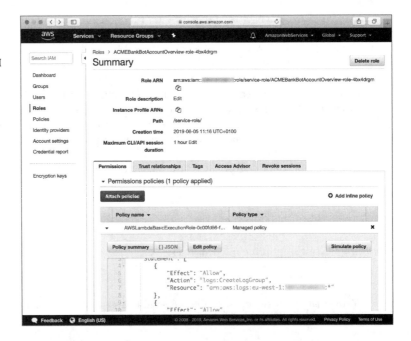

This policy document allows AWS Lambda to write logs to CloudWatch, and perform any action on any Amazon DynamoDB table. Click the Review Policy button at the bottom of the page to go to the Review Policy screen (Figure 14.16).

FIGURE 14.15
Updating the default
policy document
associated with the IAM
role created by
AWS Lambda

FIGURE 14.16
Review Policy screen

Click the Save Changes button to finish updating the IAM policy. After the policy changes
have been saved, use the Services menu to switch back to the AWS Lambda management console
and navigate to the `ACMEBotAccountOverview` Lambda function (Figure 14.17). The function
designer section of the page should now list both Amazon CloudWatch Logs and Amazon
DynamoDB as the resources that can be accessed by the function.

FIGURE 14.17
AWS Lambda func-
tion designer

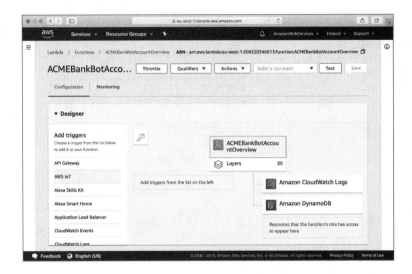

The Lambda function you have created will not do much at this point, as you have not
specified the code for the body of the function nor the triggers that should be associated with the
function. Scroll down to the function code editor and replace the boilerplate code in the code
editor with the contents of Listing 14.1.

LISTING 14.1:   ACMEBankBotAccountOverview function code

```python
import json
import boto3
import logging
import os
import sys
from boto3.dynamodb.conditions import Key, Attr

# create and configure a logger object.
logger = logging.getLogger()
logger.setLevel(logging.DEBUG)

# create an object that can be used to access Amazon DynamoDB tables
# in the same region as this AWS Lambda function.
dynamodb_resource = boto3.resource('dynamodb')

# this function returns a JSON object which when sent to Amazon Lex
# will result in the chatbot asking the end user to provide the value
# of the slot specified in 'slot_to_elicit'
def elicit_slot(slot_to_elicit, session_attributes, intent_name, slots):
    return {
        'sessionAttributes': session_attributes,
        'dialogAction': {
```

```
                'type': 'ElicitSlot',
                'intentName': intent_name,
                'slots': slots,
                'slotToElicit': slot_to_elicit
        }
    }

# this function returns a JSON object which when sent to Amazon Lex
# will result in the chatbot determining the next course of action.
def defer_next_action_to_chatbot(session_attributes, slots):
    return {
        'sessionAttributes': session_attributes,
        'dialogAction': {
            'type': 'Delegate',
            'slots': slots
        }
    }

# this function returns True if the specified customer_identifier
# exists in the ACMEBankCustomer table.
def validate_customer_identifier(customer_identifier):

    customer_table = dynamodb_resource.Table('ACMEBankCustomer')

    dynamodb_response = customer_table.query(
        KeyConditionExpression =
Key('CustomerIdentifier').eq(customer_identifier)
    )

    if dynamodb_response['Count'] == 0:
        return False

    return True


# this function returns a string that contains information
# on the accounts held by the customer and the balances in
# those accounts.
def get_account_overview(customer_identifier):

    account_table = dynamodb_resource.Table('ACMEBankAccount')

    dynamodb_response = account_table.query(
        KeyConditionExpression =
Key('CustomerIdentifier').eq(customer_identifier)
    )
```

```
        num_accounts = dynamodb_response['Count']
        if num_accounts == 0:
            return 'I could not find any accounts for you on our systems. Is there
anything else I can help you with?'

        response_string = ''
        account_array = dynamodb_response['Items']
        for i in range(num_accounts):
            account_object = account_array[i]
            account_description = 'The balance in account number {0} is
£ {1}'.format(account_object['AccountIdentifier'],
account_object['AccountBalance'])
            response_string = response_string + account_description

            if i == num_accounts - 1:
                response_string = response_string + ". Is there anything else I can
help you with?"
            else:
                response_string = response_string + ", "

        return response_string


def lambda_handler(event, context):

    # log the event to the CloudWatch log group associated
    # with this AWSLambda function.
    logger.debug(event)

    # name of the bot that is executing this function
    bot_name = event['bot']['name']

    # name of the intent that has executed this function.
    intent_name = event['currentIntent']['name']

    # ensure this lambda function is not being called by
    # the wrong bot/intent.
    if bot_name != 'ACMEBankBot':
        raise Exception('This function can only be used with the
    ACMEBankBot')

    if intent_name != 'AccountOverview':
        raise Exception('This function can only be used with the
    AccountOverview intent')

    # get session attributes
```

```python
# session attributes are not used in this code, but it is possible
  to read and
# modify values as needed.
session_attributes = event['sessionAttributes']

# get CustomerIdentifier slot
intent_slots = event['currentIntent']['slots']
customer_identifier = intent_slots["CustomerIdentifier"]

# is this function being executed for validation or fulfillment?
invocation_source = event['invocationSource']

# initialization and validation
if invocation_source == 'DialogCodeHook':

    # If the user has not provided a value for the
    # CustomerIdentifier slot, then return a response
    # that will result in the chatbot asking the user
    # to provide a value for the slot.
    if customer_identifier is None:
        return elicit_slot('CustomerIdentifier',
                            session_attributes,
                            intent_name,
                            intent_slots)


    # validate CustomerIdentifier slot.
    # if it is invalid, then ask the customer to
    # provide a value.
    if not validate_customer_identifier(customer_identifier):

        # set the invalid intent slot to None so that
        # the chatbot knows that the slot does not have
        # a value.
        intent_slots['CustomerIdentifier'] = None

        return defer_next_action_to_chatbot(session_attributes,
                            intent_slots)


# read a list of accounts for the customer
# from DynamoDB table ACMEBankAccounts and
# return a JSON object with account details.

account_overview = get_account_overview(customer_identifier)

return {
    'sessionAttributes': session_attributes,
```

```
                'dialogAction': {
                    'type': 'Close',
                    'fulfillmentState' : 'Fulfilled',
                    'message': {
                        'contentType': 'PlainText',
                        'content': account_overview
                    }
                }
            }
        }
```

Click the Save button at the top-right corner of the screen to save your code changes.

To understand the code in Listing 14.1, you need to consider the sequence of events between Amazon Lex and AWS Lambda. This function will be invoked at different times during the course of a customer's interaction with a front-end chat client application, which will in turn use one of the Amazon Lex runtime APIs to communicate with the chatbot. The first time this function will be invoked is when the AccountOverview intent is initialized. Initialization occurs when a customer types an utterance that the chatbot is able to match to the AccountOverview intent. At the point of initialization, the customer has not yet been asked to provide the value of the CustomerIdentifier slot. The input event to the AWS Lambda function resembles the following:

```
{
    'messageVersion': '1.0',
    'invocationSource': 'DialogCodeHook',
    'userId': '32p0rg8zzgoqhABCDEFG',
    'sessionAttributes': {},
    'requestAttributes': None,
    'bot': {
        'name': 'ACMEBankBot',
        'alias': '$LATEST',
        'version': '$LATEST'
    },
    'outputDialogMode': 'Text',
    'currentIntent': {
        'name': 'AccountOverview',
        'slots': {
            'CustomerIdentifier': None
        },
        'slotDetails': {
            'CustomerIdentifier': {
                'resolutions': [],
                'originalValue': None
            }
        },
        'confirmationStatus': 'None',
        'sourceLexNLUIntentInterpretation': None
    },
    'inputTranscript': 'view accounts'
}
```

You can find the complete specification for this event at `https://docs.aws.amazon.com/ lex/latest/dg/lambda-input-response-format.html`. For this discussion, the important fields are:

◆ `invocationSource`: The value `DialogCodeHook` implies that this function is being used for initialization and validation (and not fulfilment).

◆ `bot`: Contains information on the bot that created the event.

◆ `currentIntent`: Contains information on the intent within the bot that created this event. The `slots` object contains a list of slots and their current values. Note that the value of the `CustomerIdentifier` slot is `None`.

◆ `inputTranscript`: Contains the text typed by the customer in the chat client window.

The code in the `lambda_handler()` method of the AWS Lambda function starts by extracting the name of the bot and the name of the current intent, and ensuring they are what the function expects:

```
# name of the bot that is executing this function
    bot_name = event['bot']['name']

    # name of the intent that has executed this function.
    intent_name = event['currentIntent']['name']

    # ensure this lambda function is not being called by
    # the wrong bot/intent.
    if bot_name != 'ACMEBankBot':
        raise Exception('This function can only be used with the ACMEBankBot')

    if intent_name != 'AccountOverview':
        raise Exception('This function can only be used with the
AccountOverview intent')
```

This is followed by extracting the current value of the `CustomerIdentifier` slot and the invocation source:

```
# get CustomerIdentifier slot
    intent_slots = event['currentIntent']['slots']
    customer_identifier = intent_slots["CustomerIdentifier"]

    # is this function being executed for validation or fulfillment?
    invocation_source = event['invocationSource']
```

Since the value of `invocation_source` is going to contain the string `DialogCodeHook`, which implies that the function is being used for initialization and slot validation, the function inspects the current value of the `CustomerIdentifier` slot. It the value is `None`, it implies that the slot does not contain a valid value, and the function sends a response that will result in the chatbot asking the user to provide a value for the slot. This is handled in lines 119 to 130, which contain the following code:

```
# initialization and validation
    if invocation_source == 'DialogCodeHook':
```

```
# If the user has not provided a value for the
# CustomerIdentifier slot, then return a response
# that will result in the chatbot asking the user
# to provide a value for the slot.
if customer_identifier is None:
    return elicit_slot('CustomerIdentifier',
                       session_attributes,
                       intent_name,
                       intent_slots)
```

The elicit_slot function is defined elsewhere in the code. It constructs the following JSON response object and sends it to the chatbot:

```
{
    'sessionAttributes': {},
    'dialogAction': {
        'type': 'ElicitSlot',
        'intentName': 'AccountOverview',
        'slots': {
            'CustomerIdentifier': None
        },
        'slotToElicit': 'CustomerIdentifier'
    }
}
```

The chatbot reads the dialogAction object and determines that the AWS Lambda function is asking it to elicit the value of the CustomerIdentifier slot. The chatbot generates the following JSON object and sends it to the client application:

```
{
  "dialogState": "ElicitSlot",
  "intentName": "AccountOverview",
  "message": "What is your 4 digit customer number?",
  "messageFormat": "PlainText",
  "responseCard": null,
  "sessionAttributes": {},
  "slotToElicit": "CustomerIdentifier",
  "slots": {
    "CustomerIdentifier": null
  }
}
```

Recall that the chatbot is a server-side API component, and the customer uses a client application (such as a chat window in a web page) to interact with the chatbot with presentation logic residing solely in the domain of the front-end client application. The client application interprets this response from the chatbot and asks the customer to provide a value for the CustomerIdentifier slot.

When the customer types a value, the client application uses one of the Amazon Lex runtime API methods to submit the value typed by the user. The chatbot executes the AWS Lambda function a second time; this time the input event object is slightly different:

```
{
    'messageVersion': '1.0',
    'invocationSource': 'DialogCodeHook',
    'userId': 'zqw0yk3qeiw,
    'sessionAttributes': {},
    'requestAttributes': None,
    'bot': {
        'name': 'ACMEBankBot',
        'alias': '$LATEST',
        'version': '$LATEST'
    },
    'outputDialogMode': 'Text',
    'currentIntent': {
        'name': 'AccountOverview',
        'slots': {
            'CustomerIdentifier': '1000'
        },
        'slotDetails': {
            'CustomerIdentifier': {
                'resolutions': [],
                'originalValue': '1000'
            }
        },
        'confirmationStatus': 'None',
        'sourceLexNLUIntentInterpretation': None
    },
    'inputTranscript': '1000'
}
```

The key difference to point out in this event is that the value of the CustomerIdentifier slot is not None anymore; it is 1000—which is the value the customer typed into the chat window. The code path through the AWS Lambda function will be similar to the path taken during the first invocation, except that the slot now has a value, and therefore the following snippet will be executed to validate the value provided by the customer:

```
# validate CustomerIdentifier slot.
    # if it is invalid, then ask the customer to
    # provide a value.
    if not validate_customer_identifier(customer_identifier):

        # set the invalid intent slot to None so that
        # the chatbot knows that the slot does not have
        # a value.
```

```
            intent_slots['CustomerIdentifier'] = None

        return defer_next_action_to_chatbot(session_attributes,
                             intent_slots)
```

The validate_customer_identifier() function is defined elsewhere in the code. It returns True if the value provided in the CustomerIdentifier slot corresponds to a value in the CustomerIdentifier column of the ACMEBankCustomer table. The code for the validate_customer_identifier() function is reproduced here:

```
# this function returns True if the specified customer_identifier
# exists in the ACMEBankCustomer table.
def validate_customer_identifier(customer_identifier):

    customer_table = dynamodb_resource.Table('ACMEBankCustomer')

    dynamodb_response = customer_table.query(
        KeyConditionExpression =
Key('CustomerIdentifier').eq(customer_identifier)
    )

    if dynamodb_response['Count'] == 0:
        return False

    return True
```

If the validate_customer_identifier() function returns True, the AWS Lambda function will retrieve a list of accounts held by the customer, format the results into a string, and return the string back to the chatbot as an attribute in a JSON object:

```
# read a list of accounts for the customer
# from DynamoDB table ACMEBankAccounts and
# return a JSON object with account details.

account_overview = get_account_overview(customer_identifier)

return {
    'sessionAttributes': session_attributes,
    'dialogAction': {
        'type': 'Close',
        'fulfillmentState' : 'Fulfilled',
        'message': {
            'contentType': 'PlainText',
            'content': account_overview
        }
    }
}
```

The response received by the client application in this case would resemble the following:

```
{
    "dialogState": "Fulfilled",
    "intentName": "AccountOverview",
    "message": "The balance in account number 1001 is £5000, The balance in
account number 1002 is £10000. Is there anything else I can help you with?",
    "messageFormat": "PlainText",
    "responseCard": null,
    "sessionAttributes": {},
    "slotToElicit": null,
    "slots": {
        "CustomerIdentifier": "1000"
    }
}
```

Note that the `dialogState` variable in the JSON object sent to the client has the value of `Fulfilled`, which indicates that the AWS Lambda function has fulfilled the user's request. You could, if you wanted, send a JSON object in the `message` attribute, instead of a string. Your chat client would need to be able to handle the JSON object and perhaps render the information in a table within the chat window. For the purposes of the chatbot being built in this chapter, which is to be tested using the client provided by the AWS Lex management console, a formatted string message is sufficient.

CREATING THE ACMEBankBotTransactionList AWS LAMBDA FUNCTION

Navigate to the AWS Lambda dashboard and click the Create Function button to start the process of creating a new AWS Lambda function. When prompted to select a template for the function, select the Author From Scratch option and use the following options:

◆ *Name:* ACMEBankBotTransactionList

◆ *Runtime:* Python 3.6

◆ *Role:* Choose an existing role.

◆ *Existing Role:* Choose the role created earlier in this chapter.

Click the Create Function button to create the function. After the function is created, you will be taken to the Lambda function configuration page.

Locate the function designer section of the page and click the function name to reveal the code editor. Replace the boilerplate code in the code editor with the contents of Listing 14.2.

LISTING 14.2:   ACMEBankBotTransactionList function code

```
import json
import boto3
import logging
```

```python
import os
import sys
from boto3.dynamodb.conditions import Key, Attr

# create and configure a logger object.
logger = logging.getLogger()
logger.setLevel(logging.DEBUG)

# create an object that can be used to access Amazon DynamoDB tables
# in the same region as this AWS Lambda function.
dynamodb_resource = boto3.resource('dynamodb')

# this function returns a JSON object which when sent to Amazon Lex
# will result in the chatbot asking the end user to provide the value
# of the slot specified in 'slot_to_elicit'
def elicit_slot(slot_to_elicit, session_attributes, intent_name, slots):
    return {
        'sessionAttributes': session_attributes,
        'dialogAction': {
            'type': 'ElicitSlot',
            'intentName': intent_name,
            'slots': slots,
            'slotToElicit': slot_to_elicit
        }
    }

# this function returns a JSON object which when sent to Amazon Lex
# will result in the chatbot determining the next course of action.
def defer_next_action_to_chatbot(session_attributes, slots):
    return {
        'sessionAttributes': session_attributes,
        'dialogAction': {
            'type': 'Delegate',
            'slots': slots
        }
    }

# this function returns True if the specified customer_identifier
# exists in the ACMEBankCustomer table.
def validate_customer_identifier(customer_identifier):

    customer_table = dynamodb_resource.Table('ACMEBankCustomer')

    dynamodb_response = customer_table.query(
        KeyConditionExpression =
Key('CustomerIdentifier').eq(customer_identifier)
    )
```

```python
    if dynamodb_response['Count'] == 0:
        return False

    return True

# this function returns True if the specified customer_identifier
# and account_identifier combination exists in the ACMEBankAccount table.
def validate_account_identifier(customer_identifier, account_identifier):

    account_table = dynamodb_resource.Table('ACMEBankAccount')

    dynamodb_response = account_table.query(
        KeyConditionExpression =
Key('CustomerIdentifier').eq(customer_identifier) &
Key('AccountIdentifier').eq(account_identifier)
    )

    if dynamodb_response['Count'] == 0:
        return False

    return True

# this function returns a string that contains information
# on the transactions in the specified account.
def get_transaction_summary(account_identifier):

    transaction_table = dynamodb_resource.Table('ACMEAccountTransaction')

    dynamodb_response = transaction_table.query(
        KeyConditionExpression =
Key('AccountIdentifier').eq(account_identifier)
    )

    num_transactions = dynamodb_response['Count']
    if num_transactions == 0:
        return 'I could not find any transactions for this account on our
      systems. Is there anything else I can help you with?'

    response_string = ''
    transaction_array = dynamodb_response['Items']
    for i in range(num_transactions):
        transaction_object = transaction_array[i]

        transaction_number = transaction_object['TransactionIdentifier']
        transaction_amount = transaction_object['Amount']
        transaction_date = transaction_object['Date']
```

```
            transaction_type_code = transaction_object['Type']

            transaction_type_description = 'credit'
            if transaction_type_code == 'CW':
                transaction_type_description = 'cash withdrawal'
            elif transaction_type_code == 'TFR':
                transaction_type_description = 'outbound transfer'

            transaction_description = 'Transaction #{0}: {1} of £{2} on {3}'.
        format(transaction_number,
                                      transaction_type_description,
                                      transaction_amount,
                                      transaction_date)

            response_string = response_string + transaction_description

            if i == num_transactions - 1:
                response_string = response_string + ". Is there anything else I
        can help you with?"
            else:
                response_string = response_string + ", "

        return response_string


def lambda_handler(event, context):

    # log the event to the CloudWatch log group associated
    # with this AWSLambda function.
    logger.debug(event)

    # name of the bot that is executing this function
    bot_name - event['bot']['name']

    # name of the intent that has executed this function.
    intent_name = event['currentIntent']['name']

    # ensure this lambda function is not being called by
    # the wrong bot/intent.
    if bot_name != 'ACMEBankBot':
        raise Exception('This function can only be used with the
      ACMEBankBot')

    if intent_name != 'ViewTransactionList':
        raise Exception('This function can only be used with the
      ViewTransactionList intent')

    # get session attributes
```

```python
# session attributes are not used in this code, but it is possible
  to read and
# modify values as needed.
session_attributes = event['sessionAttributes']

# get CustomerIdentifier slot
intent_slots = event['currentIntent']['slots']
customer_identifier = intent_slots["CustomerIdentifier"]
account_identifier = intent_slots["AccountIdentifier"]

# is this function being executed for validation or fulfillment?
invocation_source = event['invocationSource']

# initialization and validation
if invocation_source == 'DialogCodeHook':

    # If the user has not provided a value for the
    # CustomerIdentifier slot, then return a response
    # that will result in the chatbot asking the user
    # to provide a value for the slot.
    if customer_identifier is None:
        return elicit_slot('CustomerIdentifier',
                           session_attributes,
                           intent_name,
                           intent_slots)

    # If the user has not provided a value for the
    # AccountIdentifier slot, then return a response
    # that will result in the chatbot asking the user
    # to provide a value for the slot.
    if account_identifier is None:
        return elicit_slot('AccountIdentifier',
                           session_attributes,
                           intent_name,
                           intent_slots)

    # validate CustomerIdentifier slot.
    # if it is invalid, then ask the customer to
    # provide a value.
    if not validate_customer_identifier(customer_identifier):

        # set the invalid intent slot to None so that
        # the chatbot knows that the slot does not have
        # a value.
        intent_slots['CustomerIdentifier'] = None

        return defer_next_action_to_chatbot(session_attributes,
                         intent_slots)
```

```
            # validate AccountIdentifier slot.
            # if it is invalid, then ask the customer to
            # provide a value.
            if not validate_account_identifier(customer_identifier,
account_identifier):

                    # set the invalid intent slot to None so that
                    # the chatbot knows that the slot does not have
                    # a value.
                    intent_slots['AccountIdentifier'] = None

                    return defer_next_action_to_chatbot(session_attributes,
                                    intent_slots)


        # read a list of transactions for the account
        # from DynamoDB table ACMEAccountTransaction and
        # return a JSON object with account details.

        transaction_summary = get_transaction_summary(account_identifier)

        return {
            'sessionAttributes': session_attributes,
            'dialogAction': {
                'type': 'Close',
                'fulfillmentState' : 'Fulfilled',
                'message': {
                    'contentType': 'PlainText',
                    'content': transaction_summary
                }
            }
        }
```

Click the Save button below the function editor to finish creating your Lambda function. This function operates in a similar manner to the one presented in Listing 14.1; hence it will not be discussed here in detail.

Now that you have created the Amazon DynamoDB tables and AWS Lambda functions, you can create the Amazon Lex chatbot in the next section. You may be wondering why the AWS Lambda functions were created before the chatbot. The reason is that while creating the chatbot, the Amazon Lex management console does not let you create AWS Lambda functions inline.

Creating the Chatbot

In this section, you will use the Amazon Lex management console to create a chatbot. Keep in mind that the management console makes use of the Amazon Lex model-building APIs to interact with the Amazon Lex service, and you can directly use the model-building APIs from the

AWS CLI. To get started with creating the Amazon Lex chatbot, click the Services menu and access the Amazon Lex service home page (Figure 14.18).

FIGURE 14.18
Accessing the Amazon Lex service home page

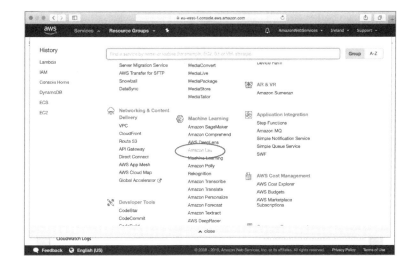

If this is the first time you are using Amazon Lex, you will be greeted with the Amazon Lex service splash screen (Figure 14.19). Click the Get Started link on the Amazon Lex splash screen.

FIGURE 14.19
Amazon Lex service splash screen

If you have used Amazon Lex in the past, then you will arrive at the Amazon Lex dashboard (Figure 14.20). Click the Create button in the Bots section of the dashboard.

FIGURE 14.20
Amazon Lex dashboard

You will arrive at the Create A Bot wizard, and will be asked to select whether you want to author the bot from scratch, or choose from one of the existing templates. Select the Custom Bot option to indicate you want to author the bot from scratch (Figure 14.21).

FIGURE 14.21
Creating a custom bot

You will be asked to provide some basic information on the new bot. Select the following options on the screen and click the Create button at the bottom on the screen to proceed:

◆ *Bot name:* ACMEBankBot

◆ *Output voice:* None

◆ *Session timeout:* 3 minutes

◆ *COPPA:* No

You will be taken to the bot editor, where you can customize the bot (Figure 14.22).

FIGURE 14.22
Amazon Lex bot editor

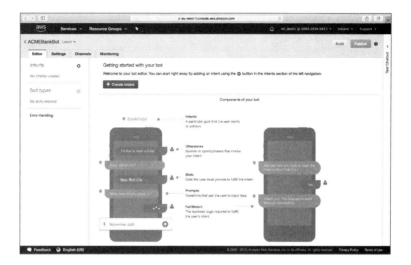

The bot that you have just created will not do anything useful as you have yet to create intents. You can think of an intent as something that a user will be able to achieve by using your bot (such as order a takeaway, purchase something, return something, etc.). The purpose of the chatbot being built in this chapter is to allow customers of a bank to get a summary of their accounts and view recent transactions. Therefore, the bot that is being built in this section will have two intents:

◆ *Account overview:* Provides information on the accounts held by the customer and the balance in each account.

◆ *View recent transactions:* Provides up to five recent transactions in an account.

Click the + button beside the intent section to begin creating the first intent, and click the Create Intent option in the pop-up dialog box that appears on the screen (Figure 14.23).

FIGURE 14.23
Configuring the slots for
your new intent.

Add intent   ✕

    ⊕ Create intent

    ⬆ Import intent

    🔍 Search existing intents

Cancel   Add

You will be asked to provide a name for the intent. Type **AccountOverview** and click the Create button (Figure 14.24).

FIGURE 14.24
Specifying the name of the new intent

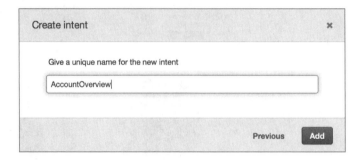

Repeat this process to create one more intent called ViewTransactionList. Once you have created both intents, your bot editor screen should resemble Figure 14.25.

FIGURE 14.25
Amazon Lex bot editor with two intents

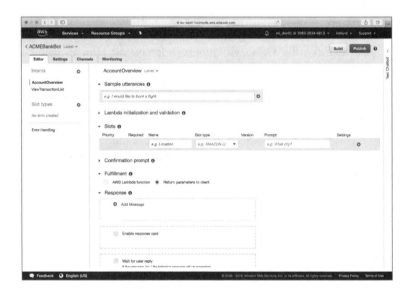

Customizing the AccountOverview Intent

Ensure the AccountOverview intent is selected in the list of intents in the bot editor and locate the Sample Utterances section (Figure 14.26) on the page. An utterance is a phrase that a user can type into your chatbot to invoke the associated intent. If the chatbot supports speech, then the user can speak the phrase. Amazon Lex uses the information you provide in the Sample Utterances section to train a machine learning model that is used to ensure that intent is robust enough to handle subtle variations of user input. The machine learning model ensures that the user can type (or speak) phrases very similar to the utterances you have configured and still invoke the correct intent. To ensure the machine learning model has sufficient training data, provide a number of sample utterances that you think could be mapped to the intent.

FIGURE 14.26
The Sample Utterances
section of the
bot editor

The example in this section will associate six utterances with the `AccountOverview` intent. If you wish, you can associate additional utterances with the intent. Type the following phrases into the Sample Utterances text field and click the + button beside the text field after each phrase to create an utterance from the phrase:

- View accounts

- Account summary

- Account list

- I would like a summary of my accounts

- I would like to view my accounts

- Show me my accounts

After you have created these utterances, the bot editor screen should resemble Figure 14.27.

Expand the Lambda Initialization And Validation section of the bot editor screen and check select the Initialization And Validation Code Hook option. You will be presented with a drop-down list of available AWS Lambda functions in your account. Select the `ACMEBankBotAccountOverview` entry in the list (Figure 14.28).

The `AccountOverview` intent requires one input from the customer: a four-character numeric customer identifier, which will be used to by the bot to locate the customer's accounts in the `ACMEBankAccount` table. Intents use the concept of slots to solicit input from users. You can think of a slot as a user-input parameter that the intent needs to perform its function. A slot can have one or more prompts associated with it; these prompts are displayed (or spoken) by the chatbot when it wants to solicit a value for the slot. Associated with the slot is a data type, known as the as the slot type. There are two types of slot types: built-in and custom. For the purposes of the customer identifier slot, we can use a built-in slot type called `AMAZON.FOUR_DIGIT_NUMBER`.

FIGURE 14.27
Utterances associated
with the
AccountOverview intent

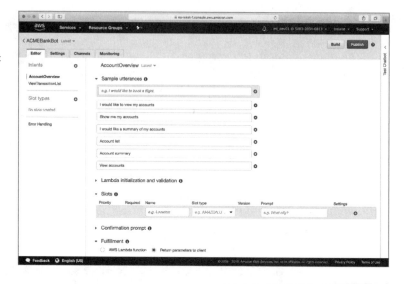

FIGURE 14.28
Specifying the validation
function for the
AccountOverview intent

Scroll down to the Slots section of the page and create a slot with the following settings:

◆ *Name:* `CustomerIdentifier`

◆ *Slot type:* `AMAZON.FOUR_DIGIT_NUMBER`

◆ *Prompt:* What is your customer identifier?

Your screen should now resemble Figure 14.29, showing the new slot listed under the Slots section.

FIGURE 14.29
Slots for the
AccountOverview intent

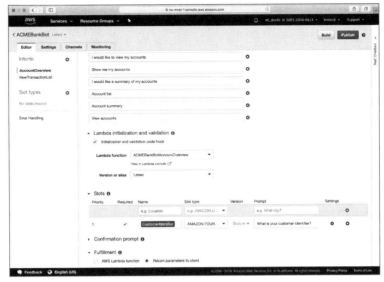

Click the gear icon beside the slot name to access the slot settings dialog box. Add an additional prompt "What is your 4-digit customer number?" to the list of prompts associated with this slot and change the number of retries to 3 (Figure 14.30). Click Save to update the slot settings.

FIGURE 14.30
CustomerIdentifier
slot settings

The prompt is a string that will be displayed (or spoken) to the user when your bot wants the user to provide a value for the slot. In this example, you have provided two prompts for the `CustomerIdentifier` slot type:

♦ What is your customer identifier?

♦ What is your 4-digit customer number?

When your bot needs the user to provide a value for the `CustomerIdentifier` slot, it will alternate between the two phrases. The maximum number of retries controls the number of additional attempts given to the customer to provide a valid value for the slot before the bot will hang up on the customer.

Scroll down the page to locate the Fulfillment section. Select the AWS Lambda Function option and select the `ACMEBankBotAccountOverview` entry in the list of available functions (Figure 14.31).

FIGURE 14.31
Specifying the
Fulfillment function
for the Account-
Overview intent

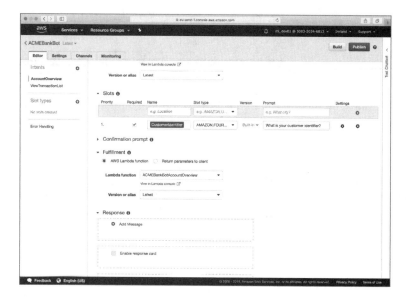

Scroll down to the bottom of the page and click the Save Intent button to save your changes.

Customizing the ViewTransactionList Intent

In the previous section you created and configured the `AccountOverview` intent. In this section you will follow a process similar to that discussed in the previous section and build the `ViewTransactionList` intent. Ensure the `ViewTransactionList` intent is selected in the list of intents in the bot editor and locate the Sample Utterances section on the page.

Create utterances out of the following phrases:

♦ I want to view a list of transactions.

♦ Show me the last few transactions.

- Show me a list of recent transactions.

- Recent account activity

- Transaction list

Expand the Lambda Initialization And Validation section of the bot editor screen and check select the Initialization And Validation Code Hook option. Select the ACMEBankBotTransactionList entry in the list of available functions (Figure 14.32).

FIGURE 14.32
Specifying the validation function for the View TransactionList intent

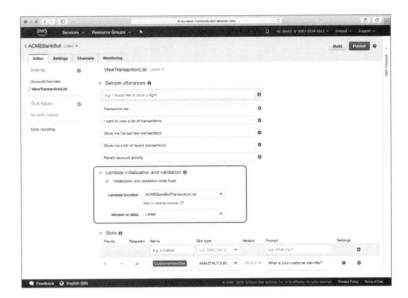

Scroll down to the Slots section of the page and create two slots as described in Table 14.3. Ensure the required attribute is selected for each slot.

TABLE 14.3:   ViewTransactionList Intent Slots

NAME	SLOT TYPE	PROMPTS
CustomerIdentifier	AMAZON.FOUR_DIGIT_NUMBER	What is your customer identifier? What is your 4-digit customer number?
AccountIdentifier	AMAZON.FOUR_DIGIT_NUMBER	What is your account number? What is your 4-digit account number?

Scroll down the page to locate the Fulfillment section. Select the AWS Lambda Function option and select the ACMEBankBotTransactionList entry in the list of available functions. (Figure 14.33).

Scroll down to the bottom of the page and click the Save Intent button to save your changes.

FIGURE 14.33
Specifying the fulfill-
ment function
for the View
TransactionList intent

Testing the Chatbot

Now that you have created the chatbot, it is time to test it out. You can test the chatbot in various ways, including the following:

- Test it using the integrated chat client in the AWS Lex management console
- Test it using Facebook Messenger, Slack, or Twilio
- Test it using the AWS CLI
- Test it from within your own desktop or mobile application

In this chapter, you will use the integrated chat client in the AWS Lex management console. You can find out more about integrating your chatbot with third-party messaging platforms at `https://docs.aws.amazon.com/lex/latest/dg/example1.html`

However, before you can test your chatbot using any of the aforementioned means, you need to build it. Building a chatbot is simply a matter of clicking the Build button at the top-right corner of the management console (Figure 14.34).

FIGURE 14.34
Building the bot

The build process can take a few minutes, after which you can test the chatbot by expanding the integrated chat client from the right-hand side of the screen and typing an utterance to invoke an intent. Figure 14.35 depicts a chat session where the `AccountSummary` intent was invoked to provide information on accounts held by a customer.

FIGURE 14.35
Testing the bot with the integrated chat client

Notice how Amazon Lex was able to invoke the `AccountSummary` intent even though the phrase typed into the chat window is "Show me accounts," which does not match any of the configured utterances exactly.

NOTE   You can download the code files for this chapter from `www.wiley.com/go/ machinelearningawscloud` or from GitHub using the following URL:

`https://github.com/asmtechnology/awsmlbook-chapter14.git`

Summary

◆   Amazon Lex is a fully managed web service that allows you to create conversation interfaces that can support both voice and text.

◆   A bot (also known as a chatbot) is a program that can accept natural-language input and is designed to simulate human conversation.

◆   You can integrate your chatbot into mobile applications using the AWS Mobile SDK, with web applications using the AWS JavaScript SDK, and into common messaging platforms such as Facebook Messenger, Slack, and Twilio.

◆   Amazon Lex chatbots are server-side applications that expose their functionality using REST APIs. While these APIs can work with both text and voice, Amazon Lex does not include a front-end interface.

◆   An intent is an object that represents an action that a user of your chatbot can perform.

◆ A slot is a parameter within an intent that the customer must provide a value for.

◆ A slot type is conceptually similar to an enumerated data type, except that Amazon Lex uses the list of enumerated values that the slot type can accept to train a machine learning model that provides the robustness needed to handle subtle variances.

◆ An utterance is a phrase associated with an intent. When a user of your chatbot types (or speaks) that phrase, Amazon Lex will initialize the intent that is preconfigured to handle the phrase.

◆ Amazon Lex provides two sets of APIs: the model-building API and the runtime API.

◆ The model-building API can be used to create, build, and deploy a chatbot application on the AWS cloud.

◆ The Amazon Lex runtime API can be used to interact with a chatbot that is deployed.

◆ Amazon Lex also provides a web-based management console that can be used to create, deploy, and test chatbots.

Chapter 15

Amazon Machine Learning

NOTE   Amazon Machine Learning is not included in AWS free-tier accounts. You can find more information on the pricing model of AWS services at `https://aws.amazon.com/pricing/`.

Amazon Machine Learning is a fully managed web service that allows you to create and deploy simple machine learning models without any programming.

Amazon Machine Learning provides a wizard-like interface that allows you to define the location of the input data, define the target attribute, and build an ML model to predict the target attribute. When you are happy with the quality of your ML model, you can deploy it on AWS managed infrastructure and access the model using an API.

Amazon Machine Learning is easy to use, but offers limited feature-engineering and model-building capabilities. Nevertheless, it is a popular choice for building linear regression and logistic regression models. In this chapter you will learn how to build, evaluate, and deploy machine learning solutions on the AWS cloud with Amazon Machine Learning.

NOTE   To follow along with this chapter, ensure you have created the S3 buckets listed in Appendix B.

You can download the code files for this chapter from `www.wiley.com/go/machinelearning-awscloud` or from GitHub using the following URL:

`https://github.com/asmtechnology/awsmlbook-chapter15.git`

Key Concepts

In this section, you learn some of the key concepts you will encounter while working with Amazon Machine Learning.

Datasources

A *datasource* is an object that stores a reference to an Amazon S3 bucket that stores your input data, along with meta information that describes the characteristics of the input data. When you create a new datasource, Amazon Machine Learning analyzes your input data to create a schema and computes descriptive statistics for the attributes in the schema. The statistics, along with other information such as the test-train split, are also stored as part of the datasource. A datasource is used to train an ML model, evaluate the model, and create batch predictions.

The statistics for each attribute can be viewed as a graph in the Amazon Machine Learning management console and are also used during the model-building process to improve the quality of the resulting ML model.

When dealing with datasources, you are likely to encounter the following terms:

- *Input data:* The input data refers to all the observations referred to by a datasource.

- *Location:* This location generally refers to a file in an Amazon S3 bucket that contains the input data. Besides Amazon S3, you can store data in Amazon RedShift databases, or MySQL databases within Amazon RDS.

- *Schema:* The schema refers to the structure of the input data, typically a list of attribute names along with their data types.

- *Observation:* An observation refers to a single unit of input data. In the case of tabular input data, an observation would correspond to an entire row in the table.

- *Attribute:* An attribute is a unique property of the input data, shared across all observations. In the case of tabular input data, an attribute would correspond to a column in the table. The data type of an attribute can be Binary, Numeric, Categorical, or Text.

- *Target attribute:* When training an ML model, the target attribute identifies the name of an attribute in the input data that contains the correct answers. When evaluating and predicting using an ML model, the target attribute represents the name of the attribute whose value you want to predict.

Amazon Machine Learning requires you to use separate datasource objects for model building and batch predictions. The datasource that is used while making batch predictions does not have a target attribute.

ML Model

A machine learning model is a mathematical model that is capable of learning patterns in data and making predictions based on those patterns. The machine learning models generated by Amazon Machine Learning are based on either linear or logistic regression and can be used for the following tasks:

- *Regression:* Predicting a continuous numeric value.

- *Binary classification:* Predicting values that have only one of two possible states.

- *Multiclass classification:* Predicting values that belong to a fixed, predefined set of possible values.

The process of building a model with Amazon Machine Learning usually involves the following steps:

1. Upload your input data to Amazon S3 and create a datasource.

2. Choose the test-train spilt. The Amazon Machine Learning default behavior is to reserve 30% of the data for testing and the remaining 70% for training.

3. Shuffle the data. Amazon Machine Learning automatically shuffles data for you.

4. Select the features and target variables; optionally apply some feature processing.

5. Select model-training parameters.

6. Create the ML model.

Building an ML model that matches your needs usually involves iterating through this ML process and evaluating a few variations in the input features, feature processing, and training parameters.

Once you have arrived at a satisfactory ML model, you will use it to make predictions. It is a good idea to store a copy of the incoming data and periodically evaluate the performance of the model on this new data. ML models will only predict accurately if the data that the model was trained on has a similar distribution to the data on which it is making predictions.

If you detect the performance of the model has degraded on the new test dataset, you would need to create a new model based on a training set that includes some of the new observations.

Regularization

Regularization is a technique that prevents models from overfitting training data by penalizing extreme weights. Overfitting occurs when your model is able to perform well on the training data but performs poorly on data it has not encountered in the past—in effect, the model has memorized the training data instead of generalizing from the data.

Amazon Machine Learning allows you to choose from two types of regularization while building models:

◆ *L1 regularization:* This form or regularization will push small weights to zero. In a linear model, a feature with zero weight does not contribute to the prediction—therefore, in effect, this form of regularization is reducing the number of features being used by the model.

◆ *L2 regularization:* This form of regularization penalizes large weights and results in smaller overall weights. It is the default type of regularization selected by Amazon Machine Learning when you build an ML model.

Training Parameters

A training parameter (also known as a hyperparameter) is a setting that controls the manner in which the ML model is built and consequently the effectiveness of the model. Amazon Machine Learning allows you to control the following training parameters:

◆ *Maximum model size:* This is the total size in bytes of the patterns generated by Amazon Machine Learning during the training of the model. The default value of this parameter is

100 MB. Choosing a model size lets you choose a trade-off between predictive accuracy and the cost you will pay to use the model to make predictions. Using a smaller model size could result in Amazon Machine Learning discarding some patterns to fit within the size limit. Larger models, on the other hand, cost more to query when making real-time predictions.

♦ *Maximum number of training passes:* This parameter controls the number of passes over the input data that Amazon Machine Learning can make to discover patterns in your data. Increasing the number of passes will result in an increase in training time and the cost of training the model. The default value of this parameter is 10, but you can increase it up to 100. If your training dataset is small, it is likely to contain fewer samples that are similar to each other, and therefore you will need more passes to obtain higher model quality.

♦ *Shuffle type:* This parameter allows you to specify whether you want Amazon Machine Learning to shuffle the input data before it is split into the training and evaluation datasources. The default option used by Amazon Machine Learning when you create a model is to use a pseudorandom shuffling algorithm. If you have already shuffled the data prior to creating the input datasource, you can set the shuffle type to None. It is worth noting that the shuffling is performed at the point Amazon Machine Learning splits the input datasource into the training and evaluation datasources. Subsequent passes of the model-building process do not shuffle the data.

♦ *Regularization type:* Regularization is a technique that prevents ML models from overfitting by penalizing large weight values. You have two forms of regularization to choose from when you build an ML model. L1 regularization pushes small weight values toward zero, in effect canceling out the effect of the associated input attribute. L2 regularization prevents very large weight values, and is the default used by Amazon Machine Learning. You can also choose to apply no regularization by setting the regularization type to None during the model-building process.

♦ *Regularization amount:* This parameter lets you control how much regularization to apply during the model-building process. Amazon Machine Learning provides three options: Mild, Moderate, and High.

Descriptive Statistics

When you create a datasource, Amazon Machine Learning computes statistical information on your data that you can use to understand your data. These statistics can be accessed from the Amazon Machine Learning console and are computed on each attribute. For numeric attributes, Amazon Machine Learning computes the following statistics:

♦ Minimum, maximum, median, and mean values

♦ Histogram

♦ Number of missing/invalid values

For binary and categorical attributes, Amazon Machine Learning computes the following statistics:

♦ Count of distinct values per category

♦ Histogram

◆ Percentage of true values (Binary data only)

◆ Most common values

For text attributes, Amazon Machine Learning computes the following statistics:

◆ Total number of words

◆ Number of unique words

◆ Range of number of words per observation

◆ Range of word lengths

◆ Most prominent words

Pricing and Availability

Amazon Machine Learning is available on a pay-per-use model and is not included in the AWS free tier. You will be charged a flat hourly fee based on the amount of compute resources consumed to create data sources, models, and evaluations. You will also be charged for making predictions with the ML models you create. Charges for services like Amazon S3 used for building datasources are billed separately. You can get more details on the pricing model at `https://aws.amazon.com/sagemaker/`.

The ability to create datasources, ML models, and evaluations and to make batch predictions is available in all AWS regions. However, the ability to make real-time predictions with the Amazon Machine Learning API is only available in the US East (N. Virginia) and EU (Ireland) regions. You can find more information on service availability at `https://docs.aws.amazon.com/machine-learning/latest/dg/regions-and-endpoints.html`.

Creating Datasources

In this section you will upload the Titanic dataset to Amazon S3 and use the Amazon Machine Learning management console to create two sources. These datasources will be used in subsequent sections of this chapter when we build an ML model to predict which passengers were more likely to survive the Titanic disaster. The first datasource will be used for model building, and the second will be used for creating batch predictions.

The Titanic dataset is a very popular dataset that contains information on the demographic and ticket information of 1309 passengers on board the Titanic, with the goal being to predict which of the passengers were more likely to survive. The full dataset is available from the Department of BioStatistics at Vanderbilt University (`http://biostat.mc.vanderbilt.edu/wiki/Main/DataSets`). Over time, researchers at Vanderbilt University have produced various versions of the dataset, with the most recent version (titanic3) being created by Thomas Cason. Thomas Cason's version is sorted by passenger name, and you can access notes on the titanic3 dataset at `http://biostat.mc.vanderbilt.edu/wiki/pub/Main/DataSets/titanic3info.txt`.

Versions of the titanic3 dataset are also available from several other sources, including a popular Kaggle competition titled Titanic: Machine Learning From Disaster (`https://www.kaggle.com/c/titanic`). The Kaggle version is included with the resources that accompany this chapter, and has the benefit of being shuffled and pre-split into a training and validation set.

The dataset consists of two files: train.csv and test.csv. Table 15.1 lists the first five rows of the train.csv file.

Let's briefly examine the attributes of the dataset:

♦ *PassengerId:* A text variable that acts as a row identifier.

♦ *Survived:* A Boolean variable that indicates if the person survived the disaster. 0 = No, 1 = Yes.

♦ *Pclass:* A categorical variable that indicates the ticket class. 1 = 1st class, 2 = 2nd class, 3 = 3rd class.

♦ *Name:* The name of the passenger.

♦ *Sex:* A categorical variable that indicates the sex of the passenger.

♦ *Age:* A numeric variable that indicates the age of the passenger.

♦ *SibSp:* A numeric variable that indicates the number of siblings/spouses traveling together.

♦ *Parch:* A numeric variable that indicates the number of parents and children traveling together.

♦ *Ticket:* A text variable containing the ticket number.

♦ *Fare:* A numeric variable that indicates the fare paid in pre-1970 British pounds.

♦ *Cabin:* A textual variable that indicates the cabin number.

♦ *Embarked:* A categorical variable that indicates the port of embarkation. C = Cherbourg, Q = Queenstown, S = Southampton.

When you create a datasource in Amazon Machine Learning, you have the option to split the data into two sets. If you choose this option, Amazon Machine Learning will create two new datasources out of the original during the model-building process. We will use this feature and have Amazon Machine Learning use 70% of the train.csv file for model building and 30% for model evaluation. We will then create another datasource for batch predictions using the test .csv file and not have Amazon Machine Learning split this datasource.

You will create two datasources in this section:

♦ Titanic_TrainingDataSource

♦ Titanic_TestDataSource

Amazon Machine Learning will split the Titanic_TrainingDataSource datasource into two when you build an ML model in the next section:

♦ Titanic_TrainingDataSource_[percentBegin=0, percentEnd=70, strategy=sequential]

♦ Titanic_TrainingDataSource_[percentBegin=70, percentEnd=100, strategy=sequential]

TABLE 15.1: The First Five Rows of the Titanic Dataset

PassengerId	Survived	Pclass	Name	Sex	Age	SibSp	Parch	Ticket	Fare	Cabin	Embarked
1	0	3	Braund, Mr. Owen Harris	male	22	1	0	A/5 21171	7.25		S
2	1	1	Cumings, Mrs. John Bradley (Florence Briggs Thayer)	female	38	1	0	PC 17599	71.2833	C85	C
3	1	3	Heikkinen, Miss Laina	female	26	0	0	STON/ O2. 3101282	7.925		S
4	1	1	Futrelle, Mrs. Jacques Heath (Lily May Peel)	female	35	1	0	113803	53.1	C123	S
5	0	3	Allen, Mr. William Henry	male	35	0	0	373450	8.05		S

Effectively, you will end up with three datasources at the end of the model-building process and use the `Titanic_TestDataSource` datasource in a subsequent section of this chapter to make batch predictions.

Before you can create the two Amazon Machine Learning datasources, you need to upload the `test.csv` and `train.csv` files into an Amazon S3 bucket. The bucket name used in this section is `awsml-amazonml-source`. Since bucket names are unique, you will need to substitute references to this bucket with your own bucket name.

Creating the Training Datasource

Log in to the AWS management console using the dedicated sign-in link for your development IAM user account. Use the region selector to select a region where the Amazon Machine Learning service is available. The screenshots in this section assume that the console is connected to the EU (Ireland) region. Click the Services menu and access the Amazon S3 service home page.

Click the `awsml-amazonml-source` bucket in the S3 management console and upload the `test.csv` and `train.csv` files to the bucket, accepting the default options in the Amazon S3 file upload dialog (Figure 15.1).

FIGURE 15.1
Uploading the Titanic dataset to an Amazon S3 bucket

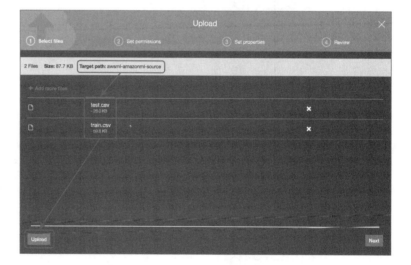

After the files have been uploaded to the bucket, click the Services menu and access the Amazon Machine Learning service home page (Figure 15.2).

Click the Get Started button on the home page to proceed (Figure 15.3).

Amazon Machine Learning provides a convenient wizard-like interface for individual tasks such as creating datasources, models, evaluations, and batch predictions. To access these wizards, click the View Dashboard button (Figure 15.4).

The Amazon Machine Learning dashboard lets you view all your datasources, models, and evaluations from one screen. Click the Create New button and select Datasource from the drop-down menu (Figure 15.5).

FIGURE 15.2
Accessing the Amazon
Machine Learning
service home page

FIGURE 15.3
The Amazon Machine
Learning service
home page

Ensure you select Amazon S3 as the source and type the name of the bucket followed by the `train.csv` file in the S3 Location field. For example, if your bucket is called `awsml-amazonml-source`, type **`awsml-amazonml-source/train.csv`** in the S3 Location field. Name the datasource `Titanic_TrainingDataSource` and click the Verify button to proceed to the next step (Figure 15.6).

During the verification process, Amazon Machine Learning will prompt you to allow access to the Amazon S3 bucket. Click the Yes button when prompted (Figure 15.7).

FIGURE 15.4
Accessing the Amazon
Machine
Learning dashboard

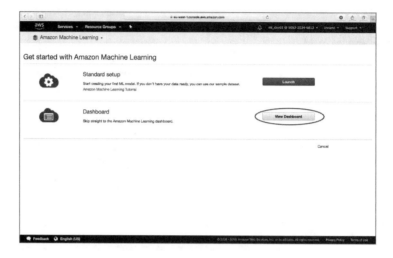

FIGURE 15.5
Accessing the Create
Datasource option from
the Amazon Machine
Learning dashboard

FIGURE 15.6
Specifying the location
of the input file

FIGURE 15.7
Granting Amazon
Machine Learning access
to your
Amazon S3 bucket

Once the verification is successful, click the Continue button to move to the Schema section of the wizard. Amazon Machine Learning will examine your data and attempt to define the schema for your data. In most cases, you will need to tweak the default schema created by Amazon Machine Learning. Since the first row of the `train.csv` file contains column names, ensure the Does The First Line In Your CSV Contain The Column Names? option is set to Yes (Figure 15.8).

FIGURE 15.8
Modifying the default
schema generated by
Amazon
Machine Learning

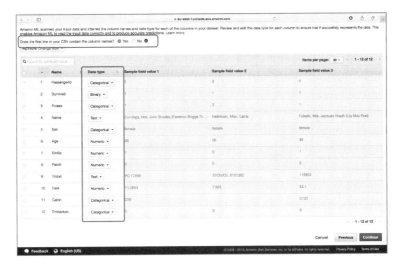

You will also need to change some of the data types inferred by Amazon Machine Learning while defining the schema. Ensure the data types for the column names match the following information and click Next:

- *PassengerId:* Categorical

- *Survived:* Binary

- *Pclass:* Categorical

◆ *Name:* Text

◆ *Sex:* Categorical

◆ *Age:* Numeric

◆ *SibSp:* Numeric

◆ *Parch:* Numeric

◆ *Ticket:* Text

◆ *Fare:* Numeric

◆ *Cabin:* Categorical

◆ *Embarked:* Categorical

On the next screen, you will be asked if you intend to use this datasource for training or evaluation. A datasource that is used for model building or evaluation must have known values of the target attribute. Ensure you select Yes in the Do You Plan To Use This Dataset To Create Or Evaluate An ML Model? option (Figure 15.9).

FIGURE 15.9
Specifying the target attribute

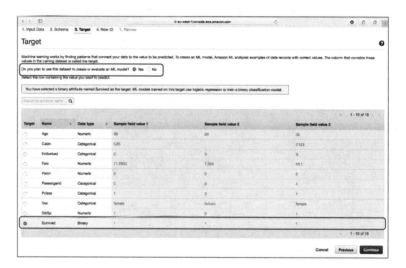

Select the Survived attribute as the target. Amazon Machine Learning will choose the ML model type based on the data type of the target attribute, according to the following rules:

◆ *Numeric:* If the target attribute is numeric, Amazon Machine Learning will generate a linear regression model.

◆ *Binary:* If the target attribute is binary, Amazon Machine Learning will generate a logistic regression model.

◆ *Categorical:* If the target attribute is categorical, Amazon Machine Learning will generate a multinomial regression model.

Amazon Machine Learning does not allow you to select a text attribute to be the target. Text attributes, therefore, are not listed in the target selection list. Click Continue to proceed.

The next step of the wizard is optional, and allows you to select an attribute that is to be used as a row identifier. Not all datasets have such an attribute. If you are using the dataset included with this lesson, answer Yes to the question Does Your Data Contain An Identifier?, and select the `PassengerId` attribute to act as the row identifier (Figure 15.10).

FIGURE 15.10
Specifying a row
identifier attribute

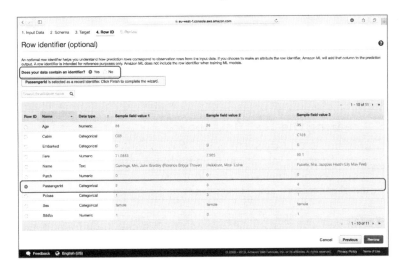

A row identifier attribute is not used during the ML model-building or evaluation process. The value of the row identifier will be included with the prediction output. The row identifier attribute must be categorical. Click Review to proceed.

The final screen of the wizard allows you to review the settings for your new datasource (Figure 15.11). Review the settings on the screen and click the Create button at the bottom of the page to create the datasource.

FIGURE 15.11
Datasource
Review screen

Creating the datasource can take several minutes. While the datasource is being created, its status will show as Pending in the Amazon Machine Learning dashboard. You can access a list of datasources using the Amazon Machine Learning dashboard, and the dashboard allows you to filter the items that are displayed using a drop-down menu (Figure 15.12).

FIGURE 15.12
Filtering the items displayed in the Amazon Machine Learning dashboard

Creating the Test Datasource

Navigate to the Amazon Machine Learning dashboard, and create a new datasource. Ensure you select Amazon S3 as the source and type the name of the bucket followed by the `test.csv` file in the S3 Location field. For example, if your bucket is called `awsml-amazonml-source`, type **`awsml-amazonml-source/test.csv`** in the S3 Location field (Figure 15.13).

FIGURE 15.13
Specifying the location of the data for the new datasource

Name the datasource `Titanic_TestDataSource` and proceed to the Schema section of the process.

Since the first row of the `test.csv` file also contains column names, ensure the Does The First Line In Your CSV Contain The Column Names? option is set to Yes on the schema definition screen (Figure 15.14).

FIGURE 15.14

Setting up the schema for the new datasource

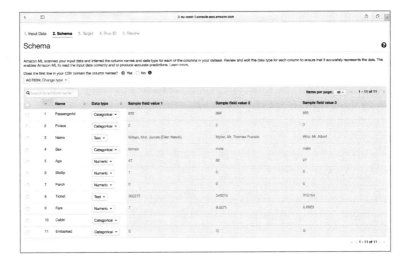

Ensure the data types for the column names match the following information:

◆ *PassengerId:* Categorical

◆ *Pclass:* Categorical

◆ *Name:* Text

◆ *Sex:* Categorical

◆ *Age:* Numeric

◆ *SibSp:* Numeric

◆ *Parch:* Numeric

◆ *Ticket:* Text

◆ *Fare:* Numeric

◆ *Cabin:* Categorical

◆ *Embarked:* Categorical

On the next screen, you will be asked if you intend to use this datasource for training or evaluation. Ensure you answer No to this question, as this datasource will be used for batch predictions, and not model building (Figure 15.15).

Select the `Survived` attribute as the target. Amazon Machine Learning will choose the ML model type based on the data type of the target attribute, according to the following rules:

◆ *For binary classification:* Logistic Regression

◆ *For multi-class classification:* Multinomial Logistic Regression

◆ *For regression:* Linear Regression

FIGURE 15.15
The new datasource does
not have a target
attribute.

FIGURE 15.15
The new datasource does
not have a target
attribute.

When asked if your data contains a row identifier, answer Yes and select the `PassengerId` attribute to act as the row identifier (Figure 15.16).

FIGURE 15.16
Specifying a row
identifier attribute

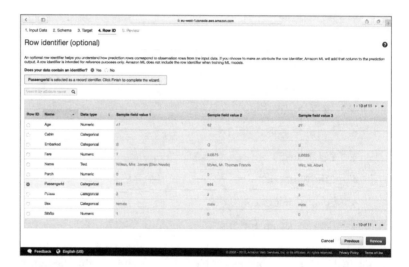

Proceed to the Review screen, and click the Create button at the bottom of the page to create the datasource. After a few minutes you will see your new datasource listed in the Amazon Machine Learning dashboard.

Viewing Data Insights

After Amazon Machine Learning has finished creating the datasource, you can access datasource statistics by clicking the name of the datasource in the dashboard (Figure 15.17).

FIGURE 15.17
Selecting the datasource
from the dashboard

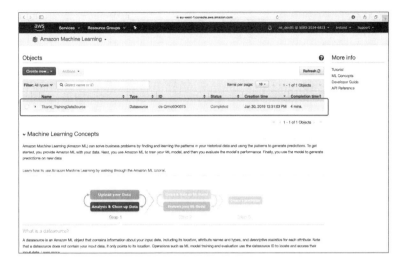

You will be taken to the datasource summary page. Click the Target Distributions link in the menu on the left side of the page to view a histogram that depicts the distribution of the target variable—in this case, the number who survived and the number who did not (Figure 15.18).

FIGURE 15.18
Histogram of the
target attribute

It is quite clear from the histogram that our dataset contains data for more people who died than survived. This suggests that there is a bias in our data, but in this case we know from historical records that this bias is not artificially introduced by our sampling techniques, and the simple fact is that more people died on the Titanic than survived. You can access summary statistics for each attribute in the datasource. Click the Categorical link in the menu on the left side of the page to view summary statistics for all categorical values (Figure 15.19).

FIGURE 15.19
Summary statistics for
categorical values

Looking at the correlation column of Figure 15.19, it is quite clear that the Sex attribute has the strongest correlation to the target attribute, and the Embarked attribute has the weakest. If you click the little histogram icon in the Preview column, you can see a detailed distribution of the values. Figure 15.20 depicts the distribution of values of the Embarked attribute.

FIGURE 15.20
Distribution of values of
the Embarked attribute

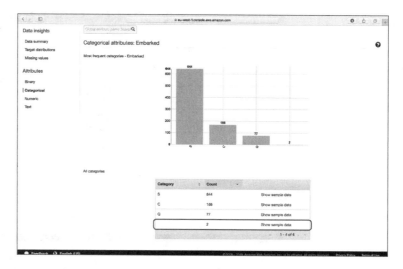

The distribution indicates that a vast majority of the people in our training dataset have embarked from Southampton, and there are only two rows of data where the port of embarkation was unspecified. Clicking the Show Sample Data link will present the two rows that do not have values for the Embarked attribute (Figure 15.21).

FIGURE 15.21

Rows that do not have a value for the Embarked attribute

You may be wondering why Amazon Machine Learning did not report these values as missing. The reason is that these are categorical attributes, and Amazon Machine Learning has assumed that missing data is just another category.

We could deal with the missing values in two ways: either guess a value, or delete the rows from the dataset. It is not possible to guess if making these changes will result in a better model at this stage. Building a good model is an iterative process; it starts with building an initial model and then, if needed, making changes to the features or model parameters to create different versions of the model. It is possible that the first model you create is good enough for your purposes. It all depends on what you want to achieve and how much time you have.

Amazon Machine Learning provides you options to control the model-building process using model parameters. You can also create different versions of datasources with better features and build models on these. In this chapter we will accept the default model parameters suggested by Amazon Machine Learning and use the ML model. Although the Embarkation feature contains missing values, the proportion of values that are missing is low, and the correlation between this attribute and the target variable is also low. Therefore, the impact of leaving these values as they are may not be significant.

Another interesting categorical attribute is Cabin. At face value, this attribute is also very poorly correlated with the target. However, looking at the distribution of values for this attribute clearly indicates that the vast majority of passengers in our dataset do not have cabin information (Figure 15.22).

FIGURE 15.22

Distribution of the Cabin attribute

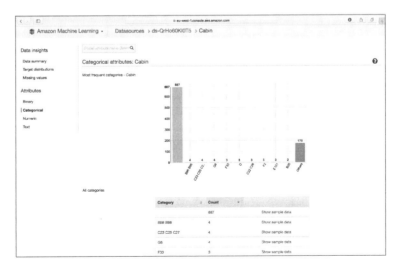

Perhaps it may be sensible to create a Boolean attribute out of this data that has 0 for all rows that do not have cabin information and 1 for the rows that do. Amazon Machine Learning has very limited feature-engineering capabilities and cannot be used for this type of feature engineering. If you want to take this on as an exercise, you can create a new CSV file using Python or Microsoft Excel and build a new datasource.

NOTE If you use Microsoft Excel on a Mac for feature engineering, ensure you save the CSV file as a Windows CSV file. There are subtle differences in how newlines are represented on Mac and Windows. Amazon Machine Learning can only build datasources out of CSV files that are saved using Microsoft Windows newline characters.

Click the Numeric link on the left-hand side of the page to access summary statistics for numeric attributes (Figure 15.23).

FIGURE 15.23

Summary statistics for numeric attributes

It is quite clear from the statistics that there are a significant number of missing values for the Age attribute. The histogram of age values indicates that they are evenly distributed around 30, which also ties in nicely with the fact that the mean and median are also close to 30 (Figure 15.24).

You could, in this case, use the median value for all the rows that are missing a value for the Age attribute, and create an additional binary value that captures the fact that the age is not known. This would again require creating a new CSV file with the changes and a new datasource. Once again, it is not possible to guess if these changes will make a better model than the one that Amazon Machine Learning will generate with default settings.

Amazon Machine Learning's default behavior when it encounters a numeric attribute with missing values is to create a new binary variable to capture the missing attribute values and use this in the model-building process. To learn more about how Amazon Machine Learning handles missing and invalid values, visit https://docs.aws.amazon.com/machine-learning/latest/dg/data-insights.html.

FIGURE 15.24
Distribution of values
for the Age attribute

FIGURE 15.24
Distribution of values
for the Age attribute

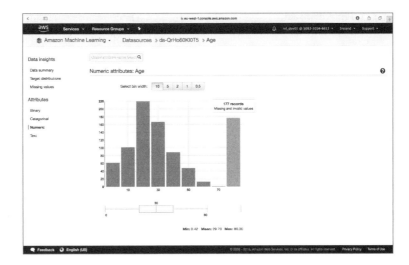

Some other statistics that stand out include that the distribution for the `Fare` attribute is extremely skewed. The range of values is between 0 and 512.3292, with the median value being only 14.4542. Also, the `Parch` and `Sibsp` attributes seem to take on a small number of values, and may perhaps have been better treated as categorical data instead of numeric. Another option could be to combine the `Parch` and `Sibsp` attributes into a new categorical attribute called `FamilySize`.

Now that we have inspected the insights provided by Amazon Machine Learning on our data, we will use this datasource as is to create an ML model.

Creating an ML Model

To create an ML model using the datasource we created earlier in this chapter, navigate to the Amazon Machine Learning dashboard and select the Create New ML Model option (Figure 15.25).

FIGURE 15.25
Creating an ML model

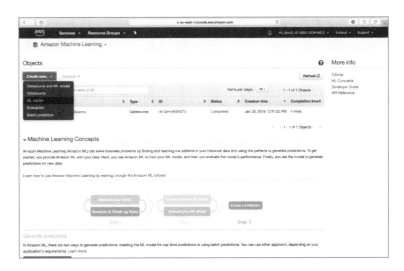

You will be asked to select a datasource. Locate the datasource that corresponds to the `train`
`.csv` file and select it from the list of available datasources (Figure 15.26).

FIGURE 15.26
Selecting a datasource

A summary of the datasource will be presented. Click Continue to proceed to the next step.
On the ML Model Settings page, provide a name for the model and select the Default training
and evaluation option (Figure 15.27).

FIGURE 15.27
Specifying ML
model settings

When you choose the default option, Amazon Machine Learning will set aside 30% of the data
in the datasource for evaluation, and the remaining 70% for training. Amazon Machine Learning
will also use default values for a number of model parameters.

Accepting the default settings is okay for creating a baseline model. You can then create additional models with different custom settings and compare the performance of these models against the baseline.

Click the Review button to proceed to the Review page. Scroll down to the bottom of the page and click the Create Model button to create the model.

It can take a few minutes to create a model. Before creating the new model, Amazon Machine Learning will create two new datasources from your datasource, with one datasource containing the 70% training set, and the other containing the 30% evaluation set.

After creating the model, Amazon Machine Learning will create an evaluation using the evaluation set. You can access the model, new data sources, and evaluation from the dashboard (Figure 15.28).

FIGURE 15.28
Amazon Machine Learning dashboard showing new data sources, the ML model, and the evaluation

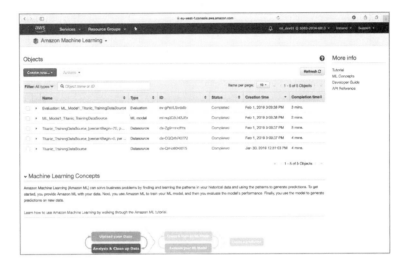

Let's now examine the characteristics of the ML model created by Amazon Machine Learning using the default settings. Click the model in the dashboard to access the Summary page for the model (Figure 15.29).

FIGURE 15.29
ML model summary

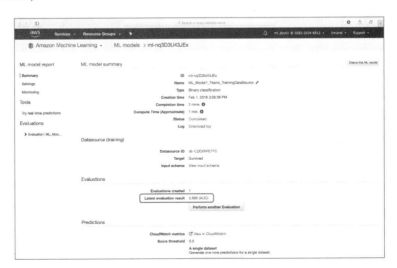

The results of the latest evaluation are presented in the Summary page. The AUC metric is listed as 0.889. Click the AUC metric for more details (Figure 15.30).

FIGURE 15.30
ML model evaluation

An AUC of 0.889 is quite good, considering an AUC score of 0.5 implies the model is randomly guessing. Click the Explore Performance button to access additional model statistics.

To tune the performance of the model, you can change the score threshold for binary classification by dragging the slider horizontally on the graph (Figure 15.31).

FIGURE 15.31
Advanced ML model
statistics

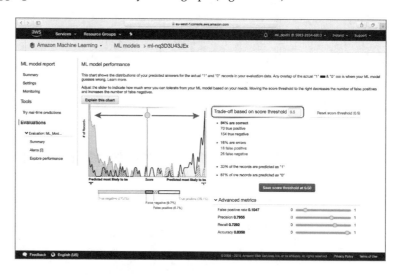

Changing the score threshold will have an impact on the accuracy, precision, and recall of the model, but not the AUC score. At the moment, with the default score of 0.5, the key performance indicators of the model are:

◆ *AUC:* 0.889

◆ *Precision:* 0.7955

◆ *Recall:* 0.7292

◆ *Accuracy:* 0.8358

False positive rate, precision, recall, and accuracy also have their own sliders, and you can use them to change one of these variables and watch the score threshold adjust to compensate.

What is the optimum score threshold to use? This is a subject of active machine learning research. It would depend on what you intend to use the model for. A model that predicts the incidence of a disease should have a very low false positive rate. In this example, we will go for a higher accuracy, and by moving the accuracy slider to the right, we can see that a score of 0.37 results in an accuracy of 0.8507, with a slightly lower precision of 0.7917 and increased recall of 0.7919 (Figure 15.32).

FIGURE 15.32
A score of 0.37 results in
a model accuracy of
0.8507 (85.07%).

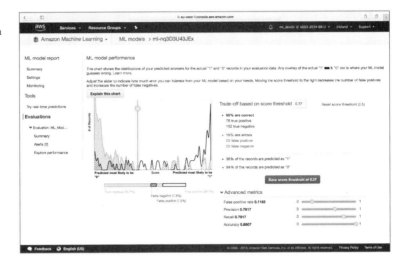

Click the Save Score Threshold button to set the score threshold for the ML model to 0.37.

Making Batch Predictions

Now that you have created an ML model, it is time to use the ML model to make predictions. Amazon Machine Learning allows you to use the console to make batch as well as single predictions. In this section you will use the `Titanic_TestDataSource` datasource to create a batch prediction.

A batch prediction involves generating a CSV file with a set of observations, and submitting the observations to Amazon Machine Learning. The results of the prediction will be stored in another CSV file in an S3 bucket. This option is suitable for situations where you do not need predictions in real time.

To create a batch prediction, navigate to the Amazon Machine Learning dashboard and select the Batch Prediction option under the Create New drop-down menu (Figure 15.33).

You will be presented with a list of ML models (Figure 15.34). Click the ML model generated in the previous section.

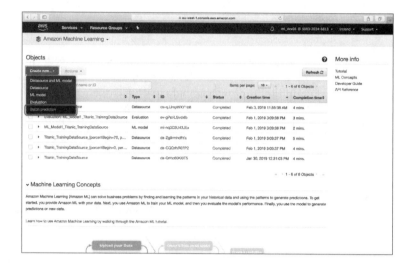

Amazon Machine Learning will present a brief summary of the ML model, including the AUC score from the most recent evaluation created with the model. Click the Continue button to proceed.

Next, you will be asked to select a datasource for batch predictions (Figure 15.35). Select the `Titanic_TestDataSource` entry from the list.

You will be presented with a summary of the datasource. Click the Continue button to proceed. If you have selected an incorrect datasource, click the Change Datasource button to select a different datasource.

Next, you will be asked to specify an existing Amazon S3 bucket where the results of the batch prediction are to be stored, and provide a name for the batch prediction operation (Figure 15.36).

FIGURE 15.35
Selecting a datasource
for batch predictions

FIGURE 15.36
Specifying an Amazon
S3 bucket where the
results of the batch
prediction are
to be stored

At the top of this screen, you will be shown the cost of the batch prediction, which in Figure 15.36 is listed as $0.10 for a CSV file with 418 rows.

In this section, the batch predictions are to be stored in a bucket called `awsml-amazonml-batchpredictions` in the EU (Ireland) region. Choose an existing bucket from your account, in the same region that your Amazon Machine Learning resources are located. Provide a name for the batch prediction that will help you identify the prediction in the dashboard. In this section, the name of the prediction is `Batch Prediction: ML_Model1_Titanic_TestDataSource`. Click the Review button to proceed to the next screen.

You will be taken to the Review screen where you can review the settings for the batch prediction as well as the cost (Figure 15.37). Click the Create button at the bottom of the page to begin the batch prediction process.

Navigate to the Amazon Machine Learning dashboard to access the batch prediction. It will take a few minutes for the predictions to be created. When the batch prediction process is complete, the corresponding row in the dashboard will list the prediction status as Complete (Figure 15.38).

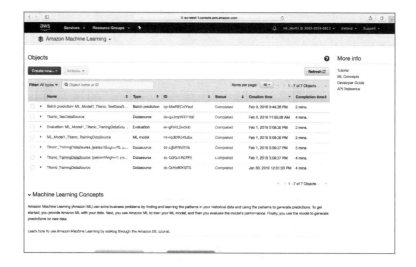

To access the results of the batch prediction operation, navigate to the Amazon S3 bucket you specified while creating the prediction operation. You will find a .gz file containing the results of the prediction (Figure 15.39).

FIGURE 15.39
Amazon S3 Bucket with
the results of the batch
prediction

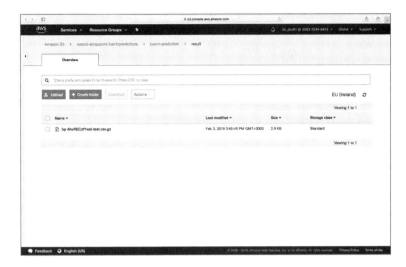

Download the file onto your computer and expand it using a suitable program. Open the
resulting CSV file with the results of the prediction. Table 15.2 lists the first 10 rows from the file.

TABLE 15.2:   The First Ten Rows of the Batch Prediction Result

TAG	BESTANSWER	SCORE
892	0	0.04036516
893	0	0.148552
894	0	0.007585382
895	0	0.01673749
896	1	0.953698
897	0	0.001477312
898	1	0.7763251
899	0	0.2489982
900	1	0.9017848
901	0	0.0003708922

The tag column contains the value of the row ID attribute, which was set up as PassengerId when the model was created. The bestAnswer column contains the prediction from the model obtained after applying the threshold to the output of the model. The score column contains the actual output of the model.

Creating a Real-Time Prediction Endpoint for Your Machine Learning Model

In addition to batch predictions, you can use your ML models for real-time predictions. Real-time predictions are synchronous and can only work with one observation at a time. You will typically use real-time predictions when you want to use the ML model generated by Amazon Machine Learning with an application that requires fast real-time predictions, such as a loan processing or credit scoring application. Your application can access the ML model as a stateless microservice, hosted on AWS infrastructure, through a RESTful interface.

To use real-time predictions with your applications, you will need to generate a real-time prediction endpoint. You will be billed for each hour the endpoint is active as well as for each prediction request you submit to the endpoint. Real-time prediction endpoints are only supported in the US East (N. Virginia) and EU (Ireland) regions.

To generate a real-time prediction endpoint, navigate to the Amazon Machine Learning dashboard, and select the check box at the start of the row that contains your ML model. Then click the Actions button and select the Create Real-Time Endpoint option from the drop-down menu (Figure 15.40).

FIGURE 15.40

Creating a real-time prediction endpoint for an Amazon Machine Learning model

You will be informed of the cost of creating the endpoint and the cost of using the endpoint for predictions (Figure 15.41). Click the Create button to create the prediction endpoint.

You can access the endpoint by clicking the name of the ML model in the AWS Machine Learning dashboard and scrolling down to the bottom of the summary page to the section titled Predictions (Figure 15.42).

FIGURE 15.41
Costs of maintaining a
real-time prediction
endpoint

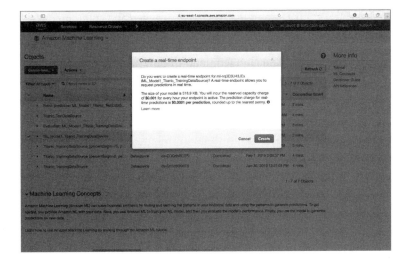

FIGURE 15.42
Accessing the real-time
prediction endpoint

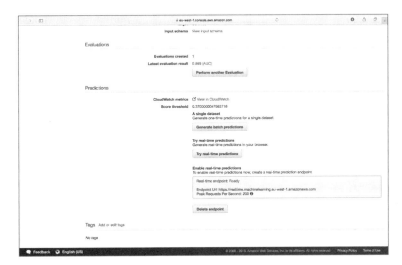

Making Predictions Using the AWS CLI

You can use the AWS CLI to access the underlying Amazon Machine Learning APIs and create datasources, build models, create evaluations, and make real-time predictions over the command line. Making real-time predictions with the AWS CLI requires setting up a real-time prediction endpoint.

In this section you will use the AWS CLI to make real-time predictions using the real-time prediction endpoint you created in the previous section. You can get more information on using other aspects of Amazon Machine Learning with the AWS CLI at `https://docs.aws.amazon .com/cli/latest/reference/machinelearning/index.html`.

This section assumes that you have installed and configured the AWS CLI to use your development IAM credentials, and to use the same region in which your Amazon S3 and Amazon Machine Learning resources are located.

To get started, launch a Terminal window on your Mac or a Command Prompt window on Windows, type the following command to retrieve a list of ML models, and press Enter:

```
$ aws machinelearning describe-ml-models
```

The output in your console window should resemble the following:

```
{
    "Results": [
        {
            "MLModelId": "ml-nq3D3U43JEx",
            "TrainingDataSourceId": "ds-CQQrlhR07P2",
            "CreatedByIamUser": "arn:aws:iam::508320346813:user/ml_dev01",
            "CreatedAt": 1549033778.022,
            "LastUpdatedAt": 1549034154.839,
            "Name": "ML_Model1_Titanic_TrainingDataSource",
            "Status": "COMPLETED",
            "SizeInBytes": 531399,
            "EndpointInfo": {
                "PeakRequestsPerSecond": 200,
                "CreatedAt": 1549229683.701,
                "EndpointUrl": "https://realtime.machinelearning.eu-west-1.
amazonaws.com",
                "EndpointStatus": "READY"
            },
            "TrainingParameters": {
                "algorithm": "sgd",
                "sgd.l1RegularizationAmount": "0.0",
                "sgd.l2RegularizationAmount": "1e-6",
                "sgd.maxMLModelSizeInBytes": "104857600",
                "sgd.maxPasses": "10",
                "sgd.shuffleType": "auto"
            },
            "InputDataLocationS3": "s3://awsml-amazonml-source/train.csv",
            "Algorithm": "sgd",
            "MLModelType": "BINARY",
            "ScoreThreshold": 0.3700000047683716,
            "ScoreThresholdLastUpdatedAt": 1549205043.711,
            "ComputeTime": 54000,
            "FinishedAt": 1549034154.839,
            "StartedAt": 1549034025.362
        }
    ]
}
```

The output is a list of all the ML models in your account, along with information on the model. Make a note of the `MLModelId` and the `EndpointUrl` attribute as you will need these to use the model over the command line.

If you get an `AccessDeniedException`, the IAM user does not have the relevant policy that allows that user to access your Amazon Machine Learning resources. In such a case, you need to ensure your IAM development user has the `AmazonMachineLearningFullAccess` policy.

To test the real-time prediction endpoint, type the following command to predict the likelihood of survival of a fictional 18-year-old male passenger, traveling alone, who boarded the Titanic at Southampton. Press Enter on your keyboard after typing the command:

```
$ aws machinelearning predict --ml-model-id ml-nq3D3U43JEx --record
'{"PassengerId":"3","Pclass":"3","Name":"Andrew
Fletcher","Sex":"male","Age":"18","SibSp":"0","Parch":"0","Embarked":"S"}' --
predict-endpoint https://realtime.machinelearning.eu-west-1.amazonaws.com
```

The results in your terminal window should resemble the following:

```
{
    "Prediction": {
        "predictedLabel": "0",
        "predictedScores": {
            "0": 0.0445670448243618
        },
        "details": {
            "Algorithm": "SGD",
            "PredictiveModelType": "BINARY"
        }
    }
}
```

The `predictedLabel` attribute contains the prediction after the score threshold has been applied. The `predictedScores` array contains a single item that contains the output of the ML model.

Using Real-Time Prediction Endpoints with Your Applications

Even though the real-time prediction endpoints generated by Amazon Machine Learning provide API-based access to the ML model, this API does not accept OAuth2 access tokens. The API accepts AWS credentials.

When you access the real-time prediction endpoint using the AWS CLI, the CLI tool uses the credentials your provided as part of the configuration process.

If you intend to use the real-time prediction endpoint from a server-side application that is hosted on AWS infrastructure (such as EC2), you can use policy-based access to ensure that the service running on the EC2 instance is able to access the real-time prediction endpoint.

If you intend to use the real-time prediction endpoint from a client application (such as a mobile app or a web app), you have two choices:

◆ Embed the credentials (AccessKeyId, SecretAccessKey) of an IAM user into the client. While this could be a quick solution during development, for most real-world production situations this option is not recommended. The only scenario where you may consider using this option in production is if you have a mechanism in place to safely transport and secure these credentials on the mobile app at runtime.

◆ Use Amazon Cognito identity pools to get a temporary set of credentials and use these credentials to access the real-time prediction endpoint.

If you would like to learn more about using the real-time prediction API, see https://docs .aws.amazon.com/machine-learning/latest/dg/requesting-real-time-predictions.html.

NOTE You can download the code files for this chapter from www.wiley.com/go/ machinelearningawscloud or from GitHub using the following URL:

https://github.com/asmtechnology/awsmlbook-chapter15.git

Summary

◆ Amazon Machine Learning is a fully managed web service that allows you to create and deploy simple machine learning models without any programming.

◆ Amazon Machine Learning is not included in the AWS free tier.

◆ Amazon Machine learning is easy to use, but offers limited feature-engineering and model-building capabilities.

◆ A datasource is an object that stores a reference to an Amazon S3 bucket that stores your input data, along with meta information that describes the characteristics of the input data.

◆ The schema refers to the structure of the input data, typically a list of attribute names along with their data types.

◆ Amazon Machine Learning can be used for regression, binary classification, and multi-class classification problems.

◆ Amazon Machine Learning provides a number of training parameters that you can use to control the quality of the model.

◆ Amazon Machine Learning provides descriptive statistics that help you analyze your input data.

◆ A batch prediction involves generating a CSV file with a set of observations, and submitting the observations to Amazon Machine Learning. The results of the prediction will be stored in another CSV file in an S3 bucket.

◆ In addition to batch predictions, you can use your ML models for real-time predictions. Real-time predictions are synchronous and can only work with one observation at a time.

◆ To use real-time predictions with your applications, you will need to generate a real-time prediction endpoint. You will be billed for each hour the endpoint is active as well as for each prediction request you submit to the endpoint.

◆ Real-time prediction endpoints are only supported in the US East (N. Virginia) and EU (Ireland) regions.

◆ You can use the real-time prediction endpoint with the AWS CLI and language-specific AWS SDKs.

Chapter 16

Amazon SageMaker

WHAT'S IN THIS CHAPTER

◆ Introduction to the Amazon SageMaker service

◆ Create an Amazon SageMaker notebook instance

◆ Train a Scikit-learn model locally on the notebook instance

◆ Train a Scikit-learn model on a dedicated instance

◆ Use Amazon SageMaker's built-in algorithms

◆ Create prediction endpoints

Amazon SageMaker is a fully managed web service that provides the ability to explore data, engineer features, and train machine learning models on AWS cloud infrastructure using Python code. Once you have trained your model, you can deploy the model to a cluster of dedicated compute instances and use the deployed model to get predictions one item at a time or create batch predictions on entire datasets.

Amazon SageMaker provides implementations of a number of cloud-optimized versions of machine learning algorithms such as XGBoost, factorization machines, and PCA (Principal Component Analysis), as well as the ability to create your own algorithms based on popular frameworks such as Scikit-learn, Google TensorFlow, and Apache MXNet. In this chapter, you will learn to use Amazon SageMaker to train and deploy machine learning models based on Scikit-learn and built-in algorithms.

NOTE Amazon SageMaker is only free for the first two months after you have signed up for a free-tier AWS account. After that period, you will be charged for compute resources.

NOTE To follow along with this chapter, ensure you have created the S3 buckets listed in Appendix B.

You can download the code files for this chapter from `www.wiley.com/go/machinelearning-awscloud` or from GitHub using the following URL:

`https://github.com/asmtechnology/awsmlbook-chapter16.git`

Key Concepts

In this section, you learn some of the key concepts you will encounter while working with Amazon SageMaker.

Programming Model

You can interact with Amazon SageMaker using one of the following methods:

◆ *The Amazon SageMaker SDK for Python:* This is a Python SDK that provides a selection of classes that can be used to interact with Amazon SageMaker for common tasks such as creating training jobs and deploying models to prediction instances. The Python SDK is object-oriented and provides a high-level API to Amazon SageMaker. By virtue of being a high-level API, the classes in this SDK provide a convenient mechanism to control Amazon SageMaker with fewer options than you would have were you to use the AWS boto3 SDK. This SDK is commonly used from Jupyter Notebooks to interact with AWS SageMaker.

◆ *The AWS boto3 SDK:* This is a Python SDK that provides a mechanism to interact will several popular AWS services, and not just Amazon SageMaker. The AWS boto3 SDK provides a lower-level interface to Amazon SageMaker and can be used to access Amazon SageMaker from an AWS Lambda function, or from a Jupyter Notebook.

◆ *Language-specific SDK:* Amazon provides a number of language-specific SDKs for programming languages such as Ruby and Java that can be used to interact with Amazon SageMaker.

◆ *AWS CLI:* You can use the AWS command-line interface to interact with Amazon SageMaker over the command line.

Amazon SageMaker Notebook Instances

Amazon SageMaker allows you to launch EC2 instances in your account that come preconfigured with a Jupyter Notebook server; a number of common Python libraries such as the Amazon SageMaker SDK, the boto3 SDK, NumPy, Pandas, Scikit-learn, and Matplotlib; and a number of different preconfigured conda kernels. These EC2 instances are referred to as Amazon SageMaker notebook instances, and the Amazon SageMaker management console provides access to the Jupyter Notebook server running on the instance. Any files that you create on your notebook instance are stored in an Elastic Block Store (EBS) storage volume that is automatically provisioned when the EC2 instance is created.

These notebook instances allow you to perform common data science tasks such as exploration and feature engineering with NumPy, Pandas, and Matplotlib. You can also use Amazon SageMaker notebook instances to programmatically create training jobs, deploy models into production, and validate the deployed models.

Training Jobs

In order to train your model on Amazon SageMaker, you need to create a training job. Training jobs create dedicated compute instances in the AWS cloud that contain model-building code, load your training data from Amazon S3, execute the model-building code on your training data, and save the trained model to Amazon S3. When the training job is complete, the compute instances that were provisioned to support the training process will automatically be terminated. You will be billed for the compute costs required to train your model. Training jobs are usually created by using the high-level Amazon SageMaker SDK from a Jupyter Notebook file that is running on a notebook instance. The compute instances that will be used to train your model are created from Docker images. Amazon SageMaker requires that model-building code and any runtime libraries are encapsulated in a Docker image with a specific filesystem structure. The compute capabilities of the instances used to train your model depend on the CPU, RAM, and GPUs allocated to the instance. Amazon SageMaker allows you to select from a number of different configurations. These configurations are called *instance types* and you can specify the instance type when creating the training job with the Amazon SageMaker SDK. You can get a list of available training instance types and their respective compute capabilities at `https://aws.amazon.com/sagemaker/pricing/instance-types/`.

Prediction Instances

After your model has been trained using a training job, you will need to deploy it into production in order to use it. Deploying a model into production involves creating one or more compute instances, deploying your model onto these instances, and providing an API that can be used to make predictions using the deployed model. Unlike instances used to train your model, instances used to support predictions are not automatically terminated and you will be billed for the time that they are active. You can deploy your model using the Amazon SageMaker management console as well as the Amazon SageMaker SDK for Python. When you deploy your model, you will be able to specify the number and type of compute instances that you wish to provision. You can get a list of available prediction instance types and their respective compute capabilities at `https://aws.amazon.com/sagemaker/pricing/instance-types/`.

Prediction Endpoint and Endpoint Configuration

A prediction endpoint is an HTTPS REST API endpoint that can be used to get single predictions from a deployed model. The HTTP endpoint is secured using AWS Signature V4 authentication. An endpoint configuration ties together information on the location of a trained machine learning model, type of compute instances, and the auto-scaling policy associated with the prediction endpoint. You need to create an endpoint configuration first and then use the endpoint configurations to deploy the model to a prediction endpoint. You cannot change an endpoint configuration while the configuration is associated with an active prediction endpoint. Endpoint configurations and prediction endpoints can be created using both the Amazon SageMaker management console and the Amazon SageMaker SDK from a notebook instance.

Amazon SageMaker Batch Transform

A prediction endpoint will only provide the ability to make predictions on one observation at a time. If you need to make predictions on an entire dataset, you can use Amazon SageMaker Batch Transform to create a batch prediction job from a trained model. You can learn more about creating batch predictions with Amazon SageMaker at `https://docs.aws.amazon.com/sagemaker/latest/dg/ex1-batch-transform.html`.

Data Channels

Training and validating a machine learning model require different sets of data. These are commonly referred to as the training set, the test set, and the validation set. In Amazon SageMaker, these different sets of data are referred to as *channels*.

Data Sources and Formats

Amazon SageMaker requires that training, test, and validation data is stored in Amazon S3 buckets. The format of the data can be either CSV files or protobuf recordIO files. The latter is the preferred format.

Built-in Algorithms

Amazon SageMaker includes cloud-optimized implementations of a number of popular machine learning algorithms. If you are working in a notebook instance, you can train models using these algorithms locally on the notebook instance using the high-level Amazon SageMaker Python library. If you want to train your models on a cluster of dedicated EC2 instances, you can create these instances from Python code in your notebook file using the Amazon SageMaker Python library and algorithm-specific Docker images provided by Amazon. As of when this chapter was written, Amazon SageMaker provides implementations of the following algorithms:

- BlazingText Algorithm
- DeepAR Forecasting Algorithm
- Factorization Machines Algorithm
- Image Classification Algorithm (based on the ResNet deep learning network)
- IP Insights Algorithm
- K-Means Algorithm
- K-Nearest Neighbors Algorithm
- LDA (Latent Dirichlet Allocation) Algorithm
- Linear Learner Algorithm
- NTM (Neural Topic Model) Algorithm
- Object2Vec Algorithm
- Object Detection Algorithm (based on VGG and ResNet deep-learning networks)
- PCA (Principal Component Analysis) Algorithm
- RCF (Random Cut Forest) Algorithm
- Semantic Segmentation Algorithm
- Sequence-to-Sequence Algorithm
- XGBoost Algorithm

Amazon SageMaker notebook instances also include sample Jupyter Notebook files that demonstrate the use of these algorithms. You can find more information on each of these algorithms at the following link: https://docs.aws.amazon.com/sagemaker/latest/dg/algos.html.

Pricing and Availability

Amazon SageMaker is available on a pay-per-use model. You pay for the Amazon EC2 compute and Amazon S3 storage requirements for your Amazon SageMaker notebook instances, Amazon SageMaker cloud model-training instances, Amazon EC2 instances that support real-time prediction endpoints, and Amazon EC2 instances that are created on demand to support batch prediction operations. Some features of this service are included in the AWS free-tier account for a period of two months after the account is created. You can get more details on the pricing model at https://aws.amazon.com/sagemaker/pricing/.

Amazon SageMaker is not available in all regions. You can get information on the regions in which it is available from the following URL: https://aws.amazon.com/about-aws/global-infrastructure/regional-product-services/.

Creating an Amazon SageMaker Notebook Instance

In this section you will learn to use the Amazon SageMaker management console to create an Amazon SageMaker notebook instance and access the Jupyter Notebook server running on that instance from your web browser. Notebook instances are fully managed ML compute EC2 instances and relevant support infrastructure that allow the instance to be reachable across the Internet.

Amazon EC2 instances use IAM role-based security to access other resources in your AWS account. The most commonly accessed resources by Amazon SageMaker notebook instances are Amazon S3 buckets that contain model-training data, validation data, and buckets into which trained model files are saved. In order for your code in your notebook instance to access another resource in your account, such as an Amazon S3 bucket, the Amazon EC2 instance will need a set of credentials that it can use to access the underlying Amazon S3 APIs. While IAM roles provide the high-level mechanism by which the Amazon EC2 instance can obtain these credentials, behind the scenes, the AWS IAM service uses another AWS service called Amazon STS (Secure Token Service) to get the actual credentials.

In most use cases involving IAM roles, you do not need to concern yourself with Amazon STS. However, because Amazon STS has both a global endpoint and region-specific endpoints, and Amazon SageMaker makes use of region-specific Amazon STS endpoints, you must ensure that the region-specific Amazon STS endpoint is enabled for the AWS region in which you create your notebook instance. If you fail to do this, the Amazon SageMaker management console will be unable to create your notebook instance.

To enable the region-specific Amazon STS endpoint that corresponds to the region in which you wish to use Amazon SageMaker, log in to the AWS management console using your root account credentials and navigate to the IAM management console. Click the Account Settings link in the menu on the left side of the IAM management console and scroll down to the section titled Security Token Service Regions (Figure 16.1).

Ensure that the row corresponding to the region in which you intend to use Amazon SageMaker is listed as Active. If it is not active, you can use the Activate hyperlink in the same row to activate the endpoint. Once you have ensured that the region-specific Amazon STS is enabled, you can proceed to create an Amazon SageMaker notebook instance. While you can continue to use your root account credentials to access the Amazon SageMaker management console, it is recommended that you log out and log back in to the AWS management console using the dedicated sign-in link for your development IAM user account.

FIGURE 16.1

Enabling region-specific Amazon STS endpoints

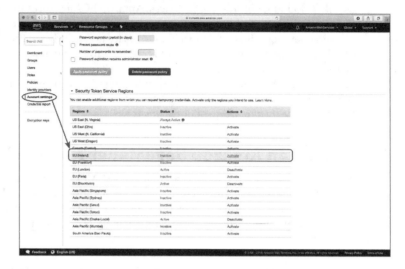

Once you have logged back in to the AWS management console, use the region selector to select a region where the Amazon SageMaker service is available. The screenshots in this section assume that the console is connected to the EU (Ireland) region. Select the Amazon SageMaker service from the Services drop-down list (Figure 16.2).

FIGURE 16.2

Accessing the Amazon SageMaker management console

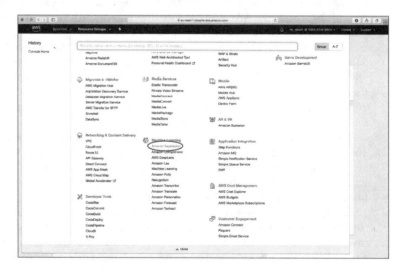

Navigate to the list of notebook instances in your Amazon SageMaker account by clicking the Notebook Instances link on the Amazon SageMaker dashboard. Click the Create Notebook

Instance button to create a new Internet-facing ML compute EC2 instance in your account with a Jupyter Notebook server hosted on the instance (Figure 16.3).

FIGURE 16.3
Navigating to the list of notebook instances

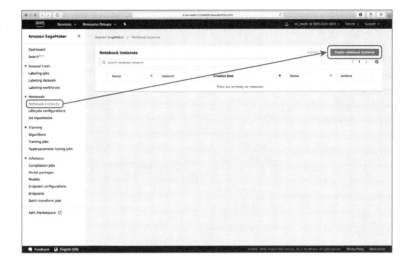

You will be asked to provide a name for the notebook instance and given an opportunity to customize some aspects of the notebook instance. By default, Amazon SageMaker will create an ml.t2-medium EC2 instance in the default Virtual Private Cloud and subnet in your AWS region. Once the EC2 instance is created, Amazon SageMaker will install an Anaconda distribution on the instance with a number of common Python packages that are required for data science. Amazon SageMaker will also configure a number of conda environments on the EC2 instance that will provide you the ability to choose from a number of commonly used combinations of Python language versions and packages.

You can choose a different type of EC2 instance, but keep in mind that the usage charge varies with EC2 instances and the ml.t2-medium EC2 instance is the cheapest option. This chapter will use a notebook instance called `kmeans-iris-flowers`. Type this value in the name field for the notebook instance (Figure 16.4) and scroll down to the Permissions And Encryption section.

FIGURE 16.4
Specifying the name of the new Amazon SageMaker notebook instance

Notebook instance settings

Notebook instance name

`kmeans-iris-flowers`

Maximum of 63 alphanumeric characters. Can include hyphens (-), but not spaces. Must be unique within your account in an AWS Region.

Notebook instance type

ml.t2.medium ▼

Elastic Inference Learn more ☑

none ▼

▶ **Additional configuration**

The Amazon EC2 instance that Amazon SageMaker will create for you uses IAM policies to govern what AWS resources in your account can be accessed by the code running on that instance. At the very least, the IAM role must provide access to one or more Amazon S3 buckets that will contain the data that you will use during data exploration, model building, and evaluation. Locate the IAM Role drop-down and choose the Create A New Role option (Figure 16.5).

FIGURE 16.5

Creating a new IAM role for the Amazon SageMaker notebook instance

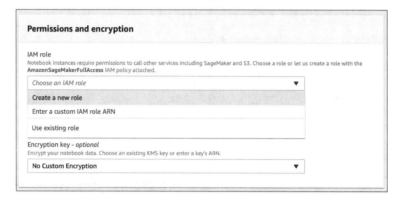

A pop-up window will appear asking you whether you want the role to allow access to specific Amazon S3 buckets. In a production scenario, you should be very specific about the bucket names you allow access to; however, for the purposes of this chapter, select the Any S3 Bucket option and click the Create Role button to create the new IAM role (Figure 16.6).

FIGURE 16.6

Specifying the permissions policy for the new IAM role for Amazon SageMaker

Create an IAM role   ✕

Passing an IAM role gives Amazon SageMaker permission to perform actions in other AWS services on your behalf. Creating a role here will grant permissions described by the **AmazonSageMakerFullAccess** ⬈ IAM policy to the role you create.

The IAM role you create will provide access to:

⊘ S3 buckets you specify - *optional*

  ○ Specific S3 buckets

      | Example: bucket-name-1, bucket-name-2, b |

      Comma delimited. ARNs, "*" and "/" are not supported.

  ◉ Any S3 bucket
      Allow users that have access to your notebook instance access to any bucket and its contents in your account.

  ○ None

⊘ Any S3 bucket with "sagemaker" in the name

⊘ Any S3 object with "sagemaker" in the name

⊘ Any S3 object with the tag "sagemaker" and value "true"   See Object tagging ⬈

⊘ S3 bucket with a Bucket Policy allowing access to SageMaker   See S3 bucket policies ⬈

                                                          Cancel   Create role

It is worth noting that even if you do not specify any specific bucket names, the IAM role will be built with a policy document that will allow access to any Amazon S3 bucket with the word sagemaker in its name. It is also worth noting that you will need to ensure that the Amazon S3 buckets you access from the notebook instance are in the same region as your notebook instance; otherwise you will incur additional cross-region data transfer charges.

Once you click the Create Role button, the pop-up window will be dismissed and a new IAM role that begins with the words AmazonSageMaker-ExecutionRole will be created in your account, and selected in the IAM Role drop-down list (Figure 16.7).

FIGURE 16.7

New IAM role for Amazon SageMaker

You can if you wish, at a later date, use the IAM management console to modify the permissions policy associated with this IAM role to control what AWS resources can be accessed from your notebook instance as well as what actions can be performed on those resources. If, in the future, you want to create a new notebook instance, you can use this same role with future instances.

Leave the rest of the options on the page at their defaults. Scroll down to the bottom of the page and click the Create Notebook Instance button to create the hosted notebook. It may take a few minutes for AWS to create a new EC2 instance and install the relevant software on the instance. Once the notebook is ready, you will see it listed in your Amazon SageMaker management console with the status of "In Service" (Figure 16.8).

It is worth noting that when the notebook instance is listed as In Service, you will be billed for the compute resources utilized to maintain the notebook instance, whether you use it or not. It is therefore recommended to stop or delete notebook instances when they are not needed. The data you store on a notebook instance is stored on a general-purpose SSD volume, and you are billed for the associated storage costs. While stopping a notebook instance will ensure you are not billed for the compute resources required to host the instance, you will continue to be billed for storage costs to the SSD volume. When you restart the notebook instance, Amazon SageMaker will provision new compute resources to host your notebook and attach the SSD volume to the new virtual server. The effect of this is that data you save on your notebook instance will persist between stopping and restarting the instance; however, you will incur costs even when the notebook instance is stopped. When a notebook instance is stopped, you can change instance settings such as the IAM role associated with the instance, the EC2 instance family used to support the instance, and so on. A deleted instance does not consume any compute resources or storage resources, and any files that you have created on the notebook instance will be lost once the instance is deleted. You can use the Actions menu to manage the state of a notebook instance as well as edit the settings of stopped instances (Figure 16.9).

FIGURE 16.8
Amazon SageMaker management console showing the new notebook instance

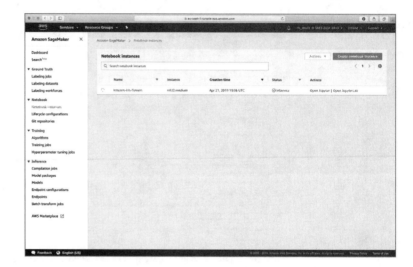

FIGURE 16.9
Amazon SageMaker notebook instance management

When a notebook is listed as In Service, you can access the Jupyter Notebook server using the Open Jupyter link. Amazon SageMaker also allows you to use JupyterLab to manage your .ipnyb notebook files. JupyterLab provides an IDE-like environment in which you can create and manage your Python .ipynb notebook files. This book does not use JupyterLab.

Preparing Test and Training Data

Creating a machine learning solution using Amazon SageMaker requires that you first explore the training data, select your features, and prepare a test and training dataset. While you can download datasets onto your notebook instance and use them within your Python notebook files for feature engineering, the final data for model building and evaluation must reside in an Amazon S3 bucket, and both the AWS boto3 SDK for Python and the Amazon SageMaker SDK for Python provide capabilities to transfer data from your notebook instance to Amazon S3 buckets. Since an Amazon S3 bucket is a must-have item for using Amazon SageMaker, the first thing you need to do is create one or more Amazon S3 buckets in your account, in the same AWS region as the Amazon SageMaker service.

In this chapter, the examples assume you have created two buckets:

◆ `awsml-sagemaker-source`

◆ `awsml-sagemaker-results`

Since bucket names need to be globally unique, if you intend to replicate the examples in this chapter you will need to substitute references to these buckets with buckets from your account.

When it comes to data exploration and feature engineering, you can perform these operations using the standard Python libraries such as NumPy, Pandas, and Scikit-learn from a Jupyter Notebook file running on your local computer or running on a cloud-based Amazon SageMaker notebook instance. You may find using a local notebook instance faster and more cost-effective for data exploration and visualization tasks. If you are using the cloud-based Amazon SageMaker notebook instance for data exploration and feature engineering, keep in mind that not only will you have to upload the data to Amazon S3, but you will also have to pay the compute costs for the notebook instance, ensure you to stop the instance when you are not using it, and deal with the latency between executing Python code on a remote server and having the results delivered to your web browser.

The machine learning model that will be built in this chapter is based on the popular Iris flowers dataset. To keep this chapter focused on model building and making predictions with Amazon SageMaker, you will not perform any feature engineering on the dataset. A copy of the Kaggle version of the Iris flowers dataset as well as files that contain the test and training sets are provided with the resources that accompany this chapter.

Log in to the AWS management console using the dedicated sign-in link for your development IAM user account. Navigate to the Amazon S3 management console and locate the `awsml-sagemaker-source` bucket (Figure 16.10).

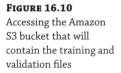

FIGURE 16.10
Accessing the Amazon S3 bucket that will contain the training and validation files

Locate the `datasets/iris_dataset/Kaggle` folder in the resources that accompany this chapter and upload the `iris_train.csv` and `iris_test.csv` files to the Amazon S3 bucket (Figure 16.11).

FIGURE 16.11
Uploading the pre-split training and test data files to the Amazon S3 bucket

Techniques to prepare training and test datasets have been covered in Chapter 5. A Jupyter Notebook file called `PreparingDatasets.ipynb` is included with the resources that accompany this chapter. This file contains the Python code that was used to generate the `iris_train.csv` and `iris_test.csv` files on an instance of Jupyter Notebook running locally on the author's computer.

Training a Scikit-Learn Model on an Amazon SageMaker Notebook Instance

In this section you will train and evaluate a machine learning model on an Amazon SageMaker notebook instance using an algorithm implemented by Scikit-learn. Training on the notebook instance implies that you only have at your disposal the vCPU and vRAM capacity of the EC2 instance that is hosting the notebook server. Amazon SageMaker also allows you to use your notebook instance to create a training job that will train your model on dedicated high-performance compute instances and deploy the trained model on a cluster of high-performance compute instances that can be accessed using a REST prediction endpoint. You will learn to train models on dedicated compute instances later in this chapter.

Training a model locally on a notebook instance is only feasible if you want to use an algorithm that is implemented by a Python library such as Scikit-learn, and are in the exploratory phase of your data science project where you work with a small dataset (or subset of a larger dataset) to pick the best algorithm and hyperparameter combinations. Training on your notebook instance is faster (and cheaper) because you do not have to wait or pay for the additional compute costs involved with dedicated training instances. Training on your notebook instance is not feasible if you are training a complex deep-learning model over a large training set. Such models will benefit from high-performance parallel training that is provided by a cluster of dedicated cloud-based instances.

The model that will be implemented in this section is a classification model using the k-means clustering algorithm. The k-means algorithm is a simple algorithm that attempts to assign input observations into k clusters. The algorithm is unsupervised and does not require pre-labeled instances; you specify the number of clusters and it assigns each member of the training dataset into one of the clusters purely based on the feature variables. It is worth noting that Amazon SageMaker also provides a built-in implementation of the k-means algorithm, but you cannot use the built-in implementation to train on your local notebook instance.

Clustering algorithms are used to find groupings in data, but they can also be used to implement instance-based learning systems. Once all the observations have been assigned to the k clusters, the mathematical centroid of each cluster can be computed and stored for future predictions. The distance between the cluster centroids and a new observation for which a prediction is desired can be computed, and the cluster corresponding to the closest centroid can be returned as the predicted result. There are some variations on the manner in which the target cluster is selected, but the general idea remains the same.

The model you will build in this section will use the Iris flowers dataset, which you uploaded to an Amazon S3 bucket in the previous section. Navigate to the list of notebook instances in your Amazon SageMaker account by clicking the Notebook Instances link on the Amazon SageMaker dashboard. Launch the kmeans-iris-flowers notebook instance and create a new Jupyter Notebook file using the conda_python3 kernel (Figure 16.12).

FIGURE 16.12
Creating a new Jupyter Notebook on an Amazon SageMaker notebook instance

A new Jupyter Notebook file called Untitled.ipnyb will be created for you on the Amazon SageMaker notebook instance. The new notebook file will also open automatically in a new browser tab. Change the title of the notebook to sklearn-local-kmeans-iris-flowers (see Figure 16.13).

FIGURE 16.13
Changing the title of a
Jupyter Notebook file

Click on the notebook title
to rename the notebook.

Scikit-learn implements the k-means algorithm in a class called KMeans in the `sklearn.cluster` package. Using Scikit-learn to train machine learning models was covered in Chapter 5, and therefore this section will assume that you know how to use Scikit-learn. Type the following code in an empty notebook cell:

```python
import boto3
import sagemaker
import io

import pandas as pd
import numpy as np

# load training and validation dataset from Amazon S3
s3_client = boto3.client('s3')
s3_bucket_name='awsml-sagemaker-source'

response = s3_client.get_object(Bucket='awsml-sagemaker-source',
Key='iris_train.csv')
response_body = response["Body"].read()
df_iris_train = pd.read_csv(io.BytesIO(response_body), header=0, delimiter=",",
low_memory=False)

response = s3_client.get_object(Bucket='awsml-sagemaker-source',
Key='iris_test.csv')
response_body = response["Body"].read()
df_iris_test = pd.read_csv(io.BytesIO(response_body), header=0,
index_col=False, delimiter=",", low_memory=False)

# separate training and validation dataset into separate features and target
variables
# assume that the first column in each dataset is the target variable.
# training a k-means classifier does not require labelled data, and therefore
# df_iris_target_train will not be used.
df_iris_features_train = df_iris_train.iloc[:,1:]
df_iris_target_train = df_iris_train.iloc[:,0]

df_iris_features_test= df_iris_test.iloc[:,1:]
df_iris_target_test = df_iris_test.iloc[:,0]
```

```
# create a KMeans multi-class classifier.
from sklearn.cluster import KMeans

kmeans_model = KMeans(n_clusters=3)
kmeans_model.fit(df_iris_features_train)

# use the  model to create predictions on the test set
kmeans_predictions = kmeans_model.predict(df_iris_features_test)
```

This code reads the `iris_train.csv` and `iris_test.csv` files from the Amazon S3 bucket called `awsml-sagemaker-source` and loads the data in these files into Pandas dataframes. Since you are going to use the k-means clustering algorithm, you do not need the target values when training the classifier, and therefore the code trains a KMeans classifier on the contents of the `df_iris_features_train` dataset alone.

Once the model is trained, you use it to make predictions on the test dataset. The clusters returned by the model are integers 0, 1, and 2 and you can use the Python `print()` function to examine the predictions:

```
# print predicted classes
print (kmeans_predictions)
[0 1 2 1 1 1 1 2 1 1 2 0 1 0 2 0 0 2 2 2 1 0 1 1 1 1 1 1 0 1 0 1 0 0 1 1 1
 2]
```

In the Iris dataset, the target attribute `species` is a categorical string. Since the k-means classifier did not use the labels associated with the training data, there is no direct relation between the cluster numbers 0, 1, and 2 as returned by the classifier and the Iris-setosa, Iris-versicolor, and Iris-virginica labels used in the Iris dataset. If you were to use the Python `print()` function to examine the labels associated with the test set, you would see that they are all strings:

```
# print expected classes
print (df_iris_target_test.values.ravel())

['Iris-setosa' 'Iris-versicolor' 'Iris-virginica' 'Iris-versicolor'
 'Iris-virginica' 'Iris-virginica' 'Iris-versicolor' 'Iris-virginica'
 'Iris-versicolor' 'Iris-virginica' 'Iris-virginica' 'Iris-setosa'
 'Iris-versicolor' 'Iris-setosa' 'Iris-virginica' 'Iris-setosa'
 'Iris-setosa' 'Iris-virginica' 'Iris-virginica' 'Iris-virginica'
 'Iris-virginica' 'Iris-setosa' 'Iris-virginica' 'Iris-versicolor'
 'Iris-versicolor' 'Iris-versicolor' 'Iris-versicolor' 'Iris-versicolor'
 'Iris-setosa' 'Iris-versicolor' 'Iris-setosa' 'Iris-versicolor'
 'Iris-setosa' 'Iris-setosa' 'Iris-versicolor' 'Iris-versicolor'
 'Iris-versicolor' 'Iris-virginica']
```

You could use the `LabelEncoder` class provided by Scikit-learn to convert the target categorical attribute from string values to integers. The following snippet converts the strings `Iris-setosa`, `Iris-versicolor`, and `Iris-virginica` into numbers 0, 1, 2 and computes the confusion matrix to get an idea of the performance of the classifier. However, this mapping was entirely your choice, and were you to select a different mapping, the numbers in the confusion matrix would change:

```
# compute confusion matrix if
# Iris-setosa = 0
```

```
# Iris-versicolor = 1
# Iris-virginica = 2

# Convert target variables 'species' from strings into integers.
from sklearn.preprocessing import LabelEncoder
labelEncoder = LabelEncoder()
labelEncoder.fit(df_iris_target_test)
df_iris_target_test = labelEncoder.transform(df_iris_target_test)

from sklearn.metrics import confusion_matrix
cm_kmeans = confusion_matrix(df_iris_target_test, kmeans_predictions)
```

```
# print confusion matrix
print(cm_kmeans)
[[10  0  0]
 [ 0  0 15]
 [ 0  8  5]]
```

The confusion matrix indicates that the model is classifying most observations correctly, except for five instances of the third class Iris-virginica that have been classed as the second class, Iris-versicolor.

Training a Scikit-Learn Model on a Dedicated Training Instance

In this section, you will use the AWS SageMaker SDK for Python from your notebook instance to create a training job that will create a dedicated training instance and train a Scikit-learn k-means classifier on the instance. The trained model will be stored in an Amazon S3 bucket, after which you will use another function provided by the Amazon SageMaker Python SDK to deploy the model to a dedicated prediction instance and create a prediction endpoint. Finally, you will use the AWS SageMaker SDK for Python to interact with this prediction endpoint from your Jupyter Notebook file to make predictions on data the model has not seen (the test set).

A dedicated training instance is an EC2 instance that is used to train a model from data in an Amazon S3 bucket and save the trained model to another Amazon S3 bucket. However, unlike a notebook instance, a dedicated training instance does not have a Jupyter Notebook server and is terminated automatically once the training process is complete. Dedicated training instances are created from Docker images. For built-in machine learning algorithms, Amazon SageMaker packages the algorithms in Docker images that include the necessary software to train a machine learning model. The location of input and output buckets, as well as any hyperparameters for model training, are usually specified as command-line arguments when the Docker container is instantiated from the image.

In addition to Docker images for built-in algorithms, Amazon SageMaker also provides Docker images that include standard machine learning libraries like Scikit-learn, Google TensorFlow, and Apache MXNet. Regardless of whether the Docker image contains an implementation of a built-in algorithm, or a general-purpose machine-learning library, the Docker images themselves are stored in Docker registries within each AWS region. You will need to provide the path to the Docker image when creating the training job. You can find the paths to the Docker registries for Scikit-learn Docker images in each supported region at https://docs. aws.amazon.com/sagemaker/latest/dg/pre-built-docker-containers-frameworks.html.

The dedicated EC2 training instances, once created, will need to assume an IAM role that will allow code running in the training instances access to other resources in your AWS account such as Amazon S3 buckets that contain the training data. Since the IAM role that is used to create your notebook instance has the correct permissions to access the relevant AWS resources, the most common approach is to use the same IAM role for the EC2 training instances.

The Docker image that allows you to create a Scikit-learn training instance does not come pre-packaged with code that builds any particular type of classifier. You can think of a Scikit-learn training instance as a barebones virtual machine that comes pre-packaged with Python, Scikit-learn, and a number of popular machine learning Python frameworks. To build a model from training data on a Scikit-learn training instance, you will need to write your model-building code in a Python script file and execute the file on the training instance. The model training script will have code that can access training data from an Amazon S3 bucket, train a model using Scikit-learn classes, and store the trained model in an Amazon S3 bucket.

To get started, launch the kmeans-iris-flowers notebook instance and use the Upload button to upload the sklearn-kmeans-training-script.py file provided with the resources that accompany this chapter (Figure 16.14).

FIGURE 16.14

Uploading a file to a notebook instance

The Python code within this file is presented here:

```python
import argparse
import pandas as pd
import os

from sklearn.cluster import KMeans
from sklearn.externals import joblib
from sklearn.preprocessing import LabelEncoder

if __name__ == '__main__':
    parser = argparse.ArgumentParser()

    # Read any hyperparameters
    parser.add_argument('--n_clusters', type=int, default=3)

    # Sagemaker specific arguments, use environment values for defaults.
    parser.add_argument('--model_dir', type=str,
        default=os.environ.get('SM_MODEL_DIR'))
    parser.add_argument('--train', type=str,
        default=os.environ.get('SM_CHANNEL_TRAIN'))

    args = parser.parse_args()
```

```
# Read input file iris_train.csv .
input_file = os.path.join(args.train, 'iris_train.csv')
df_iris_train = pd.read_csv(input_file, header=0, engine="python")

# Convert target variables 'species' from strings into integers.
labelEncoder = LabelEncoder()
labelEncoder.fit(df_iris_train['species'])
df_iris_train['species'] = labelEncoder.transform(df_iris_train['species'])

# Separate training and validation dataset into
# separate features and target variables.
#
# Assume that the first column in each dataset is the target variable.
#
# k-means does not require labelled training data, therefore
# df_iris_target_train will not be used.
df_iris_features_train = df_iris_train.iloc[:,1:]
df_iris_target_train = df_iris_train.iloc[:,0]

# Create a K-Means multi-class classifier.
kmeans_model = KMeans(n_clusters=args.n_clusters)
kmeans_model.fit(df_iris_features_train)

# Save the model.
joblib.dump(kmeans_model, os.path.join(args.model_dir,
    "sklearn-kmeans-model.joblib"))
```

```
# deserializer.
def model_fn(model_dir):
    model = joblib.load(os.path.join(model_dir, "sklearn-kmeans-model.joblib"))
    return model
```

Let's briefly look at the contents of this script. When you create a training job using the SageMaker Python SDK, you provide the name of the file that contains the training script, as well as any hyperparameters required by the script. The k-means model we will build will expect a single hyperparameter called n_clusters, which will be injected into the constructor of the Scikit-learn KMeans class.

When the EC2 instance starts up, your script file will be installed as a Python module with the same name as the name of the script file and executed using a command-line statement similar to:

```
python -m <your_script> --<your_hyperparameters>
```

For example, if the training job were created using the script file listed earlier, and the value of the n_clusters hyperparameter is specified as 3, then the command-line statement that will be executed on the training instance to kick off the training process will be:

```
python -m sklearn-kmeans-training-script --num_clusters=3
```

Within your script, you place your model training code inside an `if __name__ == '__main__':` condition block. Placing the training code inside this `if` condition block ensures that the code is only executed when the module is executed as the main module from the command line, and not when the module is executed by importing it into another Python file with a standard Python `import` statement.

Within the model-training code, you can use an `ArgumentParser` object to read any command-line arguments that were passed to the module by Amazon SageMaker. The training job that you will create later in this section will pass the number of k-means clusters as a hyperparameter. The following snippet demonstrates how you can read command-line arguments in your script file:

```
parser = argparse.ArgumentParser()

# Expect an argument called n_clusters, apply a default value if
# argument is missing.
parser.add_argument('--n_clusters', type=int, default=3)

# Parse the arguments
args = parser.parse_args()

# You can now access the n_clusters command-line argument
# using args.n_clusters
```

In addition to hyperparameters that can be used to instantiate Scikit-learn classes, your script will also need some additional Amazon SageMaker–specific information such as the location of the training dataset, and the location where the trained model should be saved. You could pass this information to the script as additional command-line arguments, or you could read some of this information from environment variables within your script.

When a training instance is created, Amazon SageMaker automatically sets up several environment variables, and these environments can also be accessed within the script. If your script needs an Amazon SageMaker–specific runtime value that has not been provided a command-line argument, a common practice is to fall back to using the environment variables as the defaults. The full list of environment variables that are available to scripts running in training instances is available at `https://github.com/aws/sagemaker-containers`.

The most common environment variables you are likely to read are:

- ◆ `SM_OUTPUT_DATADIR`: Contains a filesystem path within the training instance where your script can store temporary artifacts that are needed to create the machine learning model. This local filesystem path is behind the scenes, mapped to an Amazon S3 bucket, and therefore the files will be written to an Amazon S3 bucket.

- ◆ `SM_MODEL_DIR`: Contains a filesystem path within the training instance where your script will store the trained model. This local filesystem path is behind the scenes, mapped to an Amazon S3 bucket, and therefore the trained model will be written to an Amazon S3 bucket.

- ◆ `SM_CHANNEL_TRAINING`: Contains a filesystem path within the training instance where your script can read the training data. This local filesystem path is behind the scenes, mapped to an Amazon S3 bucket, and therefore the training data will be read from an Amazon S3 bucket.

The following snippet demonstrates how you can use the `ArgumentParser` object to read Amazon SageMaker–specific runtime information from the command-line arguments, and fall back to using environment variables if the values have not been specified on the command line:

```
parser = argparse.ArgumentParser()

# SageMaker specific arguments.
# Defaults are set in the environment variables.
parser.add_argument('--model-dir', type=str,
    default=os.environ['SM_MODEL_DIR'])
parser.add_argument('--train', type=str,
    default=os.environ['SM_CHANNEL_TRAIN'])

# Parse the arguments
args = parser.parse_args()

# You can now access the S3 bucket where the training files are stored
# via args.train
```

The actual code to create a Scikit-learn k-means classifier is similar to the code that was presented in the previous section when you trained the classifier on the local notebook instance. The model-building code in the script file starts by loading the training data present in a CSV file called `iris_train.csv` in the Amazon S3 bucket referenced by `args.train` and loads the contents of this file into a Pandas dataframe:

```
# Read input file iris_train.csv .
input_file = os.path.join(args.train, 'iris_train.csv')
df_iris_train = pd.read_csv(input_file, header=0, engine="python")
```

Next, the model-building code uses Scikit-learn's `LabelEncoder` class to convert the categorical attribute `species` from discrete strings to integers. Before conversion, the target attribute (`species`) can have one of the string values `Iris-setosa`, `Iris-versicolor`, or `Iris-virginica`. After conversion, the target attribute will have one of the integer values 0, 1, 2, respectively:

```
# Convert target variables 'species' from strings into integers.
labelEncoder = LabelEncoder()
labelEncoder.fit(df_iris_train['species'])
df_iris_train['species'] = labelEncoder.transform(df_iris_train['species'])
```

The features and target variables are then extracted from the `df_iris_train` dataframe into separate dataframe objects and a `KMeans` classifier is trained on the features. The `n_clusters` argument of the `KMeans` constructor is assigned a value of `args.n_clusters`, which is a hyper-parameter read from the command line:

```
# Separate training and validation dataset into
# separate features and target variables.
```

```
#
# Assume that the first column in each dataset is the target variable.
#
# k-means does not require labelled training data, therefore
# df_iris_target_train will not be used.

df_iris_features_train = df_iris_train.iloc[:,1:]
df_iris_target_train = df_iris_train.iloc[:,0]

# Create a K-Means multi-class classifier.
kmeans_model = KMeans(n_clusters=args.n_clusters)
kmeans_model.fit(df_iris_features_train)
```

After the model is trained, it is saved to the Amazon S3 bucket specified in `args.model_dir` using the following statement:

```
# Save the model.
joblib.dump(kmeans_model, os.path.join(args.model_dir,
    "sklearn-kmeans-model.joblib"))
```

The model will be saved to a file called `sklearn-kmeans-model.joblib`. It is worth noting that the training instance does not save the model artifacts automatically. If you do not explicitly save the model, the training instance will terminate after model training is complete and you will not have access to the model, and therefore will not be able to create a prediction instance.

The script file must also contain a function called `model_fn()`, which by convention is a function that will be used to read the model artifacts to create a prediction instance:

```
# deserializer.
def model_fn(model_dir):
    model = joblib.load(os.path.join(model_dir, "sklearn-kmeans-model.joblib"))
    return model
```

Now that you have prepared a model-training script file, it is time to use a Jupyter Notebook file to create a training job. Create a new Jupyter Notebook file on your notebook instance using the conda_python3 kernel. Change the title of the notebook to `sklearn-kmeans-iris-flowers` and type the following code in an empty notebook cell:

```
import sagemaker

# Get a SageMaker-compatible role used by this Notebook Instance.
role = sagemaker.get_execution_role()

# get a SageMaker session object, that can be
# used to manage the interaction with the SageMaker API.
sagemaker_session = sagemaker.Session()

# train a Scikit-learn KMeans classifier on a dedicated instance
# send hyperparameter n_clusters = 3.
from sagemaker.sklearn.estimator import SKLearn
```



```
sklearn = SKLearn(entry_point='sklearn-kmeans-training-script.py',
                  train_instance_type='ml.m4.xlarge',
                  role=role,
                  sagemaker_session=sagemaker_session,
                  hyperparameters={'n_clusters': 3},
                  output_path='s3://awsml-sagemaker-results/')

sklearn.fit({'train': 's3://awsml-sagemaker-source/'})
```

Execute the code in the notebook cell to launch a training job that will result in SageMaker creating a dedicated ml.m4.xlarge EC2 instance from the default Docker image for Scikit-learn model training. You can specify a different instance type, but keep in mind that more powerful instance types have higher running costs associated with them. The SKLearn class is part of the AWS SageMaker Python SDK and provides a convenient mechanism to handle end-to-end training and deployment of Scikit-learn models. The constructor for the class accepts several arguments, including the path to the Python script file that contains your model-building code, the type of training instance that you wish to create, the IAM role that should be assigned to the new instance, and model-building hyperparameters that will be passed as command-line arguments to your script running on the instance. You can learn more about the parameters of the SKLearn class at `https://sagemaker.readthedocs.io/en/stable/sagemaker.sklearn.html`.

When you execute the code in a notebook cell, Amazon SageMaker will create a new dedicated training instance and execute your script file within the instance once the instance is ready. This can be a time-consuming process and may take several minutes. While the training process is underway, you will see various status messages printed below the notebook cell (Figure 16.15).

FIGURE 16.15

Using a notebook instance to create a training job

The training process is complete when you see lines similar to the following in the output:

```
2019-04-28 19:31:46,805 sagemaker-containers INFO     Reporting training SUCCESS

2019-04-28 19:31:54 Completed - Training job completed
Billable seconds: 24
```

After the training process is complete, Amazon SageMaker will automatically terminate the instance that was created to support the training. The model that was created will be saved to the `awsml-sagemaker-results` bucket in a folder that has the structure `<job name>/output/`. You can find the value of the job name by inspecting the `job_name` attribute of the `SM_TRAINING_ENV` variable in the log messages. You can also access the full path to the model artifact by examining the value of the `module_dir` attribute:

```
SM_TRAINING_ENV={
"additional_framework_parameters":{},
"channel_input_dirs":{"train":"/opt/ml/input/data/train"},
"current_host":"algo-1",
"framework_module":"sagemaker_sklearn_container.training:main",
"hosts":["algo-1"],
"hyperparameters":{"n_clusters":3},
"input_config_dir":"/opt/ml/input/config",
"input_data_config":{
    "train":{
        "RecordWrapperType":"None",
        "S3DistributionType":"FullyReplicated",
        "TrainingInputMode":"File"
    }
},
"input_dir":"/opt/ml/input",
"job_name":"sagemaker-scikit-learn-2019-04-28-19-35-16-021",
"log_level":20,
"model_dir":"/opt/ml/model",
"module_dir":"s3://awsml-sagemaker-results/sagemaker-scikit-learn-2019-04-28-19--
35-16-021/source/sourcedir.tar.gz",
"module_name":"sklearn-kmeans-training-script",
"network_interface_name":"ethwe",
"num_cpus":4,
"num_gpus":0,
"output_data_dir":"/opt/ml/output/data",
"output_dir":"/opt/ml/output",
"output_intermediate_dir":"/opt/ml/output/intermediate",
"resource_config":{
    "current_host":"algo-1",
    "hosts":["algo-1"],
    "network_interface_name":"ethwe"
},
"user_entry_point":"sklearn-kmeans-training-script.py"
}
```

In the log messages shown here, the file referenced in the `module_dir` attribute is `s3://awsml-sagemaker-results/sagemaker-scikit-learn-2019-04-28-19-35-16-021/source/sourcedir.tar.gz`, and not `sklearn-kmeans-model.joblib` as you had specified in your Python training script. This is because Amazon SageMaker compresses the model artifacts into a `tar.gz` file before uploading to Amazon S3. If you were to download and extract the `tar.gz` file, you would find the `sklearn-kmeans-model.joblib` file inside it.

You do not necessarily have to make a note of the location of the model or the job name listed in the messages below the notebook cell. You can also view a list of trained models from the Models menu item of the AWS SageMaker management console (Figure 16.16) and access the model artifact file from there.

FIGURE 16.16

List of trained models

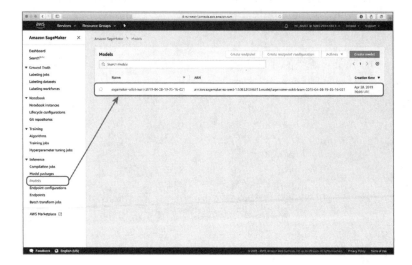

Now that you have a trained model, you can deploy the model to one or more dedicated prediction instances and then either create an HTTPS API endpoint for creating predictions on one item at a time, or create a batch transform job to obtain predictions on entire datasets. Using batch transforms is not covered in this chapter; however, you can find more information at
`https://docs.aws.amazon.com/sagemaker/latest/dg/ex1-batch-transform.html`.

You can deploy models into prediction instances using several different methods, including using the AWS SageMaker Python SDK and the AWS management console. Regardless of the manner in which you choose to deploy the model, the process of deployment involves first creating an endpoint configuration object, and then using the endpoint configuration object to create the prediction instances and the HTTPS endpoint that can be used to get inferences from the deployed model. The endpoint configuration contains information on the location of the model file, the type and number of compute instances that the model will be deployed to, and the auto-scaling policy to be used to scale up the number of instances as needed.

If you use the high-level Amazon SageMaker Python SDK to deploy your model, the SDK provides a convenience function that takes care of creating the endpoint configuration, creation of compute resources, deployment of the model, and the creation of the HTTPS endpoint. If you use the lower-level AWS boto3 Python SDK you will need to perform the individual steps in sequence yourself. Keep in mind that prediction instances incur additional costs and are not automatically terminated after you have made predictions.

Execute the following code in an empty cell of the `sklearn-kmeans-iris-flowers` notebook to deploy the trained Scikit-learn model to a single ML compute instance and create an HTTPS endpoint:

```
# create a prediction instance
predictor = sklearn.deploy(initial_instance_count=1,
instance_type="ml.m4.xlarge")
```

This code assumes that the `sklearn` object has been created in the previous notebook cell where you trained the model. This is important because the `deploy()` function does not have an argument that lets you specify the path to the model file, but instead uses whatever model file is referenced within the `sklearn` object.

When you execute this code, Amazon SageMaker will take several minutes to create an endpoint configuration, create the compute instances, deploy your model onto the instances, and create an HTTP endpoint. You can view the status of the process in log messages listed below the notebook cell:

```
INFO:sagemaker:Creating model with name: sagemaker-scikit-learn-2019-04-30-07-
13-14-329
INFO:sagemaker:Creating endpoint with name sagemaker-scikit-learn-2019-04-30-
07-13-14-329
```

Once the prediction endpoint is created, the `deploy()` function will return an object of class `SKLearnPredictor`, which provides a convenience function called `predict()` that can be used to make predictions from the HTTPS endpoint. The prediction endpoint is Internet-facing and is secured using AWS Signature V4 authentication. You can access this endpoint in a variety of ways, including the AWS CLI, tools such as Postman, and the language-specific AWS SDKs. If you use the AWS CLI, or one of the AWS SDKs, authentication will be achieved behind the scenes for you. You can learn more about AWS Signature V4 at `https://docs.aws.amazon.com/AmazonS3/latest/API/sig-v4-authenticating-requests.html`.

If you want to expose the prediction endpoint as a service to your consumers, you can create an endpoint on an Amazon API Gateway instance, and set up the API Gateway to execute an AWS Lambda function when it receives a request. You can then use one of the language-specific SDKs in the AWS Lambda function to interact with the prediction endpoint. The advantage of this approach is that your clients do not need to worry about AWS Signature V4 authentication, and an API Gateway can provide several features that are critical to managing the business-related aspects of a commercial API service, such as credential management, credential rotation, support for OIDC, API versioning, traffic management and so on.

If you are using the AWS SageMaker Python SDK from a notebook instance, you can use the `predict()` function of the `SKLearnPredictor` instance to make single predictions. Behind the scenes, the `predict()` function will use a temporary set of credentials associated with the IAM role assumed by the notebook instance to authenticate with the prediction endpoint. Execute the following code in an empty notebook cell to make predictions on the test dataset stored in the file `iris_test.csv` using the `predict()` function:

```
# load iris_test.csv from Amazon S3 and split the features
# and target variables into separate dataframes.
import boto3
import sagemaker
import io

import pandas as pd
import numpy as np

# load training and validation dataset from Amazon S3
s3_client = boto3.client('s3')
s3_bucket_name='awsml-sagemaker-source'
```

```
response = s3_client.get_object(Bucket='awsml-sagemaker-source',
Key='iris_test.csv')
response_body = response["Body"].read()
df_iris_test = pd.read_csv(io.BytesIO(response_body), header=0,
index_col=False, delimiter=",", low_memory=False)

# Convert target variables 'species' from strings into integers.
from sklearn.preprocessing import LabelEncoder
labelEncoder = LabelEncoder()
labelEncoder.fit(df_iris_test['species'])
df_iris_test['species'] = labelEncoder.transform(df_iris_test['species'])

# separate validation dataset into separate features and target variables
# assume that the first column in each dataset is the target variable.
df_iris_features_test= df_iris_test.iloc[:,1:]
df_iris_target_test = df_iris_test.iloc[:,0]


# use the prediction instance to create predictions.
predictions = predictor.predict(df_iris_features_test.values)
```

You can use the Python print() function to examine the predictions:

```
print (predictions)


[1 2 0 2 2 2 2 0 2 2 0 1 2 1 0 1 1 0 0 0 2 1 2 2 2 2 2 2 1 2 1 2 1 1 2 2 2
 0]
```

To terminate the prediction instances and the associated HTTPS endpoint, you can, once again, use the high-level interface provided by the AWS SageMaker Python SDK. Execute the following code in a free notebook cell to terminate the prediction endpoint and deactivate the prediction endpoint:

```
sklearn.delete_endpoint()

INFO:sagemaker:Deleting endpoint with name: sagemaker-scikit-learn-2019-04-28-19-35-16-
021
```

You can also use the AWS SageMaker management console to view the list of active prediction endpoints, deactivate a prediction endpoint and terminate the associated prediction instances, and create new prediction endpoints from endpoint configurations.

Training a Model Using a Built-in Algorithm on a Dedicated Training Instance

In the previous sections of this chapter you created Scikit-learn-based k-means classifiers and trained them on the notebook instance as well as on a dedicated training instance. In this section you will use your notebook instance to train a k-means classifier on the Iris flowers dataset using Amazon SageMaker's built-in implementation of the k-means algorithm. Amazon SageMaker provides cloud-optimized implementations of several popular machine learning algorithms, and k-means is one of them. The steps involved in training a model with a built-in algorithm are similar to, if not somewhat easier than, training the model on a dedicated Scikit-learn instance. Amazon SageMaker provides Docker images for each built-in algorithm. These algorithm-specific Docker images are very similar to the generic Scikit-learn Docker image, except that you do not need to deploy any model building onto them. The code is already present in the image and preconfigured to accept a standard set of inputs, such as hyperparameters and data location from command-line arguments.

The general format of the path to an algorithm-specific Docker image is as follows:

```
<ecr_path>/<algorithm>:<tag>
```

The `ecr_path` portion refers to the path to the Amazon ECR Docker registry for the region in which you want to create the training instances, the `algorithm` portion is an identifier that identifies a specific algorithm, and the `tag` portion identifies a version of the Docker image. A full list of algorithm-specific Docker images is available at `https://docs.aws.amazon.com/sagemaker/latest/dg/sagemaker-algo-Docker-registry-paths.html`.

Using the information on this page at the time this chapter was written, the path to the latest version of the Docker image that contains the built-in k-means classifier, in the eu-west-1 region, is `438346466558.dkr.ecr.eu-west-1.amazonaws.com/kmeans:latest`. It is worth noting that not all algorithms may be available in each AWS region.

If you are using the high-level interface exposed by the AWS SageMaker for Python SDK from your notebook instance, you do not need to explicitly specify the path to the Docker image. If, however, you are using some of the lower-level classes, or using the AWS boto3 SDK, you will need to provide the path to the image. This chapter does not cover using the lower-level `Estimator` class or the low-level boto3 SDK; if you would like more information on training a model based on a built-in algorithm with the low-level SDK, visit `https://docs.aws.amazon.com/sagemaker/latest/dg/ex1-train-model.html`.

The rest of this section will look at using the high-level interface exposed by the AWS SageMaker for Python SDK to create a training job using a built-in algorithm from a notebook instance. To get started, launch the `kmeans-iris-flowers` notebook instance and create a new Jupyter Notebook file on your notebook instance using the `conda_python3` kernel. Change the title of the notebook to `kmeans-iris-flowers` and type the following code in an empty notebook cell:

```
import sagemaker
import boto3
import io
```

```
import pandas as pd
import numpy as np

# Get a SageMaker-compatible role used by this Notebook Instance.
role = sagemaker.get_execution_role()

# get a SageMaker session object, that can be
# used to manage the interaction with the SageMaker API.
sagemaker_session = sagemaker.Session()

# create a training job to train a KMeans model using
# Amazon SageMaker's own implementation of the k-means algorithm
#
# set hyperparameter k = 3
from sagemaker import KMeans

input_location = 's3://awsml-sagemaker-source/iris-train.csv'
output_location = 's3://awsml-sagemaker-results'

kmeans_estimator = KMeans(role=role,
                train_instance_count=1,
                train_instance_type='ml.m4.xlarge',
                output_path=output_location,
                k=3)


# load training and validation dataset from Amazon S3
s3_client = boto3.client('s3')
s3_bucket_name='awsml-sagemaker-source'

response = s3_client.get_object(Bucket='awsml-sagemaker-source',
Key='iris_train.csv')
response_body = response["Body"].read()
df_iris_train = pd.read_csv(io.BytesIO(response_body), header=0, delimiter=",",
low_memory=False)

response = s3_client.get_object(Bucket='awsml-sagemaker-source',
Key='iris_test.csv')
response_body = response["Body"].read()
df_iris_test = pd.read_csv(io.BytesIO(response_body), header=0,
index_col=False, delimiter=",", low_memory=False)

# Convert target variables 'species' from strings into integers.
from sklearn.preprocessing import LabelEncoder
labelEncoder = LabelEncoder()
labelEncoder.fit(df_iris_train['species'])
labelEncoder.fit(df_iris_test['species'])
```

```
df_iris_train['species'] = labelEncoder.transform(df_iris_train['species'])
df_iris_test['species'] = labelEncoder.transform(df_iris_test['species'])

# separate training and validation dataset into separate features and target
datasets
# assuming that the first column of the iris_train.csv and iris_test.csv files
# contains the target attribute.
#
# since training a k-means classifier does not require labelled training data,
# you will not make use of df_iris_target_train

df_iris_features_train= df_iris_train.iloc[:,1:]
df_iris_target_train = df_iris_train.iloc[:,0]

df_iris_features_test= df_iris_test.iloc[:,1:]
df_iris_target_test = df_iris_test.iloc[:,0]


# create a training job.
train_data = df_iris_features_train.values.astype('float32')
record_set = kmeans_estimator.record_set(train_data)
kmeans_estimator.fit(record_set)
```

Execute the code in the notebook cell to launch a training job that will result in SageMaker creating a dedicated ml.m4.xlarge EC2 instance from the default Docker image that contains the code for the k-means algorithm and kick off model training. Model training will take several minutes, during which time you will see log messages appear beneath the notebook cell (Figure 16.17). Once the model is trained, Amazon SageMaker will save it to the awsml-sagemaker-results Amazon S3 bucket, and terminate the training instances.

FIGURE 16.17
Training a model based on a built-in algorithm using an AWS SageMaker notebook instance

Let's briefly examine some of the key aspects of this code snippet. You start by accessing the IAM role associated with the notebook instance using the statements:

```
role = sagemaker.get_execution_role()
```

You then instantiate a KMeans class with the IAM role, the type of training instance you want, the number of instances, the location of the output data, and the number of clusters:

```
kmeans_estimator = KMeans(role=role,
                train_instance_count=1,
                train_instance_type='ml.m4.xlarge',
                output_path=output_location,
                k=3)
```

The KMeans class is part of the AWS SageMaker SDK for Python and provides a high-level interface to create a training job with the built-in k-means algorithm. You can learn more about the KMeans class at https://sagemaker.readthedocs.io/en/stable/kmeans.html.

You then proceed to load the training and test data from the iris_train.csv and iris_test.csv files in the awsml-sagemaker-source Amazon S3 bucket into Pandas dataframes and convert the categorical target attribute species into a number:

```
# load training and validation dataset from Amazon S3
s3_client = boto3.client('s3')
s3_bucket_name='awsml-sagemaker-source'

response = s3_client.get_object(Bucket='awsml-sagemaker-source',
Key='iris_train.csv')
response_body = response["Body"].read()
df_iris_train = pd.read_csv(io.BytesIO(response_body), header=0, delimiter=",",
low_memory=False)

response = s3_client.get_object(Bucket='awsml-sagemaker-source',
Key='iris_test.csv')
response_body = response["Body"].read()
df_iris_test = pd.read_csv(io.BytesIO(response_body), header-0,
index_col=False, delimiter=",", low_memory=False)

# Convert target variables 'species' from strings into integers.
from sklearn.preprocessing import LabelEncoder
labelEncoder = LabelEncoder()
labelEncoder.fit(df_iris_train['species'])
labelEncoder.fit(df_iris_test['species'])
df_iris_train['species'] = labelEncoder.transform(df_iris_train['species'])
df_iris_test['species'] = labelEncoder.transform(df_iris_test['species'])
```

Creating the training job is achieved by calling the fit() method on the KMeans instance. However, Amazon SageMaker's implementation of k-means prefers the training data to be specified in the protobuf recordIO format. You can learn more about this format at https://docs.aws.amazon.com/sagemaker/latest/dg/cdf-training.html.

The following lines of code split the training dataset into a dataframe that contains the features and one that contains the target labels. The feature dataframe is converted to a NumPy array and then to a protobuf recordIO buffer. The recordIO buffer is provided as input to the `fit()` method to kick off the model training job:

```
df_iris_features_train= df_iris_train.iloc[:,1:]
df_iris_target_train = df_iris_train.iloc[:,0]

df_iris_features_test= df_iris_test.iloc[:,1:]
df_iris_target_test = df_iris_test.iloc[:,0]

# create a training job.
train_data = df_iris_features_train.values.astype('float32')
record_set = kmeans_estimator.record_set(train_data)
kmeans_estimator.fit(record_set)
```

The KMeans class is known as an estimator class and inherits from a base class called EstimatorBase. The AWS SageMaker SDK for Python contains subclasses of EstimatorBase corresponding to the different built-in algorithms supported by AWS SageMaker. There is also a subclass called Estimator that can be used to train a model using any of the built-in models, and provides lower-level controls such as the ability to choose a specific Docker image. You can learn more about the Estimator class at https://sagemaker.readthedocs.io/en/stable/estimators.html#sagemaker.estimator.EstimatorBase.

When the model has finished training, execute the following code in an empty notebook cell to deploy the model to a prediction instance and create an HTTPS endpoint that can be used to make predictions:

```
# deploy the model to a prediction instance
# and create a prediction endpoint.
predictor = kmeans_estimator.deploy(initial_instance_count=1,
instance_type="ml.m4.xlarge")
```

Deploying the model may take several minutes. Once the model is deployed, you can use it to make predictions on the Iris flowers test set:

```
test_data = df_iris_features_test.values.astype('float32')

predictions = predictor.predict(test_data)
print (predictions)
```

The prediction for each row in the test data is returned as a JSON object that contains information on the cluster label, and the distance of the row from the centroid of the cluster:

```
label {
  key: "closest_cluster"
  value {
    float32_tensor {
      values: 0.0
    }
  }
}
```

```
label {
  key: "distance_to_cluster"
  value {
    float32_tensor {
      values: 0.33853915333747864
    }
  }
}
```

To terminate the prediction instance and associated HTTP endpoint, execute the following code in a notebook cell:

```
# terminate the prediction instance and associated
# HTTPS endpoint.
kmeans_estimator.delete_endpoint()
```

NOTE   You can download the code files for this chapter from www.wiley.com/go/ machinelearningawscloud or from GitHub using the following URL:

https://github.com/asmtechnology/awsmlbook-chapter16.git

Summary

◆ Amazon SageMaker is a fully managed web service that provides the ability to explore data, engineer features, and train machine learning models on AWS cloud infrastructure using Python code.

◆ Amazon SageMaker provides implementations of a number of cloud-optimized versions of machine learning algorithms such as XGBoost, factorization machines, and PCA.

◆ Amazon SageMaker also provides the ability to create your own algorithms based on popular frameworks such as Scikit-learn, Google TensorFlow, and Apache MXNet.

◆ The Amazon SageMaker SDK for Python provides a convenient high-level, object-oriented interface for Python developers.

◆ Amazon SageMaker notebook instances are EC2 instances in your account that come preconfigured with a Jupyter Notebook server, and a number of common Python libraries.

◆ Training jobs create dedicated compute instances in the AWS cloud that contain model-building code, load your training data from Amazon S3, execute the model-building code on your training data, and save the trained model to Amazon S3.

◆ When the training job is complete, the compute instances that were provisioned to support the training process will automatically be terminated.

◆ Deploying a model into production involves creating one or more compute instances, deploying your model onto these instances, and providing an API that can be used to make predictions using the deployed model.

◆ Prediction instances are not automatically terminated.

◆ An endpoint configuration ties together information on the location of a trained machine learning model, type of compute instances, and an auto-scaling policy.

◆ A prediction endpoint is an HTTPS REST API endpoint that can be used to get single predictions from a deployed model. The HTTP endpoint is secured using AWS Signature V4 authentication.

◆ If you need to make predictions on an entire dataset, you can create use Amazon SageMaker Batch Transform to create a batch prediction job from a trained model.

Chapter 17

Using Google TensorFlow with Amazon SageMaker

WHAT'S IN THIS CHAPTER

- ◆ Introduction to Google TensorFlow

- ◆ Create a linear regression model with Google TensorFlow

- ◆ Introduction to artificial neural networks

- ◆ Create a neural network classifier with the Google TensorFlow Estimators API

- ◆ Train and deploy Google TensorFlow models on Amazon SageMaker

In the previous chapter you learned to use Amazon SageMaker to build and deploy machine learning models that were based on Amazon SageMaker's built-in implementation of popular machine learning algorithms, and models created with Scikit-learn. In this chapter you will learn to create models using Google TensorFlow and use Amazon SageMaker to train and deploy these models.

NOTE Amazon SageMaker is only free for the first two months after you have signed up for a free-tier AWS account. After that period, you will be charged for compute resources.

NOTE To follow along with this chapter, ensure you have created the S3 buckets listed in Appendix B.

You can download the code files for this chapter from `www.wiley.com/go/machinelearning-awscloud` or from GitHub using the following URL:

`https://github.com/asmtechnology/awsmlbook-chapter17.git`

Introduction to Google TensorFlow

TensorFlow is a machine learning library created by Google, which was initially developed by the team at Google Brain for internal use and then subsequently released as an open source project under the Apache license in November 2015. TensorFlow requires you to model your computation problem as a tree-like structure called a *computation graph*, made up of nodes and leaves. The nodes of the graph represent mathematical operations or functions, and the leaf nodes represent some kind of input into the operations. The data on which this graph operates is represented as *n*-dimensional matrices called *tensors*. You can think of a tensor as a generalization of vectors and matrices.

Operation nodes are also called *op nodes*, and while most of them take tensors as inputs and return a tensor that represents the result of the operation, some operation nodes do not return anything. These nodes that do not return any outputs usually modify the data in the entire graph in some way, such as initializing all variables with values wherever in the graph they may be.

Leaf nodes can be of three different types:

◆ *Constant:* A constant leaf node (also known as a constant tensor) is a tensor whose value cannot be changed once it has been assigned. A constant tensor is created using the `tf` `.constant()` Python function. You can learn more about creating constant tensors at https://www.tensorflow.org/api_docs/python/tf/constant.

◆ *Variable:* A variable leaf node (also known as a variable tensor) is a tensor whose value can be changed as the program executes. When building machine learning models, the parameters of the model such as weights and bias terms are represented using variable tensors. Variable tensors are instances of the `tf.Variable` class and can be created by either using the class constructor or the `tf.get_variable()` function. You can learn more about variable tensors at https://www.tensorflow.org/api_docs/python/ tf/Variable.

◆ *Placeholder:* A placeholder leaf node (also known as a placeholder tensor) is a special node whose value is a tensor that you must feed into the graph when you evaluate the graph. Placeholders for tensors are typically used to feed training data and labels into your program and are created using the `tf.placeholder()` function. You can learn more about tensor placeholders at https://www.tensorflow.org/api_docs/python/tf/ placeholder.

The process of running the TensorFlow program amounts to evaluating the computation graph in an object called a *session*. The graph is then evaluated in a session, and during the evaluation process, input data (tensors) are fed into the leaf nodes of the graph and flow through the graph toward the root node—hence the name TensorFlow. A TensorFlow session takes care of converting the computation graph into executable code and executing the graph on the CPU or GPU. The scope of the variables, constants, and tensor placeholders is restricted to the session. You can have multiple sessions with different computation graphs in each.

While this graph-based approach may seem like overkill for a simple arithmetic problem, it is extremely useful (and natural) if the computation problem that you are trying to represent is inherently graph-based, such as an artificial neural network (ANN).TensorFlow is typically used to create different types of artificial neural network models for classification and regression tasks. A detailed discussion of artificial neural networks cannot be accommodated in one chapter, but a high-level summary is provided here to help you get the general idea of how they work.

Artificial neural networks are computing tools that were developed by Warren McCulloch and Walter Pitts in 1943, and their design is inspired by biological neural networks. Figure 17.1 depicts the structure of a very simple artificial neural network.

FIGURE 17.1
Structure of an artificial neural network (ANN)

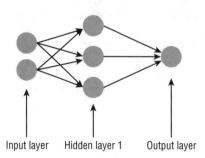

Input layer   Hidden layer 1   Output layer

ANNs are made up of units call *neurons* and are organized into a series of layers. There are three types of layers:

♦ *Input layer:* This is the layer that directly receives inputs for the computation. There is only one input layer in an artificial neural network.

♦ *Output layer:* This is the layer that provides the output of the computation. There can be one or more neurons in this layer, depending on the type of problem the network is used to solve.

♦ *Hidden layer:* This is a layer that sits between the input and the output layer. Neurons in the input layer are connected to neurons in the hidden layer, and neurons in the hidden layer are connected to neurons in the output layer. When each of the neurons in one layer is connected to every neuron in the previous layer, the network is called a *fully connected network*. A very simple neural network may not necessarily have a hidden layer, and complex neural networks such as deep-learning networks have several hidden layers, each with a large number of neurons in them.

Each of the connections between neurons has a weight value associated with it, and the weight multiplies the value of the neuron the connection originated from. Each neuron works by computing the sum of its inputs and passing the sum through a non-linear activation function. The output value of the neuron is the result of the activation function. Figure 17.2 depicts a very simple neural network with two neurons in the input layer and one neuron in the output layer.

FIGURE 17.2

A simple neural network

If x_1, x_2 are the values loaded into the neurons in the input layer, w_1, w_2 are the connection weights between the input layer and the output layer, and $f()$ is the activation function of the neuron in the output layer, then the output value of the neural network in Figure 17.2 is $f(w_1.x_1 + w_2.x_2)$.

There are many different types of activation functions with their own advantages and disadvantages. The reason to have an activation function is to ensure that the network is not just a one big linear model. When a neural network is instantiated, the weights are set to random values. The process of training the neural network involves finding out the values of the weights.

The TensorFlow Python API is structured in a series of layers (Figure 17.3), with the topmost layer known as the Estimators API. Objects in the Estimators layer provide the ability to create entire neural networks with a single Python statement.

FIGURE 17.3

TensorFlow API architecture

Estimators

Layers   Datasets   Metrics

Low-level Python API

The Estimators layer also provides a framework to train these networks. The intermediate layer consists of the Layers, Datasets, and Metrics APIs. The Layers API provides the ability to operate at the level of a neural network layer and create a complex neural network architecture by stitching together different types of layers. The lowest layer consists of low-level Python classes and functions that allow you to operate at the level of individual graph nodes such as `tf.Variable`, `tf.placeholder`, and `tf.constant`. In the next section you will create a simple linear regression model from scratch using the low-level Python API. In a subsequent section you will use the Estimators API to create a special kind of neural network called a Dense Neural Network (DNN) and use the network for a classification task. You can learn more about the TensorFlow APIs at `https://www.tensorflow.org/guide`.

Creating a Linear Regression Model with Google TensorFlow

In this section you will use an Amazon SageMaker notebook instance to train a linear regression model on the notebook instance with the low-level Python API provided by TensorFlow. The linear regression model will be trained on the Boston house prices toy dataset that is included in Scikit-learn. You can learn more about the Boston housing toy dataset at `https://scikit-learn.org/stable/datasets/index.html#datasets`. A copy of the dataset is included with the downloads that accompany this chapter. To better illustrate the process of using Google TensorFlow, the linear regression model will first be trained on a single feature of the dataset, and then modified to work with the remaining features.

To get started, log in to the AWS management console using the dedicated sign-in link for your development IAM user account. Navigate to the Amazon S3 management console and locate the `awsml-sagemaker-source` bucket (Figure 17.4).

FIGURE 17.4
Accessing the Amazon S3 bucket that will contain the training and validation files

If you have not created the `awsml-sagemaker-source` bucket yet, refer to the section titled "Preparing Test and Training Data" in the previous chapter. Locate the `datasets/boston_dataset` folder in the resources that accompany this chapter and upload the `boston_train.csv` and `boston_test.csv` files to the Amazon S3 bucket (Figure 17.5).

FIGURE 17.5
Uploading the pre-split training and test data files to the Amazon S3 bucket

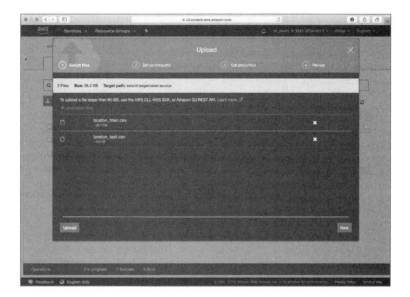

Techniques to prepare training and test datasets were covered in Chapter 5. A Jupyter Notebook file called `PreparingTheBostonDataset.ipynb` is included with the resources that accompany this chapter. This file contains the Python code that was used to generate the `boston_train.csv` and `boston_test.csv` files on an instance of Jupyter Notebook running locally on the author's computer.

After you have uploaded the files to Amazon S3, use the Services drop-down menu to switch to the Amazon SageMaker management console and create a new ml.t2-medium notebook instance called `tensorflow-models`. Amazon SageMaker will, by default, select the same IAM role that was created for you when you created the `kmeans-iris-flowers` notebook instance in the previous chapter.

NOTE　If you did not create the notebook instance in the previous chapter, you will need to create a new IAM role that will be assumed by the notebook instance. Refer to the section titled "Creating an Amazon SageMaker Notebook Instance" in the previous chapter for instructions on creating this IAM role.

When the `tensorflow-models` notebook instance is ready, you will see it listed in your Amazon SageMaker management console with the status of "In Service" (Figure 17.6).

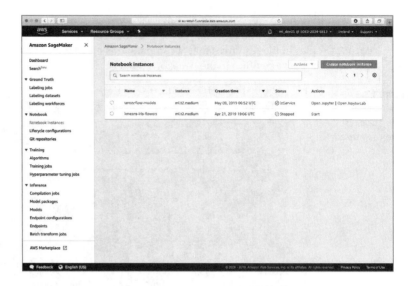

Click the Open Jupyter link to access the Jupyter Notebook server running on your
tensorflow-models notebook instance and create a new notebook file called TF_
SingleFeatureRegression_SGD using the conda_tensorflow_p36 kernel. Execute the following code snippet in an empty notebook cell to load the boston_train.csv and boston_test
.csv files from Amazon S3 into Pandas dataframes, and separate the feature variables and target
into separate dataframes:

```
import boto3
import sagemaker
import io

import pandas as pd
import numpy as np

# load training and validation dataset from Amazon S3
s3_client = boto3.client('s3')
s3_bucket_name='awsml-sagemaker-source'

response = s3_client.get_object(Bucket='awsml-sagemaker-source',
Key='boston_train.csv')
response_body = response["Body"].read()
df_boston_train = pd.read_csv(io.BytesIO(response_body), header=0,
delimiter=",", low_memory=False)

response = s3_client.get_object(Bucket='awsml-sagemaker-source',
Key='boston_test.csv')
response_body = response["Body"].read()
df_boston_test = pd.read_csv(io.BytesIO(response_body), header=0,
index_col=False, delimiter=",", low_memory=False)
```

```
# extract features and target variable into separate datasets.
df_boston_train_target = df_boston_train.loc[:,['price']]
df_boston_train_features = df_boston_train.drop(['price'], axis=1)

df_boston_test_target = df_boston_test.loc[:,['price']]
df_boston_test_features = df_boston_test.drop(['price'], axis=1)
```

The df_boston_train dataset has 14 columns. The first column is called price and is the target variable, and the remaining 13 columns are the feature variables. The description of the 13 feature variables is present at https://scikit-learn.org/stable/datasets/index .html#datasets. You can inspect the first five rows of the df_boston_train dataframe by using the dataframe's head() method (Figure 17.7).

FIGURE 17.7
Inspecting the first five rows of the Boston housing dataset

In [4]:	df_boston_train.head()												
Out[4]:													
	price	CRIM	ZN	INDUS	CHAS	NOX	RM	AGE	DIS	RAD	TAX	PTRATIO	B	LSTAT
0	24.8	0.21409	22.0	5.86	0.0	0.431	6.438	8.9	7.3967	7.0	330.0	19.1	377.07	3.59
1	16.8	0.22438	0.0	9.69	0.0	0.585	6.027	79.7	2.4982	6.0	391.0	19.2	396.90	14.33
2	13.1	23.64820	0.0	18.10	0.0	0.671	6.380	96.2	1.3861	24.0	666.0	20.2	396.90	23.69
3	25.1	0.52058	0.0	6.20	1.0	0.507	6.631	76.5	4.1480	8.0	307.0	17.4	388.45	9.54
4	32.0	0.07875	45.0	3.44	0.0	0.437	6.782	41.1	3.7886	5.0	398.0	15.2	393.87	6.68

Let's now build a linear regression model using the low-level TensorFlow Python API that attempts to predict the value of the price target attribute from a single feature variable. The complete code that you can execute in a notebook cell will be presented at the end of this section; for now, let's explore the process of building and training a model with the low-level TensorFlow API.

You can choose any feature variable. The code in this section assumes you are using the first feature of the dataset, which is called CRIM and represents the per-capita crime rate. Recall from Chapter 4 that a linear regression model attempts to fit a straight line (or hyperplane) to the set of points that make the training data and uses the line to make predictions on future values. The general equation of a linear regression model for N features is:

$$Y = w_1 X_1 + w_2 X_2 + \ldots + w_n X_n + c.$$

Where:

w_1, w_2, ... w_n are the coefficients associated with the features X_1, X_2, ... X_n respectively.

Y is the predicted value (target value).

X_i's are the input features.

c is a constant term, also known as the bias term or intercept.

Since we are trying to build a model from a single feature, this equation reduces to:

$$Y = w_1 X_1 + c.$$

The aim of model training will be to find the value of w_1 and c that will result in the best possible predictions. The quality of predictions will be measured using the mean squared error (MSE) metric, which is illustrated in Figure 17.8.

FIGURE 17.8
Mean squared
error metric

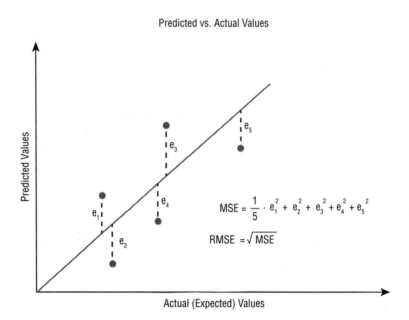

The process of building a model with TensorFlow involves defining a tree-like structure called a computation graph, and the process of training the model is achieved by evaluating the root node of the computation graph in a session and feeding the graph with the training data. Let's now define the computation graph.

Since we are building a linear regression model that takes one input feature and predicts the value of one target variable, we will need to provide two inputs to the TensorFlow graph during model training. The first will be an array of values called x1, which will contain the values in the CRIM column of the df_boston_train_features dataset. The second input to the model training process will be an array of values called y_actual that will contain the values of the price column from the df_boston_train_target dataset. Values of the price column are what we want the model to predict, but during the model-training process we will provide both the CRIM and price values and compute the optimum values of w_1 and c.

Values that you need provide as inputs to a computation graph at runtime are represented using placeholder nodes. You create placeholder nodes using the tf.placeholder() function. The following snippet creates two placeholder nodes called x1 and y_actual and adds the nodes to the default computation graph:

```
import tensorflow as tf
tf.reset_default_graph()

x1 = tf.placeholder(tf.float32, [None, 1], name="x1")
y_actual = tf.placeholder(tf.float32, [None, 1], name="y_actual")
```

NOTE The standard alias for TensorFlow in Python projects is tf. TensorFlow is typically imported into a Python project using the following statement:

```
import tensorflow as tf
```

The standard behavior of TensorFlow is to add any nodes you create to the default computation graph. It is possible to create additional graph objects and attach nodes to these other graphs.

The `tf.reset_default_graph()` statement is used to delete any nodes from the default computation graph.

TensorFlow will expect you to feed values for all placeholder nodes when you execute the computation graph in a session, and we will see how to do that shortly. All data that flows through a computation graph is represented as n-dimensional matrices called tensors, and therefore a placeholder is a tensor. The dimensions of the x1 and y_actual tensors have been specified as [None, 1], which means both x1 and y_actual are tensors that have any number of rows, and a single column. The data type of the tensor elements is defined as float32, which is a 32-bit floating-point number. You can learn more about the `tf.placeholder()` function at https://www.tensorflow.org/api_docs/python/tf/placeholder. Figure 17.9 depicts the structure of the computation graph after the two placeholder nodes are created.

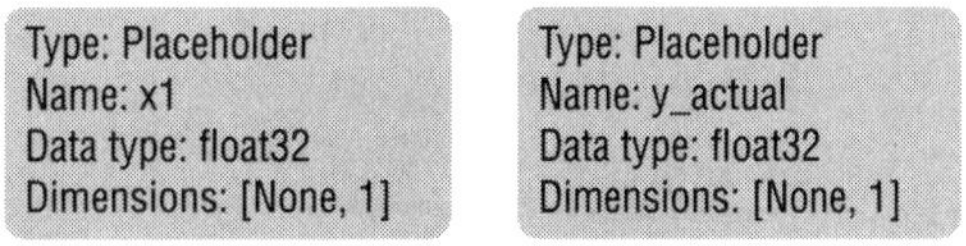

FIGURE 17.9

Computation graph with two placeholder nodes

Type: Placeholder
Name: x1
Data type: float32
Dimensions: [None, 1]

Type: Placeholder
Name: y_actual
Data type: float32
Dimensions: [None, 1]

Your linear regression model will also contain two variables: the weight w_1 corresponding to the one input feature and the intercept term c. The objective of model training will be to use the computation graph to find the values of w_1 and c. Quantities whose values can be changed as a result of executing the graph are known as variables in TensorFlow, and are represented as instances of the `tf.Variable` class. Typically, you will create `tf.Variable` instances for all quantities that you wish to compute. Just like placeholders, variables are also tensors. However, unlike placeholders, you do not feed the value of variables into the computation graph at runtime; instead, they are assigned an initial value and then the value of the variable is updated as different nodes of the graph are evaluated. You can create variables using the `tf.Variable()` constructor or the `tf.get_variable()` function. The following statements define two variables, w1 and c, using the `tf.Variable()` constructor:

```
w1 = tf.Variable(tf.zeros([1,1]), name="w1")
c = tf.Variable(tf.zeros([1]), name="c")
```

When you create a variable, you need to provide a default value; the shape of the variable tensor is inferred from the shape of the default value. The preceding statements make use of the `tf.zeros()` function to create tensors that are used as default values for the w1 and c variables. The `tf.zeros()` function creates tensors that have all elements set to 0. You can learn more about the `tf.zeros()` function at https://www.tensorflow.org/api_docs/python/tf/zeros. Even though you have specified the initial value of the variable as a constructor argument, the values are not assigned to those variables until the graph is executed in a session. Figure 17.10 depicts the structure of the computation graph after the two variable nodes are created.

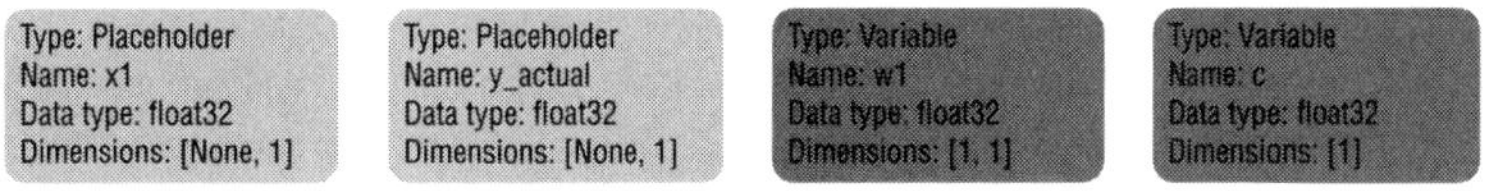

FIGURE 17.10

Computation graph with two variable nodes

Type: Placeholder
Name: x1
Data type: float32
Dimensions: [None, 1]

Type: Placeholder
Name: y_actual
Data type: float32
Dimensions: [None, 1]

Type: Variable
Name: w1
Data type: float32
Dimensions: [1, 1]

Type: Variable
Name: c
Data type: float32
Dimensions: [1]

Now that you have created placeholder nodes and variable nodes in the computation graph, you can use the `tf.matmul()` operator to create an operation node that will contain the matrix product of the tensors in the w1 and x1 nodes. You can learn more about the `tf.matmul()` operator at https://www.tensorflow.org/api_docs/python/tf/linalg/matmul. The following statement adds a new node called `temp` to the computation graph, the value of which will be the tensor obtained by multiplying the tensors w1 and x1:

```
temp = tf.matmul(x1,w1)
```

Figure 17.11 depicts the structure of the computation graph after the matrix multiplication node has been added.

FIGURE 17.11

Computation graph after the multiplication of w1 and x1 nodes

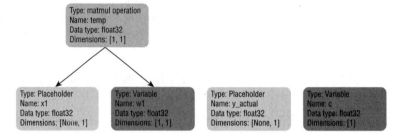

Let's now create a new operation node in the computation graph, the value of which is the sum of the `temp` tensor and the tensor in variable c. We can do this by using the + arithmetic operator as follows:

```
y_predicted = temp + c
```

Figure 17.12 depicts the structure of the computation graph after the `y_predicted` node has been added.

FIGURE 17.12

Computation graph with y_predicted

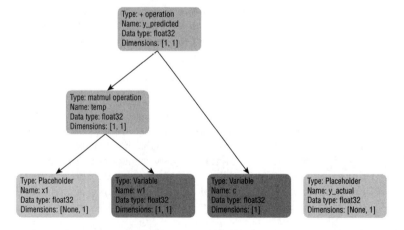

The `y_predicted` node represents your linear regression model. However, since the default values of w1 and c are tensors with zeros in them, the `y_predicted` values will all be zero, regardless of the values you feed into the x1 placeholder.

What you need to do is work out the best values for the `w1` and `c` tensors, and in order to do so, you will need to feed the expected values of the target variable `price` into the `y_actual` placeholder, compute the value of a cost function that captures the error in prediction between the actual and predicted values, and adjust the values of `w1` and `c` so as to minimize the value of the cost function.

Let's now add nodes to the computation graph to compute the value of a cost function. There are many kinds of cost functions, such as MSE, RMSE, MAE, etc., and the low-level TensorFlow API provides the ability to create operation nodes that can be combined together to compute the value of common cost functions. In this section you will use the mean squared error (MSE) cost function, and the cost function can be computed in three steps:

1. Use the – arithmetic operator to create an operation node in the graph to compute the difference between the actual and predicted values.

2. Use the `tf.square()` operator to create another operation node that can square the difference computed in the previous step.

3. Use the `tf.reduce_mean()` function to create a third operation node that can compute the mean of the values computed in the previous step.

The following code snippet adds nodes to the computation graph to perform these three steps:

```
# compute cost function
# MSE between predicted and actual values
diff = y_predicted - y_actual
square_diff = tf.square(diff)
mse_cost = tf.reduce_mean(square_diff)
```

The `tf.reduce_mean()` operator provided by TensorFlow is equivalent to the NumPy `mean()` function, and you can learn more about the `tf.reduce_mean()` operator at `https://www.tensorflow.org/api_docs/python/tf/math/reduce_mean`. Figure 17.13 depicts the structure of the computation graph after the nodes to compute the MSE cost have been added.

Now that you have a node in your graph that represents the cost function, you need to tweak the values of the variables `w1` and `c` so as to reduce the value of the cost function. One solution is to try every possible combination of `w1` and `c` and pick the one that results in the lowest value of the cost function. This approach will return the best possible values of `w1` and `c` but can be impractical to compute because of the sheer number of possibilities. If searching for the best possible values is not practical, you will need to search for good-enough values, and in order to do so you will need to apply an optimization strategy to reduce the size of the search space. Various optimization algorithms are used by data scientists and the one you are going to use in this section is called gradient descent (GD) optimization.

An in-depth discussion of gradient descent optimization is outside the scope of this book. You can learn more about the gradient descent technique at `https://developers.google.com/machine-learning/crash-course/reducing-loss/gradient-descent`. Gradient descent is a popular optimization algorithm and is based on an assumption that the three-dimensional plot of the values of the cost function `mse_cost`, `w1`, and `c` is bowl shaped (concave), and it has a single minimum value. With this assumption, the gradient descent algorithm computes the value of the derivate (gradient) of the point `[mse_cost, w1, c]` and uses the sign of the derivative to work out the direction in which the value of the cost function should be moved. A positive value would indicate that the optimal point on the surface of the bowl-shaped curve is higher up (toward the rim of the bowl), and a negative value would indicate that the optimal point is somewhere lower down toward the trough. A new point is then selected on the bowl-shaped curve by moving a small amount in the direction indicated by the gradient and the corresponding w1 and c values are selected. This process then repeats iteratively for a fixed number of iterations, and the best value arrived at during the iterations is selected.

FIGURE 17.13
Computation graph that contains nodes to compute the MSE cost function

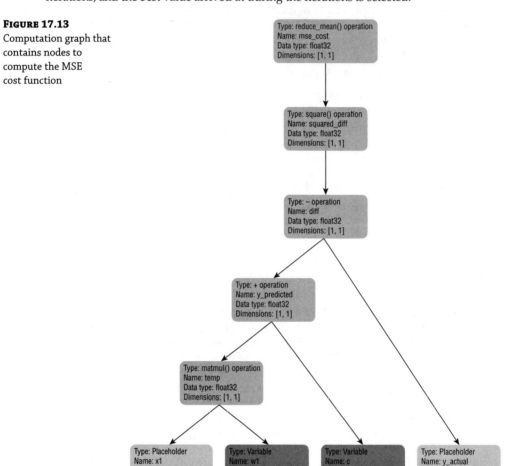

Fortunately, you do not need to implement the gradient descent algorithm from scratch in TensorFlow, and instead can create an instance of the tf.GradientDescentOptimizer class to get an optimizer object, and then use the minimize() method of the optimizer object to get an operation node that can both compute the gradient and use the gradient to tweak the values of the variables that impact the value of the cost function. The following snippet demonstrates the use of the tf.GradientDescentOptimizer class to add an operation node to the computation graph. You can learn more about this class at https://www.tensorflow.org/api_docs/python/tf/train/GradientDescentOptimizer.

```
# create a root node - a gradient descent optimizer, setup to optimize the
# mse_cost
learning_rate = 0.000001
train_step = tf.train.GradientDescentOptimizer(learning_rate).minimize(mse_cost)
```

Figure 17.14 depicts the structure of the computation graph after the optimizer operation has been added.

FIGURE 17.14
Computation graph that contains the operation to optimize the cost function

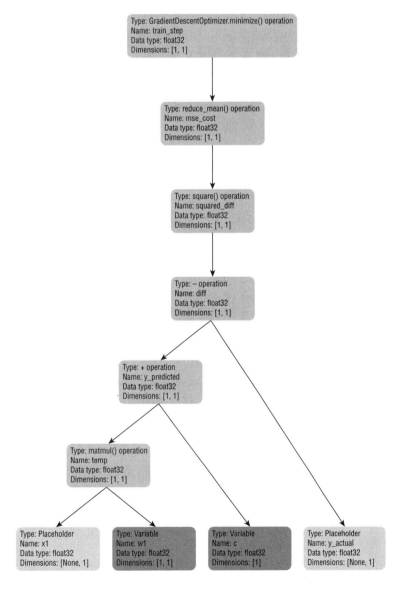

Now that you have created the computation graph, you need to run the graph in a session, which involves creating a tf.Session object, initializing the variables of the graph, feeding values into the placeholders, and evaluating the values of one or more nodes of the graph.

The following snippet prepares two arrays, xin and yin, that contain the values you will feed into the placeholder nodes once you run the computation graph in a session:

```
# extract CRIM feature and target variable into arrays so that
# these can be fed into the computation graph via the placeholders
# created earlier.
xin = df_boston_train_features['CRIM'].values
yin = df_boston_train_target['price'].values
```

It is important to note that you do not have to start evaluating the graph at the root node and can choose to evaluate the value of any node in the graph. TensorFlow will evaluate the values of any child nodes needed to compute the value of the node you want to evaluate. Instead of initializing every variable in your computation graph one by one, you can use the tf.global_variables_initializer() function to add an initializer node to the computation graph. This node when executed within a session will initialize all the variables in the computation graph with default values. The following snippet creates a tf.Session object, and initializes the values of all the variables in the default computation graph using the tf.global_variables_initializer() function:

```
with tf.Session() as sess:
    # use a global_variable_initializer node to initialize
    # variables all variables in the graph (w1 and c)
    init_node = tf.global_variables_initializer()
    sess.run(init_node)
```

The call to the tf.global_variables_initializer() function adds an initializer node to the graph, but the actual variable initialization happens when the next line, sess.run(init_node), is executed. The run() method of the tf.Session object can be used to execute any node of the computation graph. You can learn more about tf.Session at https://www.tensorflow.org/api_docs/python/tf/Session.

NOTE The reason to use the with-as statement is to ensure that you do not explicitly need to close the session object once you have finished using it.

If you did not want to use the with-as statement, the equivalent lines of code would have been:

```
sess = tf.Session()
init_node = tf.global_variables_initializer()
sess.run(init_node)
  sess.close()
```

Forgetting to call sess.close() will result in the resources associated with the session not being freed, and in order to avoid the problem altogether, Python programmers use the with-as statement when creating sessions.

With the variables initialized, the following code snippet will feed each item of the xin and yin Python arrays into the x1 and y_actual placeholder nodes one element at a time, and it will evaluate the train_step node of the graph. The values of the w1 and c graph variables that result in the lowest value of the cost function will be stored in the best_w1, best_c, and lowest_cost Python variables. These statements must be executed within the scope of the with-as statement:

```
# for each observation, evaluate the node called train_step
# which will in turn update w1 and c so as to minimize
# the cost function.

num_elements = df_boston_train_features.shape[0]
best_w1 = 0.0
best_c = 0.0
lowest_cost = 100000.00

for i in range(num_elements):
    input_dict={x1:[[xin[i]]], y_actual:[[yin[i]]]}
    sess.run(train_step, feed_dict=input_dict)

    computed_w1 = sess.run(w1)
    computed_c = sess.run(c)
    computed_cost = sess.run(mse_cost, feed_dict=input_dict)

    if computed_cost < lowest_cost:
        lowest_cost = computed_cost
        best_w1 = computed_w1
        best_c = computed_c

    print ("End of iteration %d, w1=%f, c=%f, cost=%f" % (i, computed_w1,
computed_c, computed_cost))
    print ("End of training, w1=%f, c=%f, lowest_cost=%f" % (best_w1, best_c,
lowest_cost))
```

In this snippet, a Python for loop is used to enumerate the contents of the xin and yin array and feed each element into placeholder nodes x1 and y_actual, one element at a time. TensorFlow requires that the values of any relevant placeholder nodes are fed into the computation graph using a dictionary object in the call to the sess.run() function. To understand how the model is trained, assume that for the first iteration i = 1, xin[i] = 10 and yin[i] = 20. Substituting these values, the call to sess.run() becomes

```
sess.run(train_step, feed_dict={x1:[[10]], y_actual:[[20]]})
```

The node being evaluated in the call to sess.run() is the train_step node is defined as:

```
train_step = tf.train.GradientDescentOptimizer(learning_rate).minimize(mse_cost)
```

In order to evaluate the train_step node, TensorFlow will need to access the tensor in the mse_cost node, and as a result, will need to evaluate the mse_cost node of the graph. The mse_cost node is defined as:

```
mse_cost = tf.reduce_mean(square_diff)
```

TensorFlow will now evaluate the value of the square_diff node, which is defined as:

```
square_diff = tf.square(diff)
```

This recursive evaluation process will continue until TensorFlow needs to evaluate the xin and yin placeholder nodes. When that happens, TensorFlow will use the values 10 and 20 provided in the feed_dict parameter to sess.run() for these placeholder nodes. The initial values of the w1 and c variable nodes will be 0, and the mse_cost tensor will be computed using these values. When the GradientDescentOptimizer node is evaluated, it will adjust the values of the w1 and c variable nodes to reduce the value of mse_cost by a small amount. Since the global_variables_initializer node is not executed in the for loop, the variables will retain their values across iterations of the loop.

Once the train_step node has been evaluated, the tensors in the w1 and c graph nodes will contain the optimized model parameters. To read these values, you will need to evaluate the w1 and c nodes in separate sess.run() statements:

```
computed_w1 = sess.run(w1)
computed_c = sess.run(c)
```

Even though TensorFlow has computed the value of the w1 and c nodes while evaluating the train_step node, the subsequent calls to sess.run(w1) and sess.run(c) will result in TensorFlow evaluating the computation graph again. Since these variable nodes do not have any dependent nodes, there will be no recursion involved, and TensorFlow will return the value of the tensors stored in these variable nodes.

Astute readers may have noticed that by feeding xin and yin values one element at a time, the gradient descent optimization process is trying to optimize the cost function for each element independently, and not trying to optimize for a better overall prediction across all the values of xin and yin. When gradient descent optimization is used in this manner, for one data point at a time, it is known as *stochastic gradient descent*.

All of the model building, training, and optimization steps discussed so far in this section are presented together in the following snippet. The complete code is also available in the TF_SingleFeatureRegression_SGD notebook file included with this chapter's resources:

```
# train a linear regression model on a single feature
# the general equation for linear regression is:
# y = w1x1 + w2x2 + ... wnxn + c
#
# in case of a single feature, the equation reduces to:
# y = w1x1 + c

import tensorflow as tf
tf.reset_default_graph()

#
# define a TensorFlow graph
#

# what you will provide:
# x1 =  one-dimensional column array of features
```

```python
# y_actual = one-dimensional column array of expected values/labels
x1 = tf.placeholder(tf.float32, [None, 1], name="x1")
y_actual = tf.placeholder(tf.float32, [None, 1], name="y_actual")

# what you  are interested in:
# w1, c weight and bias term (intercept)
w1 = tf.Variable(tf.zeros([1,1]), name="w1")
c = tf.Variable(tf.zeros([1]), name="c")

# compute y_predicted = w1x1 + c
temp = tf.matmul(x1,w1)
y_predicted = temp + c


# compute cost function
# MSE between predicted and actual values
diff = y_predicted - y_actual
square_diff = tf.square(diff)
mse_cost = tf.reduce_mean(square_diff)

# create a root node - a gradient descent optimizer, setup to optimize the
# mse_cost function.
learning_rate = 0.000001
train_step = tf.train.GradientDescentOptimizer(learning_rate).minimize(mse_cost)

# extract CRIM feature and target variable into arrays so that
# these can be fed into the computation graph via the placeholders
# created earlier.
xin =  df_boston_train_features['CRIM'].values
yin =  df_boston_train_target['price'].values


#
# execute the graph
#
with tf.Session() as sess:
    # use a global_variable_initializer node to initialize
    # variables all variables in the graph (w1 and c)
    init_node = tf.global_variables_initializer()
    sess.run(init_node)

    # for each observation, evaluate the node called train_step
    # which will in turn update w1 and c so as to minimize
    # the cost function.

    num_elements = df_boston_train_features.shape[0]
    best_w1 = 0.0
    best_c = 0.0
```

```
lowest_cost = 100000.00

for i in range(num_elements):
    input_dict={x1:[[xin[i]]], y_actual:[[yin[i]]]}
    sess.run(train_step, feed_dict=input_dict)

    computed_w1 = sess.run(w1)
    computed_c = sess.run(c)
    computed_cost = sess.run(mse_cost, feed_dict=input_dict)

    if computed_cost < lowest_cost:
        lowest_cost = computed_cost
        best_w1 = computed_w1
        best_c = computed_c

    print ("End of iteration %d, w1=%f, c=%f, cost=%f" % (i, computed_w1,
computed_c, computed_cost))
    print ("End of training, w1=%f, c=%f, lowest_cost=%f" % (best_w1, best_c,
lowest_cost))
```

If you execute this code in an empty notebook cell, you will see log messages below the notebook cell, listing the values of w1, c, and the cost function at each iteration. A section of the log messages corresponding to the last few iterations is presented here:

```
End of iteration 371, w1=0.038582, c=0.016661, cost=83.229652
End of iteration 372, w1=0.038587, c=0.016705, cost=483.073090
End of iteration 373, w1=0.038598, c=0.016748, cost=465.388062
End of iteration 374, w1=0.039058, c=0.016770, cost=122.635811
End of iteration 375, w1=0.039264, c=0.016800, cost=219.331360
End of iteration 376, w1=0.039390, c=0.016831, cost=237.831055
End of iteration 377, w1=0.039394, c=0.016871, cost=403.164185
End of iteration 378, w1=0.039399, c=0.016916, cost=518.887878
End of training, w1=0.016363, c=0.005673, lowest_cost=15.077192
```

As you can see, the cost function is fluctuating randomly with each iteration—sometimes it goes up, and sometimes it goes down. This is because we are feeding the dataset one point at a time.

At the end of the training, the values of best_w1 and best_c1 represent the parameters of the trained model and can be used to make predictions on the test set using the linear regression equation $Y = w_1X_1 + c$. This is demonstrated in the following snippet:

```
# use best_w1 and best_c to make predictions on all observations in the test set
predictions = df_boston_test_features['CRIM'].values * best_w1 + best_c
```

Once you have the predictions, you can use Scikit-learn to compute the MSE across all the predictions over the test set using the values of best_w1 = 0.016363 and best_c = 0.005673 as follows:

```
# compute MSE on test set
from sklearn.metrics import mean_squared_error
```

```
mse_test = mean_squared_error(np.transpose(df_boston_test_target.values),
predictions)
```

The value of the mean squared error can be examined using the Python print statement, and comes out as a rather high value—which indicates that the model is performing quite poorly:

```
print (mse_test)
601.8169340697825
```

This poor performance is to be expected for a number of reasons, the top two of which are that we are using just one feature of the dataset, and our optimization step is not trying to reduce the value of the cost function over the entire dataset. This code can easily be modified to work with multiple features of the dataset and perform batch gradient descent. The modified version of this code is provided in the TF_MultiFeatureRegression_BatchGradientDescent notebook file as part of the resources that accompany this chapter. The model training and optimization code is presented here, with the key differences highlighted in boldface:

```
# train a linear regression model on a single feature
# the general equation for linear regression is:
# y = w1x1 + w2x2 + ... wnxn + c
#
# in case of a single feature, the equation reduces to:
# y = w1x1 + c

import tensorflow as tf
tf.reset_default_graph()


#
# define a TensorFlow graph
#

# what you will provide:
# x1 =  one-dimensional column array of features
# y_actual = one-dimensional column array of expected values/labels
x1 = tf.placeholder(tf.float32, [None, 1], name="x1")
y_actual = tf.placeholder(tf.float32, [None, 1], name="y_actual")

# what you  are interested in:
# w1, c weight and bias term (intercept)
w1 = tf.Variable(tf.zeros([1,1]), name="w1")
c = tf.Variable(tf.zeros([1]), name="c")

# compute y_predicted = w1x1 + c
y_predicted = tf.matmul(x1,w1) + c

# compute cost function
# MSE between predicted and actual values
mse_cost = tf.reduce_mean(tf.square(y_predicted - y_actual))
```

```
# create a root node - a gradient descent optimizer, setup to optimize the
# mse_cost function.
learning_rate = 0.00001
train_step = tf.train.GradientDescentOptimizer(learning_rate).minimize(mse_cost)

#
# execute the graph
#
with tf.Session() as sess:
    # use a global_variable_initializer node to initialize
    # variables all variables in the graph (w1 and c)
    init = tf.global_variables_initializer()
    sess.run(init)

    # extract CRIM feature and target variable into arrays
    xin =  df_boston_train_features['CRIM'].values
    yin =  df_boston_train_target['price'].values

    xin = np.transpose([xin])
    yin = np.transpose([yin])

    # for each observation, evaluate the node called train_step
    # which will in turn update w1 and c so as to minimize
    # the cost function.
    best_w1 = 0.0
    best_c = 0.0
    lowest_cost = 100000.00

    num_epochs = 100000
    for i in range(num_epochs):
        input_dict={x1:xin, y_actual:yin}
        sess.run(train_step, feed_dict=input_dict)

        computed_w1 = sess.run(w1)
        computed_c = sess.run(c)
        computed_cost = sess.run(mse_cost, feed_dict=input_dict)

        if computed_cost < lowest_cost:
            lowest_cost = computed_cost
            best_w1 = computed_w1
            best_c = computed_c

        print ("End of epoch %d, w1=%f, c=%f, cost=%f" % (i, computed_w1,
computed_c, computed_cost))
    print ("End of training, best_w1=%f, best_c=%f, lowest_cost=%f" % (best_w1,
best_c, lowest_cost))
```

As you can see, the entire contents of `xin` and `yin` are fed into the computation graph, and not just once, but 100,000 times. Presenting the entire training set multiple times ensures that the gradient descent optimizer is able to find better values of `w1` and `c`. The number of times the training set is presented during model optimization is called the number of training epochs, and this value is hardcoded to `100000` in the preceding snippet. In effect, the `learning_rate` and `num_epochs` Python variables are hyperparameters of the linear regression model.

If you execute this code in an empty notebook cell, you will see log messages below the notebook cell, listing the values of `w1`, `c`, and the cost function at the end of each training epoch. A selection of the log messages corresponding to different training epochs is presented here:

```
End of epoch 0, w1=0.001066, c=0.000448, cost=588.218872
End of epoch 1, w1=0.002129, c=0.000896, cost=588.085815
End of epoch 2, w1=0.003191, c=0.001344, cost=587.953125
End of epoch 3, w1=0.004251, c=0.001791, cost=587.820862
End of epoch 4, w1=0.005309, c=0.002239, cost=587.689026
...
...
End of epoch 380, w1=0.293133, c=0.165376, cost=557.741821
End of epoch 381, w1=0.293664, c=0.165798, cost=557.695679
End of epoch 382, w1=0.294195, c=0.166221, cost=557.649658
End of epoch 383, w1=0.294725, c=0.166643, cost=557.603760
End of epoch 384, w1=0.295254, c=0.167066, cost=557.557983
End of epoch 385, w1=0.295782, c=0.167488, cost=557.512268
End of epoch 386, w1=0.296309, c=0.167911, cost=557.466675


...
...
End of epoch 99995, w1=-0.222613, c=19.488510, cost=90.642677
End of epoch 99996, w1=-0.222616, c=19.488585, cost=90.642120
End of epoch 99997, w1=-0.222619, c=19.488659, cost=90.641563
End of epoch 99998, w1=-0.222622, c=19.488733, cost=90.640999
End of epoch 99999, w1=-0.222625, c=19.488808, cost=90.640442
End of training, best_w1=-0.222625, best_c=19.488808, lowest_cost=90.640442
```

As you can see, the cost function is not randomly fluctuating with each epoch anymore, but instead is steadily decreasing, which is more in line with what you would expect from an optimization process.

At the end of the training, the values of `best_w1=-0.222625` and `best_c1=19.488808` represent the parameters of the trained model and can be used to make predictions on the test set using the linear regression equation $Y = w_1 X_1 + c$. This is demonstrated in the following snippet:

```
# use best_w1 and best_c to make predictions on all observations in the test set
predictions = df_boston_test_features['CRIM'].values * best_w1 + best_c
```

Once you have the predictions, you can use Scikit-learn to compute the MSE across all the predictions over the test set using the values of `best_w1=-0.222625` and `best_c1=19.488808` as follows:

```
# compute MSE on test set
from sklearn.metrics import mean_squared_error
```

```
mse_test = mean_squared_error(np.transpose(df_boston_test_target.values),
predictions)
```

The value of the mean squared error can be examined using the Python print statement, and comes out to be a significantly lower value—which indicates that the model is performing significantly better:

```
print (mse_test)

85.05865369536087
```

Training and Deploying a DNN Classifier Using the TensorFlow Estimators API and Amazon SageMaker

In the previous section, you learned to create a linear regression model from scratch using the low-level TensorFlow Python API. In this section you will use the high-level TensorFlow Estimators API to train a Dense Neural Network (DNN)–based classifier on the popular Iris flowers dataset.

You will write your TensorFlow code in a Python script file and upload it to your Amazon SageMaker notebook instance. You will then use the AWS SageMaker SDK for Python from a Jupyter Notebook running on your notebook instance to create a training job. The training job will create a dedicated training instance on the AWS cloud and deploy your TensorFlow model-training code onto the instance. When the training completes, your trained model will be stored in an Amazon S3 bucket, after which you will use another function provided by the AWS SageMaker Python SDK to deploy the trained model to a dedicated prediction instance and create an HTTPS prediction endpoint. Finally, you will use the AWS SageMaker SDK for Python to interact with this prediction endpoint from your Jupyter Notebook file to make predictions on data the model has not seen.

A dedicated training instance is an EC2 instance that is used to train a model from data in an Amazon S3 bucket and save the trained model to another Amazon S3 bucket. However, unlike a notebook instance, a dedicated training instance does not have a Jupyter Notebook server and is terminated automatically once the training process is complete. Dedicated training instances are created from Docker images. Amazon SageMaker provides Docker images for training and deploying models that have been created using the TensorFlow Estimators API. The Docker image used for training includes TensorFlow, Python, and a number of other libraries such as NumPy and Pandas. The Docker image used to deploy trained models includes TensorFlow Serving, which is a server product from Google that allows TensorFlow models to be deployed in production environment and accessed via REST APIs. Amazon's Docker images are stored in Docker registries within each AWS region. You can find the paths to the Docker registries for TensorFlow Docker images in each supported region at https://docs.aws.amazon.com/sagemaker/latest/dg/pre-built-docker-containers-frameworks.html.

The dedicated EC2 training instances, once created, will need to assume an IAM role that will allow code running in the training instances access to other resources in your AWS account, such as Amazon S3 buckets that contain the training data. Since the IAM role that is used to create your notebook instance has the correct permissions to access the relevant AWS resources, the most common approach is to use the same IAM role for the EC2 training instances.

To get started, launch the `tensorflow-models` notebook instance and use the Upload button to upload the `TF_DNN_iris_training_script.py` file provided with the resources that accompany this chapter (Figure 17.15).

FIGURE 17.15
Uploading a file to a notebook instance

The Python code within this file is presented here:

```python
import argparse
import numpy as np
import pandas as pd
import os
import tensorflow as tf

def estimator_fn(run_config, params):

    feature_columns = [tf.feature_column.numeric_column(key='sepal_length'),
                tf.feature_column.numeric_column(key='sepal_width'),
                tf.feature_column.numeric_column(key='petal_length'),
                tf.feature_column.numeric_column(key='petal_width')]


    return tf.estimator.DNNClassifier(feature_columns=feature_columns,
                                hidden_units=[10, 10],
                                n_classes=3,
                                config=run_config)


def train_input_fn(training_dir, params):

    # read input file iris_train.csv .
    input_file = os.path.join(training_dir, 'iris_train.csv')
    df_iris_train = pd.read_csv(input_file, header=0, engine="python")

    # convert categorical target attribute 'species'  from  strings to integers
    df_iris_train['species'] = df_iris_train['species'].map({'Iris-
setosa':0,'Iris-virginica':1,'Iris-versicolor':2})

    # extract numpy data from a DataFrame
    labels = df_iris_train['species'].values
```

```python
    features = {
        'sepal_length': df_iris_train['sepal_length'].values,
        'sepal_width': df_iris_train['sepal_width'].values,
        'petal_length': df_iris_train['petal_length'].values,
        'petal_width': df_iris_train['petal_width'].values
    }

    return features, labels


def eval_input_fn(training_dir, params):

    # read input file iris_test.csv .
    input_file = os.path.join(training_dir, 'iris_test.csv')
    df_iris_test = pd.read_csv(input_file, header=0, engine="python")

    # convert categorical target attribute 'species'  from  strings to integers
    df_iris_test['species'] = df_iris_test['species'].
map({'Iris-setosa':0,'Iris-virginica':1,'Iris-versicolor':2})

    # extract numpy data from a DataFrame
    labels = df_iris_test['species'].values

    features = {
        'sepal_length': df_iris_test['sepal_length'].values,
        'sepal_width': df_iris_test['sepal_width'].values,
        'petal_length': df_iris_test['petal_length'].values,
        'petal_width': df_iris_test['petal_width'].values
    }


    return features, labels


def serving_input_fn(params):

    feature_spec = {
        'sepal_length': tf.FixedLenFeature(dtype=tf.float32, shape=[1]),
        'sepal_width': tf.FixedLenFeature(dtype=tf.float32, shape=[1]),
        'petal_length': tf.FixedLenFeature(dtype=tf.float32, shape=[1]),
        'petal_width': tf.FixedLenFeature(dtype=tf.float32, shape=[1])
    }

    return
tf.estimator.export.build_parsing_serving_input_receiver_fn(feature_spec)()
```

The high-level TensorFlow Estimators API is contained in the `tf.estimators` package. You can create a model using one of the pre-made Estimators contained in this package or create your own custom Estimator. As of when this chapter was written, Amazon SageMaker only allows you to build and deploy models that are built using the Estimators API onto prediction instances. If you use the low-level TensorFlow Python API, you can train your model on a notebook instance but cannot deploy it onto the Amazon cloud and create an HTTPS prediction endpoint. It is possible to create a custom `Estimator` object and use this to wrap your low-level model-building code, but this is an advanced topic and beyond the scope of this book. If you want to learn more about building custom Estimators, refer to `https://www.tensorflow.org/guide/custom_estimators`.

The model that you will be training in this section will use a pre-made Estimator called `tf.estimators.DNNClassifier`. The advantage of using pre-made Estimators is that you do not need to build a computation graph or manage a session. You can use a pre-made Estimator with minimal effort, out of the box, without necessarily understanding how it works. Since all `Estimator` objects implement a common interface, it is possible to switch to different model architectures with minimal effort. The neural network classifier will consist of an input layer with 4 neurons, 2 hidden layers with 10 neurons each, and an output layer with 3 neurons. All neurons in a layer are fully connected with the neurons in the previous layer. The architecture of the neural network is depicted in Figure 17.16.

FIGURE 17.16
Architecture of neural-network–based classification model

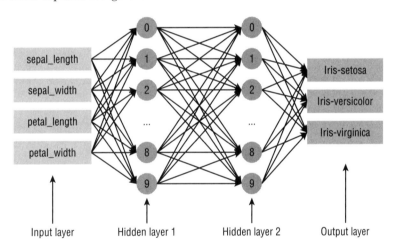

The four input neurons correspond to the four features of the Iris dataset, and each of these neurons accepts continuous numeric floating-point input values. The three output neurons correspond to the three target classes, and the values of these will also be a continuous numeric floating-point value, which will represent the class-wise prediction probability.

Let's briefly examine the training script file `TF_DNN_iris_training_script.py`. Amazon SageMaker requires that a script file to train a TensorFlow model implements the following functions:

◆ Any one of these three functions:

   ◆ `estimator_fn`: This function is used when you are building a model using a pre-built TensorFlow Estimator. The function is expected to return an instance of a pre-built TensorFlow `Estimator` object that will train the model.

◆ `keras_model_fn`: This function is used when you are building a model using the Keras library.

◆ `model_fn`: This function is used when you are building a model from scratch. The function is expected to return an `EstimatorSpec` object, which will be used to generate an `Estimator` object.

◆ `train_input_fn`: This function is responsible for reading training data from your data sources, preprocessing the data, and converting the data into a format that the Estimator can use.

◆ `eval_input_fn`: This function is responsible for reading evaluation data from your data sources, preprocessing the data, and converting the data into a format that the Estimator can use.

◆ `serving_input_fn`: This function is responsible for preprocessing the data that you submitted with your prediction requests and preparing them for the model.

Since you are creating a model using a pre-built Estimator, your script implements `estimator_fn` as follows:

```
def estimator_fn(run_config, params):

    feature_columns = [tf.feature_column.numeric_column(key='sepal_length'),
                    tf.feature_column.numeric_column(key='sepal_width'),
                    tf.feature_column.numeric_column(key='petal_length'),
                    tf.feature_column.numeric_column(key='petal_width')]


    return tf.estimator.DNNClassifier(feature_columns=feature_columns,
                                hidden_units=[10, 10],
                                n_classes=3,
                                config=run_config)
```

To create the neural network classifier, you instantiate the DNNClassifier class from the `tf.estimator` package. The constructor for the class requires an array called `feature_columns` that describes the input features. The contents of this array must be feature column objects and will be used by the DNNClassifier instance to construct the input layer of the neural network. Since the input features are all continuous, numeric values, each element of the array that you pass into the `feature_columns` argument is an instance of NumericColumn and is created using the `tf.feature_column.numeric_column()` function. You can learn more about creating feature columns for different types of inputs at https://www.tensorflow.org/api_docs/python/tf/feature_column.

The DNNClassifier instance also requires you to specify the number of neurons in each of the hidden layers and the number of output classes, which are specified in the `hidden_units` and `n_classes` constructor arguments, respectively. You can get more information on the DNNClassifier class at https://www.tensorflow.org/api_docs/python/tf/estimator/DNNClassifier.

The training input function is used during model training and is responsible for reading training data from your data source, performing any necessary feature engineering, and preparing the data in a format that is compatible with the input feature columns. The training input function is implemented in a function called `train_input_fn` as follows:

```
def train_input_fn(training_dir, params):

    # read input file iris_train.csv .
    input_file = os.path.join(training_dir, 'iris_train.csv')
    df_iris_train = pd.read_csv(input_file, header=0, engine="python")

    # convert categorical target attribute 'species'  from  strings to integers
    df_iris_train['species'] = df_iris_train['species'].map({'Iris-
setosa':0,'Iris-virginica':1,'Iris-versicolor':2})

    # extract numpy data from a DataFrame
    labels = df_iris_train['species'].values

    features = {
        'sepal_length': df_iris_train['sepal_length'].values,
        'sepal_width': df_iris_train['sepal_width'].values,
        'petal_length': df_iris_train['petal_length'].values,
        'petal_width': df_iris_train['petal_width'].values
    }

    return features, labels
```

The training input function makes use of Pandas to load the `iris_train.csv` file from the Amazon S3 bucket called `awsml-sagemaker-source` into the `df_iris_train` dataframe using the `pd.read_csv` function. The full path to the Amazon S3 bucket will be provided by Amazon SageMaker in the `training_dir` parameter when this training script is deployed onto a training container.

The outputs of a neural network classifier are numeric values, and not strings; therefore, you will need to convert the values in the target column `species` of the dataframe from strings to numbers. This is achieved using the dataframe's `map()` function. Occurrences of the string `Iris-setosa` in the `species` column will be replaced by the integer 0, `Iris-virginica` with 1, and `Iris-versicolor` with 2.

Training input functions need to return a tuple with two values. The first member of the tuple is a dictionary called `features`, where each key corresponds to the name of an input feature column (as specified in the Estimator function), and the corresponding value is an array of values for that feature. The second member of the tuple is an array of target values. There are many ways to construct this tuple, including the TensorFlow datasets API, but in this example, I have constructed the tuple from scratch.

The evaluation input function is used during the model-evaluation phase and is responsible for reading evaluation data from your data source, performing any necessary feature engineering, and preparing the data in a format that is compatible with the input feature columns. The

evaluation input function is implemented in a function called `eval_input_fn` and is similar to
the training input function, except that it reads the `iris_test.csv` file:

```
def eval_input_fn(training_dir, params):

    # read input file iris_test.csv .
    input_file = os.path.join(training_dir, 'iris_test.csv')
    df_iris_test = pd.read_csv(input_file, header=0, engine="python")

    # convert categorical target attribute 'species'  from  strings to integers
    df_iris_test['species'] = df_iris_test['species'].map({'Iris-
setosa':0,'Iris-virginica':1,'Iris-versicolor':2})

    # extract numpy data from a DataFrame
    labels = df_iris_test['species'].values

    features = {
        'sepal_length': df_iris_test['sepal_length'].values,
        'sepal_width': df_iris_test['sepal_width'].values,
        'petal_length': df_iris_test['petal_length'].values,
        'petal_width': df_iris_test['petal_width'].values
    }


    return features, labels
```

The serving input function is used when you use the trained model to make predictions. The
purpose of the serving input function is to prepare the data that you provide, while making
predictions with the model, into a format that the model can use. The serving input function is
implemented as follows:

```
def serving_input_fn(params):

    feature_spec = {
        'sepal_length': tf.FixedLenFeature(dtype=tf.float32, shape=[1]),
        'sepal_width': tf.FixedLenFeature(dtype=tf.float32, shape=[1]),
        'petal_length': tf.FixedLenFeature(dtype=tf.float32, shape=[1]),
        'petal_width': tf.FixedLenFeature(dtype=tf.float32, shape=[1])
    }

    return
tf.estimator.export.build_parsing_serving_input_receiver_fn(feature_spec)()
```

You can learn more about serving models with TensorFlow Serving at
`https://www.tensorflow.org/tfx/serving/serving_basic`.

Now that you have prepared a model-training script file, it is time to use a Jupyter Notebook
file to create a training job. Create a new Jupyter Notebook file on your notebook instance using

the conda_tensorflow_p35 kernel. Change the title of the notebook to TF_DNN_iris_flowers and type the following code in an empty notebook cell:

```
import sagemaker

# Get a SageMaker-compatible role used by this Notebook Instance.
role = sagemaker.get_execution_role()

# get a SageMaker session object, that can be
# used to manage the interaction with the SageMaker API.
sagemaker_session = sagemaker.Session()

# train a TensorFlow Estimator based model on a dedicated instance
from sagemaker.tensorflow import TensorFlow


tf_estimator = TensorFlow(entry_point='TF_DNN_iris_training_script.py',
                          train_instance_count=1,
                          train_instance_type='ml.m4.xlarge',
                          role=role,
                          framework_version='1.12',
                          training_steps=500,
                          evaluation_steps=10,
                          output_path='s3://awsml-sagemaker-results/')


tf_estimator.fit('s3://awsml-sagemaker-source/')
```

Execute the code in the notebook cell to launch a training job that will result in the creation of a dedicated ml.m4.xlarge EC2 instance from the default Docker image for TensorFlow model training. You can specify a different instance type, but keep in mind that more powerful instance types have higher running costs associated with them. The TensorFlow class is part of the AWS SageMaker Python SDK and provides a convenient mechanism to handle end-to-end training and deployment of TensorFlow models. The constructor for the class accepts several arguments, including the path to the Python script file that contains your model building code, the type of training instance that you wish to create, the IAM role that should be assigned to the new instance, and model-building hyperparameters. All TensorFlow Estimators require both the training_steps and evaluation_steps parameters, which control the number of training and evaluation epochs. In addition, individual Estimators may have specific hyperparameters that you can pass as a hyperparameter dictionary similar to how you passed hyperparameters while training Scikit-learn models in the previous chapter.

You can learn more about the parameters of the TensorFlow class at https://sagemaker .readthedocs.io/en/stable/sagemaker.tensorflow.html.

When you execute the code in a notebook cell, Amazon SageMaker will create a new dedicated training instance and execute your script file within the instance once the instance is ready. This can be a time-consuming process and may take several minutes. While the training process is underway, you will see various status messages printed below the notebook cell (Figure 17.17).

FIGURE 17.17

Using a notebook
instance to create a
training job

The training process is complete when you see lines similar to the following in the output:

```
2019-05-12 18:59:49,097 INFO - tensorflow - SavedModel written to: s3://awsml-
sagemaker-results/sagemaker-tensorflow-2019-05-12-18-57-13-796/checkpoints/
export/Servo/1557687587/saved_model.pb
2019-05-12 18:59:49,217 INFO - tensorflow - Loss for final step: 6.2997513.
2019-05-12 18:59:49,403 INFO - tf_container - Downloaded saved model at
/opt/ml/model/export/Servo/1557687587

2019-05-12 18:59:56 Uploading - Uploading generated training model
2019-05-12 18:59:56 Completed - Training job completed
Billable seconds: 39
```

After the training process is complete, Amazon SageMaker will automatically terminate the instance that was created to support the training. The model that was created will be saved to the awsml-sagemaker-results bucket, and the full path to the saved model is printed in the log messages. You can also view a list of trained models from the Models menu item of the AWS SageMaker management console (Figure 17.18) and access the model artifact file from there.

Now that you have a trained model, you can deploy the model to one or more dedicated prediction instances and then either create an HTTPS API endpoint for creating predictions on one item at a time, or create a batch transform job to obtain predictions on entire datasets. Using batch transforms is not covered in this chapter; however, you can find more information at https://docs.aws.amazon.com/sagemaker/latest/dg/ex1-batch-transform.html.

You can deploy models into prediction instances in several different ways, including using the AWS SageMaker Python SDK and the AWS management console. Regardless of the manner in which you choose to deploy the model, the process of deployment involves first creating an endpoint configuration object, and then using the endpoint configuration object to create the prediction instances and the HTTPS endpoint that can be used to get inferences from the deployed model. The endpoint configuration contains information on the location of the model file, the type and number of compute instances that the model will be deployed to, and the auto-scaling policy to be used to scale up the number of instances as needed.

FIGURE 17.18

List of trained models

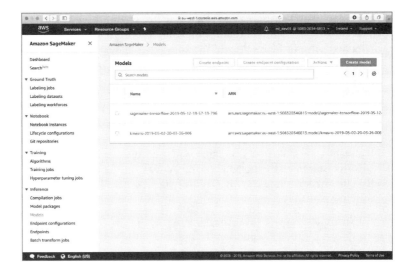

If you use the high-level Amazon SageMaker Python SDK to deploy your model, the SDK provides a convenience function that takes care of creating the endpoint configuration, creation of compute resources, deployment of the model, and the creation of the HTTPS endpoint. If you use the lower-level AWS Boto Python SDK, you will need to perform the individual steps in sequence yourself. Keep in mind that prediction instances incur additional costs and are not automatically terminated after you have made predictions.

Execute the following code in an empty cell of the notebook to deploy the trained model to a single ML compute instance and create an HTTPS endpoint:

```
# create a prediction instance
predictor = tf_estimator.deploy(initial_instance_count=1,
instance_type="ml.m4.xlarge")
```

This code assumes that the tf_estimator object has been created in the previous notebook cell where you trained the model. This is important because the deploy() function does not have an argument that lets you specify the path to the model file, but instead uses whatever model file is referenced within the tf_estimator object.

When you execute this code, Amazon SageMaker will take several minutes to create an endpoint configuration, create the compute instances, deploy your model onto the instances, and create an HTTPS endpoint. Once the prediction endpoint is created, the deploy() function will return an object of class TensorFlowPredictor, which provides a convenience function called predict() that can be used to make predictions from the HTTPS endpoint. The prediction endpoint is internet-facing and is secured using AWS Signature V4 authentication. You can access this endpoint in a variety of ways, including the AWS CLI, tools such as Postman, and the language-specific AWS SDKs. If you use the AWS CLI, or one of the AWS SDKs, authentication will be achieved behind the scenes for you. You can learn more about AWS Signature V4 at `https://docs.aws.amazon.com/AmazonS3/latest/API/sig-v4-authenticating-requests.html`.

If you want to expose the prediction endpoint as a service to your consumers, you can create an endpoint on an Amazon API Gateway instance and set up the Amazon API Gateway to execute an AWS Lambda function when it receives a request. You can then use one of the language-specific SDKs in the AWS Lambda function to interact with the prediction endpoint. The advantage of this approach is that your clients do not need to worry about AWS Signature V4 authentication, and an Amazon API Gateway can provide several features that are critical to managing the business-related aspects of a commercial API service such as credential management, credential rotation, support for OIDC, API versioning, and traffic management.

If you are using the AWS SageMaker Python SDK from a notebook instance, you can use the `predict()` function of the `TensorFlowPredictor` instance to make single predictions. Behind the scenes, the `predict()` function will use a temporary set of credentials associated with the IAM role assumed by the notebook instance to authenticate with the prediction endpoint. Execute the following code in an empty notebook cell to use the `predict()` function to predict the class of an Iris flower:

```
input_dict = {'sepal_length': 63.4,
              'sepal_width': 3.2,
              'petal_length': 4.5,
              'petal_width': 11.5 }

# use the prediction endpoint to get a single prediction
prediction = predictor.predict(input_dict)
```

You can use the Python `print()` function to examine the predictions:

```
print (prediction)

{'result': {'classifications': [{'classes': [{'label': '0', 'score': 1.0},
{'label': '1'}, {'label': '2', 'score': 5.525393273616511e-15}]}]}, 'model_spec':
{'name': 'generic_model', 'version': {'value': 1557687587}, 'signature_name':
'serving_default'}}
```

To terminate the prediction instances and the associated HTTPS endpoint, you can, once again, use the high-level interface provided by the AWS SageMaker Python SDK. Execute the following code in a free notebook cell to terminate and deactivate the prediction endpoint:

```
tf_estimator.delete_endpoint()
```

You can also use the AWS SageMaker management console to view the list of active prediction endpoints, deactivate a prediction endpoint and terminate the associated prediction instances, and create new prediction endpoints from endpoint configurations.

NOTE You can download the code files for this chapter from `www.wiley.com/go/machinelearningawscloud` or from GitHub using the following URL:

`https://github.com/asmtechnology/awsmlbook-chapter17.git`

Summary

- TensorFlow is a machine learning library created by Google, which was initially developed by the team at Google Brain for internal use, and then subsequently released as an open source project under the Apache license in November 2015.

- TensorFlow requires you to model your computation problem as a tree-like structure called a computation graph, made up of nodes and leaves.

- A constant leaf node (also known as a constant tensor) is a tensor whose value cannot be changed once it has been assigned.

- A variable leaf node (also known as a variable tensor) is a tensor whose value can be changed as the program executes.

- A placeholder leaf node (also known as a placeholder tensor) is a special node whose value is a tensor that you must feed into the graph when you evaluate the graph.

- Artificial neural networks (ANNs) are computing tools that were developed by Warren McCulloch and Walter Pitts in 1943, and their design is inspired by biological neural networks.

- The TensorFlow Python API is structured in a series of layers, with the topmost layer known as the Estimators API.

- Objects in the Estimators layer provide the ability to create entire neural networks with a single Python statement.

- You can train and deploy a machine learning model that uses the Estimators API on Amazon SageMaker.

Chapter 18

Amazon Rekognition

WHAT'S IN THIS CHAPTER

♦ Introduction to the Amazon Rekognition service

♦ Use the Amazon Rekognition management console

♦ Use the AWS CLI to interact with Amazon Rekognition

♦ Call Amazon Rekognition APIs from AWS Lambda

Amazon Rekognition is a fully managed web service that provides access to a deep-learning models for image and video analysis. Using Amazon Rekognition you can create projects that can analyze the content of images and videos to implement features such as object detection, object location, scene analysis, activity detection, and content filtering. In this lesson you will learn to use the Amazon Rekognition APIs from the management console, the AWS CLI, and an AWS Lambda function.

NOTE To follow along with this chapter ensure you have created the S3 buckets listed in Appendix B.

You can download the code files for this chapter from `www.wiley.com/go/machinelearning-awscloud` or from GitHub using the following URL:

`https://github.com/asmtechnology/awsmlbook-chapter18.git`

Key Concepts

In this section you will learn some of the key concepts you will encounter while working with Amazon Rekognition.

Object Detection

Object detection is a discipline within computer vision that focuses on creating algorithms that allow computers to analyze the content of digital images and prepare a list of objects found in the image. Traditionally these algorithms have relied on having a database of template objects and using matching techniques to match templates in the database against the content of the image. Recent advances in deep learning have led to the creation of more reliable and robust algorithms. Object detection with Amazon Rekognition results in a set of string labels that describe the content of the image, and is referred to as label detection in Amazon Rekognition.

Object Location

Object location is a discipline within computer vision that builds upon object detection algorithms and provides information on the location of objects found within the image. The location is usually specified as a bounding box with respect to one of the corners of the image.

Scene Detection

Scene detection (also known as scene description) is a discipline in artificial intelligence that attempts to build upon the results of object detection and location algorithms to arrive at a textual description of a digital image. For instance, an object detection algorithm may detect a person and a bicycle in an image. An object location algorithm will then be able to define the bounding boxes of these objects in the image. A scene detection algorithm could use these results to describe the scene as "Man riding a bicycle on a sunny day." Scene detection using convolutional neural networks (CNNs) is an area of active research.

Activity Detection

Activity detection is a discipline in artificial intelligence that attempts to create algorithms that analyze the contents of a video frame by frame and arrive at a description of an activity that occurs in the video. The key difference between activity detection and scene detection is that scene detection works on a single isolated image, whereas activity detection examines a sequence of images.

Facial Recognition

Facial recognition algorithms attempt to examine a digital image (or a video feed) to detect and locate known human faces. The recognition aspects of these algorithms require that the algorithm has access to a database of faces and only attempts to locate the faces that exist in the database. Faces are usually added to the database as part of a training operation. In the past, the main algorithm in facial recognition involved using Haar wavelet descriptors; however, today the main approach to facial recognition involves using convolutional neural networks, which have produced accuracies that approach that of a human being tasked to recognize the same faces.

Face Collection

A face collection is an indexed container of information that describes human faces. Face collections are used with Amazon Rekognition APIs such as `DetectFaces` that implement facial recognition.

API Sets

Amazon Rekognition provides two sets of APIs: the Amazon Rekognition Image APIs and the Amazon Rekognition Video APIs. As their names suggest, these APIs are to be used with single images or videos, respectively. Inputs and outputs to both API sets are JSON objects; however, Amazon Rekognition Image APIs are synchronous whereas Amazon Rekognition Video APIs are asynchronous. Asynchronous API operations allow you to start an operation by calling an initiation API (such as `StartFaceDetection`) and then publish the completion status of the operation to an Amazon SNS topic. On receiving a notification from Amazon SNS you can then use a get API for the type of operation you initiated (such as `GetFaceDetection`).

Non-Storage and Storage-Based Operations

Non-storage API operations are those operation where Amazon Rekognition does not persist any information during the analysis process, or the result of the analysis. You provide input images or videos, and the API operation reads the inputs and provides the results with nothing being persisted by Amazon Rekognition. Storage-based operations, on the other hand, store the results of the operation within Amazon Rekognition and are typically used when building a face collection for subsequent facial recognition operations. The APIs that build the face collection are storage based; however, the actual facial recognition APIs are not.

Model Versioning

Amazon Rekognition makes use of deep-learning CNN models to implement its APIs. Amazon continually improves these models and frequently releases new versions. If you are using the Amazon Rekognition Image APIs, you do not need to keep track of the model versions used by Amazon Rekognition as the latest version will automatically be used. However, if you are using Amazon Rekognition Video APIs that use a previously built face collection or if you are adding faces to an existing collection, you will only be able to use the version of the model that was used when the collection was created. Face collections created using one model version cannot be translated to (and used with) a different model version.

Pricing and Availability

Amazon Rekognition is available on a pay-per-use model. Use of the image APIs is charged based on the number of images processed; use of the video APIs is charged based on the minutes of videos processed. If you store faces in a collection, you will also be charged for the number of faces stored. This service is included in the AWS free-tier account. You can get more details on the pricing model at `https://aws.amazon.com/rekognition/pricing/`.

Amazon Rekognition is not available in all regions. You can get information on the regions in which it is available from the following URL: `https://aws.amazon.com/about-aws/global-infrastructure/regional-product-services/`.

Analyzing Images Using the Amazon Rekognition Management Console

In this section you will use the Amazon Rekognition management console to perform object detection on images. Due to the nature of the operations they perform, Amazon Rekognition APIs are typically accessed using one of the AWS SDKs directly from your projects, or via an AWS Lambda function that is triggered in response to an event.

The Amazon Rekognition management console provides an easy-to-use interface that lets you try out the Rekognition APIs on individual images and video sequences.

Log in to the AWS management console using the dedicated sign-in link for your development IAM user account. Use the region selector to select a region where the Amazon Rekognition service is available. The screenshots in this section assume that the console is connected to the EU (Ireland) region. Click the Services menu and access the Amazon Rekognition service home page (Figure 18.1).

FIGURE 18.1

Accessing the Amazon
Rekognition service
home page

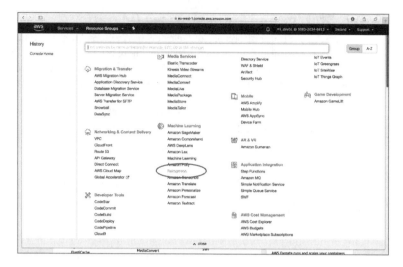

Expand the menu on the left side of the page if it is not visible and click the Object And Scene
Detection link under the Demos category (Figure 18.2).

FIGURE 18.2

Accessing the Object and
Scene Detection demo

You can use one of the sample images provided by Amazon or use your own. The images
used in this chapter are included with the files that accompany this chapter. Upload the `bicycle_01`
image from the sample images and observe the list of object labels detected by Amazon
Rekognition (Figure 18.3).

Each label is listed along with a confidence score between 0 and 100, with labels with higher
confidence at the top of the list. When you use the management console to access the Rekognition
APIs, the console creates a JSON request on your behalf and sends the request to the relevant
Rekognition image (or video) API. The response from the API is also a JSON object, which the
management console parses before displaying the labels on the web page.

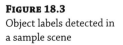

FIGURE 18.3

Object labels detected in a sample scene

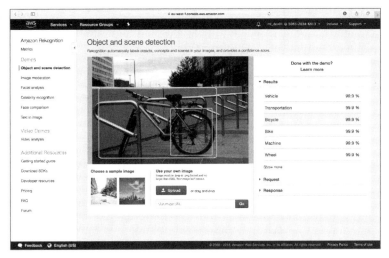

You can access the raw JSON request and response by expanding the Request and Response sections of the web page. The request object in this example contains a single attribute called Image that contains the Base64-encoded contents of the image file that you have uploaded:

```
{
"Image": {"Bytes": "..."}
}
```

The response object is considerably larger, and contains information on the object labels and their confidence scores:

```
{
    "LabelModelVersion": "2.0",
    "Labels": [  {
        "Confidence": 99.98981475830078,
        "Instances": [],
        "Name": "Vehicle",
        "Parents": [{"Name": "Transportation"}]
    },
    {
        "Confidence": 99.98981475830078,
        "Instances": [],
        "Name": "Transportation",
        "Parents": []
    },
    {
        "Confidence": 99.98981475830078,
        "Instances": [{
            "BoundingBox":{
            "Height": 0.6593928337097168,
            "Left": 0.04068286344408989,
```

```
            "Top": 0.2880190312862396,
            "Width": 0.7587363719940186
            },
            "Confidence": 99.98981475830078
            }],
        "Name": "Bicycle",
        "Parents": [
            {"Name": "Vehicle" },
            {"Name": "Transportation"}]
    },
    {
    "Confidence": 99.98981475830078,
    "Instances": [],
    "Name": "Bike",
    "Parents": [{"Name": "Vehicle" },
    {"Name": "Transportation" }]
    },
    {
    "Confidence": 99.92826080322266,
    "Instances": [],
    "Name": "Machine",
    "Parents": []
    },
    {
    "Confidence": 99.92826080322266,
    "Instances": [{
        "BoundingBox": {
        "Height": 0.44183894991874695,
        "Left": 0.5008670091629028,
        "Top": 0.4816884696483612,
        "Width": 0.2692929804325104
        },
        "Confidence": 99.92826080322266 }],
    "Name": "Wheel",
    "Parents": [{ "Name": "Machine" } ]
    },
    {
    "Confidence": 55.68204879760742,
    "Instances": [],
    "Name": "Mountain Bike",
    "Parents": [
        {"Name": "Vehicle"},
        {"Name": "Bicycle"},
        {"Name": "Transportation"}]
    }
    ]
}
```

Each label is represented as an item in an array, and consists of a name, confidence score, information on bounding box coordinates if applicable, and the name of the parent label if Amazon Rekognition detects a hierarchical relationship between labels. For instance, the Wheel label has a parent label called Machine:

```
{
        "Confidence": 99.92826080322266,
        "Instances": [ {
            "BoundingBox": {
            "Height": 0.44183894991874695,
            "Left": 0.5008670091629028,
            "Top": 0.4816884696483612,
            "Width": 0.2692929804325104
            },
            "Confidence": 99.92826080322266
        }],
        "Name": "Wheel",
        "Parents": [ { "Name": "Machine" } ]
}
```

You can use the Metrics link to view aggregate graphs on six metrics over a period of time (see Figure 18.4).

FIGURE 18.4
Amazon Rekognition
aggregate metric graphs

The six metrics and associated graphs are listed in Table 18.1.

To view the Amazon Rekognition metric graphs, the IAM user that you are using must have appropriate Amazon CloudWatch and Amazon Rekognition permissions; at the very least the user should have the `AmazonRekognitionReadOnlyAccess` and `CloudWatchReadOnlyAccess` permissions.

The aggregate graphs that you see in the Rekognition metrics pane are powered by Amazon CloudWatch metric reports. You can learn more about monitoring Amazon Rekognition at the following URL: `https://docs.aws.amazon.com/rekognition/latest/dg/rekognition_monitoring.html`.

TABLE 18.1:   Aggregate Metric Graphs

NAME OF GRAPH	METRIC NAME
Successful calls	SuccessfulRequestCount
Client errors	UserErrorCount
Server errors	ServerErrorCount
Throttled	ThrottledCount
Detected labels	DetectedLabelCount
Detected faces	DetectedFaceCount

Interactive Image Analysis with the AWS CLI

You can use the AWS CLI to access the underlying Amazon Rekognition APIs and perform image and video analysis over the command line. The Amazon Rekognition APIs accept JSON inputs and provide JSON responses. Since the Amazon Rekognition APIs work on images or videos—which are fundamentally large-sized objects—the most common approach to submit images or videos to the Amazon Rekognition APIs is to upload them to an Amazon S3 bucket and submit the Amazon S3 object ARN (Amazon Resource Name) as a parameter in the JSON request payload.

Another option is to encode the bytes of the image or video object as a BASE64 string and include the BASE64 string in the JSON request payload. This technique is not recommended, and it is better to separate image/video upload from the actual Amazon Rekognition API call.

The examples in this section will upload the images to an Amazon S3 bucket before calling the Amazon Rekognition APIs. The bucket that will be used in this section is called awsml-rekognition-awscli-source. Since bucket names are unique, you will need to substitute references to this bucket with your own bucket name. This section also assumes you have installed and configured the AWS CLI to use your development IAM credentials.

To upload an image to an Amazon S3 bucket with the AWS CLI, launch a Terminal window on your Mac or a Command Prompt window on Windows, and type a statement similar to the following:

```
$ aws s3 cp <source-file-name> s3://<bucket-name>
```

Replace <source-file-name> with the full path to the image file on your computer, and <bucket-name> with the name of your Amazon S3 bucket. For example, the following command will upload a file called tower-bridge-01.jpg to a bucket called awsml-rekognition-awscli-source:

```
aws s3 cp \
/Users/abhishekmishra/Desktop /tower_bridge_01.jpg  \
s3://awsml-rekognition-awscli-source
```

The image will take a few seconds to upload. You can verify that the image has uploaded by listing the contents of the bucket using the following command:

```
$ aws s3 ls s3://awsml-rekognition-awscli-source
```

Once you have confirmed that the image has been uploaded to your Amazon S3 bucket, type the following command to perform object analysis on the image using the Amazon Rekognition image APIs. Replace the name of the Amazon S3 bucket and object as necessary:

```
aws rekognition detect-labels --image \
'{"S3Object":{"Bucket":"awsml-rekognition-awscli-source", \
"Name":"tower_bridge_01.jpg"}}'
```

The command-line statement invokes the DetectLabels API with a single input parameter called image, which is a JSON object:

```
{
        "S3Object":{
        "Bucket":"awsml-rekognition-awscli-source",
        "Name":"tower_bridge_01.jpg"}
}
```

Press the Enter key on your keyboard to execute the command. The result of executing this command is a list of labels along with their confidence scores as a JSON object:

```
{
    "Labels": [
        {
            "Name": "Building",
            "Confidence": 99.22096252441406,
            "Instances": [],
            "Parents": []
        },
        {
            "Name": "Bridge",
            "Confidence": 97.9942855834961,
            "Instances": [
                {
                    "BoundingBox": {
                        "Width": 0.8991885185241699,
                        "Height": 0.580137312412262,
                        "Left": 0.09563709050416946,
                        "Top": 0.2453334629535675
                    },
                    "Confidence": 96.43193817138672
                }
            ],
            "Parents": [
                {
                    "Name": "Building"
                }
            ]
        },
```

```
        {
            "Name": "Architecture",
            "Confidence": 91.6387939453125,
            "Instances": [],
            "Parents": [
                {
                    "Name": "Building"
                }
            ]
        },
        {
            "Name": "Outdoors",
            "Confidence": 83.56424713134766,
            "Instances": [],
            "Parents": []
        },
        {
            "Name": "Suspension Bridge",
            "Confidence": 80.96751403808594,
            "Instances": [],
            "Parents": [
                {
                    "Name": "Bridge"
                },
                {
                    "Name": "Building"
                }
            ]
        },
        {
            "Name": "Arch",
            "Confidence": 76.18531799316406,
            "Instances": [],
            "Parents": [
                {
                    "Name": "Building"
                },
                {
                    "Name": "Architecture"
                }
            ]
        },
        {
            "Name": "Arched",
            "Confidence": 76.18531799316406,
            "Instances": [],
            "Parents": [
```

```
                {
                    "Name": "Building"
                },
                {
                    "Name": "Architecture"
                }
            ]
        },
        {
            "Name": "Nature",
            "Confidence": 73.91722869873047,
            "Instances": [],
            "Parents": []
        },
        {
            "Name": "Arch Bridge",
            "Confidence": 70.39462280273438,
            "Instances": [],
            "Parents": [
                {
                    "Name": "Architecture"
                },
                {
                    "Name": "Arch"
                },
                {
                    "Name": "Bridge"
                },
                {
                    "Name": "Building"
                }
            ]
        },
        {
            "Name": "Urban",
            "Confidence": 58.88948440551758,
            "Instances": [],
            "Parents": []
        },
        {
            "Name": "Metropolis",
            "Confidence": 58.88948440551758,
            "Instances": [],
            "Parents": [
                {
                    "Name": "Urban"
                },
```

```
                        {
                            "Name": "Building"
                        },
                        {
                            "Name": "City"
                        }
                    ]
                },
                {
                    "Name": "City",
                    "Confidence": 58.88948440551758,
                    "Instances": [],
                    "Parents": [
                        {
                            "Name": "Urban"
                        },
                        {
                            "Name": "Building"
                        }
                    ]
                },
                {
                    "Name": "Town",
                    "Confidence": 58.88948440551758,
                    "Instances": [],
                    "Parents": [
                        {
                            "Name": "Urban"
                        },
                        {
                            "Name": "Building"
                        }
                    ]
                }
            ],
            "LabelModelVersion": "2.0"
    }
```

If you were to include the --max-labels and --min-confidence arguments in addition to the --image argument in the command-line statement, you could restrict the response to contain fewer labels, and those that are above a minimum confidence score. The following command-line statement demonstrates how these additional attributes can be used:

```
$aws rekognition detect-labels \
--image  '{"S3Object":{"Bucket":"awsml-rekognition-awscli-source", \
  "Name":"tower_bridge_01.jpg"}}' \
--max-labels 4 \
--min-confidence 98.75
```

Press the Enter key on your keyboard to execute the command. After a few seconds, the output on your computer should resemble the following:

```
{
    "Labels": [{
        "Name": "Building",
        "Confidence": 99.22096252441406,
        "Instances": [],
        "Parents": []
        }],
    "LabelModelVersion": "2.0"
}
```

If no labels are found, the DetectLabels operation will return a JSON object with an empty Labels array.

Using Amazon Rekognition with AWS Lambda

In the previous sections of this chapter you have learned to use Amazon Rekognition using the management console and the AWS CLI. While using these APIs interactively certainly provides results, you cannot integrate AWS Rekognition with your own projects in this way.

To integrate Amazon Rekognition in a real-world project, you will most likely pick one of two approaches:

◆ Use one of the language-specific AWS SDKs and call the Amazon Rekognition APIs directly from your code.

◆ Create an AWS Lambda function that will call the Amazon Rekognition APIs when triggered.

In this section you will create an Amazon DynamoDB table and an AWS Lambda function that will be triggered when an image is uploaded to an Amazon S3 bucket. Once triggered, the AWS Lambda function will read the uploaded image from the Amazon S3 bucket and use Amazon Rekognition image APIs to extract a list of objects detected in the image. The names of the objects will then be written to the Amazon DynamoDB table along with the image filename. The Amazon DynamoDB table will serve as a content-based index and could be used by an application to search for images that contain a particular object.

In real-world scenarios, there may be several other events that you could use to trigger the AWS Lambda function, such as an HTTP request being received by an API Gateway. Triggering an AWS Lambda function in the scenarios just described is not covered in this book.

NOTE   To follow along with this section ensure you have created the S3 buckets listed in Appendix B.

You can download the code files for this chapter from www.wiley.com/go/machinelearning-awscloud or from GitHub using the following URL: https://github.com/asmtechnology/awsmlbook-chapter18.git

Creating the Amazon DynamoDB Table

To get started, log in to the AWS management console using the dedicated sign-in link for your development IAM user account and use the region selector to select a region where the Amazon Rekognition service is available. The screenshots in this section assume that the console is connected to the EU (Ireland) region. Click the Services menu and access the Amazon DynamoDB service home page (Figure 18.5).

FIGURE 18.5

Accessing the Amazon DynamoDB management console

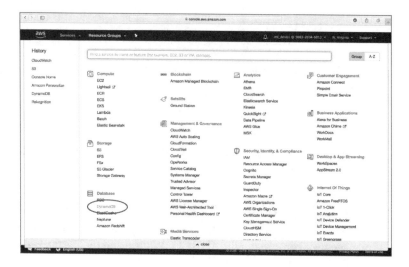

Ensure the Amazon DynamoDB console is set to work with the same region that contains your Amazon S3 bucket. Create a new table called `imageindex` with a partition key attribute called `label` and a sort key attribute called `filename` (see Figure 18.6). If you have never used Amazon DynamoDB, or need a refresher on the concepts, refer to Chapter 11 before continuing with this section.

FIGURE 18.6

Amazon DynamoDB table name and primary key attributes

Uncheck the Use Default Settings option on the page and scroll down to locate the Read/ Write Capacity Mode section (Figure 18.7). Ensure the table is set to use provisioned capacity units, and uncheck the auto scaling options for read and write capacity units.

FIGURE 18.7
Amazon DynamoDB
Table Read/Write
Capacity Mode section

Click the Create Table button at the bottom of the page to finish creating the table. You should see the new table listed alongside any existing tables in the Amazon DynamoDB management console (Figure 18.8).

FIGURE 18.8
Amazon DynamoDB
management console
displaying a
list of tables

Creating the AWS Lambda Function

Click the Services menu and access the AWS Lambda service home page. Ensure the management console is configured to use the same region in which your Amazon S3 buckets and Amazon DynamoDB tables have been created. Click the Create function button to start the process of creating a new AWS Lambda function. If you are new to AWS Lambda, or would like to refresh your skills, refer to Chapter 12 before continuing with the rest of this section.

After clicking the Create Function button, you will be asked to select a template for the function (Figure 18.9). Select the Author From Scratch option.

FIGURE 18.9
Creating an AWS Lambda function from scratch

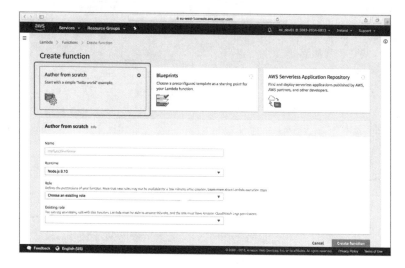

Name the function **DetectLabels**, use the Runtime drop-down to select the Python 3.6 runtime, and select the Create A New Role With Basic Lambda Permissions from Execution Role drop-down (Figure 18.10).

FIGURE 18.10
Lambda Function Name and Runtime settings

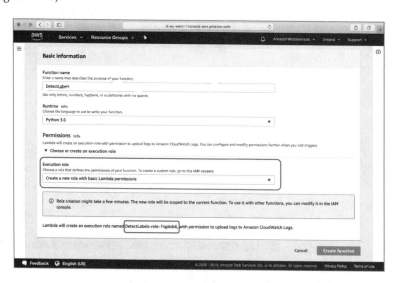

AWS will create a new IAM role for your function with a minimal set of permissions that will allow your function to write logs to AWS CloudWatch. The name of this IAM role is

displayed below the Execution Role drop-down in Figure 18.10 and will be similar to
DetectLabels-role-xxxxx. Make a note of this name as you will need to modify the role to
allow access to Amazon S3, Amazon DynamoDB, and Amazon Rekognition. Click on the
Create Function button at the bottom of the page to create the AWS Lambda function and
the IAM role.

After the AWS Lambda function is created, use the services menu to switch to the IAM
management console and navigate to the new IAM role that was just created for you when you
created the Lambda function. Locate the permissions policy document associated with the role
and click on the Edit Policy button (Figure 18.11).

FIGURE 18.11

Viewing the default
policy document
associated with the IAM
role created by
AWS Lambda

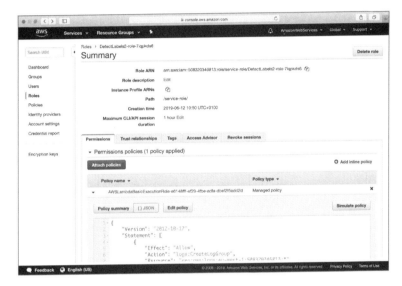

You will be taken to the policy editor screen. Click on the JSON tab to view the policy document as a JSON file (Figure 18.12).

FIGURE 18.12

Updating the default
policy document
associated with the IAM
role created by
AWS Lambda

Add the following objects to the Statement array:

```
{
    "Action": [
        "rekognition:DetectLabels"
    ],
    "Effect": "Allow",
    "Resource": "*"
},
{
    "Action": [
        "s3:GetObject"
    ],
    "Effect": "Allow",
    "Resource": "arn:aws:s3:::*"
},
{
  "Effect": "Allow",
        "Action": [
"dynamodb:PutItem",
            "dynamodb:GetItem",
            "dynamodb:Query",
            "dynamodb:UpdateItem"
        ],
        "Resource": "*"
}
```

Your final policy document should resemble this:

```
{
    "Version": "2012-10-17",
    "Statement": [
        {
            "Effect": "Allow",
            "Action": "logs:CreateLogGroup",
            "Resource": "arn:aws:logs:eu-west-1:5083XXXX13:*"
        },
        {
            "Effect": "Allow",
            "Action": [
                "logs:CreateLogStream",
                "logs:PutLogEvents"
            ],
            "Resource": [
                "arn:aws:logs:eu-west-1:5083XXXX813:log-
group:/aws/lambda/DetectLabels2:*"
            ]
        },
```

```
        {
            "Action": [
                "rekognition:DetectLabels"
            ],
            "Effect": "Allow",
            "Resource": "*"
        },
        {
            "Action": [
                "s3:GetObject"
            ],
            "Effect": "Allow",
            "Resource": "arn:aws:s3:::*"
        },
        {
      "Effect": "Allow",
            "Action": [
    "dynamodb:PutItem",
                "dynamodb:GetItem",
                "dynamodb:Query",
                "dynamodb:UpdateItem"
            ],
            "Resource": "*"
        }
    ]
}
```

This policy document allows AWS Lambda to write logs to CloudWatch, call the Amazon Rekognition DetectLabels API, read objects from any Amazon S3 bucket, read and write items to any Amazon DynamoDB table, and execute queries on any Amazon DynamoDB table in your account.

You can allow access to additional Amazon Rekognition APIs by adding the relevant actions after "rekognition:DetectLabels". You can get a list of available Amazon Rekognition actions that can be used in policy documents at https://docs.aws.amazon.com/rekognition/latest/dg/api-permissions-reference.html.

Click on the Review Policy button at the bottom of the page to go to the Review Policy screen (Figure 18.13).

Click on the Save Changes button to finish updating the IAM policy. After the policy changes have been saved, use the Services menu to switch back to the AWS Lambda management console and navigate to the DetectLabels Lambda function.

Locate the function designer section of the page and add the Amazon S3 trigger to the function. The function designer should resemble Figure 18.14 and should list Amazon CloudWatch Logs, Amazon S3, Amazon DynamoDB, and Amazon Rekognition as the resources that can be accessed by the function.

Scroll down to the Configure Triggers section and choose an Amazon S3 bucket that will serve as the event source. In this example, the source bucket is called awsml-rekognition-awslambda-source. Ensure the Event Type is set to Object Created (All) and click the Add button to finish configuring the S3 event trigger (Figure 18.15).

FIGURE 18.13
Review Policy screen

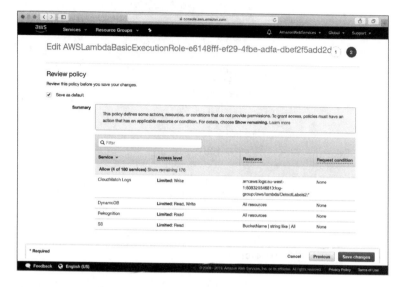

FIGURE 18.14
AWS Lambda function designer

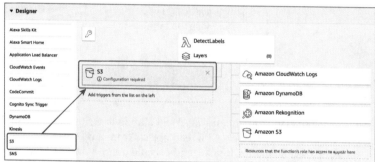

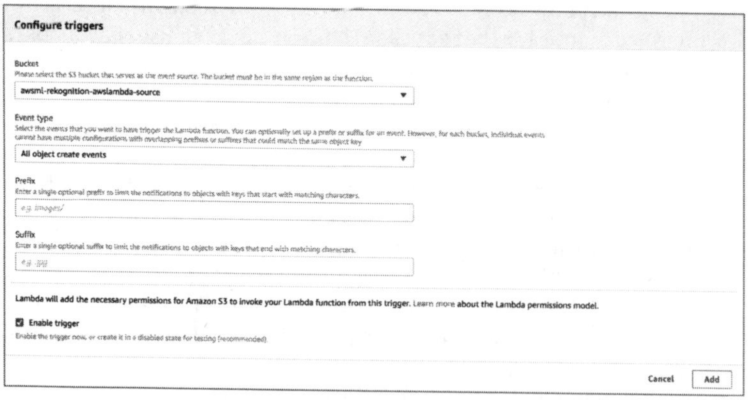

FIGURE 18.15
Configuring the S3 event trigger

Click the Save button at the top of the page to save your changes. By creating the trigger, you have set up the Lambda function to be executed every time a new file is uploaded to the source S3 bucket.

To update the Lambda function code, scroll down to the function designer and click the function name to reveal the code editor (Figure 18.16).

FIGURE 18.16
Configuring the AWS
Lambda function code

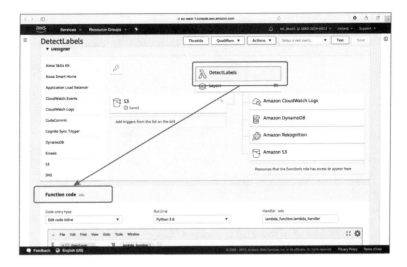

Replace the boilerplate code in the code editor with the contents of Listing 18.1.

LISTING 18.1:   Python 3.6 AWS Lambda Function Code to Perform Label Detection with
Amazon Rekognition

```python
import json
import boto3
import os
import sys
import uuid
import logging

def lambda_handler(event, context):

    logger = logging.getLogger()
    logger.setLevel(logging.INFO)

    rekognition_client = boto3.client('rekognition')
    dynamodb_client = client = boto3.client('dynamodb')

    logger.info('Found event{}'.format(event))

    for record in event['Records']:
```

```
# Read the value of the eventSource attribute.
#
# You can use this to conditionally handle events
# from different triggers in the same lambda function.
event_source = record['eventSource']
logger.info(event_source)

# read S3 bucket and object key
bucket = record['s3']['bucket']['name']
key = record['s3']['object']['key']

logger.info('Found bucket ' +  bucket)
logger.info('Found key ' + key)

# use Amazon Rekognition to detect labels in the image
rekognition_results = rekognition_client.detect_labels(
    Image = {'S3Object': {'Bucket': bucket,'Name': key}},
    MaxLabels = 5,
    MinConfidence = 70)

# write results of label detection to DynamoDB
for label in rekognition_results['Labels']:

    text = label['Name']
    confidence = str(label['Confidence'])

    logger.info('Found label ' + text)

    dynamodb_response = dynamodb_client.put_item(
        Item={'label': {'S': text},'filename': {'S': key},
'confidence': {'N':confidence}},
        ReturnConsumedCapacity='TOTAL',
        TableName='imageindex')

    logger.info('DynamDBResponse ' + format(dynamodb_response))


# return the entities that were detected.
return {
'statusCode': 200,
}
```

Click the Save button below the function editor to finish creating your Lambda function. To test this function, use the Services drop-down menu to switch to Amazon S3 and navigate to the bucket that you have associated with the AWS Lambda function trigger. Upload an image file into the bucket. After uploading the image to Amazon S3, switch over to the Amazon DynamoDB management console and inspect the contents of the imageindex table. You should see one new item in the table for each label detected by Amazon Rekognition (Figure 18.17).

FIGURE 18.17
Examining the results of
the AWS
Lambda function

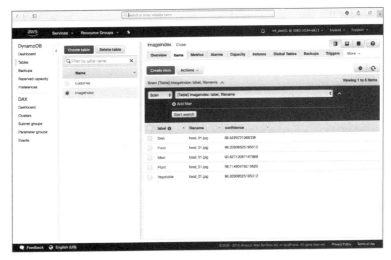

If you upload a few images to the S3 bucket, you will soon have a number of rows in the Amazon DynamoDB table. You can then execute a query on the table to retrieve all images that contain a specific object (see Figure 18.18).

FIGURE 18.18
Querying the Amazon
DynamoDB table will
allow you to search for
images based on
their content.

The output bucket is hardcoded in Listing 18.1. You should change it to the appropriate value if you are using a different bucket name. The bucket names and files used in this example are:

- *Source bucket:* `awsml-rekognition-awslambda-source`
- *DynamoDB Table:* `imageindex`
- *Input file:* `food_01.jpg`

NOTE You can download the code files for this chapter from www.wiley.com/go/
machinelearningawscloud or from GitHub using the following URL:
https://github.com/asmtechnology/awsmlbook-chapter18.git

Summary

◆ Amazon Rekognition is a fully managed web service that provides access to a deep-
learning–based models for computer vision tasks such as object location, scene analysis,
and video analysis.

◆ Amazon Rekognition APIs consist of two subsets: the Amazon Rekognition Image APIs
and the Amazon Rekognition Video APIs.

◆ Amazon Rekognition Image APIs operate synchronously, whereas Amazon Rekognition
Video APIs operate asynchronously.

◆ The asynchronous model of Amazon Rekognition Video APIs relies on using Amazon SNS
topics to notify listeners of the completion status of an operation.

◆ Non–storage-based APIs do not store any data on Amazon Rekognition. Storage-based
APIs, on the other hand, store information in Amazon Rekognition.

◆ Amazon Rekognition Video APIs that provide the capability to build face collections are
storage-based APIs.

◆ When creating a face collection, you are tied into the version of the model used by
Amazon Rekognition at the point the collection is created. You cannot update the model
version used by a face collection.

Appendix A

Anaconda and Jupyter Notebook Setup

In this appendix, you learn to install Anaconda Navigator on your computer, set up a Python environment that includes several common machine learning libraries, and configure Jupyter Notebook.

Installing the Anaconda Distribution

Anaconda is a Python distribution (pre-built and preconfigured collection of packages) that is commonly used for data science. The Anaconda distribution includes the conda package manager in addition to the preconfigured Python packages and other tools. The conda package manager can be used from the command line to set up Python environments and install additional packages that do not come installed by default with Anaconda.

Anaconda Navigator is a GUI tool that is included in the Anaconda distribution and makes it easy to configure, install, and launch tools such as Jupyter Notebook. Although we make use of Anaconda Navigator in this book, keep in mind that you can do everything through the command line using the conda command.

To begin the Anaconda Navigator installation process, visit `https://www.anaconda.com` and click the Downloads link at the top-right corner of the page (Figure A.1).

FIGURE A.1
Anaconda home age

On the downloads page, locate the download the link for a version that includes Python 3.7 or higher (Figure A.2). Click the download link to download the installer for your operating system.

FIGURE A.2
Downloading the appropriate version of Anaconda

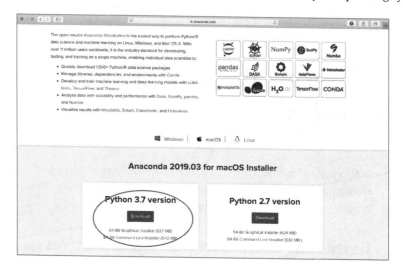

Locate the installer on your computer's download folder and launch it to begin the installation process (Figure A.3).

FIGURE A.3
Anaconda installer on macOS X

At some point in the installation process, you will be asked if you want to install Microsoft Visual Studio Code (Figure A.4). Visual Studio Code is a free IDE that supports Python and several other languages. In this book we do not use Visual Studio Code. If you wish to install Visual Studio Code, you can do so either during the Anaconda distribution installation process, or later on from the Anaconda Navigator user interface.

FIGURE A.4
The Anaconda Installer
provides the option to
install Microsoft Visual
Studio Code

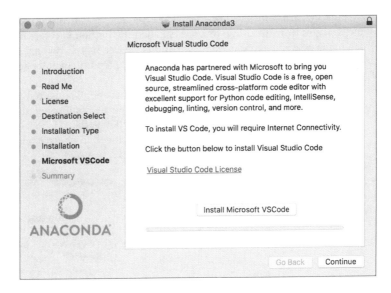

The Anaconda distribution will be installed on your computer when the installer completes
successfully (Figure A.5).

FIGURE A.5
Anaconda has been
successfully installed.

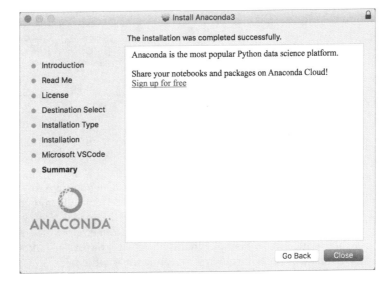

Creating a Conda Python Environment

A fresh Anaconda installation comes with a single conda Python environment called *base (root)*
that includes a set of pre-installed packages. In this section you will create a new conda Python
environment and install a set of packages that have been used for the examples in this book. A
conda Python environment is an isolated environment and allows you to install packages
without modifying your system Python installation.

Python's officially sanctioned package manager is called PiP (Pip Installs Packages) and gets its packages from an online repository called the Python Package Index (PyPI). Conda is a language-agnostic package manager and is used to install packages within conda environments. This is an important distinction—conda cannot help you install packages on your system Python installation.

A number of tools that are included with Anaconda Navigator, such as Jupyter Notebook and Spyder IDE, will pick up the conda environments available on your computer and allow you to switch between different environments with little overhead.

To get started with creating a new environment, launch Anaconda Navigator and switch to the Environments section of the user interface (Figure A.6).

FIGURE A.6

Environment settings in Anaconda Navigator

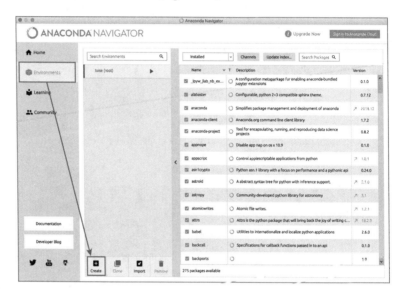

You will see the base (root) environment created by the Anaconda installer along with all the packages contained in the environment. Click the Create button to create a new conda environment.

Provide a name for the new conda environment (Figure A.7), and ensure the Python language is checked and the Python version is set to 3.7 or higher. Ensure the R language check box is unchecked. The examples in this book assume the conda environment is called `AWS_ML_Book`. However, you are free to use your own name. Remember to select the appropriate environment while trying out the examples in this book. Click the Create button on the Create New Environment dialog box to finish creating the environment.

After a few minutes, a new conda environment will be created on your computer and you will see it listed in Anaconda Navigator (Figure A.8).

Clicking the new environment will display a list of packages in this environment. By default, all new conda environments are created with a minimal set of packages.

FIGURE A.7
Creating a new Conda
Python environment

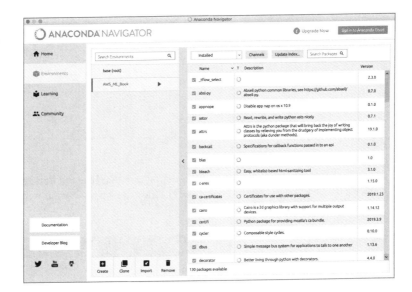

FIGURE A.8
Switching to the AWS_
ML_Book Conda
environment

Installing Python Packages

In this section you will install a number of Python packages in your new conda environment. To start, ensure your conda environment is selected in the Anaconda Navigator application. Select the All option in the package type combo box (Figure A.9).

FIGURE A.9
Displaying all available
Python packages

Use the search text box to search for the Pandas package. Locate the Pandas package in the search result, select it, and click the Apply button (Figure A.10).

FIGURE A.10
Searching for a package

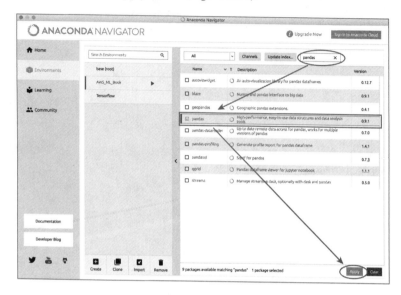

Anaconda Navigator will present a dialog box that lists the Pandas package and all dependencies that will be installed (Figure A.11). Click the Apply button to finish installing the Pandas package and its dependencies.

FIGURE A.11
Package dependencies
dialog box

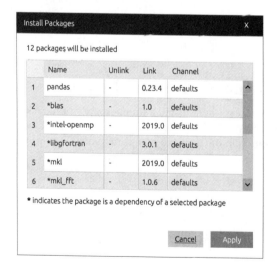

Use the same technique to install the following additional packages along with their respective dependencies:

♦ matplotlib

♦ pillow

♦ scikit-learn

♦ tensorflow

♦ seaborn

♦ graphviz

♦ pydotplus

♦ python-graphviz

NOTE   If your computer has an Nvidia GPU, you will have the option to install a GPU-accelerated version of TensorFlow called TensorFlow-GPU.

Installing Jupyter Notebook

In this section, you will install Jupyter Notebook in the conda environment that you created earlier in this appendix. Launch Anaconda Navigator and switch to the Home tab. Locate the Jupyter Notebook icon and click the Install button (Figure A.12). This action will install Jupyter Notebook in the default base (root) environment.

FIGURE A.12
Installing
Jupyter Notebook

After Jupyter Notebook has been installed, launch a Terminal window on your Mac (or Command Prompt in Windows) and type the following command to list all conda environments on your computer. Press the Enter key after typing the command:

```
$ conda info --envs
```

The output on your computer should resemble the following:

```
AMBP:~ abhishekmishra$ conda info --envs
# conda environments:
#
base                        *  /anaconda3
AWS_ML_Book                    /anaconda3/envs/AWS_ML_Book
```

You should see the conda environment you created earlier in this chapter listed along with any other conda environments that exist on your computer.

Type the following command to switch to the conda environment you created earlier. Replace AWS_ML_Book with the name of the environment you have created. Press the Enter key after typing the command:

```
$ conda activate AWS_ML_Book
```

Type the following command to install Jupyter Notebooks in the conda environment you just activated with the previous command:

```
$ conda install jupyter
```

The output on your computer should resemble the following:

```
$ conda install jupyter
Solving environment: done

## Package Plan ##

  environment location: /anaconda3/envs/AWS_ML_Book

  added / updated specs:
    - jupyter


The following packages will be downloaded:

    package                    |          build
    ---------------------------|-----------------
    widgetsnbextension-3.4.2   |         py36_0        1.7 MB
    ipywidgets-7.4.2           |         py36_0        151 KB
    qtconsole-4.4.2            |         py36_0        157 KB
    pyqt-5.9.2                 | py36h655552a_2        4.4 MB
    jupyter-1.0.0              |         py36_7          6 KB
    sip-4.19.8                 | py36h0a44026_0        252 KB
    jupyter_console-6.0.0      |         py36_0         35 KB
    ---------------------------------------------------------
                                          Total:        6.7 MB
```

```
The following NEW packages will be INSTALLED:

    dbus:              1.13.2-h760590f_1
    expat:             2.2.6-h0a44026_0
    gettext:           0.19.8.1-h15daf44_3
    glib:              2.56.2-hd9629dc_0
    icu:               58.2-h4b95b61_1
    ipywidgets:        7.4.2-py36_0
    jupyter:           1.0.0-py36_7
    jupyter_console:   6.0.0-py36_0
    libiconv:          1.15-hdd342a3_7
    pcre:              8.42-h378b8a2_0
    pyqt:              5.9.2-py36h655552a_2
    qt:                5.9.6-h45cd832_2
    qtconsole:         4.4.2-py36_0
    sip:               4.19.8-py36h0a44026_0
    widgetsnbextension: 3.4.2-py36_0
```

```
Proceed ([y]/n)?
```

You will be presented with a summary of the packages that will be installed in the environment and asked if you want to proceed. Press the Y key on your keyboard and then press Enter to continue.

After Jupyter Notebook has finished installing in the new conda environment, type the following command to create a new kernel specification in Jupyter Notebook. A kernel specification will allow you to switch to your new conda environment from within Jupyter Notebook. Replace AWS_ML_BOOK with the name of your environment. Press the Enter key after typing the command:

```
$ python -m ipykernel install --user --name AWS_ML_BOOK --display-name "Python
(AWS_ML_BOOK)"
```

You should see a message on your computer confirming that the kernel specification has been installed:

```
Installed kernelspec AWS_ML_BOOK in /Users/abhishekmishra/Library/Jupyter/
kernels/aws_ml_book
```

Type the following command to install the nb-conda-kernels package from the conda-forge repository (also known as a channel). Press the Enter key after typing the command:

```
$ conda install --channel=conda-forge nb_conda_kernels
```

You will once again be asked to confirm whether you want to download and install the nb_conda_kernels package along with dependencies. Press the Y key on your keyboard when asked to finish installing the packages.

You can now use Anaconda Navigator to launch Jupyter Notebook. The notebook is launched in your default web browser and configured to display the contents of your users directory (Figure A.13).

FIGURE A.13
Jupyter Notebook
running in a
web browser

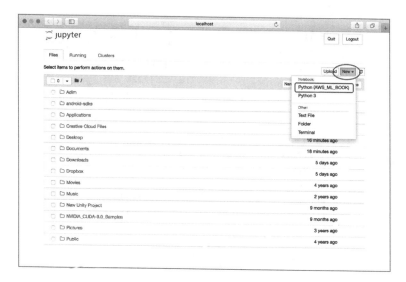

Clicking the New button in the Jupyter Notebook page within your web browser will display a drop-down menu allowing you to create a new notebook using one of the kernels installed on your computer. A kernel corresponding to the new conda environment you created earlier in this chapter should be listed in the drop-down menu.

You can also launch Jupyter Notebook using the command line by typing the following command in a Terminal (or Command Prompt) window and pressing Enter:

```
$ jupyter notebook
```

Summary

♦ Anaconda is a Python distribution (pre-built and preconfigured collection of packages) that is commonly used for data science. The Anaconda distribution includes the conda package manager in addition to the preconfigured Python packages and other tools.

♦ Anaconda Navigator is a GUI tool that is included in the Anaconda distribution and makes it easy to configure, install, and launch tools such as Jupyter Notebook.

♦ A conda Python environment is an isolated environment and allows you to install packages without modifying your system Python installation.

Appendix B

AWS Resources Needed to Use This Book

This appendix contains a list of AWS resources that you will need to set up under your own account in order to make the most of the content of this book.

Creating an IAM User for Development

In this section you will create an IAM user for development tasks. This user will have policies that allow access to a broad range of tasks on your resources. For instance, in a production scenario you will not use policies that provide access to all your Amazon S3 resources or allow all actions on every Amazon DynamoDB table. However, when you are developing a solution you can use a special development user, and then create production users with restrictive policies when you are closer to testing and releasing.

To get started, log in to the IAM management console using either an IAM user with administrative privileges or your root account credentials. Click the Users link in the IAM dashboard to load the user management page. Click the Add User button to start the process of creating a user under your root account (see Figure B.1).

FIGURE B.1
Creating an IAM user

Specify a username and ensure you have enabled both Programmatic Access and AWS Management Console Access (see Figure B.2).

Provide a custom password that will be used by the IAM user while logging in to the management console and ensure the Require Password Reset check box is enabled.

Once you have specified a username and access type, you will be asked to configure permissions for the user. Ensure the option labeled Add User To Group is selected and click the Create Group button (see Figure B.3).

FIGURE B.2
User details screen

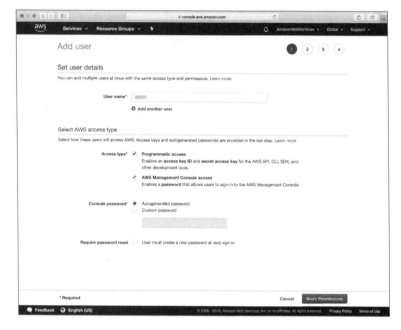

FIGURE B.3
Creating a new group for
the IAM user

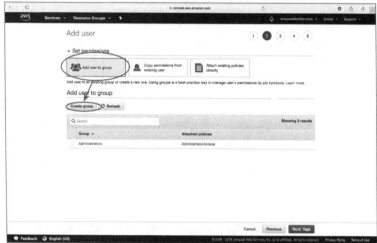

Name the new group **MLDevelopers** and add the following policies to the group:

◆ AmazonMachineLearningFullAccess

◆ AmazonSageMakerFullAccess

◆ ComprehendFullAccess

◆ AmazonS3FullAccess

◆ AmazonDynamoDBFullAccess

◆ AWSLambdaFullAccess

♦ AmazonLexFullAccess

♦ AmazonRekognitionFullAccess

Click the Create Group button to finish creating the group. On clicking the Create Group button, you will be taken back to the previous screen and will see your new group listed alongside existing groups (Figure B.4). Ensure the new user is added to the MLDevelopers group.

FIGURE B.4
Adding the new IAM user to the MLDevelopers group

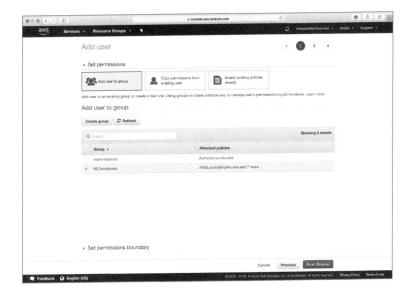

Click the Next button to display the review screen and click the Create User button in the review screen to finish creating the user. You will be presented with a confirmation screen like the one in Figure B.5 that contains the name of the user just created as well as access credentials.

FIGURE B.5
User confirmation screen

Use the Download .csv button to download the full set of credentials for the user, and click the Close button to go back to the IAM home screen.

Creating S3 Buckets

In this section, you will use the AWS management console to create a set of S3 buckets that will be used in other chapters of the book. Log in to the IAM console using your dedicated IAM user-specific sign-in link and navigate to the S3 service home page (Figure B.6).

FIGURE B.6
Accessing the S3
management console

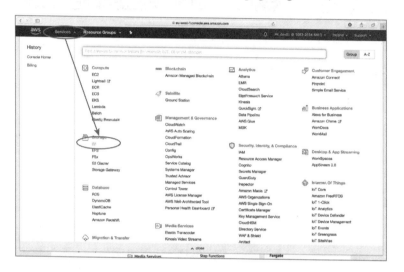

Recall from Chapter 9 that the S3 service is available in all regions, so you do not need to select a region in the management console. A bucket, on the other hand, is region-specific, and you will need to select the region in which you want to create the bucket.

Create the following buckets in a region of your choice. All the examples in this book use the EU (Ireland) region. If you decide to choose another region, keep in mind that some AWS services may not be available in your chosen region.

◆ awsml-comprehend-entitydetection-result

◆ awsml-comprehend-entitydetection-source

◆ awsml-rekognition-awscli-source

◆ awsml-rekognition-awslambda-source

The name you choose for your bucket must be globally unique, and prefixing a reverse-domain name is a common practice to ensure unique naming. Use a suitable prefix while creating the buckets.

You do not need to configure bucket versioning, logging, or cost allocation tags for any of these buckets at this stage (Figure B.7). When prompted, leave the settings at their default values.

FIGURE B.7
Configuring versioning, logging, and cost allocation tags

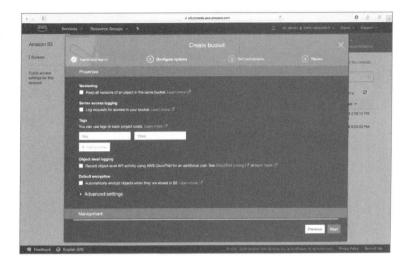

When you reach the screen that allows you to configure access permissions for the bucket, ensure you apply the following settings:

◆ *Block new public ACLs and uploading public objects:* Unchecked

◆ *Remove public access granted through public ACLs:* Unchecked

◆ *Block new public bucket policies:* Unchecked

◆ *Block public and cross-account access:* Unchecked

Your screen should resemble Figure B.8.

FIGURE B.8
Configuring bucket permissions

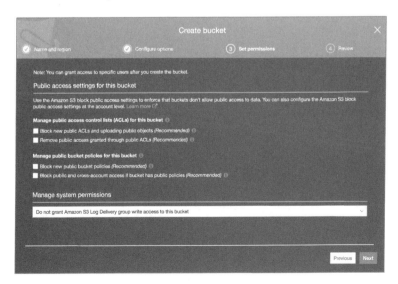

Click the Next button and proceed to create each bucket using the same settings as described in this section.

Appendix C

Installing and Configuring the AWS CLI

This appendix includes instructions for installing and configuring the AWS CLI on Max OS X and Windows.

The AWS Command Line Interface (CLI) is a tool that lets you manage your AWS services using a command-line interface, over the internet. In this appendix you will learn to download, install, and configure the appropriate version of the AWS CLI on your computer.

Mac OS Users

If you are a Mac OS user, you can use a bundled installer to install the AWS CLI on your computer. The bundled installer requires Python2 version 2.6.5+ or Python3 version 3.3+ to be pre-installed on the computer.

To check the Python version on a Mac OS computer, open a Terminal window, type the following command, and hit Enter:

```
python --version
```

If you do not have a suitable version of Python installed on your computer, follow the instructions available at the following URL to get/update Python on your computer:

```
http://docs.aws.amazon.com/cli/latest/userguide/installing
.html#install-python
```

Installing the AWS CLI

Type the following commands in a Mac OS Terminal window, or at the equivalent shell prompt on your system:

```
$ curl "https://s3.amazonaws.com/aws-cli/awscli-bundle.zip" -o "awscli-
bundle.zip"
$ unzip awscli-bundle.zip
$ sudo ./awscli-bundle/install -i /usr/local/aws -b /usr/local/bin/aws
```

If you do not have unzip installed, or do not have administrative privileges on your computer, you can use one of the techniques listed at the following URL to install the AWS CLI on your computer:

```
http://docs.aws.amazon.com/cli/latest/userguide/installing.html
```

Once you have installed the AWS CLI on your computer, type the following line to test the installation:

```
$ aws help
```

Your screen should display a list of aws commands along with a brief description of each (see Figure C.1).

FIGURE C.1

List of AWS CLI commands, Mac OS

Typing the aws instruction takes you into the AWS CLI shell. To exit the AWS CLI shell and come back to your operating system's default shell, press **q** on your keyboard.

Configuring the AWS CLI

Before you can use the AWS CLI, to you need to configure the CLI tool on your computer. Type the following command in a Terminal window on your Mac, or appropriate shell prompt on your computer:

```
$ aws configure
```

You will be asked to provide the Access Key ID and Secret Access Key for an IAM user that has adequate permissions to access your resources. You will also be asked to provide a default AWS region and output options:

```
Abhisheks-MacBook:~ abhishekmishra$ aws configure
AWS Access Key ID [****************COFA]:
AWS Secret Access Key [****************PcqG]:
Default region name [eu-west-1]:
Default output format [None]:
Abhisheks-MacBook:~ abhishekmishra$
```

The Access Key ID and Secret Access Key were created for you when you created the IAM user, and you were prompted to record the information and save it in a safe place. If you do not remember your Access Key ID/Secret Access Key, you can use the IAM management console to generate a new set.

The region name is a string that identifies an AWS region. Table C.1 lists the values that you can type and the corresponding regions they represent.

TABLE C.1:   AWS Region Names

REGION NAME	AWS CLI STRING
US East (N. Virginia)	us-east-1
US East (Ohio)	us-east-2
US West (N. California)	us-west-1
US West (Oregon)	us-west-2
Canada (Central)	ca-central-1
Asia Pacific (Mumbai)	ap-south-1
Asia Pacific (Singapore)	ap-southeast-1
Asia Pacific (Sydney)	ap-southeast-2
Asia Pacific (Tokyo)	ap-northeast-1
Asia Pacific (Seoul)	ap-northeast-2
Asia Pacific (Osaka)	ap-northeast-3
EU (Frankfurt)	eu-central-1
EU (Ireland)	eu-west-1
EU (London)	eu-west-2
EU (Paris)	eu-west-3

TABLE C.1: AWS Region Names *(CONTINUED)*

REGION NAME	AWS CLI STRING
China (Beijing)	cn-north-1
China (Ningxia)	cn-northwest-1
South America (São Paulo)	sa-east-1

The output option can be either JSON (default), or text.

You have now successfully installed and configured the AWS CLI tools on your Mac.

Windows Users

For Windows users, Amazon provides an installer package that can be used to install the CLI on a computer running Windows XP or a newer operating system. The AWS CLI is not supported on computers running older versions of Windows.

Installing the AWS CLI

Use the following link to download a Windows installer for your computer. Both 32-bit and 64-bit installers are available:

```
https://docs.aws.amazon.com/cli/latest/userguide/install-windows.html
```

Launch the installer and follow the on-screen instructions to complete the installation. By default, the AWS CLI will be installed at `C:\Program Files\Amazon\AWSCLI` (64-bit) or `C:\Program Files (x86)\Amazon\AWSCLI` (32-bit).

To test the installation of the CLI, launch the command prompt, type the following command at the prompt, and press Enter:

```
> aws help
```

Your screen should display a list of aws commands along with a brief description of each (see Figure C.2).

Type **q** to go back to the command prompt.

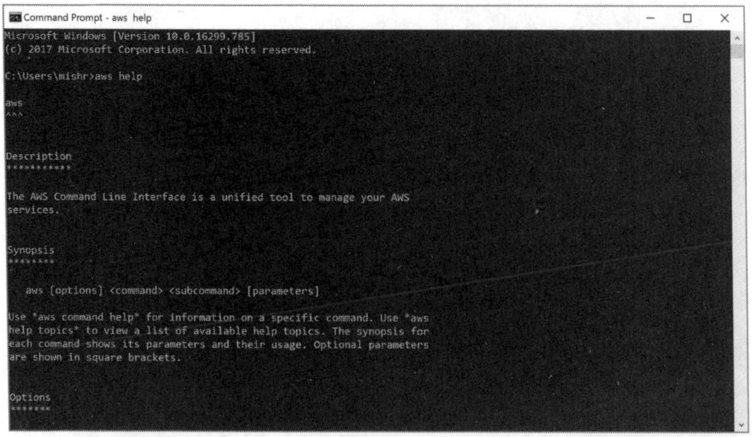

FIGURE C.2
List of AWS CLI commands, Windows

Configuring the AWS CLI

Before you can use the AWS CLI, you need to configure the CLI tool on your computer with access keys for an IAM user account. Type the following command at the command prompt:

```
> aws configure
```

You will be asked to provide the Access Key ID and Secret Access Key for an IAM user that has adequate permissions to access an EC2 instance. You will also be asked to provide a default AWS region and output options:

```
Microsoft Windows [Version 10.0.16299.785]
(c) 2017 Microsoft Corporation. All rights reserved.

C:\Users\mishr>aws configure
AWS Access Key ID [None]: AKIAIR2R5O3F4VHVCOFA
AWS Secret Access Key [None]: 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
Default region name [None]:

Default output format [None]:
C:\Users\mishr>
```

The Access Key ID and Secret Access Key were created for you when you created the IAM user, and you were prompted to record the information and save it in a safe place. If you do not remember your Access Key ID/Secret Access Key, you can use the IAM management console to generate a new set.

The region name is a string that identifies an AWS region. Table C.2 lists the values that you can type and the corresponding regions they represent.

TABLE C.2:   AWS Region Names

REGION NAME	AWS CLI STRING
US East (N. Virginia)	us-east-1
US East (Ohio)	us-east-2
US West (N. California)	us-west-1
US West (Oregon)	us-west-2
Canada (Central)	ca-central-1
Asia Pacific (Mumbai)	ap-south-1
Asia Pacific (Singapore)	ap-southeast-1
Asia Pacific (Sydney)	ap-southeast-2
Asia Pacific (Tokyo)	ap-northeast-1
Asia Pacific (Seoul)	ap-northeast-2
Asia Pacific (Osaka)	ap-northeast-3
EU (Frankfurt)	eu-central-1

TABLE C.2:   AWS Region Names   *(CONTINUED)*

REGION NAME	AWS CLI STRING
EU (Ireland)	eu-west-1
EU (London)	eu-west-2
EU (Paris)	eu-west-3
China (Beijing)	cn-north-1
China (Ningxia)	cn-northwest-1
South America (São Paulo)	sa-east-1

The output option can be either JSON (default), or text.

Appendix D

Introduction to NumPy and Pandas

In this appendix you will learn to use two popular Python libraries used by data scientists: NumPy and Pandas. These libraries are commonly used during the data exploration and feature engineering phase of a project. The examples in this appendix require the use of Jupyter Notebooks.

NOTE   To follow along with this appendix, ensure you have installed Anaconda Navigator and Jupyter Notebook as described in Appendix A.

You can download the code files for this chapter from www.wiley.com/go/ machinelearningawscloud or from GitHub using the following URL:

https://github.com/asmtechnology/awsmlbook-appendixd.git

NumPy

NumPy is a math library for Python that allows for fast and efficient manipulation of arrays. The main object provided by NumPy is a homogeneous multidimensional array called ndarray. All the elements of an ndarray must be of the same data type, and dimensions are referred to as axes in NumPy terminology.

To use NumPy in a Python project, you typically add the following import statement to your Python file:

```
import numpy as np
```

The lowercase alias np is a standard convention for referring to NumPy in Python projects.

Creating NumPy Arrays

You can create an ndarray in a number of ways. To create an ndarray object out of a three-element Python list, use the np.array() statement. The following code snippet, when typed in a Jupyter Notebook, will result in a NumPy array created with three elements:

```
# creating an ndarray
x = np.array([10, 27, 34])
print (x)

[10 27 34]
```

Note the use of the square brackets within the parentheses. Omitting the square brackets will result in an error. The ndarray x has one axis and three elements. Unlike arrays created using the Python library class called `array`, NumPy arrays can be multidimensional. The following statements create a NumPy array with two axes, and print the contents of the ndarray object:

```
# creating a two-dimensional ndarray
points = np.array([[11, 28, 9], [56, 38, 91], [33,87,36], [87,8,4]])
print (points)

[[11 28  9]
 [56 38 91]
 [33 87 36]
 [87  8  4]]
```

The ndarray created by the preceding statement will have two axes, and can be represented for visualization purposes as a two-dimensional matrix with four rows and three columns:

11	28	9
56	38	91
33	87	36
87	8	4

The first axis contains four elements (the number of rows), and the second axis contains three elements (the number of columns). Table D.1 contains some of the commonly used attributes of ndarrays.

TABLE D1: Commonly Used Ndarray Attributes

ATTRIBUTE	DESCRIPTION
ndim	Returns the number of axes.
shape	Returns the number of elements along each axis.
size	Returns the total number of elements in the ndarray.
dtype	Returns the data type of the elements in the ndarray.

All elements in an ndarray must have the same data type. NumPy provides its own data types, the most commonly used of which are `np.int16`, `np.int32`, and `np.float64`. Unlike Python, NumPy provides multiple data types for a particular data class. This is similar to the C language concept of `short`, `int`, `long`, `signed`, and `unsigned` variants of a data class. For example, NumPy provides the following data types for signed integers:

◆ byte: This is compatible with a C char.

◆ short: This is compatible with a C short.

◆ intc: This is compatible with a C int.

◆ int_: This is compatible with a Python int.

◆ longlong: This is compatible with a C long long.

◆ intp: This data type can be used to represent a pointer. The number of bytes depends on the processor architecture and operating system your code is running on.

◆ int8: An 8-bit signed integer.

◆ int16: A 16-bit signed integer.

◆ int32: A 32-bit signed integer.

◆ int64: A 64-bit signed integer.

Some NumPy data types are compatible with Python; these usually end in an underscore character (such as int_, float_). You can find a complete list of NumPy data types at https:// docs.scipy.org/doc/numpy-1.15.1/reference/arrays.scalars.html#arrays-scalars-built-in.

You can specify the data type when creating ndarrays as illustrated in the following snippet:

```
#creating a one-dimensional array, whilst specifying the data type
y = np.array([10, 27, 34], dtype=np.float64)
print (y)
```

```
[10. 27. 34.]
```

When you specify the elements in the array at the time of creation, but do not specify the data type, NumPy attempts to guess the most appropriate data type. The default data type is float_, which is compatible with a Python float.

When creating a NumPy array, if you do not know the values of the elements, but know the size and number of axes, you can use one of the following functions to create ndarrays with placeholder content:

◆ zeros: Creates an ndarray of specified dimensions, with each element being zero.

◆ ones: Creates an ndarray of specified dimensions, with each element being one.

◆ empty: Creates an uninitialized ndarray of specified dimensions.

◆ random.random: Creates an array of random values that lie in the half open interval [0.0, 1.0).

As an example, if you wanted to create an ndarray with four rows and three columns, where each element is an int16 with value 1, you would use a statement similar to the following:

```
# create an array with ones
a = np.ones((4,3), dtype=np.int16)
print (a)

[[1 1 1]
 [1 1 1]
 [1 1 1]
 [1 1 1]]
```

The following statement would create an ndarray with two rows and three columns populated with random numbers. The data type of random numbers is `float_`:

```
# create an array with random numbers
r = np.random.random([2,3])
print (r)


[[0.48746158 0.93214926 0.1450121 ]
 [0.69303901 0.43758922 0.62645661]]
```

NumPy provides methods to create sequences of numbers. The most commonly used are:

◆ arange: Creates a single-axis ndarray with evenly spaced elements.

◆ linspace: Creates a single-axis ndarray with evenly spaced elements.

The arange function is similar to the Python range function in functionality. The arange function takes four arguments: the first value is the start of the range, the second is the end of the range, the third is the step increment between numbers within the range, and the fourth is an optional parameter that allows you to specify the data type.

For example, the following snippet creates an ndarray, the elements of which lie in the range [0,9(.Each element in the ndarray is greater than the previous element by three:

```
# use the arange function to create a sequence of numbers
sequence1 = np.arange(0, 9, 3)
print (sequence1)


[0 3 6]
```

The upper limit of the range is not included in the numbers that are generated by the arange function. Therefore, the ndarray generated by the preceding statement will have the following elements, and not include the number 9:

0, 3, 6

If you want a sequence of integers from 0 up to a specific number, you can call the arange function with a single argument. The following statements achieve identical results:

```
# these arange statements achieve identical results.
sequence2 = np.arange(5)
sequence3 = np.arange(0,5,1)


print (sequence2)
[0 1 2 3 4]

print (sequence3)
 0 1 2 3 4]
```

The linspace function is similar to arange in that it generates a sequence of numbers that lie within a range. The difference is that the third element is the number of values that are required between the start and end values. The following statement creates an ndarray with three elements, between 0 and 9:

```
# the linspace function can also be used to obtain a sequence
sequence4 = np.linspace(0, 9, 3)
print (sequence4)

[0.    4.5    9. ]
```

Unlike the arange function, the linspace function ensures that the specified lower and upper bounds are part of the sequence.

Modifying Arrays

NumPy provides several functions that allow you to modify the contents of arrays. While it is not possible to cover each of them in this appendix, the most commonly used operations will be discussed.

ARITHMETIC OPERATIONS

NumPy allows you to perform element-wise arithmetic operations between two arrays. The result of the operation is stored in a new array. The +, -, /, and * operators retain their arithmetic meaning. The following code snippet demonstrates how to perform arithmetic operations on two ndarrays:

```
# Elementwise Arithmetic operations can be performed on ndarrays
array1 = np.array([[1,2,3], [2, 3, 4]])
array2 = np.array([[3,4,5], [4, 5, 6]])

Sum = array1 + array2
Difference = array1 - array2
Product = array1 * array2
Division = array1 / array2

print (Sum)
[[ 4  6  8]
 [ 6  8 10]]

print (Difference)
[[-2 -2 -2]
 [-2 -2 -2]]

print (Product)
[[ 3  8 15]
 [ 8 15 24]]

print (Division)
[[0.33333333 0.5        0.6       ]
 [0.5        0.6        0.66666667]]
```

You can use the +=, -=, *=, and /= operators to perform in-place element-wise arithmetic operations. The results of these operations are not stored in a new array. The use of these operators is demonstrated in the following snippet:

```
# in-place elementwise arithmetic operations
array1 = np.array([1,2,3], dtype=np.float64)
array2 = np.array([3,4,5], dtype=np.float64)
array3 = np.array([4,5,6], dtype=np.float64)
array4 = np.array([5,6,7], dtype=np.float64)

# in-place arithmetic and can be performed using arrays of the same size
array1 += np.array([10,10,10], dtype=np.float64)
array2 -= np.array([10,10,10], dtype=np.float64)
array3 *= np.array([10,10,10], dtype=np.float64)
array4 /= np.array([10,10,10], dtype=np.float64)

# in-place arithmetic can be performed using a scalar value
array1 += 100.0
array2 -= 100.0
array3 *= 100.0
array4 /= 100.0

print (array1)
[111. 112. 113.]

print (array2)
[-107. -106. -105.]

print (array3)
[4000. 5000. 6000.]

print (array4)
[0.005 0.006 0.007]
```

The exponent operator is represented by two asterisk symbols (**). The following statements demonstrate the use of the exponent operator:

```
# the exponent operator
array1 = np.arange(4, dtype=np.float64)
array1 **= 4
print (array1)

[ 0.  1. 16. 81.]
```

COMPARISON OPERATIONS

NumPy provides the standard comparison operators <, >, <= , >=, ! = , and==. The comparison operators can be used with ndarrays of the same size or a scalar. The result of using a comparison operator is an ndarray of Booleans. The use of comparison operators is demonstrated in the following snippet:

```
array1 = np.array([1,4,5])
array2 = np.array([3,2,5])

# less than
print (array1 < array2)
[True False False]

# less than equal to
print (array1 <= array2)
[True False  True]

# greater than
print (array1 > array2)
[False  True False]

# greater than equal to
print (array1 >= array2)
[False  True  True]

# equal to
print (array1 == array2)
[False False  True]

# not equal to
print (array1 != array2)
[ True  True False]
```

MATRIX OPERATIONS

NumPy provides the ability to perform matrix operations on ndarrays. The following list contains some of the most commonly used matrix operations:

◆ inner: Performs a dot product between two arrays.

◆ outer: Performs the outer product between two arrays.

◆ cross: Performs the cross product between two arrays.

◆ transpose: Swaps the rows and columns of an array.

The use of matrix operations is demonstrated in the following snippet:

```
array1 = np.array([1,4,5], dtype=np.float_)
array2 = np.array([3,2,5], dtype=np.float_)

# inner (dot product)
print (np.inner(array1, array2))
36.0

# outer product
print (np.outer(array1, array2))
[[ 3.  2.  5.]
 [12.  8. 20.]
 [15. 10. 25.]]

# cross product
print (np.cross(array1, array2))
[ 10.  10. -10.]
```

Indexing and Slicing

NumPy provides the ability to index elements in an array as well as slice larger arrays into smaller ones. NumPy array indexes are zero-based. The following code snippet demonstrates how to index and slice one-dimensional arrays:

```
# create a one-dimensional array with 10 elements
array1 = np.linspace(0, 9, 10)

print (array1)
[0. 1. 2. 3. 4. 5. 6. 7. 8. 9.]

# get the third element. Indexes are zero-based.
print (array1[3])
3.0

# extracts elements 2 , 3, 4 into a sub array
print (array1[2:5])
[2. 3. 4.]

#extract first 6 elements of the array (elements 0 to 5)
print (array1[:6])
[0. 1. 2. 3. 4. 5.]

# extract elements 5 onwards
print(array1[5:])
[5. 6. 7. 8. 9.]
```

```
# extract every alternate element, step value is specified as 2
print (array1[::2])
[0. 2. 4. 6. 8.]

# reverse all the elements in array1
print (array1[::-1])
[9. 8. 7. 6. 5. 4. 3. 2. 1. 0.]
```

Indexing a multidimensional array requires you to provide a tuple with the value for each axis. The following code snippet demonstrates how to index and slice multidimensional arrays:

```
# create a two-dimensional array with 12 elements
array1 = np.array([[1,2,3,4], [5,6,7,8], [9, 10, 11, 12]])

print (array1)
[[ 1  2  3  4]
 [ 5  6  7  8]
 [ 9 10 11 12]]

# get the element in the second row, third column. Indexes are zero-based.
print (array1[1,2])
7

# get all the elements in the first column
print (array1[:,0])
[1 5 9]

#get all the elements in the first row
print (array1[0,:])
[1 2 3 4]

# get a sub 2-dimensional array
print (array1[:3, :2])
[[ 1  2]
 [ 5  6]
 [ 9 10]]
```

Pandas

Pandas is a free, open source data analysis library for Python and is one of the most commonly used tools for data munging. The key objects provided by Pandas are the series and dataframe. A Pandas series is similar to a one-dimensional list and a dataframe is similar to a two-dimensional table. One of the key differences between Pandas dataframes and NumPy arrays is that the columns in a dataframe object can have different data types, and can even handle missing values.

To use Pandas in a Python project, you typically add the following import statement to your Python file:

```
import pandas as pd
```

The lowercase alias pd is a standard convention for referring to Python in Python projects.

Creating Series and Dataframes

You have many ways to create a series and a dataframe object with Pandas. The simplest way is to create a Pandas series out of a Python list, as demonstrated in the following snippet:

```
# create a Pandas series from a Python list.
car_manufacturers = ['Volkswagen','Ford','Mercedes-Benz','BMW','Nissan']
pds_car_manufacturers = pd.Series(data=car_manufacturers)
print (pds_car_manufacturers)


0        Volkswagen
1              Ford
2     Mercedes-Benz
3               BMW
4            Nissan
dtype: object
```

A Pandas series contains an additional index column, which contains a unique integer value for each row of the series. In most cases, Pandas automatically creates this index column, and the index value can be used to select an item using square brackets [ ]:

```
print (pds_car_manufacturers[2])

Mercedes-Benz
```

If your data is loaded into a Python dictionary, you can convert the dictionary into a Pandas dataframe. A dataframe built from a Python dictionary does not, by default, have an integer index for each row of the dataframe. The following example shows how to convert a Python dictionary into a Pandas dataframe:

```
# create a Pandas series from a Python dictionary
#
# Pandas does not generate a series index.
cars = {'RJ09VWQ':'Blue Volkswagen Polo',
        'WQ81R09':'Red Ford Focus',
        'PB810AQ':'White Mercedes-Benz E-Class',
        'TU914A8':'Silver BMW 1 Series'}

pds_cars = pd.Series(data=cars)

print (pds_cars)
RJ09VWQ            Blue Volkswagen Polo
WQ81R09                  Red Ford Focus
```

```
PB810AQ    White Mercedes-Benz E-Class
TU914A8            Silver BMW 1 Series
dtype: object
```

Even though the dataframe does not have a numeric index, you can still use numbers to select a value:

```
print (pds_cars[2])
```

White Mercedes-Benz E-Class

Since the dataframe was created from a Python dictionary, the keys of the dictionary can be used to select a value:

```
print (pds_cars['WQ81R09'])
```

Red Ford Focus

The reason you are able to use the keys from the dictionary object is that Pandas is clever enough to create an Index object for your dataframe. You can use the following statement to view the contents of the index of the dataframe:

```
print (pds_cars.index)
```

Index(['RJ09VWQ', 'WQ81R09', 'PB810AQ', 'TU914A8'], dtype='object')

In most real-world use cases, you do not create Pandas dataframes from Python lists and dictionaries; instead, you will want to load the entire contents of CSV file straight into a dataframe. The following snippet shows how to load the contents of a CSV file that is included with the resources that accompany this lesson into a Pandas dataframe:

```
# load the contents of a file into a pandas Dataframe
input_file = './titanic_dataset/original/train.csv'
df_iris = pd.read_csv(input_file)
```

The dataframe created in this case is a matrix of columns and rows. You can get a list of column names by using the `columns` attribute:

```
# print the names of the columns
print (df_iris.columns)
```

**Index(['PassengerId', 'Survived', 'Pclass', 'Name', 'Sex', 'Age', 'SibSp',
       'Parch', 'Ticket', 'Fare', 'Cabin', 'Embarked'],
dtype='object')**

You can also create a dataframe by selecting a subset of named columns from an existing dataframe, as shown in the following example:

```
# create a Dataframe with a subset of the columns in df_iris
df_iris_subset = df_iris[['PassengerId', 'Survived', 'Pclass',
'Sex','Fare', 'Age']]
```

Getting Dataframe Information

Pandas provides several useful functions to inspect the contents of a dataframe, get information on the memory footprint of the dataframe, and get statistical information on the columns of a dataframe. Some of the commonly used functions to inspect the contents of a dataframe are listed here:

- shape(): Use this function to find out the number of columns and rows in a dataframe.

- head(n): Use this function to inspect the first n rows of the dataset. If you do not specify a value for n, the default used is 5.

- tail(n): Use this function to inspect the last n rows of the dataset. If you do not specify a value for n, the default used is 5.

- sample(n): Use this function to inspect a random sample of n rows from the dataset. If you do not specify a value for n, the default used is 1.

The following code snippet demonstrates the use of the shape(), head(), tail(), and sample() functions:

```
# how many rows and columns in the dataset
print (df_iris_subset.shape)
(891, 6)

# print first 5 rows
print (df_iris_subset.head())

        PassengerId  Survived  Pclass     Sex      Fare   Age
0                 1         0       3    male    7.2500  22.0
1                 2         1       1  female   71.2833  38.0
2                 3         1       3  female    7.9250  26.0
3                 4         1       1  female   53.1000  35.0
4                 5         0       3    male    8.0500  35.0

# print last 3 rows
print (df_iris_subset.tail(3))

        PassengerId  Survived  Pclass     Sex    Fare   Age
888             889         0       3  female   23.45   NaN
889             890         1       1    male   30.00  26.0
890             891         0       3    male    7.75  32.0

# print a random sample of 10 rows
print (df_iris_subset.sample(10))

    PassengerId  Survived  Pclass     Sex      Fare   Age
710         711         1       1  female   49.5042  24.0
127         128         1       3    male    7.1417  24.0
222         223         0       3    male    8.0500  51.0
795         796         0       2    male   13.0000  39.0
```

673	674	1	2	male	13.0000	31.0
115	116	0	3	male	7.9250	21.0
451	452	0	3	male	19.9667	NaN
642	643	0	3	female	27.9000	2.0
853	854	1	1	female	39.4000	16.0
272	273	1	2	female	19.5000	41.0

Pandas provides several useful functions to get information on the statistical characteristics and memory footprint of the data. Some of the most commonly used functions to obtain statistical information are:

◆ describe(): Provides information on the number of non-null values, mean, standard deviation, minimum value, maximum value, and quartiles of all numeric columns in the dataframe.

◆ mean(): Provides the mean value of each column.

◆ median(): Provides the median value of each column.

◆ std(): Provides the standard deviation of the values of each column.

◆ count(): Returns the number of non-null values in each column.

◆ max(): Returns the largest value in each column.

◆ min(): Returns the smallest value in each column.

The following snippet demonstrates the use of some of these statistical functions:

```
# get statistical information on numeric columns
print (df_iris_subset.describe())

       PassengerId    Survived      Pclass        Fare         Age
count   891.000000  891.000000  891.000000  891.000000  714.000000
mean    446.000000    0.383838    2.308642   32.204208   29.699118
std     257.353842    0.486592    0.836071   49.693429   14.526497
min       1.000000    0.000000    1.000000    0.000000    0.420000
25%     223.500000    0.000000    2.000000    7.910400   20.125000
50%     446.000000    0.000000    3.000000   14.454200   28.000000
75%     668.500000    1.000000    3.000000   31.000000   38.000000
max     891.000000    1.000000    3.000000  512.329200   80.000000


# mean of all columns
print (df_iris_subset.mean())

PassengerId    446.000000
Survived         0.383838
Pclass           2.308642
Fare            32.204208
Age             29.699118
dtype: float64
```

```
# the following statement is identical to the previous one,
# as axis = 0 implies columns.
print (df_iris_subset.mean(axis=0))

PassengerId    446.000000
Survived         0.383838
Pclass           2.308642
Fare            32.204208
Age             29.699118
dtype: float64

#correlation between columns
print (df_iris_subset.corr())

             PassengerId  Survived    Pclass      Fare       Age
PassengerId     1.000000 -0.005007 -0.035144  0.012658  0.036847
Survived       -0.005007  1.000000 -0.338481  0.257307 -0.077221
Pclass         -0.035144 -0.338481  1.000000 -0.549500 -0.369226
Fare            0.012658  0.257307 -0.549500  1.000000  0.096067
Age             0.036847 -0.077221 -0.369226  0.096067  1.000000

# number of non-null values in each column
print (df_iris_subset.count())

PassengerId    891
Survived       891
Pclass         891
Sex            891
Fare           891
Age            714
dtype: int64
```

The info() function provides information on the data type of each column and the total memory required to store the dataframe. The following snippet demonstrates the use of the info() function:

```
# get information on data types and memory footprint
print (df_iris_subset.info())

<class 'pandas.core.frame.DataFrame'>
RangeIndex: 891 entries, 0 to 890
Data columns (total 6 columns):
PassengerId    891 non-null int64
Survived       891 non-null int64
Pclass         891 non-null int64
Sex            891 non-null object
Fare           891 non-null float64
Age            714 non-null float64
dtypes: float64(2), int64(3), object(1)
memory usage: 41.8+ KB
```

The `isnull()` function can be used to highlight the null values in a dataframe. The output of the `isnull()` function is a dataframe of the same dimensions as the original, with each location containing a Boolean value that is true if the corresponding location in the original dataframe is null. The use of the `isnull()` function is demonstrated in the following snippet:

```
# highlight the null values in a random sample of data
print (df_iris_subset.sample(10).isnull())

     PassengerId  Survived  Pclass    Sex   Fare    Age
385        False     False   False  False  False  False
530        False     False   False  False  False  False
166        False     False   False  False  False   True
334        False     False   False  False  False   True
603        False     False   False  False  False  False
807        False     False   False  False  False  False
819        False     False   False  False  False  False
99         False     False   False  False  False  False
767        False     False   False  False  False  False
480        False     False   False  False  False  False
```

If you want to quickly find out the number of null values in each column of the dataframe, use the `sum()` function with the `isnull()` function, as demonstrated in the following snippet:

```
# find out if there are any missing values in the data
print (df_iris_subset.isnull().sum())

PassengerId      0
Survived         0
Pclass           0
Sex              0
Fare             0
Age            177
dtype: int64
```

Selecting Data

Pandas provides powerful functions to select data from a dataframe. You can create a dataframe (or series) that contains a subset of the columns in an existing dataframe by specifying the names of the columns you want to select:

```
# extract a single column as a series object
pds_class = df_iris_subset[['Pclass']]
print (pds_class.head())

   Pclass
0       3
1       1
2       3
3       1
4       3
```

```
# extract a specific subset of named columns into a new dataframe
df_test1 = df_iris_subset[['PassengerId', 'Age']]
print (df_test1.head())

   PassengerId   Age
0            1  22.0
1            2  38.0
2            3  26.0
3            4  35.0
4            5  35.0
```

You can create a dataframe that contains a subset of the rows in an existing dataframe by specifying a range of row index numbers:

```
# extract first 3 rows into a new data frame
df_test2 = df_iris_subset[0:3]
print (df_test2.head())

   PassengerId  Survived  Pclass     Sex     Fare   Age
0            1         0       3    male   7.2500  22.0
1            2         1       1  female  71.2833  38.0
2            3         1       3  female   7.9250  26.0
```

You can use the iloc() function to extract a sub matrix from an existing dataframe:

```
# extract first 3 rows and 3 columns into a new dataframe
df_test3 = df_iris_subset.iloc[0:3,0:3]
print (df_test3.head())

   PassengerId  Survived  Pclass
0            1         0       3
1            2         1       1
2            3         1       3
```

You can also use comparison operators to extract from a dataframe all rows that fulfill a specific criterion. For example, the following snippet will extract all rows from the df_iris_ subset dataframe that have a value greater than 26 in the Age column:

```
# extracting all rows where Age > 26 into a new dataframe
df_test4 = df_iris_subset[df_iris_subset['Age'] > 26]
print (df_test4.count())

>>> PassengerId    395
Survived       395
Pclass         395
Sex            395
Fare           395
Age            395
dtype: int64
```

In addition to the functions covered in this chapter, Pandas provides several others, including functions that can be used to sort data and techniques to use a standard Python function as a filter function over all the values of a dataframe. To find out more about the capabilities of Pandas, visit `http://pandas.pydata.org`.

Index